The Battle of Peach Tree Creek

Civil War America

PETER S. CARMICHAEL, CAROLINE E. JANNEY,
and AARON SHEEHAN-DEAN, *editors*

This landmark series interprets broadly the history and culture of the Civil War era through the long nineteenth century and beyond. Drawing on diverse approaches and methods, the series publishes historical works that explore all aspects of the war, biographies of leading commanders, and tactical and campaign studies, along with select editions of primary sources. Together, these books shed new light on an era that remains central to our understanding of American and world history.

Hood's First Effort to Save Atlanta

· ·

EARL J. HESS

The
Battle of
PEACH
TREE
CREEK

THE UNIVERSITY OF NORTH CAROLINA PRESS

Chapel Hill

This book was published with the
assistance of the FRED W. MORRISON FUND
of the University of North Carolina Press.

© 2017 Earl J. Hess

Manufactured in the United States of America

Set in Miller and Sentinel by Tseng Information Systems, Inc.
The University of North Carolina Press has been
a member of the Green Press Initiative since 2003.

Cover illustration: The 111th Pennsylvania at Peach Tree Creek.
From John Richards Boyle, *Soldiers True: The Story of the One
Hundred and Eleventh Regiment Pennsylvania Veteran Volunteers,
and of Its Campaigns in the War for the Union, 1861–1865* (1903).

Library of Congress Cataloging-in-Publication Data
Names: Hess, Earl J., author.
Title: The battle of Peach Tree Creek : Hood's first effort to
save Atlanta / Earl J. Hess.
Other titles: Civil War America (Series)
Description: Chapel Hill : The University of North Carolina Press, [2017] |
Series: Civil War America | Includes bibliographical references and index.
Identifiers: LCCN 2017007289| ISBN 9781469634197 (cloth : alk. paper) |
ISBN 9781469634203 (ebook)
Subjects: LCSH: Peachtree Creek, Battle of, Ga., 1864. | Hood, John Bell,
1831–1879. | Georgia—History—Civil War, 1861–1865. | United States—
History—Civil War, 1861–1865—Campaigns.
Classification: LCC E476.7 .H465 2017 | DDC 973.7/371—dc23
LC record available at https://lccn.loc.gov/2017007289

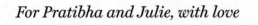

For Pratibha and Julie, with love

Contents

. . . .

Illustrations

. . . .

Maps

. . . .

Preface

· ·

The midday sun was at its height on the afternoon of July 20, 1864, as the men of George H. Thomas's Army of the Cumberland settled into positions south of Peach Tree Creek. The crossing had consumed many hours and was conducted in stages the day before and that morning. Now it was time for some of Thomas's units to construct rude fieldworks, send out skirmishers, and consolidate their hold on the high ground just south of the stream. For other units, commanded by men who assumed there would be no fighting that day, there was an opportunity to lounge in the bottomland of the creek, fix a meal, and relax under the shade of trees.

But then, without warning, battle flags appeared from the woods south of Thomas's new position, followed by division upon division of butternut-clad men. The Army of Tennessee was on the move, and its new commander, John Bell Hood, was making his first strike to save Atlanta. After falling back sixty miles from Dalton since early May, the Confederates attempted their first major attack on William T. Sherman's army group as the enemy closed in on the outskirts of Atlanta. Hood hoped to take advantage of the fact that his enemy had just made a difficult crossing of Peach Tree Creek. His Confederates certainly took the Unionists by surprise. All along the developing battle front the Federals scrambled to get ready; two potentially dangerous gaps in the line of the Twentieth Corps were waiting to be exploited by the onrushing enemy, and some other bits of high ground still had not been secured by Union commanders along the line.

In short, there was reason for the Confederates to hope that Hood's plan might work to their benefit. Only two days in command of the Army of Tennessee, Hood had precious little time to acclimate himself to a position he had not wanted and for which he possessed few attributes to fill. But he did his best to plan, position, and inspire his men despite widespread dissatisfaction at the relief of their beloved general Joseph E. Johnston and the elevation of someone who had served in the Army of Tennessee for only four months. Whether his men could fulfill Hood's hope for a dramatic turnaround in Rebel fortunes during the Atlanta campaign would be worked out before dusk fell on that hot and bloody day of fighting north of the city.

This book tells the story of the battle of Peach Tree Creek—the battle of July 20, 1864, north of Atlanta. A successor to my studies of Kennesaw Mountain and Ezra Church, this book is also based on exhaustive research in primary sources and an examination of the ground. Its purpose is not only to detail the battle's history in narrative fashion but to analyze and evaluate the major features of that history. Each phase of the Atlanta campaign possessed important aspects to explain the course of events from the May confrontation at Dalton to the final battle at Jonesboro in late August and early September. None of those phases were necessarily decisive in shaping the campaign, but all of them contributed to its contours and results. We need to understand each phase in its turn and how it contributed to the larger picture if we hope to understand one of the largest, most important, and most interesting campaigns of the Civil War.

The battle of Peach Tree Creek was heavily dominated by the sudden replacement of Johnston with Hood on July 17–18. In that event the Army of Tennessee lost its most respected commander (although one who did not hesitate to discipline the troops with executions for desertion) and gained a man whose capabilities were largely unknown. William J. Hardee, the only one of the army's corps commanders with great experience in his job, was miffed at Hood's ascension to command. Hardee's colleagues (Alexander P. Stewart and Benjamin F. Cheatham) had not yet fought a battle with their new corps commands. Hood mandated an overly complex movement en echelon by divisions, and the attack took place several hours later than planned. The Confederates advanced with little information about the placement of their enemy, knew nothing of a one-and-a-half-mile gap in Sherman's line, and were ill-informed that Sherman's left wing was closing in along the eastern approaches to Atlanta. That latter development forced Hood to curtail the fighting at Peach Tree Creek earlier than anticipated.

Despite these disadvantages, the Confederates brought to bear a huge preponderance of manpower upon one division of Thomas's army and found two gaps in the Twentieth Corps line as they approached the Federals south of Peach Tree Creek. Their failure to exploit these advantages doomed the Rebel effort that afternoon. A combination of poor Confederate troop handling, lack of offensive spirit, and very effective Union countermeasures evened the odds and resulted in a spirited Union victory. Hood completely failed in his objective, and the Army of the Cumberland achieved one more important success on the battlefield.

Morale loomed large as an element in the story of Peach Tree Creek. The Confederates suffered depressed spirits to a significant degree, and they were comparatively unused to offensive action thus far in the campaign. In fact the Army of Tennessee had not conducted a major attack since the battle of Chickamauga ten months before. Most Rebel soldiers did not know what to make of their new army commander. In contrast, the Federals had enjoyed unusually high morale for a long while before the Atlanta campaign began, and they had complete faith in Sherman's ability to conduct the risky movements necessary to approach the city. They loved and trusted Thomas. We should keep in mind that the Federals were used to winning campaigns and battles, and the Confederates were not—an important factor in assessing troop morale. In terms of battle spirit, Peach Tree Creek matched the opponents at a time when the Confederates were at an important disadvantage, and the Federals were, as usual, riding high.

Looking objectively at the course of the fighting at Peach Tree Creek, it is striking that so many Confederate brigades in William J. Hardee's Corps moved forward only part way across the contested ground before stopping well short of the Union line and doing little more than firing for the rest of the afternoon. Hardee greatly outnumbered the lone Fourth Corps division opposing him, commanded by John Newton, yet he utterly failed to capitalize on that unusual advantage. Even the men of Alexander P. Stewart's Army of Mississippi, advancing to the left of Hardee, failed to exploit the two gaps in Joseph Hooker's Twentieth Corps line. Ironically, about one-third of the troops in Winfield S. Featherston's Mississippi Brigade did not even attempt to move into the gap they found, choosing to remain at the captured Union skirmish line rather than advance farther toward the enemy. Although some Rebel units would later attack well on July 22 and at Ezra Church on July 28, Peach Tree Creek marked the beginning of a deterioration of combat spirit among many other units in the Army of Tennessee.

The Federals of William Ward's Union division responded remarkably well, surging forward up a steep slope to grapple in many places hand to hand with Featherston's men, but they also tended to exaggerate the intensity of the fighting that developed. Ironically, Ward's three brigades competed with only two-thirds of Featherston's Brigade in this contest. Without taking anything away from the inspired fighting conducted by Ward's division, it has to be pointed out that even in Stewart's command a significant lack of fighting spirit hampered the Confederate effort on July 20.

Confederate fighting spirit increased after Peach Tree Creek but not in a uniform way. As the disruption caused by Johnston's relief faded and Hood endured an agonizing transition period into army command, some units attacked with a good deal of determination on July 22 east of Atlanta when the Army of Tennessee came closer than at any other time in the campaign to winning an important victory over Sherman. Other units also attacked with a good deal of determination at Ezra Church on July 28. In both engagements, however, improved morale failed to translate into tactical success, and in each of them some Confederate units failed to press home their assaults. Peach Tree Creek represented the beginning of a trend in the Atlanta campaign, resulting in uneven battle spirit within Confederate ranks. As a result, the course of the campaign continued to be dominated by the Federals until the final agony at Jonesboro led to Hood's evacuation of Atlanta on September 2, 1864.

Like all the battles that took place during the Atlanta campaign, Peach Tree Creek held the potential for decisive results. But, like all of them, those results were not realized. It would be misleading to argue that any one engagement in this long campaign was the decisive moment in Sherman's struggle for Atlanta. Each one contributed in its own way toward shaping the course of the campaign and influencing its outcome. The purpose of this study is to determine how the battle of July 20 affected the events in Georgia, why it became a failure for one side and a success for the other, and how the battle affected the 46,000 men directly engaged in combat that hot afternoon in late July, more than 150 years ago.

I wish to thank all the staff members of the archival institutions listed in the bibliography for their assistance in making their valuable holdings accessible during the course of gathering material for this book. Also a note of thanks to all the graduate student researchers who aided me in accessing material at archives I was unable to visit personally.

The two scholars who read the manuscript for the University of North Carolina Press, Peter S. Carmichael and A. Wilson Greene, deserve a deep note of thanks from me for their helpful suggestions.

Most of all my deep gratitude to my wife Pratibha for all she means to me. She and I also are responsible for all the maps that appear in this book.

The Battle of Peach Tree Creek

I am getting very wearied of this eternal retiring.
—W. H. T. Walker

1

To the Chattahoochee

By the middle of July 1864, the Atlanta campaign had stretched into the longest and most grueling military effort in the Civil War's Western Theater. Maj. Gen. William T. Sherman had started from the vicinity of Chattanooga with some 100,000 men organized as an army group. Maj. Gen. George H. Thomas's Army of the Cumberland was the largest of the three armies in this group with about 60,000 men, and Maj. Gen. James B. McPherson's Army of the Tennessee consisted of about 30,000 men after the Seventeenth Corps joined it in early June. Maj. Gen. John M. Schofield's Army of the Ohio, consisting only of the Twenty-Third Corps, was the smallest of the three with about 10,000 troops. These three armies were drawn from the military departments embraced by Sherman's command, the Military Division of the Mississippi.[1]

Sherman had benefited from the tutelage of Lieut. Gen. Ulysses S. Grant, who now served as general-in-chief of the United States Army. Grant made his headquarters with Maj. Gen. George G. Meade's Army of the Potomac so as to direct its operations against Gen. Robert E. Lee's Army of Northern Virginia in the East. His conduct of the Overland campaign astonished the country with its fierce attacks against Lee's well-fortified positions. In driving south from the Wilderness to Petersburg, Grant lost 64,000 troops in six weeks of rugged campaigning, inflicting a proportionate number of casualties on Lee and laying semi-siege to an important rail center thirty miles south of Richmond.[2]

Sherman admired Grant's aggressive approach to the thorny problem posed by Lee and the Army of Northern Virginia, but he also was stunned by the human cost of that approach. He preferred a more cautious method of dealing with Gen. Joseph E. Johnston's Army of Tennessee, which consisted of about 60,000 men after Lieut. Gen. Leonidas Polk joined Johnston in mid-May with his Army of Mississippi. Polk's command essentially formed a third corps for Johnston's army, even though it technically constituted an independent force drawn from the Department of Mississippi and East Louisiana.[3]

Sherman crafted an effective strategy, working it out through trial and error during the course of the Atlanta campaign. The foundation of that strategy was maneuver, for his larger force had many opportunities to find either of Johnston's flanks whenever the Confederates took up a fortified position. Sherman experimented with several attacks, but they always were local rather than general in nature. Localized attacks tended to minimize casualties and reduce the resonance of failure; they never neutralized Sherman's ability to continue operations after they failed. In contrast, Grant tended to attack more often and trusted too much on general assaults. He often gave little time to Meade for planning these massive efforts and too little attention was paid to heavy skirmishing and trying to reach Lee's flanks in subtle movements. Of course, the well-known vigilance and aggressive tactics that characterized Lee's handling of the Army of Northern Virginia in previous campaigns contributed to Grant's sense of urgency; he could ill afford to be idle or complacent in front of the Army of Northern Virginia. But the result of Grant's campaign thus far was apparent stalemate outside Petersburg with a military force that had lost about half the men in its ranks when it started the Overland campaign. The military effectiveness of the Army of the Potomac had been severely reduced by June and July, greatly contributing to the slow pace and often failed offensives of Grant's efforts at Petersburg.[4]

Just as Lee's reputation and conduct contributed to the nature of Grant's operations in Virginia, the reputation and conduct of Joseph E. Johnston helped to shape the way Sherman conducted the Atlanta campaign. The two commanders had met before, in the Jackson campaign that followed the fall of Vicksburg in July 1863. At that time, Grant sent Sherman with a sizable force to deal with Johnston's troops (who later constituted the core of Polk's Army of Mississippi during the Atlanta campaign). Johnston refused to offer

William T. Sherman, commander of the Military Division of the Mississippi, whose calculations did not include having to deal with a Confederate attack at Peach Tree Creek on July 20. (Library of Congress, LC-DIG-cwpb-07315)

battle to Sherman as he fell back from the Big Black River twenty-eight miles to Jackson, having already failed to mount an effective effort to relieve the siege of Vicksburg, despite urgent entreaties from authorities in Richmond to do so. Johnston acted strictly on the defensive in the short campaign for Jackson, preferring to rely on the ring of fortifications that barely protected the capital of Mississippi. When Sherman made moves to cross the Pearl River and cut off his retreat east of the city, Johnston evacuated Jackson on the night of July 16. The Jackson campaign was a foretaste of Johnston's handling of the Army of Tennessee in the Union drive toward Atlanta.[5]

While Sherman retained a healthy respect for Johnston's skill as an army administrator, he knew that his opponent was not an aggressive tactician.[6] As long as he could maintain his tenuous line of communications (a rail line stretching 350 miles to Louisville) and keep his army intact, Sherman could afford to take his time in approaching Atlanta.

Several rivers not only posed obstacles to Sherman's advance but marked geographic divisions along his march toward Atlanta. The Oostanaula River, which flowed from northeast toward the southwest near Resaca about twenty miles south of Chattanooga, marked the limit of Appalachian terrain. The area north of this stream consisted of high ridges that dominated the countryside, but Sherman had little difficulty maneuvering through it, using the long ridges to shield his flanking movements around the imposing Confederate positions. The Etowah River, draining toward the west some forty miles south of Chattanooga, marked the limit of a transition zone between Appalachia and the Piedmont. This was an area of more open and fertile country, also posing few difficulties to Sherman's advance.[7]

When the Federals crossed the Etowah River on May 23, temporarily cutting away from the railroad, they entered a Piedmont region of rolling terrain often engulfed with thick pine forests and dotted by isolated villages. This territory slowed Sherman enormously and aided Johnston's defensive tactics. The Federals often did not discover their enemy until within a few yards of their works, and Sherman's massive army group found it difficult to maneuver across the narrow, primitive roads. When rains set in, the situation grew worse, and Federal progress slowed to a crawl. Only by working their way in short stages were the Unionists able to regain the railroad by June 7. Then Sherman continued to move in short stages southward until forcing Johnston onto the dominating heights of Kennesaw Mountain. He again experimented by launching a major attack, the largest of the campaign, on June 27. His 15,000 troops hardly dented the Confederates' well-constructed earthen line, and suffered 3,000 casualties in the attempt. Only when he mounted a major movement away from the railroad to turn Johnston's left flank did the Confederates give up Kennesaw Mountain and fall back on July 2.[8]

Johnston now gave up ground in smaller increments, exhibiting more determination to make his Fabian tactics work by tenaciously holding every possible defensive position. He fell back from the Kennesaw Mountain Line only a short distance to Smyrna Station, giving up that line on July 4 and

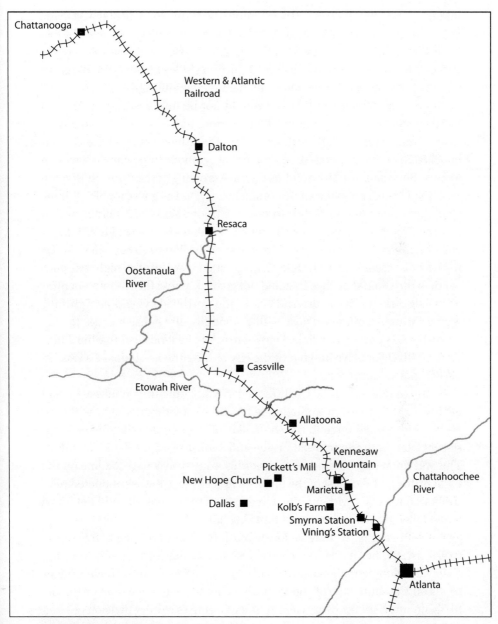

Chattanooga to Atlanta

taking up the Chattahoochee River Line along the north bank of that stream. It took Sherman two months to get this far, ninety miles on a straight line from Chattanooga and only ten miles north of Atlanta. Along the way the Federals lost about 21,000 men, and Johnston suffered about 9,000 casualties, far less than the Union and Confederate losses in Virginia.[9]

But Sherman's success thus far should not be underestimated. He had pried enemy forces out of ten fortified positions and was busy devising ways to eject them from the eleventh line. After that, the crossing of the Chattahoochee River itself represented an event of symbolic importance. It was, in a sense, Sherman's Rubicon. Julius Caesar's crossing of the Rubicon River in 49 BC had been a major event in Roman history; as the governor of Cisalpine Gaul, he was forbidden by law to take his troops across the border of that province and toward Rome or risk being branded an enemy of the state. In crossing the river to seize power, Caesar knew he had to either win or suffer the worst consequences. For Sherman the stakes were not so high, but once south of the Chattahoochee he could not go back across the river except after capturing Atlanta. To be driven back to the north side would be rightfully seen as a major military defeat with potentially dire consequences for the Northern war effort as a whole. Once across, the Federals had to whip Johnston decisively or drive him out of the city by other means to make a success of the Atlanta campaign.

Sherman dealt with the Chattahoochee River Line the same way he had dealt with the other ten Confederate positions—by threatening the flanks. He crossed a small force to the south side of the river at Isham's Ford, upstream from both the railroad bridge and Johnston's right flank, on July 8. This was enough for Johnston to order his army to evacuate the line on the night of July 9. Like most of the previous evacuations, it was conducted relatively smoothly and without interference from the enemy who did not know it had taken place until the early morning hours.[10]

But Johnston failed to tenaciously block the many crossing points of the river; instead, he pulled his troops close to Atlanta for rest and to watch enemy developments. This gave ample room for Sherman to create bridgeheads on the south side of the Chattahoochee at several locations with virtually no interference. Brig. Gen. Kenner Garrard's cavalry division crossed at Roswell about twelve miles upstream from the railroad bridge on July 9. By the next day, Schofield's Twenty-Third Corps crossed at the mouth of Soap Creek, using Isham's Ford to get across the stream. On July 12, Maj. Gen. David S. Stanley's Fourth Corps division, Army of the Cumberland, crossed at Isham's Ford and moved more than three miles south to secure the bluffs on the east side of the Chattahoochee River opposite Power's Ferry,

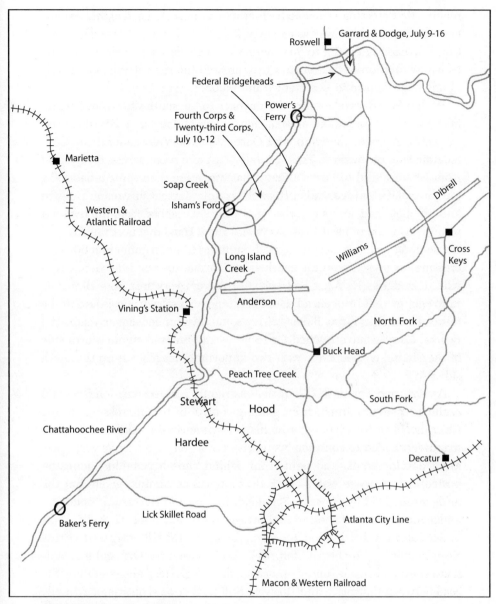

Chattahoochee River Area

making that crossing available to Sherman as well. After the 58th Indiana laid a pontoon bridge at Power's Ferry, Brig. Gen. Thomas J. Wood's Fourth Corps division crossed it to join Stanley on the south side. Brig. Gen. John Newton's division of the Fourth Corps crossed the river at Roswell on July 13 and moved down to join Stanley and Wood.[11]

Within four days of Johnston's drawback to the south side of the Chattahoochee, Sherman had all of Maj. Gen. Oliver O. Howard's Fourth Corps, the entire Army of the Ohio, and Garrard's cavalry division on the Confederate side of the river. The Federals possessed a connected bridgehead from Isham's Ford to Power's Ferry that was more than three miles wide, plus an isolated bridgehead at Roswell six miles farther upstream. Howard and Schofield had access to a road network that reached from the river out toward road junctions at Cross Keys and Buck Head due north of Atlanta. Those junctions gave access to roads running in nearly any direction. Increasing his presence on the south side, Sherman moved Maj. Gen. Grenville M. Dodge's Left Wing, Sixteenth Corps over the river at Roswell by July 14 to enlarge that bridgehead. He also extended cavalry troops south of the railroad bridge as far as Baker's Ferry some seven miles downstream. The Federal army group stretched for some twenty miles along the north side of the Chattahoochee River with two important bridgeheads on the south side.[12]

As historian Thomas L. Connelly has rightly pointed out, Johnston did nothing to stop Sherman from gaining control of useful crossings of the Chattahoochee River. Judging by his performance, the Confederate commander intended to continue his passive resistance to Sherman's advance, await developments, and fight from behind chosen positions. Johnston posted his cavalry to watch the Federals north of Atlanta, given that the bridgeheads held by Howard, Schofield, Dodge, and Garrard portended a major move north of the railroad bridge. Brig. Gen. John H. Kelly, commander of a cavalry division, took Col. George G. Dibrell's brigade to Cross Keys by July 10. To Dibrell's left, Kelly positioned Brig. Gen. John S. Williams's cavalry brigade some distance north of Buck Head and straddling the road between that place and Roswell. Still farther to Williams's left, Kelly positioned Col. Robert H. Anderson's cavalry brigade so that Anderson's left flank touched the Chattahoochee near the mouth of Long Island Creek.[13]

Maj. Gen. Joseph Wheeler, who commanded the Cavalry Corps, Army of Tennessee, was responsible for the overall positioning of these mounted units under Johnston's general direction. They were posted to guard against a major Union move south from Roswell but were in position so as to quickly confront any Federal move out of the Isham's Ford–Power's Ferry bridgehead as well. Johnston's directions to Wheeler were simple: "Please watch the force you mention as on this side of the river, and whenever it moves forward impede its march as much as you can, destroying bridges after you. Give notice of all the roads by which they march, also."[14]

Despite the missed opportunity inherent in failing to block these crossing points of the river with large infantry forces, Johnston displayed an air of calm routine in posting his cavalry and issuing orders. But his withdrawal across the Chattahoochee caused anything but calm among the residents of Atlanta. "Our presence on the south side of the Chatahoochee [*sic*] created considerable alarm," wrote Irenus Watson Landingham, a member of Lieut. Gen. John Bell Hood's corps staff, "and the good people of that city have been getting to the rear in a hurry." As soon as he settled the Army of Tennessee south of the river and just a short distance north of the city, Johnston ordered surplus government stores removed from Atlanta to safer locations south. This logical step simply increased the sense of panic among the citizens. News of the shifting of stores also penetrated the rank and file and led many soldiers to wonder if Johnston had any intention of fighting for possession of the city. J. Walker Coleman of the 1st Tennessee was not surprised to learn that the residents despaired of their safety and were trying to leave Atlanta. Many officers shared Coleman's view. Maj. Gen. W. H. T. Walker, who commanded a division in Lieut. Gen. William J. Hardee's Corps, was convinced that the civilians had become disheartened by Johnston's fall back from Dalton to the gates of Atlanta, but he assured his daughter that most of his men were still in good heart and willing to fight.[15]

Johnston paid no attention to public opinion as he calmly prepared for the future. After crossing the Chattahoochee, he concentrated on improving the City Line that encircled Atlanta. Started the previous summer of 1863, and laid out and supervised by engineer Capt. Lemuel P. Grant, only the basic trench line studded with many forts on high ground existed when the Army of Tennessee crossed the river. Johnston told his chief engineer to assist Grant in the improvements, including cutting embrasures so the artillery could be protected from enemy sharpshooters. He also asked for the shipment of several heavy guns from Mobile and selected an outer line north of the City Line to oppose the Federals when they moved down from Roswell and Power's Ferry. Johnston gave indication that he intended to hold the city as long as possible and that the City Line could be made a formidable position barring Sherman's entry into Atlanta.[16]

But the city's supply lines were vulnerable. Johnston had been unable to prevent Sherman from outflanking him thus far in the campaign, and there was every reason to believe the Federal commander would continue using maneuver and flanking rather than frontal attacks as his modus operandi once he moved south of the Chattahoochee. In fact, Sherman had no intention of battering his army group against Grant's line of fortifications. As early as June 30 he had informed his wife that he would operate against the city's lines of communication instead of against its earthworks. Sherman expressed it well to Maj. Gen. Henry W. Halleck, chief of staff of the United States Army, when he wrote on July 6 that, "instead of attacking Atlanta direct, or any of its forts, I propose to make a circuit, destroying all its railroads. This is a delicate movement and must be done with caution."[17]

The presence of three corps and one cavalry division at Roswell and Power's Ferry telegraphed to the enemy that Sherman intended to move on the city from the north. Was there an alternative? Maj. Gen. Jacob D. Cox, who commanded a division in Schofield's Twenty-Third Corps, carefully examined that question after the war. Cox noted that two railroads entered Atlanta from the south. The Atlanta and West Point Railroad came from Montgomery, Alabama, and joined the Macon and Western Railroad at East Point six miles south of the city. From there traffic on both roads used the track of the Macon and Western Railroad into Atlanta. The Georgia Railroad entered Atlanta from the east, coming from Augusta, Georgia, while the Western and Atlantic Railroad, already in Federal hands, came from Chattanooga, northwest of Atlanta.[18]

Cox envisioned the possibility of Sherman crossing the Chattahoochee River downstream from the railroad bridge. Such a crossing would have given him a relatively short march to reach the railroad south of Atlanta. But Cox foresaw that then Johnston could have relied on the Georgia Railroad and his connection with Augusta. The Confederate commander could also have given up Atlanta and defended every town on the Georgia Railroad as he retired toward Augusta. Missing from Cox's analysis, however, was the knowledge that Johnston had positioned two of his corps (Hardee's and Hood's) to the northwest of Atlanta. They could have quickly confronted any Union move toward the railroad south of the city.[19]

Moreover, Sherman feared that a major crossing downstream from the railroad bridge would expose his own line of communications to a Confederate cavalry force that crossed the Chattahoochee north of the bridge. Moreover, he always had to keep in mind a significant threat: Robert E. Lee might be able to detach troops from the Army of Northern Virginia and use the Confederate rail network to shift reinforcements to Johnston. If so, those troops would likely arrive by way of the Georgia Railroad rather than by the southern route to Atlanta. The strategic situation as well as the tactical environment therefore seemed to dictate a move upstream of the railroad bridge, an approach from the north, and an attempt to cut the Georgia Railroad before hitting the other lines.[20]

The difficulties of this approach were apparent to Sherman, and Cox explained them well in his postwar history of the campaign. Atlanta lay on high ground that constituted the watershed of terrain draining north toward the Chattahoochee River and south toward the Ocmulgee River. But the ground north of Atlanta did not drain directly into the river; it mostly drained into Peach Tree Creek, which ran generally east to west about four miles north of Atlanta. The creek dominated the area and represented a good defensive position for the Confederates. It emptied into the Chattahoochee River just upstream from the railroad bridge where its mouth was, in Cox's words, "a wide and muddy bed."[21]

Not only did the creek pose a serious obstacle to the Federal advance, in terms of both the depth of its valley and the possibility of Confederate resistance, but a northern approach would have to come out of the two bridgeheads already established south of the Chattahoochee. Cox noted that any Union force moving from Roswell would have to march three to four times more miles to reach the Georgia Railroad than would troops marching from the Isham's Ford–Power's Ferry bridgehead to Peach Tree Creek. Sherman faced the problem of coordinating the movement of his army group over a wide area within reach of the enemy so as not to open a dangerous hole in his line of approach that could be exploited by the Confederates. His left would have to move a long distance from Roswell toward Decatur, while his right would have to move a very short distance to the mouth of Peachtree Creek. With inadequate information about the road system, this would be a difficult task.[22]

Before tackling this problem, Sherman offered his troops much needed time for rest. They had been marching, digging, and fighting for more than two months. "Seventy odd days is a long time in such a life as we are leading, with just enough of rest and comfort to keep us from breaking down altogether," complained Luther P. Bradley, a brigade commander in Newton's division. While quartermasters and commissaries stockpiled supplies at forward depots located in newly occupied places such as Allatoona, Marietta, and Vining's Station, the rank and file took it easy for a few days. Scurvy became apparent in some units due to the lack of fresh vegetables, and clothing was universally ragged and worn out. Officers dealt with these problems as best they could in the short time available before the campaign moved into its next phase south of the Chattahoochee River. Morale was high in Sherman's ranks; the course of the campaign thus far had inspired most Federals to assume they would be successful in capturing the city, and they expected the place to fall soon after they crossed the river.[23]

Most Confederates also expected something important to happen soon after their enemy crossed the Chattahoochee. Ellison Capers, commander of the 24th South Carolina, thought Johnston would hit the Federal flank as his enemy maneuvered north of Atlanta while closing in on the city. Capers feared that if Johnston did not take the tactical offensive, he might evacuate Atlanta and retire east. W. H. T. Walker more than conjectured about Johnston's intentions; he was deeply worried that his commander would not fight. "I am getting very wearied of this eternal retiring," he told his wife on July 12, "Where it is to stop I don't know." Walker was certain the men remained in good spirits and were eager to fight. A company commander in the 28th Mississippi Cavalry named Sidney S. Champion also thought the rank and file was solidly in favor of a major battle, and he was certain a "great stand up fight will be made" on the south side of the Chattahoochee.[24]

While many Confederates worried about Johnston's long retreat from Dalton, most of them retained faith in his leadership and hoped that, with the army's back to Atlanta, there would be no more retreats. But that sense of cautious optimism was not shared by Confederate authorities in Richmond. In fact, Johnston's long withdrawal from Dalton had created an atmosphere of crisis in the Confederate capital. President Jefferson Davis had a deep history of frustration and conflict with Johnston stemming from the period following the Confederate victory at First Manassas. Johnston had disappointed everyone in Richmond when he failed to relieve the siege of Vicksburg the previous summer. Davis had consented to Johnston's replacement of Gen. Braxton Bragg to command the Army of Tennessee because he felt there was no better alternative, but his fears grew with each retrograde movement south from Dalton. Johnston made the situation worse by failing to mollify Richmond and harping on the need for sending Confederate cavalry from Mississippi to cut Sherman's line of communications in Tennessee. That cavalry had its hands full dealing with several Union expeditions penetrating the state from Memphis. Davis in turn urged Johnston to use his own cavalry command to strike at Sherman's line of communications, but the general felt he needed the horsemen to extend and protect his flanks in the face of Sherman's more numerous army group. What little communication was exchanged between the general and the president tended to have a testy, worried tone on the part of Davis and an air of frustrating calm on the part of Johnston.[25]

The Chattahoochee River was a Rubicon of sorts for the Confederate general as well; when Johnston fell back to the south side, Davis felt he had gone one river too far. The Confederate president sent Bragg, now his military advisor to visit the Army of Tennessee. Bragg had helped to organize that army and had commanded it from the spring of 1862 until the disastrous defeat at Missionary Ridge in late November 1863. Always controversial, Bragg nevertheless possessed talent as an administrator and had become an important part of Davis's presidential staff. When Bragg reached Atlanta on July 13, he confirmed that all Confederate troops were south of the Chattahoochee, "and indications seem to favor an entire evacuation of this place."[26]

When Bragg met with Johnston on July 14, they had a rather strange series of interactions. Davis's emissary did not disclose the real reason for his visit, preferring to observe Johnston to see if there were any signs of fight in the general. For his part, Johnston also failed to take Bragg into his confidence. They conversed about a wide range of topics without engaging in meaningful discussion about the most important issue of the moment. Bragg also conferred with the two corps leaders in the Army of Tennessee, William J. Hardee and John Bell Hood, on July 14. He spoke as well with Alexander P. Stewart, who had been named as Leonidas Polk's permanent replacement in charge of the Army of Mississippi after Polk was killed by Union artillery fire at Pine Mountain on June 14. This army, consisting of troops drawn from the Department of Mississippi and East Louisiana, had been on detached service cooperating with Johnston's Army of Tennessee since mid-May.[27]

Bragg's conference with the corps leaders produced no startling developments except for an interesting letter written by Hood. Apparently spurred on by Bragg's visit, Hood more openly criticized Johnston's handling of the campaign than he had previously dared. In a long letter addressed to Bragg and dated July 14, Hood blasted Johnston for failing to take advantage of numerous opportunities to strike Sherman since Dalton. The Army of Tennessee lost 20,000 men in his estimation even though it had not yet fought a general battle with the Yankees. Hood adamantly opposed abandoning Atlanta. "We should attack him, even if we should have to recross the river to do so. I have, general, so often urged that we should force the enemy to give us battle as to almost be regarded reckless by the officers high in rank in this army, since their views have been so directly opposite. I regard it as a great misfortune to our country that we failed to give battle to the enemy many miles north of our present position."[28]

This letter was the culmination of a sordid series of actions and attitudes that had gripped Hood since the young general had been elevated to command a corps in the Army of Tennessee. A West Point graduate who had racked up a sterling record as a brigade and division commander under Lee in Virginia, Hood suffered debilitating injuries on the battlefield. He lost the use of an arm at Gettysburg and suffered amputation of a leg after Chickamauga. Bragg became enamored of him as a soldier and strongly urged Hood's appointment to the corps command. Davis needed little urging because he had developed a personal acquaintance with Hood during the winter of 1863–64. Both men seemed to have looked on Hood as a breath of fresh air for an army that had been battered by in-fighting between Bragg and his corps leaders, Hardee and Polk.[29]

But Hood had not done well as a corps commander. Ironically, he was responsible for some of Johnston's decisions to retreat rather than fight. Johnston assigned Hood the task of moving forward to strike Sherman on May 19 near Cassville, only to call off the offensive when Hood reported that Union troops unexpectedly appeared near his right flank. Later that evening, Hood and Polk badgered Johnston into giving up a good defensive position on top a high ridge outside Cassville because Federal artillery had gained enfilade fire on their lines. Johnston later regretted caving in to his generals on that occasion. Hood missed another chance to attack along the New Hope Church–Pickett's Mill–Dallas Line when the Federals moved troops quickly enough to protect their left flank. Moreover, when Hood did launch an attack at Kolb's Farm on June 22, it was without orders from Johnston and without preparation. The result was a bloody repulse with 1,000 casualties. The only thing Hood gained from it was to block Sherman's attempt to find and turn the Confederate left flank, something he could have accomplished with a skirmish line and the loss of a few dozen troops.[30]

Hood's letter to Bragg of July 14 was duplicitous and irresponsible. Johnston was not as supine as Hood pretended, and Hood was not so vigorous a proponent of the offensive as he professed. Worst of all, Hood appeared to be above his ability as a corps commander both in terms of how he handled the three divisions under his charge and in terms of how he dealt with his colleagues and superior. He got along very well with Polk because both men were intriguers who enjoyed making trouble behind the scenes (Polk had been the chief thorn in Bragg's side for months). Hood seems to have bought into Polk's habits and mimicked the bishop general's penchant for trading on his deep personal friendship with Davis against anyone he did not like.[31]

Hood was far less adept at playing this game than Polk, and he overstretched himself in the July 14 letter to Bragg. It is quite possible that, on the basis of this letter, Bragg decided Johnston had to go and Hood had to replace him. Hood's motives in this have been a bone of contention among historians ever since. Many have assumed Hood connived for the command of the army all along. Hood biographer Richard McMurry goes so far as to say that he deliberately lied in the letter and wonders if Bragg was his accomplice or his dupe. There is another line of interpretation—that Hood really was not angling for the command. He had given no indication in any way that he wanted to lead the Army of Tennessee, but he certainly did not like Johnston or the way the campaign had evolved thus far. Hood simply went too far in his letter concerning the game he had learned to play from Polk—influencing great events through personal influence with decision makers. Polk had been quite careful in what he put down on paper, but Hood had no discretion in this matter. Bragg and Davis had largely come to the decision to drop Johnston in any case, but Hood's letter may have led them to conclude that Hood was the best replacement for him. If so, it most likely was not part of a plan on Hood's part for, as we shall see in the next chapter, Hood was genuinely surprised at the appointment and tried to persuade Davis to change his mind about elevating him to army command before he only reluctantly accepted the appointment.[32]

Bragg wrote a long letter to Davis on July 15 before he left Atlanta. In it he spelled out Johnston's failures, noting that he had two conferences with the general. "He has not sought my advice, and it was not volunteered. I cannot learn that he has any more plan for the future than he has had in the past. It is expected that he will await the enemy on a line some three miles from here, and the impression prevails that he is now more inclined to fight." For his part, Johnston later recalled his visits with Bragg in the same way. Indeed, Bragg had been quite cagey with Johnston about the true nature of his visit to Atlanta, and that created a good deal of surprise and resentment on Johnston's part when later he realized what was happening. Bragg advised Davis to appoint Hood to the command. His recommendation of Hood was less enthusiastic than his recommendation had been for Hood's corps command, but he thought the young man had the right spirit for the job.[33]

Ironically, Bragg's July 15 letter did not play a direct role in Davis's decision because Bragg sent it by a courier who did not reach Richmond before the Confederate president decided to relieve Johnston. But Bragg's recommendations were fully in line with Davis's views and could only have added strength to his conviction. Davis made up his own mind as the result of a garbled report that the Federals were building a fortified line south of the Chattahoochee River toward the Georgia Railroad. This report arrived in Richmond on July 16, before the Yankees had crossed the river in force. Yet it prompted Davis to urgently telegraph Johnston. "I wish to hear from you as to present situation, and your plan of operations so specifically as will enable me to anticipate events." Unlike Lee, Johnston had never informed Davis of his tactical or strategic plans for dealing with the enemy, and the Confederate president was understandably worried.[34]

"As the enemy has double our number," Johnston telegraphed on July 16, "we must be on the defensive. My plan of operations must, therefore, depend upon that of the enemy. It is mainly to watch for an opportunity to fight to advantage. We are trying to put Atlanta in condition to be held for a day or two by the Georgia militia, that army movements may be freer and wider." Johnston further explained the reality behind the report that set Davis a flutter: Wheeler reported that some troops from Schofield's Twenty-Third Corps had moved about three miles east of Isham's Ford and made some breastworks.[35]

Johnston's telegram was honest and frank, and it demonstrated why he had not communicated his plans before July 16. The truth was Johnston had no real plan to deal with Sherman other than to wait and see what would develop and fall back whenever there was a threat to his position. His few and furtive efforts to take the tactical offensive often were spoiled by Hood, and Johnston did not seem to care a great deal about them. His Fabian strategy had prolonged the campaign and kept the Army of Tennessee intact, but it had destroyed whatever political capital he held with the Richmond authorities. Because Bragg had not been frank with him, Johnston also was blissfully unaware that his career as commander of the main Confederate army in the West was about to end.

Davis waited another day to ponder the momentous decision he was about to make, but in the end he could see no other way than to change commanders. It was a desperate move on the eve of Sherman's massive sweep south of the Chattahoochee River, and the fate of Atlanta and perhaps of the Western Confederacy lay in the balance.

I feel the weight of the responsibility so suddenly and
unexpectedly devolved upon me.—John B. Hood

The men are bitterly opposed to the change and Swear
that they will not fight under Hood.—Hugh Black

To-morrow I want a bold push for Atlanta.—William T. Sherman

2

. . . .

Across the Chattahoochee,
July 17–18

Sherman set July 17, a clear and hot day, as the beginning of
the last phase of his drive toward Atlanta. Three corps of his
army group prepared to move across the Chattahoochee River
that day. Maj. Gen. John M. Palmer's Fourteenth Corps and
Maj. Gen. Joseph Hooker's Twentieth Corps, both of Thomas's
Army of the Cumberland, planned to cross within the Isham's
Ford–Power's Ferry bridgehead, while Maj. Gen. John A.
Logan's Fifteenth Corps and Maj. Gen. Frank P. Blair's Seventeenth Corps of McPherson's Army of the Tennessee planned
to cross at Roswell. As soon as the entire army group was on the
south side, it was to move forward along well-planned routes
to cover the northern and eastern approaches to Atlanta.
McPherson and Garrard would march about sixteen miles
until reaching Decatur and the Georgia Railroad east of the
city. Thomas's large army had anywhere from one to ten miles
to move until covering nearly the entire front north of Atlanta,
while Schofield would try to fill in the gap between the two
larger armies. There was a screen of Confederate cavalry in the
way, and Federal officers would have difficulty finding roads
that allowed all units to move forward without exposing dan-

gerous gaps in the approach, but the Federals had conducted similarly dangerous moves before in the campaign.[1]

Sherman wanted Thomas to get at least as far as Nancy's Creek by dark of July 17. That stream flowed southwest and entered Peach Tree Creek about a half mile from the Chattahoochee. Thomas's men would have to march from one to four miles to reach Nancy's Creek. Continuing beyond the stream on July 18, Thomas would find Buck Head four miles farther east. As soon as he reached this important crossroads, Sherman wanted him to redirect his columns southward and explore the area along the Buck Head and Atlanta Road to "see what is there. A vigorous demonstration should be made" to distract the enemy from McPherson's long march.[2]

The single pontoon bridge at Power's Ferry proved inadequate for the crossing of two corps in one day. Engineers laid two more pontoon bridges at Pace's Ferry, two miles north of the railroad bridge and about four miles south of Power's Ferry, on July 17. Howard sent Thomas J. Wood's division of the Fourth Corps to cover the laying of these bridges early that morning. Wood pushed away Confederate pickets and formed a line straddling the road leading east from Pace's Ferry as the 58th Indiana constructed them. Both structures were in place by early afternoon, and then Palmer's Fourteenth Corps crossed one and Hooker's Twentieth Corps used the other. When Maj. Gen. Jefferson C. Davis's division of Palmer's command relieved Wood at 4 P.M., the latter returned to Howard. Davis then skirmished forward along the Pace's Ferry Road until dusk, driving Confederate cavalry skirmishers until he rested about one mile from the Chattahoochee River.[3]

As the Federals moved across the stream, these temporary bridges swayed with the movement. The banks on both sides rose from six to fifteen feet above the level of the swift current. The chaplain of the 58th Indiana recalled that the sand along the banks gave the water a distinct yellow color. He also noted that sharp rocks on the river bottom sometimes tore the canvas covering of the pontoon boats when the Indiana troops were careless in maneuvering them into place.[4]

Davis took position about a mile from the crossing and near Kyle's Bridge over Nancy's Creek. Supporting divisions soon trudged up to form a line, Palmer posting his men on the right. Palmer also sent skirmishers down as far as the junction of Nancy's Creek and Peach Tree Creek. This point would serve as the pivot upon which Thomas had to move his army the next day. The ground was cut up with ravines and heavily covered by forest. Morale was high among Thomas's men. There was a "general impression . . . that we should be in Atlanta by the 20th, and with almost no fighting," recalled James A. Connolly, a division level staff officer in the Fourteenth Corps.[5]

Hooker's Twentieth Corps troops crossed the river a bit later than Palmer's men and set out toward Nancy's Creek. Although some units marched across the pontoons as late at 9 P.M., many Twentieth Corps men found the Chattahoochee River "a beautiful stream, swift and banks very steep." The two bridges served Sherman's purpose well; consisting of seventeen pontoon boats each, they provided swift passage over the last river before reaching Atlanta. Once on line to the left of Palmer's corps, Hooker's troops found the landscape choked with trees and so irregular in outlay that they crowded together on the high ground to form a feasible defensive position for the night.[6]

Howard already had his Fourth Corps south of the Chattahoochee River and moved it out of the Isham's Ford–Power's Ferry bridgehead on July 17. By evening his troops took position to the left of Hooker's command fronting Nancy's Creek. Schofield's Twenty-Third Corps also already lay south of the river; moving out of the same bridgehead, it kept pace with Howard and took position to the left of the Fourth Corps. Confederate cavalry skirmishers annoyed both corps as they maneuvered into position along the Nancy's Creek line.[7]

McPherson set out from the Roswell bridgehead early on July 17. Pushing back Confederate skirmishers, he made good progress until reaching the vicinity of Nancy's Creek. Dodge's Left Wing, Sixteenth Corps, positioned on McPherson's right, now found resistance so heavy that its advance stalled at the creek. Dodge reinforced his skirmish line and managed to push across the stream by 6 P.M., establishing a bridgehead on the Confederate side. He was then about a mile away from Schofield's left flank, but Cox sent out skirmishers to make contact with Dodge's troops and cover the gap between Sherman's wings.[8]

During the few days before Sherman's final crossing of the Chattahoochee, Johnston had rearranged his cavalry screen north of Atlanta. Kelly's Division moved to the east side of the city to guard the Georgia Railroad. It is unclear exactly which cavalry units tried to screen Sherman's approach north of Atlanta, but at least three brigades were available. Brig. Gen. Frank C. Armstrong's Brigade of Brig. Gen. William H. Jackson's Cavalry Division opposed McPherson, while Brig. Gen. John S. Williams's Brigade of Kelly's Division stood before Thomas. Brig. Gen. Samuel W. Ferguson's Brigade of Jackson's Division occupied a spot between Armstrong and Williams with "a wide interval" between his command and Williams's. It is possible that Wheeler also used elements of Maj. Gen. William T. Martin's Division on July 17. Even so, it is clear that Johnston devoted few troops to screening and delaying the Union approach. W. C. Dodson, who wrote a eulogizing book about Wheeler in 1899, related a wild story about his hero attacking through the ranks of Federal infantrymen and driving back "an entire division" on July 17, giving up only three miles of territory to the overwhelming foe. It was nothing but fantasy; the Federals had little difficulty pushing the cavalry screen back at will. Even Dodge, who encountered more resistance, managed to advance beyond Nancy's Creek. Wheeler more accurately reported that his men fought from behind "successive lines of breast-works" against heavy odds and, at best, temporarily repulsed Federal skirmish lines now and then.[9]

By the end of July 17, Sherman completed his crossing of the Chattahoochee River and moved out of the bridgeheads at Roswell, Isham's Ford–Power's Ferry, and Pace's Ferry. His troops made it to their first-day objective, Nancy's Creek, and formed a relatively connected position near its banks with one bridgehead on the other side in McPherson's sector. Accomplished with minimal fighting, it is no wonder so many Yankees assumed Atlanta would fall soon; Johnston displayed no aggressive intent. Sherman hoped Schofield could reach Decatur and McPherson, the Georgia Railroad east of that town, while Thomas headed for Buck Head on July 18.[10]

Johnston continued his normal mode of operations, selecting good defensive ground some distance from the immediate presence of the enemy and waiting for their approach. Peach Tree Creek seemed like a good obstacle to the Federal advance. Stories abounded as to why it received its name. One had it that a Native American village located near its junction with the Chattahoochee was the source. Called Standing Peach Tree, this Creek village may have derived its name from a tall pine tree located on a hill northeast of the union of Chattahoochee River and Peach Tree Creek. The pine had a good deal of pitch, which the natives tapped; "pitch tree" was corrupted into "peach tree." It is also possible that a genuine peach tree once stood on that hill, although local historian Franklin Garrett has pointed out that the pine tree was indigenous to the area and the peach tree was not. Fort Peach Tree stood near the junction of river and creek for several years from 1814 on, solidifying the distinctive name that came to be attached to the creek.[11]

Johnston later argued that he had no choice but to await the enemy along the banks of this stream. If he had tried to deploy north of the creek, its "broad and muddy channel . . . would have separated the two parts of the army" because Johnston had to protect the south side of the Chattahoochee downstream from the creek's mouth. By placing his men south of the creek, he could form a continuous line along both the creek and the river. Johnston instructed his engineers to select a position on high ground a short distance south of Peach Tree Creek to place the army when necessary. From here, he

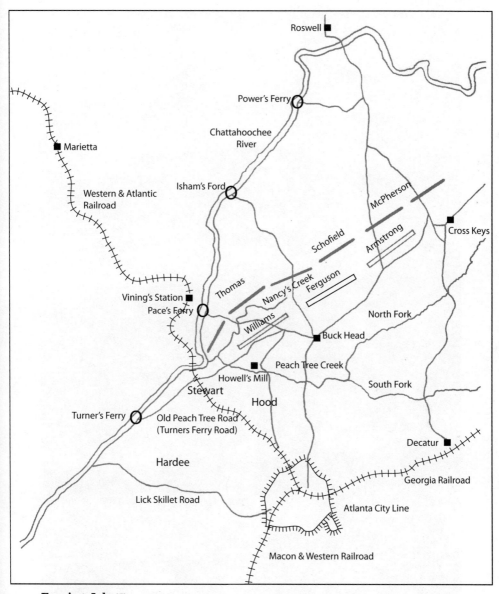

Roswell

Power's Ferry

Chattahoochee
River

Marietta

McPherson

Isham's Ford

Schofield

Cross Keys

Western & Atlantic
Railroad

Armstrong

Thomas

Nancy's Creek

Ferguson

Vining's Station

North Fork

Pace's Ferry

Williams

Buck Head

Howell's Mill

Peach Tree Creek

South Fork

Stewart

Hood

Turner's Ferry

Old Peach Tree Road
(Turners Ferry Road)

Decatur

Hardee

Georgia Railroad

Lick Skillet Road

Atlanta City Line

Macon & Western Railroad

Evening, July 17

Joseph E. Johnston, commander of the Army of Tennessee, who lost his job because of his passive handling of the Atlanta campaign. (Library of Congress, LC-DIG-cwpb-06280)

wrote after the war, the Army of Tennessee "might engage the enemy if he should expose himself in the passage of the stream." The engineers selected positions for each corps and pointed them out to staff officers. Johnston also issued orders to his corps leaders on the morning of July 17 to be ready to move at a moment's notice.[12]

Johnston was well aware of Sherman's moves on July 17 and continued preparations to meet the enemy. He was consulting with Col. S. W. Presstman, his chief engineer, late that evening at army headquarters located at the Nelson house three miles from Atlanta on the road to Marietta. A telegram arrived at either 9 P.M. or an hour later, depending on which source one relies upon. The telegram was sent by Adj. Gen. Samuel Cooper in Richmond. It conveyed the news that Jefferson Davis had decided to relieve Johnston of his command and replace him with Hood, who was elevated to the temporary rank of full general. The reason for this change, in Cooper's words, was that "you have failed to arrest the advance of the enemy to the vicinity of Atlanta, far in the interior of Georgia, and express no confidence that you can defeat or repel him." Like a good soldier, Johnston quickly drafted a farewell to the army, although he waited before issuing it to the troops.[13]

Hood also received a telegram that night at his headquarters near the Turner's Ferry Road. Delivered at 11 P.M., it was sent by Secretary of War James A. Seddon and announced his elevation to army command. "You are charged with a great trust," Seddon told Hood. "You will, I know, test to the upmost your capacities to discharge it. Be wary no less than bold. It may yet be practicable to cut the communication of the enemy or find or make an opportunity of equal encounter whether he moves east or west. God be with you."[14]

Not long after that, Johnston sent a note of congratulation to Hood. In replying to it at 1 A.M. of July 18, Hood frankly told his commander that he was surprised by the order and wanted to consult with him early in the morning. In his memoirs, published nearly twenty years later, Hood was more explicit about his feelings at this crucial moment in his life. "This totally unexpected order so astounded me, and overwhelmed me with a sense of the responsibility thereto attached, that I remained in deep thought throughout the night." Historians have often assumed Hood had angled for the command, but there is more than enough convincing evidence that the appointment truly was unexpected and even unwanted. F. Halsey Wigfall, a member of Hood's corps staff, confirmed it in a letter to his mother. "The first time I saw him that day, I shook hands with him and congratulated him. He spoke very sadly and said he hardly knew if it were a subject of congratulation."[15]

Further confirmation that Hood did not want the command lies in his

John Bell Hood, who succeeded Johnston in command of the Army of Tennessee on July 18 and launched a quick strike against the Federals two days later at Peach Tree Creek. (Library of Congress, LC-DIG-cwpb-07468)

efforts to postpone or derail the appointment. He started for Johnston's headquarters before dawn of July 18 and met Alexander P. Stewart on the way. The two engaged in earnest conversation about the change of commanders as they continued their ride to army headquarters. Arriving just after dawn, Hood asked Johnston the reason for the change. Johnston replied that he was not entirely certain, other than that Davis insisted on it. Hood then urged Johnston to pocket the order and continue to lead the army at least until Sherman's current movements had run their course. Stewart apparently was the one who initially suggested this to Hood before the pair reached army headquarters. Johnston correctly pointed out that such an action was impossible unless the president's order was rescinded, so Hood wrote a telegram to Davis requesting the order be set aside. "I deem it dangerous to change the commanders of this army at this particular time, and to be to the interest of the service that no change should be made until the fate of Atlanta is decided." Stewart and Hardee signed the telegram as well.[16]

The generals sent this round-robin telegram at 9 A.M., but it would take several hours to receive a reply. Meanwhile, Hood prevailed on Johnston to retain command until they heard from their president. The deposed commander took time during the day to pen a telegram to Richmond defending his course of action during the campaign. He argued that Sherman outnumbered his army by a greater degree than Grant outnumbered Lee, yet Sherman's pace was slow compared to Grant's. "Confident language by a military commander is not usually regarded as evidence of competency," he lectured Cooper.[17]

Johnston tried to ease Hood's transition to army command on July 18 while the pair waited for Davis's reply to the corps commanders' telegram. "I explained my plans to him: First, to attack the Federal army while crossing Peach Tree Creek. If we were successful great results might be hoped for, as the enemy would have both the creek and the river to intercept their retreat. Second, if unsuccessful, to keep back the enemy by intrenching, to give time for the assemblying of the State troops promised by Governor Brown; to garrison Atlanta with those troops, and when the Federal army approached the town attack it on its most exposed flank with all the Confederate troops." At least this is how Johnston explained it in his report dated October 20, 1864. Ironically, if he had been as explicit in his telegram to the Confederate president on July 16, Davis might have hesitated to relieve him of command. Johnston consistently told this story in subsequent narratives of the events that day, as well as a letter written in late August 1864, leading historians such as Thomas Robson Hay to assume he had fully informed Hood of plans to attack the Army of the Cumberland at Peach Tree Creek.[18]

But Hood never indicated that Johnston told him this information on July 18. Hay assumes the young general was overwhelmed by the appointment and did not pay close attention to everything that was said. The fact that Johnston is the only source of information concerning his plans to attack at Peach Tree Creek (and he never wrote anything to that effect before being relieved) has led other historians to doubt if he had any real intention of attacking at all. Howell Cobb, who commanded the post at Macon eighty miles south of Atlanta, was convinced Johnston meant to fight. Writing to his wife on July 14, Cobb asserted, "From all I can learn I am satisfied he intends to make a decided stand at Atlanta, and I believe it will be a successful one."[19]

If we look at Johnston's past record, it is true he launched a major attack on the Army of the Potomac when it came close to Richmond during the Peninsula campaign. That attack at Seven Pines on May 31 and June 1, 1862, failed to turn the enemy back. Johnston never attacked Sherman's command during the Jackson campaign of July 1863, giving up the city without even a small offensive battle. Historian Thomas L. Connelly sees no "solid evidence" that Johnston planned to take the offensive, only "a general idea of attacking Sherman." But given his strong assertion of intent to assault at Peach Tree Creek, even if that assertion postdated the event, one tends to credit Johnston at least with some degree of aggressive spirit on July 17 and 18.[20]

Johnston indicated that Hood had urgently asked him to continue giving orders until Davis's telegram settled the issue of command, and he consented to do so. There was real need for someone to be in charge who knew where each corps lay and who was informed about the exact location of the line recently selected by the army's engineers south of Peach Tree Creek. Hood was ignorant of all those details. Johnston busied himself with issuing orders for the troops to move and assume their places in this line; the Army of Tennessee obeyed these orders without knowing what truly was going on at army headquarters.[21]

Davis's telegram arrived at 2 P.M., and it contained predictable news. He sent a copy to each of the three corps leaders and was frank in explaining why he decided to replace Johnston. Davis also revealed a keen awareness of the import of this move and admitted that he had hesitated perhaps too long to make it. The decision boiled down to a choice between continuing a policy that seemed disastrously ineffective and making a change for a different style of leadership. Davis pleaded with each of the corps leaders to set aside personal opinions, accept the decision, and try hard to make it work. "The order has been executed," he concluded, "and I cannot suspend it without making the case worse than it was before the order was issued."[22]

Even with such a firm statement as this in his pocket, Hood still tried to avert the responsibility of command. He once again pleaded with Johnston to ignore Davis and continue managing affairs, and Johnston understandably refused. Then Hood frankly told the older man that he was woefully uninformed about everything necessary to make decisions that day and asked him to at least stay with the army for a few days so he could offer counsel. According to Hood, Johnston was so moved by this plea that he could see tears in the older man's eyes. Johnston agreed to stay, but he wanted to ride into Atlanta that evening and attend to some matters before coming back to help him.[23]

We probably will never know for sure whether Johnston agreed to counsel Hood; we do know that he stayed the night of July 18 in Atlanta with his wife. F. Halsey Wigfall also rode to Atlanta that evening and spoke with Johnston, who displayed no evidence of concern or bitterness at the turn of events. "Indeed he seemed in rather better spirits than usual though it must have been at the cost of much exertion." Johnston also told Wigfall that he intended to go to Columbia the next day. He changed his mind on July 19, taking passage on a freight train for Macon at 6:30 P.M. Howell Cobb persuaded the couple to stay at his house. Mrs. Johnston had a headache, and her husband was now feeling the full emotional impact of events. "Still he indulges in no spirit of complaint, speaks kindly of his successor and very hopefully of the prospect of holding Atlanta," Cobb reported to his wife.[24]

Hood remained bitter for the rest of his life about the manner in which Johnston left him in command. "He deserted me in violation of his promise to remain and afford me the advantage of his counsel, whilst I shouldered all responsibility of the contest." Historians have generally doubted that Johnston promised to remain and offer his advice, even though some of them think Johnston should have been willing to do this on his own. Hood was compelled to issue orders assuming command of the army on the afternoon of July 18. "I feel the weight of the responsibility so suddenly and unexpectedly devolved upon me," Hood wrote in an address to the troops. "I look with confidence to your patriotism to stand by me."[25]

Attention was now focused on him as it had never been before. A newspaper correspondent described Hood in a dispatch dated July 19. He appeared "a tall bony man, with light blue eyes, and brown hair, a heavy suit of beard of the same color falling upon his bosom and an expression of imperturbable benevolence all over his open face. He sto[o]ps a little from the use of his crutch, but moves about with ease."[26]

If Hood seemed imperturbable on July 19, his own account of his work on the afternoon of July 18 would contradict such an air of calm. According to his memoirs, Hood was frantic, working hard to locate the other two corps in the Army of Tennessee, opening up lines of communication with them and with the far-flung locations of the army's cavalry units. But it is strange that Hood never mentioned the Army of Tennessee staff in this regard. They would have been as well informed of these matters as Johnston, and most of them stayed at army headquarters to serve under Hood. The new commander also did not know the exact location of Sherman's units as of late on July 18. Hood later assumed that Wheeler must have kept Johnston informed of this vital intelligence, but Johnston failed to pass it on to him. Only when reading Sherman's memoirs after the war did Hood realize the Federals hit the Georgia Railroad by 2 P.M. of July 18. Johnston did not leave the army for Atlanta until 4 P.M. that day. "I reiterate," Hood asserted in his memoirs, "that it is difficult to imagine a commander placed at the head of an Army under more embarrassing circumstances than those against which I was left to contend."[27]

Hood also complained in his postcampaign report that Johnston had left him with only 48,000 men (Johnston claimed the number totaled 51,000). Hood argued that the troops were "enfeebled in ... spirit by long retreat and by severe and apparently fruitless losses." In his memoirs, Hood went further and argued that the rank and file of the Army of Tennessee were "wedded to the 'timid defensive' policy, and naturally regarded with distrust a commander likely to initiate offensive operations." Moreover, the army was "unfitted for united action in pitched battle" because of its experience thus far in the campaign.[28]

Many of the army's highest-ranking officers were dissatisfied with Hood's accession to command. Hardee had never gotten along well with the young newcomer and felt aggrieved at his elevation. Maj. Gen. Samuel G. French, who had served under Johnston in Mississippi, visited Hood and told him he was sorry to see Johnston go. French told Hood that he and Johnston had had long conversations about the most effective strategy to win the war; preserving the main field armies and holding out until the North exhausted itself in money and spirit. But French assured Hood that he would serve "faithfully and cheerfully" under him. "Although he took my hand and thanked me, I was ever afterwards impressed with the belief that he never forgave me for what I said."[29]

The feelings of the common soldier in the Army of Tennessee about Johnston and Hood have been the subject of much study. The tendency has been to view them as overwhelmingly pro-Johnston, dejected and even demoralized by his removal, and at best noncommittal toward Hood when the news of the change in commanders became widely known on July 18. Richard

McMurry has injected a needed corrective by pointing out that a careful search through contemporary letters and diaries indicates a minority of soldiers had become dissatisfied with Johnston's retreats by mid-July.[30]

Those men who deplored the removal of their hero commonly used terms such as "shocked" and "astounded" at the news that Johnston had been replaced by Hood. "I am afraid it may do harm at this moment," commented Taylor Beatty, "because the army still has confidence in Johnston & does not know Hood." Most men had no idea why the change was made, but others acquired very accurate intelligence on that score. Col. John C. Carter, a brigade commander in Hardee's Corps, spread the word to Andrew Jackson Neal and others in the army. "They have made ole J. Johnston quit us because he falls back," moaned a man in the 29th Georgia, "I am sorrow of it."[31]

One of Hood's greatest problems lay in the fact that his accession to command created a large wellspring of resentment among the rank and file at the loss of a beloved leader. "I never have seen or heard of an army so wrapped up in a commander as this army proved itself to be," asserted Lieut. Hamilton Branch of the 54th Georgia. Branch told his mother that the men acted "as if they had lost their best friend and the general remark was, well this army is lost, and everyone seemed to be whipped." Lieut. Emmett Ross of the 20th Louisiana expressed the opinion of many when he wrote home on July 19 that the men retained full confidence in Johnston despite his long retreat. The source of this confidence lay more in the way he treated the army than in his combat record. Johnston played the role of a benevolent father, feeding the army well, sparing men's lives on the battlefield, and very much acting like a competent commander. He seemed to be a marked contrast to Braxton Bragg, a breath of fresh air in an army that had suffered far too long under the weight of bitter feuds among its generals and one failed campaign after another.[32]

Many men communicated their feelings publicly and in ways that Johnston could not ignore. Brig. Gen. Clement H. Stevens, who commanded a brigade in Hardee's Corps, wrote a letter to the general deploring his removal as soon as the news was made public. Troops of W. H. T. Walker's Division and Brig. Gen. Jesse J. Finley's Florida Brigade cheered and unfurled their flags as they marched past army headquarters on their way to take up sectors of the Peach Tree Creek Line. A regimental band in Finley's Brigade stopped to serenade Johnston as well. "The men are bitterly opposed to the change," wrote Hugh Black in Finley's command, "and Swear that they will not fight under Hood."[33]

The gloom of July 18 and 19 was caused by the loss of Johnston; many men in the Army of Tennessee had at that time no dissatisfaction with his replacement. Hood was as yet an untried general as far as most members of the army were concerned, and most of them were willing to give him a chance. Some soldiers recognized that Johnston was hampered by the fact that the Richmond authorities did not trust him, and they assumed Hood had no such problem.[34]

The new general would have his chance to prove himself, and after the string of big battles to come in late July, judgment on his ability tended to sour. One can read in many letters and diary entries deep disappointment in the outcome of those bloody battles coexisting with some degree of satisfaction that they at least temporarily stopped Sherman's efforts to cut the army's lines of communication around the city.[35]

After the war ended in bitter defeat, Hood's accession to command emerged in soldier memoirs as a black event that doomed the Army of Tennessee. If one concentrated only on these postwar accounts, the reality of soldier morale on July 18 would be terribly skewed. Even if one concentrated only on accounts produced on July 18 and 19, it is clear that most men in the Army of Tennessee deeply regretted the loss of Johnston and at best were willing to give Hood a try. Some were so bitter that they could not for the time see themselves fighting for Hood.[36]

The Army of Tennessee was on the verge of a new phase in the Atlanta campaign, bound for offensive action under a general as yet untried and unknown to most of the troops. This was difficult enough, but the army was still mourning the exit of the most beloved commander in its history. From the standpoint of morale, the army was in poor shape with a large enemy force moving quickly within striking distance north of Atlanta. Davis's action was poorly timed, through no real fault of his; he had hesitated to take this step for quite a long while to be certain it was the right move. Not until Johnston retired across the Chattahoochee did Davis lose *"all hope of a battle,"* as he told William D. Gale on July 30. Davis also had no idea when Sherman would move across the river.[37]

As the Confederate army absorbed the unexpected turmoil, the Federals continued their massive sweep toward Atlanta. Sherman instructed Thomas to move to Buck Head and form a line facing south with his entire army. He identified the Old Peach Tree Road as the objective for July 18. This thoroughfare started at Turner's Ferry about three miles downstream from the Chattahoochee River railroad bridge and ran northeast until crossing Peach Tree Creek near Moore's Mill, near its junction with Nancy's Creek. The Old Peach Tree Road then stretched to Buck Head and beyond. Thomas was to advance south of this road so as to make it available as a ready means of communication along his line. The next obstacle south of the Old Peach

Tree Road was the valley of Peach Tree Creek. While Thomas maneuvered into position, Schofield and McPherson were to break away from Nancy's Creek and head for the Georgia Railroad. This meant a march of some eight miles before McPherson reached the track between Decatur and Stone Mountain and Schofield reached Decatur. "I want that railroad as quick as possible," Sherman wrote.[38]

Thomas issued clear instructions to his subordinates for the day's operations. Howard's Fourth Corps would lead the Army of the Cumberland, seize Buck Head, and then form east of the town and south of Old Peach Tree Road, facing south. Hooker's Twentieth Corps would follow and form in similar manner west of Buck Head. Brig. Gen. Richard W. Johnson's division of Palmer's Fourteenth Corps had the job of stretching out to maintain contact with Hooker, but Palmer's other two divisions, led by Brig. Gen. Jefferson C. Davis and Brig. Gen. Absalom Baird, would essentially maintain the positions they had assumed on the evening of July 17, anchoring Thomas's right flank.[39]

Howard received these instructions just as his corps started to move out at 4:30 A.M., July 18, with Brig. Gen. John Newton's Second Division in the lead. Newton met Confederate cavalry skirmishers two miles from camp and pressed them to Nancy's Creek by 7 A.M. The bridge was partially destroyed and part of Williams's Confederate cavalry brigade was positioned atop a bluff on the south side with four pieces of artillery behind breastworks. Brig. Gen. Luther P. Bradley, whose command led Newton's division, brought up his own guns and arranged for a push over the stream with three regiments, the 65th Ohio, 125th Ohio, and 3rd Kentucky. When the infantry set out at 9:40 A.M., it drove the enemy away, but the Federals had to rebuild the bridge by stripping timber from a nearby barn before they moved on at 11 A.M.[40]

An hour before Newton resumed his advance toward Buck Head, one of Thomas's staff officers delivered a civilian to Sherman's headquarters. The man was a spy who had managed to get out of Atlanta and into Union lines with a newspaper dated July 18, announcing that Hood had replaced Johnston. Sherman knew that Hood had been in the same class at West Point as Schofield, so he asked him about the new commander. Sherman "learned that he was bold even to rashness, and courageous in the extreme; I inferred that the change of commanders meant 'fight.'" Sherman took comfort in noting that Hood graduated forty-fourth in the class of 1853, whereas Schofield had graduated seventh and McPherson first. After the war Sherman could afford to comment that Jefferson Davis had done him a favor by replacing Johnston with Hood, for he was more wary of the former and did not mind meeting the latter in open battle. But it is difficult to tell how much bravado he felt on July 18 while superintending his tricky move toward Atlanta. Col. Andrew J. Mackay, chief quartermaster of the Fourteenth Corps, knew Hood well before the war. "A man who will bet a thousand dollars without having a pair in his hand," he told Richard W. Johnson, "will fight when he has the troops with which to do it."[41]

Sherman received another bit of intelligence on July 18, a document found in a Rebel camp by his advancing troops that indicated the Army of Tennessee had 44,400 men under arms. The estimate undervalued the strength of Hood's army by 4,000 to 7,000 men. It did not change Sherman's mode of moving forward; he had to be prepared for anything now that Hood was in charge.[42]

Newton continued pushing Williams's cavalry east of Nancy's Creek until his van, with Howard along, reached Buck Head at 12:30 P.M. The crossroads did not impress any of the Federals, who noticed a tavern, two or three stores, and a handful of houses. Howard established Newton in two lines east of town and advanced them far enough south to embrace the Old Peach Tree Road as ordered. When Stanley's and Wood's divisions arrived by midafternoon, they also were placed in line with Stanley holding Howard's left, Wood occupying his center, and Newton his right. The advance east of Nancy's Creek had been relatively easy, with only light skirmishing. A Southern newspaper reporter gave Williams far too much credit for hard fighting, claiming the brigade killed and wounded 500 Yankees on July 18; Howard actually suffered only six men wounded that day. John Wesley Marshall of the 97th Ohio in Newton's division spent more time "picking blackberries" than in worrying about the enemy.[43]

Hooker's Twentieth Corps moved out on July 18 with Brig. Gen. William T. Ward's Third Division crossing Nancy's Creek late in the morning. The other two divisions, commanded by Brig. Gen. Alpheus S. Williams and Brig. Gen. John W. Geary, crossed during the afternoon. Hooker instructed Ward to send a brigade toward Buck Head but not long after informed Ward that Howard's Fourth Corps troops had already occupied the town. Ward then moved his division forward and took position to Howard's right, facing south and embracing the Old Peach Tree Road, at 5 P.M.[44]

As Williams and Geary closed up to extend the line Ward began, the men of the Twentieth Corps remarked on the rough nature of the terrain, covered as it often was by thick underbrush. As they approached the Old Peach Tree Road, however, they were struck by the nature of the roadbed, wide and firmly trod, one of the best thoroughfares they had seen in Georgia. The landscape south of the road also had more clearings and substantial houses, an intermediate zone between the wilderness to the north and the thriving city of Atlanta to the south. William Clark McLean noticed a small field with corn already twelve feet tall. "I never saw such corn," he remarked in his diary. More than one Twentieth Corps man picked as many blackberries as he could that day; "the boys have quite a feast," Albert M. Cook of the 123rd New York reported.[45]

When Hooker's men took position just south of Old Peach Tree Road that evening, they constructed breastworks to secure their line. Ward held the left, Geary the center and Williams the right. Some units worked well into the night until the men felt their barricades were high enough to protect them.[46]

Palmer's Fourteenth Corps largely maintained its position while shifting only one division to maintain contact with Hooker's men. Col. Anson G. McCook's brigade led Johnson's division forward, crossing Nancy's Creek and pushing back Confederate cavalry skirmishers, until it reached the Old Peach Tree Road at 2 P.M. At this point McCook was very near Peach Tree Creek, so he moved south along Howell's Mill Road and drove the enemy across that stream. The Confederates burned the bridge at Howell's Mill, about two miles up from the mouth of the creek, preventing McCook from pushing farther south. McCook took position on the high ground north of Peach Tree Creek and constructed breastworks. The other brigades of Johnson's division came forward to extend the line west.[47]

Johnson filed a report with Palmer about the day's accomplishment, noting that Peach Tree Creek appeared to be deep and had very steep banks, rendering it unwise to cross without a bridge. He knew the Confederates were on the south side but had no information as to their strength. The miller at Howell's Mill told the Federals the Rebels were on the high bluff behind tree cover; McCook's skirmishers could catch only a few glimpses of them. Johnson reported a small gap in Thomas's line between McCook's brigade and Williams's division of the Twentieth Corps.[48]

The rest of Palmer's command moved up behind and to the right of Johnson. Baird's division took position as a reserve near Howell's Mill. Davis wheeled his division across Nancy's Creek and moved a short distance toward the north side of Peach Tree Creek. He was responsible for the stretch of ground from Johnson's right flank, below Howell's Mill and down to the mouth of Peach Tree Creek. Confederate skirmishers kept up a lively fight with Davis in the area of Moore's Mill, half a mile upstream from the mouth of the creek, but the Federals pushed them across the watercourse and dug in on the north side. Only on Davis's far right, where the Confederates had no skirmishers near the south bank of Peach Tree Creek, did the

Federals cross the stream. Col. John G. Mitchell sent two companies of the 121st Ohio from his brigade to construct works on the south side of the creek on the night of July 18. Thomas could report that his army accomplished Sherman's objectives for the day.[49]

As Thomas moved in easy stages toward the Old Peach Tree Road, Schofield moved south of Nancy's Creek until stopping along the North Fork of Peach Tree Creek three miles away. Brig. Gen. Milo S. Hascall's division took position at Johnson's Mill, four miles short of Decatur. He sent a brigade to reconnoiter down the road linking the mill with Atlanta to see what lay ahead. On the evening of July 17 a gap had existed between Schofield's left and McPherson's right; now a gap of one mile developed between Schofield's right and Howard's left. The Army of the Ohio clearly was not large enough to maintain contact to right and left. The Fourth Corps sent out patrols to cover one of those gaps and give the alert in case the enemy discovered and tried to exploit it.[50]

Despite all Sherman's efforts, his troops were unable to advance toward Atlanta in a continuous line. This was not surprising considering the difficulties of maneuvering tens of thousands of men over this large area. The units had to march along roads and hope to wind up at the end of the day in lines that were at least close to being connected. Ironically, Thomas had the luxury of keeping Baird's division in reserve on his right wing. If Baird had extended the line, the one-mile gap between Howard and Schofield would have nearly closed.

McPherson's Army of the Tennessee moved out from Nancy's Creek on the morning of July 18, detached from Schofield, and moved southeast toward the railroad between Decatur and Stone Mountain. Garrard's cavalry division led the way, followed by Logan's Fifteenth Corps. By late afternoon Logan was near the railroad and, at McPherson's direction, sent a detachment to tear up a short stretch of the track. These Federals were the first to lay hands on the Georgia Railroad. Meanwhile, Dodge's Left Wing, Sixteenth Corps pushed Confederate cavalry skirmishers away as he advanced from Nancy's Creek and drove the enemy across the North Fork of Peach Tree Creek. Dodge then bivouacked for the night on the north bank with Schofield to his right across the mile-long gap and Blair's Seventeenth Corps to his left.[51]

While Sherman's troops were fulfilling their objectives for the advance on July 18, the Army of Tennessee also was on the move. Johnston had set it in motion before giving up command to Hood so that the Peach Tree Creek Line could become a reality. For Stewart's Army of Mississippi, there was relatively little motion because it already was essentially occupying the

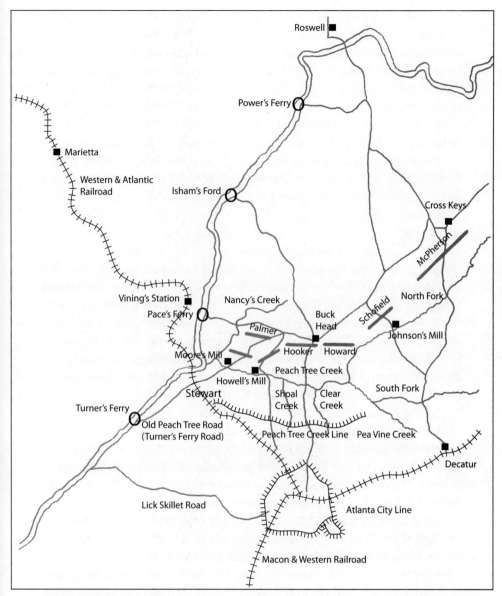

Roswell

Power's Ferry

Marietta

Western & Atlantic
Railroad

Isham's Ford

Cross Keys

McPherson

Vining's Station

Nancy's Creek

Buck
Head

Schofield

North Fork

Pace's Ferry

Palmer

Johnson's Mill

Moore's Mill

Hooker

Howard

Howell's Mill

Peach Tree Creek

Stewart

Shoal
Creek

Clear
Creek

South Fork

Turner's Ferry

Old Peach Tree Road
(Turner's Ferry Road)

Peach Tree Creek Line

Pea Vine Creek

Decatur

Lick Skillet Road

Atlanta City Line

Macon & Western Railroad

Evening, July 18

ground allotted to its troops in that line. Stewart had rested most of his command between the railroad and the Pace's Ferry Road to the east ever since the army crossed the Chattahoochee River. Each division was to place two brigades on line with one brigade held as a reserve. For the time being, Stewart told his subordinates only to take up the position, not to fortify it, clearly signaling his expectation that an attack would soon be ordered.[52]

Samuel G. French's Division anchored Stewart's and the army's left flank. As of July 18, French had one brigade on picket along the south bank of the river from the railroad bridge up to Peach Tree Creek, and then along its south bank some distance east. Another brigade had already formed a main line from the railroad east, and his third brigade acted as a reserve.[53]

Hardee's Corps was resting northwest of Atlanta when Johnston's order to take up the Peach Tree Creek Line arrived on July 18. The men had to move several miles to take post to Stewart's right, but Hardee instructed the troops to wait until the next day to construct fortifications along the new line. Hood's Corps also had to move from bivouac areas northwest of Atlanta to extend the developing Confederate position. Maj. Gen. Carter L. Stevenson took command of the corps when Hood assumed charge of the army on the afternoon of July 18. Stevenson marched the troops several miles to take post to the right of Hardee's Corps. It was during all this marching about that several brigades happened to pass Johnston's headquarters on the Marietta Road and cheered him a fond goodbye.[54]

The developing Peach Tree Creek Line faced entirely north because neither Johnston nor Hood had yet become aware of McPherson's long march to the Decatur–Stone Mountain area. As far as they were concerned, Thomas's Army of the Cumberland posed the most immediate threat to Atlanta. The entire Army of Tennessee was arrayed to face Thomas by the evening of July 18. The line crossed several major roads approaching the city as well as several significant streams. Starting near the railroad, it traversed the Howell's Mill Road and Shoal Creek (or Tanyard Branch), before crossing the Buck Head and Atlanta Road. The line also crossed Clear Creek and ended at Pea Vine Creek. Jacob Cox thought the "ground was well chosen." Hood tried to take full credit for the Peach Tree Creek Line in his report, arguing that the Army of Tennessee had been lying around scattered camps when he assumed command with hardly a thought that they would soon be called on to do battle after a long series of retreats and missed opportunities for fighting.[55]

Later, with the benefit of hindsight, Hood also tried to argue that the creation of the Peach Tree Creek Line compelled Sherman to extend his army group so as to get around its right flank and approach Atlanta from the east.

The truth was quite different. Sherman's plan to hit the Georgia Railroad already had borne fruit by the evening of July 18, and he had always intended to approach the city from the east as well as from the north.[56]

Wheeler directed the cavalry that opposed Thomas, Schofield, and at least Dodge on July 18. He fell back before the Federals, burning bridges wherever possible. By the evening of July 18, the Army of Tennessee occupied the Peach Tree Creek Line and took over picketing and skirmishing duties from the cavalry. At that point, Wheeler shifted Armstrong, Williams, Ferguson, and any other mounted units he had north of the city to the east side of Atlanta. Kelly's Division, already there to guard the Georgia Railroad, was positioned too close to the city to interfere with Logan. As a result, the Federals were able to tear up some track east of Decatur without opposition. It is quite possible that Wheeler did not know Logan had touched the Georgia Railroad that afternoon. If Wheeler did not know, Johnston would not have known either, and Hood unfairly blamed his former commander for not telling him that important fact.[57]

As far as Hood understood the situation on the evening of July 18, Thomas was the real threat. He informed Seddon that the lines were well drawn between the enemy and his new command, "the creek intervening between the armies." Confederate corps commanders arranged for skirmish lines to be sent to the valley of Peach Tree Creek opposite their units.[58]

Although the Army of Tennessee was still reeling from the news that its beloved leader was gone, it became obvious to most members that a change in policy would occur. "A fight now is obliged to come off," W. H. T. Walker told his wife. Walker had a long and friendly relationship with Johnston and "dislike exceedingly to see him leave us." But he accepted the decision from Richmond and marveled that "Hood has 'gone up like a rocket.' It is to be hoped ... that 'he will not come down like the stick.' He is brave, wither he has the capacity to command armies (for it required a high order of talent) time will develop." Walker knew full well that Hardee, his corps commander, was mortified by Hood's promotion. Hardee's "star has always been in the ascendant and he always the most dashing light around the throne. I wonder how he likes to have it obscured & suffer an eclipse by the passing of this new planet between him and the sun."[59]

Did the change in commanders need to take place? Some historians side with Johnston, while others admit that his handling of the Army of Tennessee was a failure. Whether Johnston should have kept Davis more closely in touch with his plans is a moot point because Johnston essentially had no plans for the campaign other than to conserve his army, take no chances, and draw the enemy deeper into Georgia without fighting a battle unless he had almost no chance to lose it. Sherman allowed him few opportunities to take the offensive, and Johnston acted far too passively on the defensive, not even bothering to contest the crossings of the Chattahoochee River. The consensus of opinion among the most recent historians tends to be that Davis was compelled to fire Johnston from his important position and probably should have done so earlier.[60]

Was Hood the best choice to replace Johnston? Some historians, such as Thomas Robson Hay, argue he was the only feasible choice. More recent historians tend to be as critical of Hood's promotion as they are of Johnston's failings. At the very least, Davis went out on a limb when he chose Hood. Widely admired for his spirit and fighting ability, even many of his friends wondered if he had the intelligence, aptitude, or patience for directing the second most-important field army in the Confederacy. Hood had not done well as a corps commander, and his sneaky habit of criticizing Johnston behind his commander's back should have been a warning sign rather than an inducement for Davis to elevate him to this important position of trust.[61]

There certainly were other choices, even though Hardee had already made it clear the previous December that he did not want to be saddled with the responsibility of army command. Stewart was a dependable and capable officer. From outside the army, Lieut. Gen. Richard Taylor, a significant factor in the Confederate victory in the Red River campaign a few months before, could have been shifted from his department command in Alabama and Mississippi. Lee might have been compelled to give up one of the corps commanders in the Army of Northern Virginia. Davis's choices were limited more by his own mind than by the supply of capable officers available. If the Confederate government could not muster a suitable general to command its major army in the West other than by choosing someone whose first reaction was to cancel the promotion and who felt so overwhelmed that he could barely cope with it, then something was seriously wrong with the entire Confederate army. There is no comparable story to be found in the history of the Union war effort.

There was no sense of alarm, despondency, or concern for the future in the Federal camp as there was among the Confederates. "To-morrow I want a bold push for Atlanta," Sherman told Thomas, "and have made my orders, which, I think, will put us in Atlanta or very close to it." He wanted the Army of the Cumberland to cross Peach Tree Creek on July 19 while Schofield and McPherson cooperated in seizing Decatur and tearing up the Georgia Railroad on their march west toward the city. "I am fully aware of the necessity of making the most of time," Sherman informed Henry Halleck, "and shall keep things moving."[62]

We are expecting a battle every moment, as Hood is
said to have been placed in command because he
wanted to fight.—Taylor Beatty

Dear father and mother, I am mortally wounded. I die like
a soldier, and hope to meet you all in heaven.—Frank Miser

3

Across Peach Tree Creek, July 19

Much like the day before, July 19 dawned clear and hot. Many
Federals continued to believe Atlanta would fall with the
current move toward the city, but Sherman did not foresee
Thomas taking the place just yet. His idea was that the Army
of the Cumberland should cross Peach Tree Creek and distract Hood's attention from Schofield and McPherson. Sherman worried about the extended nature of his deployment
and wanted Thomas to move his left flank enough to close the
gap between the Army of the Cumberland and the Army of
the Ohio. Thomas planned to cross the creek and fill the gap
on July 19.[1]

Peach Tree Creek was a relatively small stream, fifteen to
twenty feet wide, but it had steep banks and a sandy bottom
"which threatened to engulf any who should be so unwise as
to trust to it for a footing," wrote Harry Stanley of the Twentieth Corps. Some of its bottomland was cleared and planted in
corn. The terrain north and south of the valley was irregular
and partly cleared; the rest was covered with timber and thick
underbrush. Sherman believed the stream was fordable east of
the road that linked Buck Head with Atlanta, but west of that
road bridges were necessary. While one Federal soldier later

asserted that the enemy had dammed the creak to raise the water level, there is no evidence that this took place.[2]

Howard's plan for the day called for Wood's division to move south down the road linking Buck Head with Atlanta and attempt a crossing of the creek. Stanley and Newton were to move left in the direction of Decatur at least as far as the North Fork of Peach Tree Creek to begin filling the gap between Thomas and Schofield. Wood sent two brigades south along the Buck Head and Atlanta Road, commanded by Col. William H. Gibson and Col. Frederick Knefler. One mile south of Buck Head they encountered Confederate skirmishers of Brig. Gen. Lucius E. Polk's Brigade, Maj. Gen. Patrick Cleburne's Division. The Federals drove the Rebel skirmishers an additional mile to the creek, arriving about 6:30 A.M. The Confederates retired to the south side of the stream and burned the bridge, "which must have been a considerable structure," Wood reported. The Rebels took shelter behind light fortifications on the southern bluff of the valley. About a mile south of the Confederate works, a good deal of smoke arose from the men who held the Peach Tree Creek Line as they cooked their morning meals.[3]

Howard reported Wood's progress to Thomas and gave his opinion that the crossing would be very difficult, given the nature of the stream and the fortifications south of the crossing. Thomas nevertheless sent orders for the division to push across the creek as soon as possible. By 1 P.M. Knefler received the order to force his brigade over the stream. It was unfordable near the burned bridge, so Knefler found a spot a bit downstream where a timbered ravine extended down to the bank. This spot was farther west than the Confederate earthwork on the south side and largely unseen by the Rebels. Knefler's pioneers gathered poles about thirty feet long to place as stringers across the stream. Then he selected fifty men each from the 79th Indiana and the 9th Kentucky and placed them under Maj. George W. Parker of the former regiment. The 100 men carried fence rails down to the water. After the pioneers worked quietly to lay the stringers, they positioned the rails crosswise over them to construct a footbridge. Knefler's 100 picked troops then moved over and advanced south as skirmishers.[4]

The rest of the brigade deployed skirmishers as well; they demonstrated at the burned bridge and distracted enemy attention while the footbridge took shape. Parker's 100 men flanked the Confederates out of their fortifications and captured the heights on the south side of Peach Tree, although Parker was wounded in the process. About thirty-five Confederates fell into Union hands, including Lieut. Col. William J. Hale of the 2nd Tennessee. Gibson's brigade also managed to construct a footbridge a bit downstream from Knefler's crossing and joined the Union force on the southern bluff.

Federal artillery supported Wood's crossing, dominating the Confederate guns that replied. Prisoners told the Federals that the skirmishing and sniping performed by Knefler's brigade compelled them to keep close behind their works. But for this, they might have noticed Parker's flanking movement sooner. All in all, Wood was quite pleased with the operation. "Considering that ... the passage was really made in the presence of a considerable force, it may be truly asserted that no handsomer nor more artistic operation was made during the campaign." Wood lost about twenty-five men in the crossing.[5]

The Federals quickly formed a bridgehead on the bluff south of Peach Tree Creek with Gibson's brigade positioned in line east of the road and to the stream. Knefler formed west of the road, his line extending in a curve like Gibson's to the creek. As soon as the Confederates recovered from their surprise and retreat, they sent a strong skirmish line forward to determine how far the enemy had advanced. By then Gibson and Knefler were securely in place.[6]

The last unit of Wood's division came south to the creek before the day ended. Brig. Gen. William B. Hazen's brigade left Buck Head at 1 P.M. and arrived at Peach Tree Creek in time to serve as a reserve for the crossing. As soon as Gibson and Knefler were firmly positioned on the south side, Hazen's pioneers began to rebuild the burned bridge. They were nearly finished by dusk when Wood adjusted his units. He sent Hazen to the south side and pulled Gibson and Knefler back to the north side under cover of darkness. The latter two brigades then marched back to Buck Head to retrieve camp equipage they had left there that morning. Hazen was fully aware that a large enemy force lay a short distance south, so his men worked to strengthen the hasty fortifications Gibson and Knefler had constructed.[7]

While Wood crossed Peach Tree Creek along the Buck Head and Atlanta Road, John Newton sent a small reconnaissance from Buck Head southeast along a secondary road toward the North Fork of Peach Tree Creek that morning. Brig. Gen. Nathan Kimball dispatched the 74th Illinois and 24th Wisconsin, which found the bridge over the North Fork burned and Confederate skirmishers dug in on the opposite bank. Kimball recalled the regiments in time for Newton to execute a new order. He was to move his entire division south of Buck Head to replace Wood's division at the bridgehead so recently established. Newton left Buck Head by 6 P.M. and arrived at Peach Tree Creek by dusk. His pioneers finished reconstructing the bridge after Hazen crossed the creek to relieve Gibson and Knefler. At 11 P.M., Newton sent Kimball's brigade across the bridge to reinforce Hazen in the bridgehead. Apparently, it was only because Gibson and Knefler needed their camp equipage at Buck Head that Howard allowed this shifting of divisions back and forth to take place. Only because of that circumstance, Newton instead of Wood would be involved in the fight that would come off at Peach Tree Creek the next day.[8]

Stanley's division made modest progress in its effort to move southeast and find Schofield's corps. Marching farther east than Kimball's small reconnoitering party that morning, Col. William Grose's brigade led Stanley's advance along a different road that led toward Decatur. Grose found a bridge over the North Fork of Peach Tree Creek already burning when he got to that point, and Confederate skirmishers were dug in on the other side of the stream. Howard received word from Sherman by 2:50 P.M. that Schofield also was on the move somewhere east of Stanley's position and attempting to contact Stanley. Howard then ordered Stanley to push across the North Fork and continue his advance if possible. The Federals crossed the fork and drove the Confederates away. Some of the bridge had been saved, and the rest was quickly repaired by Union pioneers, but Schofield seemed not to be in reach.[9]

While the Fourth Corps performed various tasks during the course of July 19, Hooker ordered Geary to move his division across Peach Tree Creek a bit to the west of the Buck Head and Atlanta Road. Geary moved his men toward Howell's Mill at dawn only to find that skirmishers of Davis's Fourteenth Corps division were already in place there battling Confederate skirmishers on the south side of the creek. When Geary informed Hooker of this fact, the corps commander told him to move to Davis's left. Geary found a likely crossing place three-quarters of a mile east of Howell's Mill and massed his division in the timber near the stream. He deployed skirmishers on the north side of the creek but cautioned them not to expose themselves or open fire just yet, wanting to screen his position from the enemy. Hooker and Geary personally placed the two batteries attached to the division, urging the gunners to construct breastworks for their own protection, as the division pioneers gathered stringers and rails for a bridge.[10]

Geary's twelve guns, belonging to Capt. Henry Bundy's 13th New York Independent Battery and Lieut. Thomas E. Sloan's Battery E, Pennsylvania Light Artillery, opened fire at 3 P.M. The skirmishers now opened fire as well. The noise and smoke helped to cover the fact that Geary's pioneers sprang into action and hurriedly lay down the stringers and rails needed to cross infantrymen over the creek. "All was done very quickly," Geary reported.[11]

Soon the footbridge was strong enough to support the weight of Col. David Ireland's brigade as it rushed across the temporary structure, led by Col. Henry A. Barnum's 149th New York. Barnum wasted no time in forming a skirmish line with three of his companies, the rest moving closely behind in support. The 149th New York advanced up the bluff on the south side and took the Confederate skirmishers by surprise. The 16th South Carolina and part of the 46th Georgia, both from Brig. Gen. States R. Gist's Brigade of Walker's Division, held the Rebel skirmish line at this point. Barnum drove the Carolinians and Georgians from their fortifications. The rest of Ireland's brigade soon followed to form a bridgehead on the south side, reversing the Confederate skirmish pits. Barnum captured twenty-three prisoners and some entrenching tools.[12]

Geary crossed the rest of his division after Ireland's advance. Col. Charles Candy's brigade used the rude footbridge at 6 P.M. and extended Ireland's line to the right, his right flank resting on the creek. Candy also constructed breastworks. Col. Patrick H. Jones moved his brigade over the creek that night and took position to Ireland's left, his own left flank connecting with the creek as well.[13]

Alpheus Williams moved his division forward on the evening of July 19, starting at about 6 P.M. His men marched five miles along a circuitous route before reaching the vicinity of Howell's Mill by 10 P.M. It was too late to cross and form a larger bridgehead on the south side, so Williams bivouacked for the night on the north side of the stream.[14]

William T. Ward's division also moved south to Peach Tree Creek on July 19. At 3 P.M., while still part way to the stream, James Wood's brigade halted and massed to hear an important message. A staff officer informed the brigade that Sherman wanted everyone to know Hood had replaced Johnston. The new commanders' classmates in the Union army had warned that he was "of an impetuous, rash and confident disposition," according to Capt. Hartwell Osborn of the 55th Ohio. "Be prepared for sudden and unexpected attacks." Rather than daunted by the news, Osborn's men were happy that Sherman kept them informed of the latest developments. "It was as if Uncle Billy had taken his soldiers into his confidence. Courage rose high in the ranks." Osborn's first sergeant, "a bronzed and well tried soldier, turned to me and said, 'Well, Captain, they mean to come out of their works. I think we'll get a few of them now.'"[15]

Wood took position to the left of Williams's division when he reached Peach Tree Creek that evening and bivouacked on the north side for the night. Pioneers from all brigades of Ward's division began to make bridges over the stream under cover of darkness.[16]

By the end of the day Hooker had done little more than Howard in bridging Peach Tree Creek and had created only a presence south of the stream instead of massing his entire command. Howard could do no more than position two brigades south of the creek because he was charged with the responsibility of trying to find Schofield off to the east. There was no similar excuse for Hooker to be so lax as to cross only one of his three divisions against light opposition. Thomas instructed Hooker to push Williams and Ward over the creek early on July 20, connect with the Fourteenth Corps to the right and the Fourth Corps to the left, and advance toward Atlanta.[17]

Palmer and his men in the Fourteenth Corps did a better job of crossing Peach Tree Creek on July 19 than did Hooker and the Twentieth Corps and did so against greater opposition. Thomas wanted Palmer to cross the stream with one division supported by the others, and Palmer ordered Davis to take the lead. Davis initially tried to do so at Howell's Mill but found enemy resistance too great. The mill building, two stories supported by stout walls, stood like a fortress. Clark Howell had constructed it in 1852, and the building combined a gristmill, sawmill, plane machine, and cotton gin. From a ridge located close to the mill on the south side, Confederate skirmishers commanded the building with their fire.[18]

It would be too costly to fight across Peach Tree Creek at Howell's Mill, so Thomas instructed Davis to move downstream where a better crossing was reported at the mouth of Green Bone Creek. Col. Caleb J. Dilworth's brigade led the division to the place, and Thomas, Palmer, and Davis accompanied Dilworth. Confederate skirmishers on the south bank opened fire, and "a well-spent ball" hit Davis's boot, stinging his foot. The other generals kidded their subordinate about "getting the first hit."[19]

Dilworth placed Lieut. Col. Charles W. Clancy's 52nd Ohio in the lead and planned to move the rest of his brigade over the creek as fast as possible to support it. Clancy made a crude footbridge from logs. The stream was about twenty-five feet wide and eight feet deep at this spot. The bluff on the south side was fifty feet tall, but "a light strip of undergrowth" on each bank helped to screen the Federals.[20]

Clancy moved his troops over the footbridge under Dilworth's personal supervision. Then he deployed five companies under Maj. James T. Holmes as skirmishers, instructing Holmes to push the enemy from the bluff and continue south until reaching a ridge that was visible 300 to 500 yards from the stream. It was a distinctive feature because a few houses were built on the cleared top of the ridge. In a spirited move, the 52nd Ohio accomplished its task, rushing forward in the face of persistent skirmish fire and seizing the ridge. Once there Clancy ordered breastworks constructed to secure the top, where he placed seven companies of his regiment, sending three companies forward to establish a skirmish line. Dilworth wanted Clancy to move his skirmishers even farther forward as soon as possible and saw to it that the rest of the brigade started to cross the creek.[21]

Dilworth caught the Confederates during a shift in the units responsible for holding this sector. A small Arkansas brigade led by Brig. Gen. Daniel H. Reynolds of Maj. Gen. Edward C. Walthall's Division, Stewart's Army of Mississippi, had earlier that day been positioned farther east, fronting the sector where Geary's division was to cross. But Gist's Brigade had relieved him at 1 P.M. before Geary moved over the creek. Reynolds then shifted his command west to cover a sector two miles long between Gist to the east and Brig. Gen. John Adams's Brigade of Maj. Gen. William W. Loring's Division, Stewart's Army of Mississippi, to the west.[22]

Reynolds had to leave eighty men on the skirmish line when he shifted because they could not easily be removed during the day without dangerously exposing them to enemy fire. Those eighty men became the eastern boundary of his new sector. On the west, Reynolds relieved the 15th Mississippi and two companies of the 6th Mississippi with his 25th Arkansas, which became the western boundary of his new sector, ending 300 yards short of Moore's Mill. Reynolds also placed the 9th Arkansas to extend the skirmish line formed by the 25th Arkansas toward the east. Even though the men were placed five to ten paces apart, the two regiments could not cover the two-mile sector; a gap existed between the 9th Arkansas and the eighty men left behind. But Reynolds allowed the remainder of his brigade to rest a bit to the rear, while he became more familiar with his new position and planned how to firm up the skirmish line.[23]

At this point in time, Clancy's 52nd Ohio moved aggressively from its crossing of Peach Tree Creek and pushed back the 9th Arkansas until the Federals gained the ridge with the houses on it. At the first indication of trouble, Reynolds rushed back to his resting regiments and reacted quickly to the Federal push. He ordered the 9th Arkansas to counterattack and try to regain its former position, sending the 2nd Arkansas Mounted Rifles (dismounted) behind it as support. The 25th Arkansas to the west was not affected by Clancy's advance and remained in place. The 9th Arkansas put a great deal of pressure on the 52nd Ohio, especially the left and center of Clancy's line, but the Ohio men held on to the ridge from behind their slim breastworks and repelled the Arkansans.[24]

As the two Arkansas regiments vainly tried to restore the Confederate skirmish line, Reynolds formed the rest of his brigade in line and prepared a second attack. As soon as the two regiments returned, Reynolds added them to the 1st Arkansas Mounted Rifles (dismounted) and the 4th Arkansas, making four regiments in his brigade line. The 25th Arkansas remained detached about 200 yards off to the west, but Reynolds sent word to its commander to cooperate with his intended advance as best he could. Reynolds's men "moved into line at a double-quick, and yet there was no confusion, although they knew the enemy were advancing and were but a short distance from them at the time." Just then word arrived that Col. Michael Farrell of the 15th Mississippi offered to cooperate with Reynolds. Farrell had been resting his men after they were relieved by the 25th Arkansas. Getting wind of action to his right, Farrell was willing to use his own regiment and the two companies of the 6th Mississippi to help. Reynolds eagerly accepted and asked Farrell to coordinate his movements with that of the 25th Arkansas.[25]

Reynolds was fully aware that the enemy was in force south of the creek and that his own brigade had only a few hundred men available for duty. He hesitated to bring on a larger engagement but wanted to restore his skirmish line. Therefore, the general instructed both wings of his brigade line to advance while the center remained stationary, thereby hoping to pressure the enemy where they were likely to be vulnerable without committing all of his small force to a risky battle.[26]

When the Confederates advanced, they found Clancy's skirmishers only seventy-five yards away from their starting point. The Federals were taken by surprise, and many of them became prisoners, including Clancy himself. But the initial Rebel success began to unravel as troops of the 9th Arkansas on the far right began to give way because they ran out of ammunition. When Reynolds learned of this, he feared the enemy would take advantage of it, advance, and cut him off from his ambulances and ordnance train. Reynolds sent his wounded to the rear and his prisoners to Adams's Brigade, made sure more rounds were issued, and then stabilized his line.[27]

But Reynolds mounted a second advance, and this time nearly overwhelmed the 52nd Ohio. Correctly seeing that he was opposed by several regiments, Holmes took command of the regiment when Clancy turned up missing. What was left of his skirmish line was driven back onto the skirmish reserve, and that was driven back into the regimental main line.[28]

Holmes was saved by the timely arrival of the 85th Illinois, the next regiment in Dilworth's brigade column to cross Peach Tree Creek and move up to the ridge with the houses on it. Maj. Robert G. Rider pushed his regiment forward and took position to the right of the 52nd Ohio just in time to meet Reynolds's big push. As the Confederate left wing approached the regiment, hand-to-hand fighting broke out. Losses were heavy in the right wing of the 85th Illinois, and there is evidence that some parts of it fell back to the creek bluff, but Holmes held his 52nd Ohio in place, and the rest of Rider's regiment also stood firm until the Confederates fell back. The Union right was saved, and the left was helped a great deal by the lack of ammunition among the 9th Arkansas, which delayed the advance of Reynolds's right wing.[29]

The battle for the ridge was a very close affair. "Without the Eighty-fifth Illinois," Holmes wrote long after the war, "the Fifty-second Ohio would all have been killed or captured." Davis's movement across the creek also "would have ended in disaster and failure," Holmes thought. His regiment lost eighty-two men in this spirited little fight, amounting to almost one-third of all casualties the 52nd suffered during the four-month campaign for Atlanta.[30]

Dilworth energetically pushed more regiments up the ridge to secure Holmes's position, quickly outracing Reynolds in the effort to mass troops at the key point of the struggle. The 125th Illinois was next in his brigade column; it moved up to a supporting position behind Holmes's 52nd Ohio. Then came the 86th Illinois, which extended the Union line to the left, and the 22nd Indiana, which extended it to the right. Firing continued on the Union right wing, wounding Maj. Thomas Shea of the 22nd Indiana and compelling Dilworth to shift his reserve, the 125th Illinois, to shore up his right.[31]

Reynolds was unable to bring all the Confederate units available to him into play. The 25th Arkansas, 15th Mississippi, and the two companies of the 6th Mississippi failed to take advantage of their position several hundred yards to the west to find and flank Dilworth's brigade. Farrell connected his right flank with the left of the 25th Arkansas, which had fallen back from the skirmish line to form a regimental battle line. The two regiments advanced with the two companies of the 6th Mississippi, but they had to move obliquely to the right through woods in hope of connecting with Reynolds's left flank. They drifted too far to the west to do so and fell back when the bulk of Dilworth's brigade crossed the creek and extended the Union right wing in their direction. Adams brought other units of his brigade toward the scene of action, but they arrived too late to take part in the fight.[32]

While Confederate commanders on the ground could not coordinate their efforts, the Federals worked smoothly to bring more troops to the area. Davis quickly moved Col. John G. Mitchell's brigade over Peach Tree Creek to support Dilworth. Mitchell sent three regiments to extend the left wing of the Union line and another to extend the right wing. Mitchell's troops continued skirmishing with Reynolds's men until dusk. Davis kept his last brigade, led by Brig. Gen. James D. Morgan, farther east to confront the Confederates who still stubbornly defended the crossing of the creek at Howell's Mill.[33]

Dilworth and his men, especially those of the 52nd Ohio, deserved the high praise they received in official reports for the short but bloody battle of July 19. "The loss was heavy on both sides," commented Jefferson C. Davis, "considering the numbers engaged and the short time the fight lasted." Dilworth reported losing 245 men of his brigade, 125 of them were seriously enough wounded to be transported to the Federal hospitals at Vining's Station north of the Chattahoochee River.[34]

The battle made July 19 "an eventful day in the history of this brigade," second only to the terrible drama of its assault on Johnston's fortified line at Kennesaw Mountain on June 27. Elias Dimmit of the 52nd Ohio was jolted by a premonition that he would die that day. Sometime during the engagement, a bullet ranged through his knapsack and into his body, killing him. Frank Miser of the same regiment was badly wounded and left on the ground for some time before he could be helped. His comrades later found him dead, but Miser had scrawled a message on a piece of paper. "Dear father and mother, I am mortally wounded. I die like a soldier, and hope to meet you all in heaven." Miser's last message to his family remained a bittersweet memory for his comrades for the rest of their lives. During the night that followed this engagement and well into the morning of the next day, Dilworth's troops cared for the wounded and buried their dead.[35]

Morgan's brigade made little headway in the area of Howell's Mill on the evening of July 19. Col. Charles M. Lum sent sharpshooters from his 10th Michigan down to the creek on both sides of the mill, but they reported the stream too deep, its current too rapid, and the opposing bluffs too near for a crossing. Confederate skirmishers not only held the bluff but occupied the mill building. Lum's men observed all they could while daylight lasted, and then Capt. John Algoe organized a select group of soldiers into three squads of ten men each. At dusk, one squad advanced upstream and another downstream, while Algoe led the third squad directly toward the mill building. Advancing quietly, they managed to break down the door before they were detected, but the Confederate skirmishers inside escaped through another door, ran across the mill dam, and disappeared into the growing darkness. The Confederate line on the south bluff was close enough so that a rain of rifle balls descended on the mill area for quite some time, and Algoe lost two men to it. Two companies of the 10th Michigan relieved Algoe's troops at midnight and worked to destroy the flume, thereby letting the water flow more freely past the dam to lower the level of Peach Tree Creek.[36]

For the time being, Davis's was the only Fourteenth Corps presence on the south side of the stream. His troops consolidated their tenuous hold by continuing to fortify their position on the ridge. They advanced skirmishers a short distance forward of the main line in the darkness and made a series of works consisting of rails with dirt thrown over them big enough to protect eight to ten skirmishers each. A few wounded and well men crawled back to the Federal skirmishers under cover of night, having lain between the lines since the fight that afternoon. Dilworth's command also constructed a proper bridge over Peach Tree Creek to facilitate communication with the north side. The troops obtained timber by tearing down a nearby house and, while working, noticed the body of a young Federal soldier floating down from the Twentieth Corps sector. They could not identify him but interred the body with their own men who had been killed in the battle.[37]

On the Confederate side of the field, Adams visited Reynolds about dusk and urged him to relieve the 15th Mississippi and the two companies of the 6th Mississippi. Adams also wanted his 20th Mississippi back, a regiment he had brought up to Farrell's position after the battle had ended. Reynolds explained that he had little more than 600 troops to cover a sector two miles wide. Furthermore, he was worried about a gap in the Rebel position to his right and had asked Walthall for reinforcements but could not guess when or if they would arrive. His main line was little more than 200 yards from the Federals. Adams returned to his sector but later sent a message once again urging Reynolds to help him. Just then, the 1st Alabama arrived from Brig. Gen. William A. Quarles's Brigade. Reynolds used that regiment to relieve the 15th Mississippi, 20th Mississippi, and the two companies of the 6th Mississippi at 11 P.M.[38]

Adams later created a controversy by denigrating Reynolds's handling of the affair. On the basis of Farrell's report (Adams had no opportunity to observe the battle personally), the brigade leader claimed that Reynolds requested Farrell to help him. He argued that the 15th Mississippi advanced and compelled the surrender of an entire Union regiment; but Farrell had to release most of them and retire because Reynolds's men failed to advance and support him. The 15th Mississippi retired but claimed to have captured all the Federals who had gotten to its rear area, including Lieut. Col. Clancy of the 52nd Ohio. Adams believed that a haul of 1,000 Federal prisoners could have been taken if Reynolds had acted with more skill. This story was widely believed among the men of Adams's Brigade.[39]

Reynolds was flabbergasted when he learned of all this and retorted a few days later with a full description of the affair. He discounted the story completely and pointed out that the prisoners his men captured, who were sent to Adams's Brigade for safekeeping, were later credited as a joint capture of the two brigades by one of Adams's staff officers. In fact, Reynolds argued that if Farrell had commanded his regiment more effectively to cooperate with his own command, the Confederates might have been able to achieve an impressive tactical victory on July 19. Adams had not the temperament for the position his brigade held that day. He complained that Reynolds's command was too small to support his right, and he also complained that Brig. Gen. Matthew D. Ector's Brigade of French's Division to his left was too small to protect that flank as well. He also argued that Walthall's Division and Walker's Division should have counterattacked on the night of July 19 and driven the Federals back to the north side of Peach Tree Creek. Adams's alarmist reports were taken seriously by Loring, but they did not resonate at higher command levels.[40]

Hood was pleased to learn that Reynolds had struck vigorously against the Fourteenth Corps crossing that afternoon, relaying the news to Richmond as the first evidence of a new spirit in the army since he took command. Reynolds spent the night gathering abandoned small arms within reach of his brigade. The moon shone brightly that night, and the Confederates had to be careful so as to avoid a shot from Federal pickets. His men also constructed breastworks of rails with dirt thrown over them. Reynolds reported losing fifty-nine men in the battle that lasted from 3 P.M. until 7:30 P.M., a much lighter loss than Dilworth suffered. Hood had reason to be encouraged by such a differential, but it also points out, once again, the wisdom of a forward and aggressive defense at natural obstacles such as Peach Tree Creek. If every Federal crossing of the stream was attended with such resistance and loss of life, it would have taken the edge off the extremely high Union troop morale, drained some manpower, and slowed Thomas's progress.[41]

As Davis led the Fourteenth Corps across Peach Tree Creek, the other two divisions of Palmer's command waited and then followed. Early on the morning of July 19, Palmer told Baird to reconnoiter in the direction of Atlanta. Baird's party found that all the bridges over Peach Tree Creek were destroyed. He then waited nearly all day; when Davis crossed the creek, he received orders to follow. Baird moved Col. Moses B. Walker's brigade across a ford located just upstream from Davis's position. The water was waist-deep here, but the 89th Ohio led Walker's brigade through it, followed by the 82nd Indiana, sometime after 6 P.M. The Ohio men deployed as skirmishers and pushed the Confederate skirmishers back to enlarge Davis's small bridgehead, connecting to Davis's left flank. Baird realized that the bridgehead on the south side was still too small for both divisions. He retained his other two brigades on the north side for a while until the combined effect of Geary's crossing and Davis's crossing compelled the Confederate skirmishers to fall back even more, allowing room for further Federal deployment on the south side. Baird crossed his remaining two brigades near Howell's Mill after constructing a bridge. It was midnight before his entire division was over and dug in south of the stream.[42]

Johnson was delayed in crossing his division over Peach Tree Creek. Finally, late in the evening, his men began to move across near Howell's Mill following Baird's troops. Johnson took position to Baird's left in an attempt to reach far enough east to connect with Hooker's right flank. He was unable to do so because Hooker had not yet crossed all his corps.[43]

At the end of the day, Thomas had barely made enough progress over Peach Tree Creek to facilitate Sherman's overall plan. Most of the crossings had been contested, with Dilworth fighting a bloody battle to secure Davis's hold on the south side. Moreover, Sherman began to worry about the gap in his general line, which continued between Schofield and Howard. Reacting to an erroneous report that Thomas had retained many troops on the north side of Nancy's Creek, he berated his subordinate for not spreading the men out well enough so that Howard could close the gap and maintain firm contact with Schofield. He envisioned Buck Head as the center of Thomas's line and wanted the entire Fourth Corps to cross both forks of Peach Tree Creek to find the Twenty-Third Corps. Even though Thomas had no troops north of Nancy's Creek, he still was unable to stretch out far enough. Both Schofield and McPherson were in the area but shielded by Confederate ignorance of their exact positions.[44]

The gap was not really Thomas's or anyone else's fault. According to Cox, Sherman admitted that the maps he used were inaccurate, making it difficult to estimate distances and plot locations for each of the corps in the army group. Everything east turned out to be farther away from locations such as Howell's Mill than anticipated, and Cox also correctly pointed out that there were in fact two Howell's Mills, one on Nancy's Creek and the other well-known one on Peach Tree Creek.[45]

With far less opposition, Schofield managed to move a substantial distance on July 19. Hascall's division had stopped at Johnson's Mill on the North Fork of Peach Tree Creek the evening before. Now he led the corps advance southward to a fork in the road; the left-hand fork led directly to Decatur, and the right-hand fork angled toward Atlanta. After skirmishing to secure the junction, Hascall began moving toward Decatur, while Cox moved toward Atlanta.[46]

Hascall pushed steadily on, crossing the South Fork of Peach Tree Creek. He sent Brig. Gen. Joseph A. Cooper's brigade into Decatur by 3 P.M. Cooper's men set to work, burning a train of cars and tearing up the track. A short while after Cooper secured the town, Dodge's Sixteenth Corps troops

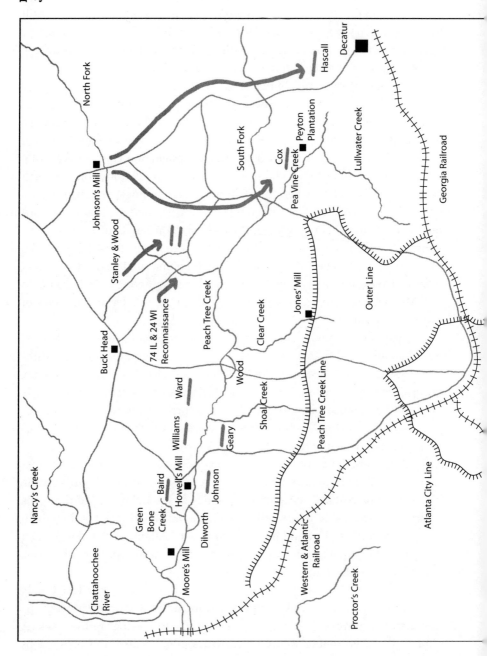

marched in from the west to relieve the Twenty-Third Corps brigade. Cooper rejoined Hascall, and the division bivouacked near Decatur on the road to Atlanta.[47]

While Hascall moved to the Georgia Railroad, Cox marched his division directly toward Atlanta from the road junction south of Johnson's Mill. He crossed the South Fork of Peach Tree Creek late in the afternoon and continued a short distance to the crossing of Pea Vine Creek. This small tributary flowed north into the South Fork. Cox bivouacked on the Peyton Plantation for the night.[48]

Schofield was anxious to make contact with Howard. During the morning of July 19, he sent a message to Howard with a member of his staff and an orderly. The pair rode west and north, approaching what Sherman later called the second crossing of the North Fork of Peach Tree Creek up from the junction of the two forks that formed the main stream. Two companies of the 75th Illinois from Grose's brigade of Stanley's division happened to be reconnoitering the road at that time, and the two mounted men approached from a direction the Federals naturally assumed would be used by the enemy. They could see that the two soldiers wore United States uniforms but when ordered to halt, the pair wheeled around and tried to ride away. They apparently assumed the 75th Illinois men were Confederates. A volley of rifle balls was unloosed and the orderly, at least, was wounded. But the two messengers managed to get away without further injury and reported the incident to Schofield, who correctly concluded that his men had been fired on by Howard's command. The gap between the Fourth and Twenty-Third Corps was ever wider, and there was no contact of any kind between the two units, no screen to shield the hole in Sherman's line from prying Confederates.[49]

McPherson's Army of the Tennessee had an easy time of it on July 19. With no opposition to hinder him, McPherson concentrated on tearing up miles of track east of Decatur leading into the town. He then was in a fair way to link up with Schofield and move west toward Atlanta the next day.[50]

July 19 brought a good deal of confirmation that Johnston had been replaced by Hood. One of Dodge's scouts came in, "having left Atlanta that morning," and brought a newspaper along with items about the change in Confederate commanders. Dodge sent the newspaper to Sherman, who was thus able to read Johnston's farewell to the Army of Tennessee. Wood's men also captured an Atlanta newspaper, while scouts and spies continued to feed reports about the change of leadership to various Union officers. Prisoners taken by Geary that day told Hooker of the change and further admitted that the incident had created "great dissatisfaction in Hardee's corps."[51]

Perhaps the realization that Hood was in charge increased Sherman's anxiety on July 19, for he fretted a good deal about the gap in his line and about whether Thomas was in position to help Schofield and McPherson if the enemy attacked. Traveling with the Twenty-Third Corps, he was sure that the way was clear for Howard to cross both forks of Peach Tree Creek but saw no sign of the Fourth Corps. "With McPherson, Howard, and Schofield, I would have ample to fight the whole of Hood's army," he told Thomas, "leaving you to walk into Atlanta, capturing guns and everything. But with Schofield and McPherson alone, the game will not be so certain." He wanted two divisions of the Fourth Corps to cross the two forks of Peach Tree Creek, or perhaps the corps could move south from the bridgehead Wood created along the Buck Head and Atlanta Road and form a junction with Schofield.[52]

No matter which way the junction was made, Sherman needed assurance from Thomas that he was mostly across Peach Tree Creek and able to link up with Schofield the next day. That would put him in position to support a drive by the Army of the Tennessee and the Twenty-Third Corps against the east face of the Atlanta perimeter. In several dispatches, Thomas fully informed Sherman of his progress that day. This reassured Sherman, who explained his overall conception of the next day's moves. "If Hood fights behind forts close to the town, I will swing in between Atlanta and the river; but if he fights outside, we must accept battle." Sherman was thinking in terms of Hood fighting Schofield and McPherson, not Thomas. This was natural, considering the Armies of the Ohio and the Tennessee were already on one of only two rail lines still bringing food and supplies into Atlanta.[53]

By midnight of July 19, Thomas had managed to get one division of the Fourth Corps, one division of the Twentieth Corps, and three divisions of the Fourteenth Corps across the moat formed by Peach Tree Creek. Only one of those crossings was fiercely contested by more than a skirmish line. Sherman's movement toward Atlanta would have developed quite differently if Hood had moved his entire army to the south bank of Peach Tree Creek rather than adopt Johnston's Peach Tree Creek Line farther south. It is possible Thomas would have had to fight a series of bloody battles to cross the stream, delaying Sherman's plan and exacting a cost in blood and morale on the Federals. As it was, five of the nine divisions in the Army of the Cumberland were securely on the south side with modest losses, and there was every prospect that the rest could cross with little delay the next day.[54]

The satisfactory nature of the day's operations further increased optimism in the Federal camp. The news that McPherson had begun tearing up the Georgia Railroad became widely known throughout the ranks. "It was thought that if this was true, [Hood] would be compelled to either fight or retreat," commented James M. Randall of the 21st Wisconsin. Sherman admitted in his memoirs that the progress achieved on July 19 also made him wonder if Hood would fall back as readily as Johnston. "I really thought the enemy intended to evacuate the place," he wrote.[55]

Hood, of course, had no intention of giving up Atlanta, but his men still pined for Johnston on July 19. "Strange is it not that he should still live in the minds of his late followers," commented Surg. P. F. Whitehead in Loring's Division. "To Hood no objections are made, every one thinks that he will *fight here*, and to use one of Mr. Lincoln's vulgarisms, he will 'either make a spoon or spoil a horn.'" A rumor spread like wildfire through the ranks that Johnston had resumed command of the army. "The report cheered the despondent hearts," noted artillery officer Thomas J. Key of Arkansas, "but I was of the impression that it was done to prevent desertions and to cause the troops to fight with their former bravery."[56]

Hood moved his headquarters to a house just north of Atlanta and on the road to Buck Head. He was careful to keep in touch with the authorities in Richmond, urging them, as did Johnston, to move cavalry from Mississippi onto Sherman's supply line. Hood was not satisfied with Carter L. Stevenson as commander of his old corps; in fact, he did not trust any of the division leaders in that corps for higher command. Hardee recommended Cheatham as the best choice, so Hood gave him the command on a temporary basis, even though Cheatham "did not desire it." If it was necessary to choose a man who already held the rank of lieutenant general, Hood suggested Stephen D. Lee (who commanded the Department of Mississippi and East Louisiana) or Wade Hampton (who led Lee's Cavalry Corps in Virginia). Among officers holding the rank of major general, Hood recommended Mansfield Lovell, even though he was still under a cloud for the loss of New Orleans in the spring of 1862. It would take several days for the Richmond authorities to decide on Lee, who took charge of Hood's old corps on July 27, too late to participate in the coming battle near Peach Tree Creek.[57]

Not long after Cheatham took charge of Hood's Corps, the new army leader tried to lay plans for an attack on Thomas. At 11 A.M. on July 19, one of his staff members informed Wheeler that, unless unforeseen circumstances cropped up, the army would strike at 1 P.M. that afternoon. Cheatham held the right of the Peach Tree Creek Line, and Wheeler was to help him deal with any Federals who may approach from the east. Hood was too ambitious; it was not yet possible to attack. As the stated time for the assault came and went, disturbing news reached army headquarters from Wheeler. The cavalry officer informed Hood before 2:15 P.M. that the Federals had reached the Georgia Railroad and were tearing it up and moving toward

Decatur. This news was nearly twenty-four hours late. "It is important to get exact information of the state of affairs in that vicinity," another staff officer informed Wheeler. Hood wanted him to send out scouts to determine if Sherman's entire infantry line was across the forks of Peach Tree Creek and, if so, exactly where the Federals were located and in what strength. Wheeler asked for reinforcements, and by the evening of July 19 Hood contemplated sending Cleburne's Division from Hardee's Corps, although no orders to that effect were yet issued.[58]

After mulling over the alarming news that the Federals were already on the Georgia Railroad and heading west, Hood instructed Cheatham to shift his corps line so at least one division faced east. The east end of the Peach Tree Creek Line (which also was the right flank of Cheatham's Corps) lay two miles north of the Georgia Railroad. Late on the evening of July 19, Brig. Gen. John C. Brown moved his division south to establish a new line, his left flank resting at the east end of the Peach Tree Creek Line and forming an angle with it. Brown's rightmost brigade, led by Brig. Gen. Arthur M. Manigault, managed to place its right flank one and a half miles north of the railroad. Wheeler's cavalry lay to Manigault's right. Brown's Division represented a refused right flank for the Peach Tree Creek Line, but Cheatham was not yet deployed so as to fully cover the eastern approach to Atlanta. Moreover, because Cheatham kept the other two divisions in place facing north, he had to thin out the rest of his corps line to only one rank in places in order to shift Brown this far south.[59]

For most Confederates, July 19 proved to be a day of continued fortifying and, for some units, minor shifting of position. News of Thomas's crossing filtered through the ranks and everyone expected a battle very soon. Hood issued a circular to his corps commanders urging them to place strong skirmish lines near Peach Tree Creek. "The object is to enable a small force to resist the enemy's crossing for some time." Other than Reynolds, it cannot be said that any other Confederate officer tried to do this on July 19.[60]

Hood had to postpone his attack on Thomas until July 20. He called a conference of his corps leaders and Maj. Gen. Gustavus W. Smith, commander of the Georgia Militia, to take place at his headquarters on the Buck Head and Atlanta Road on the evening of July 19. His instructions were to assault at 1 P.M. the next day, driving directly northward against Thomas. In his memoirs, Hood explained that his intention was to "crush Sherman's right wing, as we drove it into the narrow space between the creek and the river." He believed that Schofield and McPherson would have had to move ten or twelve miles to support Thomas, thus isolating the Army of the Cumberland from immediate aid.[61]

These instructions could have been disseminated by written orders, but Hood had two other objectives in calling a conference, the first during his tenure as army commander. First, he wanted "to deliver most explicit instructions [to his corps commanders] in regard to their respective duties." He asked each man directly if he understood the orders, and all of them responded affirmatively. "I was very careful in this respect, inasmuch as I had learned from long experience that no measure is more important, upon the eve of battle, than to make certain, in the presence of the commanders, that each thoroughly comprehends his orders."[62]

The second objective lay in Hood's attempt to time the attack precisely when he predicted that only a part of Thomas's army would have time to take position on the south side of Peach Tree Creek. He reckoned that by 1 P.M., many Federal units would have crossed but not yet have secured their positions with heavy earthworks. Timing was all important in this scheme, and the troops needed to know that, if they saw breastworks, they were to attack without restraint just the same. That, Hood reasoned, could be imparted to the corps leaders only through a personal meeting. The army commander wanted to catch the enemy "in the act of throwing up such works, and just in that state of confusion to enable our forces to rout them by a bold and persistent attack."[63]

There was another, unstated, reason for Hood's desire to have a personal conference with his subordinates. He was brand new to the job, about to embark on a risky move for which he had poor preparation. He knew that many members of his army questioned the change of leadership. It was far from a comfortable situation for the young commander, and he undoubtedly felt the need to establish a clear and supportive relationship with his chief subordinates. As biographer Richard McMurry has pointed out, Hardee resented Hood's elevation; Stewart had not yet led his corps in action; Cheatham was a supporter of Johnston and had assumed corps command for the first time in his life only a few hours before the conference. Hood's chief of staff, Brig. Gen. William W. Mackall, was a strong supporter and friend of Johnston.[64]

The rank and file could not know what was going on at army headquarters on the evening of July 19, but they knew that action was in the air. "We are expecting a battle every moment," Taylor Beatty wrote in his diary, "as Hood is said to have been placed in command because he wanted to fight."[65]

At one I attack the . . . enemy. He has pressed our lines until he is within a short distance of Atlanta, and I must fight or evacuate. I am going to fight. The odds are against us, but I leave the issue with the God of Battles.—John Bell Hood

4

. . . .

Preparations for Battle, July 20

With each passing day of Sherman's operations south of the Chattahoochee, the temperature and humidity continued to climb. Some soldiers remembered July 20 as "intolerably warm, scarcely a breath of air stirring," while others recalled it as "an intensely hot day." Clouds obscured the sky at times, but in most ways it was a typical summer day in the Deep South.[1]

As was his habit, Sherman developed definite ideas about how to push operations on the third day since his crossing of the Chattahoochee. Even though Thomas provided a sketch showing his troop positions, Sherman still believed his subordinate had too much manpower on the right wing of the Army of the Cumberland. He wanted Thomas to move Stanley's and Wood's divisions farther to the left, wheeling so as to cover the space between Thomas's left flank and Schofield's corps in the area embraced by the forks of Peach Tree Creek. "In other words, I wish you to strengthen your left and risk more to your right, for the reason that as Atlanta is threatened the enemy will look to it rather than the river." Sherman contemplated a general advance closer to the city on July 20 with all units forming a connected line and the main threat posed to Hood coming from Schofield and McPherson. "Each army commander will accept battle on anything like fair terms," he wrote in special field orders, "but if the army reach within cannon-range of the city without receiving artillery or musketry fire he will halt, form a strong line, with batteries in position, and await orders." Sherman announced that he would continue to travel with Schofield's command on July 20. Engineer troops completed a wagon bridge over the Chattahoochee River and took up the last pontoon bridge on July 20, making Federal logistical support more secure.[2]

Thomas gave Howard his marching orders for the day when the latter visited Army of the Cumberland headquarters at dawn. Newton was to place the rest of his division in the bridgehead south of Peach Tree Creek along the Buck Head and Atlanta Road, relieving Hazen's brigade, and then advance cautiously south. After Hazen rejoined Wood's division, Stanley and Wood were to move out in fulfillment of Sherman's directive to connect with Schofield and cover the area around the forks of Peach Tree Creek. Howard issued orders to his subordinates at 6 A.M. Stanley was to take the lead with Wood following close behind him, and Howard intended to travel with Stanley that day. Given Newton's detached position, Howard told him to report directly to Thomas for orders. Joseph Fullerton, Howard's adjutant general, informed Newton that Stanley and Wood would try to make connection with his left flank as soon as possible, but for the time being Newton's division was the left end of Thomas's connected line. "From present appearances the battle will be fought by the forces to your left," Fullerton told Newton.[3]

The first order of business for Newton was to mass his entire division south of Peach Tree Creek. Kimball's brigade had already crossed the stream the evening before and held the bridgehead with Hazen's brigade during the night. Kimball replaced Hazen's men in the light breastworks with his own troops at 8 A.M. Then Col. John W. Blake's brigade followed by Brig. Gen. Luther P. Bradley's brigade crossed the bridge and moved into place to the left and rear of Kimball. Hazen's troops filed north over the bridge when the way was clear and made their way to Wood's location.[4]

Thomas kept close tabs on events that morning, spending time at Hooker's headquarters and consulting personally with Newton on the Buck Head and Atlanta Road. Newton was ready to advance his division farther south but needed to wait until he could form a connection with Twentieth Corps units to the west. Sending a staff officer to find Hooker, Newton discovered that the only Twentieth Corps division located south of Peach Tree Creek was Geary's command and that a gap existed between Geary and his own division. Hooker informed Newton that he intended to move Ward's division into that gap later in the day, and as soon as the Federals could present a connected front of some kind Newton intended to advance.[5]

Sherman received word a bit after 11 A.M. that one of his cavalry officers, Maj. Gen. George Stoneman, had spoken with a black man who fed him much information about what was happening on the Confederate side of the campaign. The fellow told Stoneman that the Union cavalry presence northwest of Atlanta had panicked the Rebels and they were preparing to retreat to Macon. The city was held only by the Georgia Militia, and the Army of Tennessee was "utterly demoralized and easily frightened," in Stoneman's words. Displaying a great deal of common sense, Sherman completely discounted this testimony as unreliable and proceeded with his operational plan, knowing that Hood and his men would not be so easily frightened.[6]

Hooker completed the movement of his other two divisions over the creek shortly after the noon hour. Although both divisions rested for several hours on the bottomland on the south side of the stream, they did send skirmish lines forward. Ward's division skirmishers connected Geary's skirmish line with Newton's, thus creating a screen covering the gap between the two commands. This was good enough for Newton. He reinforced his skirmish line under Col. Wallace W. Barrett of the 44th Illinois. Barrett controlled the 36th Illinois, 74th Illinois, and 88th Illinois from Kimball's brigade. Blake contributed to this skirmish formation by placing the 97th Ohio as a second skirmish line and providing the 27th Kentucky as a skirmish reserve.[7]

Barrett set out about 1 P.M. and pushed the Confederate skirmishers along the Buck Head and Atlanta Road on the double-quick. His men advanced 600 yards to a ridge that was higher than Newton's present position. From there, Barrett saw that another, slightly higher ridge lay 400 yards farther south. He decided to continue moving forward and easily occupied this rise of ground too, capturing a surgeon and an ambulance along the way.[8]

The ridge that Barrett occupied was the best ground in the area, commanding the ground north toward Peach Tree Creek and not commanded by any ground farther south toward Atlanta. Newton quickly moved his entire division forward to occupy the ridge. Kimball also rotated regiments on the skirmish line to bring in fresh men. The 15th Missouri, 24th Wisconsin, and 73rd Illinois replaced Barrett's five regiments, and Kimball placed Col. Joseph Conrad of the 3rd Missouri in charge of the new skirmishers.[9]

Newton admired the new place his division had taken. Calling it a "fine natural position," he saw that the ridge began near the valley of Clear Creek, a tributary that flowed northward into Peach Tree Creek about a mile east of his division. The ridge seemed to extend indefinitely west, parallel to and about three-fourths of a mile south of Peach Tree Creek. A spur of high ground connected the ridge with the bridge over Peach Tree; the Buck Head and Atlanta Road ran along the top of this spur. Low and rolling ground lay to either side of the spur. Ridge and spur seemed of vital importance in maintaining a firm hold on lines of communication north to Buck Head and in terms of planting a solid anchor for the left end of Thomas's line along Peach Tree Creek.[10]

Newton formed his division to hold the ridge in case of trouble. Kimball aligned mostly to the right of the road, although he placed the 88th Illinois to the left of it. Four guns of Lieut. Charles W. Scovill's Battery A, 1st Ohio Light Artillery took position on the road between the 88th Illinois and the rest of Kimball's infantry. Blake aligned his brigade to the left of the 88th Illinois, extending eastward. He refused the left end of his line because there were no friendly troops east of the division. Blake also placed the 28th Kentucky in reserve. Kimball did not refuse his right flank because he expected Ward's division of Hooker's corps to move up and connect to it at any moment.[11]

As Newton put it, his men "commenced naturally to throw up log and rail barricades." Indeed, the hasty construction of field fortifications had become such a commonplace event that most Union soldiers did it automatically. It had for some, in the words of an anonymous correspondent of the *Cincinnati Commercial*, become "the ruling passion of the campaign." Kimball reported that his men stacked arms and "fell to work with the greatest activity" to protect themselves.[12]

When Bradley moved his brigade up to the new position on the high ridge, he formed it in a column of regiments along the road. As a reserve force, it would be easy to move the troops to right or left in this formation. Compared to the line ahead, Bradley's column resembled the stem of a T in the division formation with the cross piece aiming south toward the Confederate line. Some men in Bradley's column reported they also began to make light breastworks. According to William D. Hynes of the 42nd Illinois, the order to do so was not uniformly distributed. Many of the men had grown so used to constructing earthworks that they never used in battle as to become "very unconcerned in the matter" on July 20. They preferred to rest and "did not work with much spirit." As a result, while Kimball and Blake had some protection for their connected line, Bradley essentially had no shelter worth speaking of in his column.[13]

Newton understandably was worried about the area east of his position, as yet uncovered by friendly forces. He called on Blake to send a regiment out into the area, and soon Lieut. Col. Willis Blanch's 57th Indiana deployed as skirmishers from the left flank of Blake's brigade east to Clear Creek. Blanch sent a detachment to the east side of the creek, but it found no Confederates. Blanch's left flank was about 600 yards from Blake's left flank, but at least there was a thin screen of Union troops extending to Clear Creek. Blake also sent Maj. Charles M. Hammond's 100th Illinois to the left and rear where it held the area near the junction of Clear Creek and Peach Tree Creek, further shoring up Newton's vulnerable flank.[14]

While Newton was positioning his division on the ridge, Conrad's three regiments replaced Barrett's five regiments on the skirmish line. Conrad moved out almost immediately under Newton's order to explore what lay ahead. His 15th Missouri advanced left of the road and the 73rd Illinois to the right, with the 24th Wisconsin as a reserve. The two regiments pushed a few Confederate skirmishers back a quarter of a mile before meeting obstacles. The 73rd Illinois stopped in the garden of a house, and Rebel skirmishers fired so heavily that the bullets striking the garden fence "made quite a rattling, disagreeable noise," according to the regimental historian. Conrad also stopped the 15th Missouri and refused its left flank for added protection. Scouts sent forward reported seeing a nearly continuous line of enemy earthworks—the Peach Tree Creek Line—and Conrad passed this information back to division headquarters. When Newton relayed it to army headquarters, Thomas told him to stay where he was for the time being. It was by now almost 3 P.M.[15]

Newton had gone as far as anyone felt comfortable, but the progress of Stanley and Wood continued to disappoint higher-ranking officers. Stanley left at 7 A.M. and moved to the South Fork of Peach Tree Creek an hour and a half later. Here he found some Confederate skirmishers. An officer from Schofield's staff also found Stanley at about that time, 8:30 A.M., representing the first contact between Fourth Corps and Twenty-Third Corps generals in days. The officer told Stanley that Schofield was moving on a road one mile east, that the road eventually converged with the road Stanley was taking, and the two forces ought to link up at that point. This contact was in stark contrast to what had happened the day before when Schofield sent a staff officer and a courier to find Stanley at the North Fork of Peach Tree Creek. On that occasion, a misunderstanding led a detachment of the 75th Illinois from Stanley's division to fire on the pair, wounding at least the courier.[16]

Stanley found it difficult to continue along the road. His men had to rebuild the burned bridge over the South Fork after his skirmishers waded the creek and drove enemy skirmishers away. Then at 10 A.M. Stanley's division crossed the stream and cautiously moved forward, meeting Rebel skirmishers half an hour later. The Federals drove their enemy from slight rail breast-works and continued forward, but Rebel artillery now opened from a line of continuous earthworks one-third of a mile beyond the fortified Confederate skirmish line.[17]

Stanley was approaching the new east-facing Confederate line that Brown's Division had started to form on the evening of July 19. By the after-noon of July 20, however, Cheatham had shifted his corps until most of his units faced east. The result was that Confederate infantry now extended from the eastern flank of the north-facing Peach Tree Creek Line down to near the Georgia Railroad. Prisoners told Stanley that Stevenson's Division stood in his way. As afternoon shaded off into evening, the Federals tried to deploy as many units as possible to face this new Confederate line. The area among the two forks of Peach Tree Creek was heavily timbered, forcing both Stanley and Wood to keep to the roads. Effective Confederate skirmishing had slowed their progress. That evening, Wood placed Knefler's brigade to Stanley's right and kept Hazen's brigade in reserve on the north side of the South Fork of Peach Tree Creek. It was impossible to extend the line west-ward to link with Newton.[18]

But Stanley managed to make a tenuous connection with Schofield by evening, although it was difficult to do so. Cox's division of the Twenty-Third Corps had crossed the South Fork of Peach Tree Creek and advanced to the Peyton Plantation, near the crossing of Pea Vine Creek, by the eve-ning of July 19. On the morning of July 20, Cox advanced a short distance against heavy Confederate skirmishing until he realized the road he was on ran nearly parallel to the continuous line of earthworks held by Cheatham's Corps on the west side of Pea Vine Creek. He had to stop his progress and de-ploy his entire division west of the road fronting that line. Cox placed three brigades in line with his fourth to the rear as a reserve.[19]

Later in the afternoon, Hascall's division moved up and deployed to Cox's left, extending Schofield's line toward the expected arrival of McPherson's Army of the Tennessee. Schofield ordered Hascall to detach one of his bri-gades and send it to Cox's right in an effort to make contact with Stanley. Hascall sent Col. William E. Hobson's brigade, but Hobson received his in-structions directly from Schofield. His task was to find and secure the junc-tion of the two roads Schofield and Stanley were using. Hobson deployed a skirmish line supported by the rest of his brigade and moved out in the direction Schofield pointed to him. He met stiff resistance and had to re-inforce his skirmishers, but the Federals were able to drive the enemy back to the road junction. There Hobson believed the Confederates were hold-ing the crossroads in force. He advanced his entire brigade in two lines and, after eight minutes of heavy skirmishing, took the junction. Hobson's men made rail breastworks to secure their hard-won objective and repulsed a Confederate counterattack. Later that evening, skirmishers from Stanley's division appeared but did not have the strength to relieve Hobson's men, so the Twenty-Third Corps troops remained at the crossroads indefinitely.[20]

The link with Stanley was slim at best, but there yet was no link with McPherson to the south. One of Logan's staff officers rode to Schofield's headquarters to at least open communications, informing Schofield that Logan was moving toward Atlanta one and a half miles from Hascall's left flank along the road directly linking Decatur with the city. Sherman had hoped to sew up his line more firmly than this by the end of the day, but he had to accept the many obstacles to fast movement and coordination of dispersed parts of his army group as a fact of military life.[21]

For reasons still unclear, Hooker took his time in moving the rest of his Twentieth Corps across Peach Tree Creek and forming a solid line on the south side. At the beginning of July 20, he already had Geary's division in place on good ground, but Ward and Williams had not yet moved over the stream, leaving two prominent holes in Thomas's line. Howard had started Fourth Corps operations at dawn, and Palmer was ready to move his Fourteenth Corps south as soon as Hooker got in motion. But there was an unaccountable air of lassitude among Twentieth Corps officers during most of the day.

Hooker's delay caused a good deal of anxiety at Army of the Cumberland headquarters. Brig. Gen. William D. Whipple, Thomas's chief of staff, repeatedly informed the army commander that Palmer was waiting for hours to move forward, and Thomas finally lectured Hooker at 3 P.M., telling him that Newton had waited only until Hooker's skirmish line was completed before advancing but Palmer had to wait until the Twentieth Corps main line was formed before moving south. Thomas wanted it done immediately, so army operations could proceed. Hooker responded defensively and with unclear language to argue that his command was in place. In short, he prevaricated because by midafternoon the Twentieth Corps main line was still not formed and those two gaps to either side of Geary's division still existed. In fact, Thomas told Newton to stop his forward advance in part because Newton had hit stiff resistance and in part because he wanted Hooker's main line to come up and support the lone Fourth Corps division. In his messages to Sherman's headquarters, however, Thomas covered up for Hooker and stated that his entire army was across Peach Tree Creek before the afternoon of July 20 (which was true) and that "the line was adjusted" (which was at best only partly true).[22]

Joseph Hooker, whose Twentieth Corps was not fully ready to meet the enemy on the afternoon of July 20 despite having several hours in which to prepare. (Library of Congress, LC-DIG-cwpb-06979)

Fortunately for the Union cause that day, Hooker managed to at least get the rest of his corps over the obstacle posed by Peach Tree Creek on July 20. Ward scouted the possible crossings and decided to move his division over the bridge behind Newton's division, where the Buck Head and Atlanta Road crossed the stream. The 22nd Wisconsin and 136th New York moved ahead and skirmished forward to establish themselves on the ridge between Newton and Geary. Then the division began to cross at 11 A.M., nearly five hours after the Fourth Corps had begun its own operations that morning. Once over the bridge, Hooker ordered Ward to rest his men in cornfields along the bottom land of the creek, at the foot of the bluff. Ward placed Col. Benjamin Harrison's First Brigade on the right, Col. John Coburn's Second Brigade in the center, and Col. James Wood Jr.'s Third Brigade on the left. Ward's command formed multiple lines, but Hooker's orders were to wait until further instructions arrived. As Wood understood it, "a farther advance was not at that time necessary." Stephen Fleharty of the 102nd Illinois re-called that "we did not anticipate any very serious work—nothing more than a slight skirmish, when we should advance to construct works at the crest of the hill."[23]

Ward's skirmishers had little difficulty clearing the way south. They easily took the first rise of ground south of Peach Tree Creek against light opposi-tion. Then they crossed a ravine and ascended the next rise of ground, meet-ing stiffer resistance from Confederate skirmishers. The Federals took some prisoners and secured this ridge to connect with Newton's division to the east and Geary's division to the west. This ridge was the best defensive posi-tion in the area; a road and a rail fence ran along the top from east to west. The 79th Ohio of Harrison's brigade detailed some men to escort Confeder-ate prisoners to the rear. The Ohio troops also were told to round up Union stragglers from Ward's march that day. The weather was hot, and the divi-sion had marched in a circuitous way to get to Newton's bridge. The 79th Ohio men found sixty stragglers and returned them to their regiments.[24]

While this was going on, Ward's men took it easy in the corn field that lined the southern bottomland of Peach Tree Creek, which extended as much as 200 yards from the stream. They were shielded from the skirmish action by the abrupt rise of the bluff land, but occasionally a few long-range shots from the Confederate skirmishers plunged into the bottoms. Many men took this opportunity to bathe in the red, muddy water of Peach Tree Creek. Even if they did not become clean, at least the washing cooled their skin in the in-creasing heat of the day. Other men kindled fires and began to boil coffee, the eternal stimulant of Civil War soldiers, and ate their midday meal.[25]

Williams's division crossed Peach Tree Creek quite early on July 20. The van of the column marched across the bridge Geary's division had constructed at about 6 A.M., while the tail of the column moved to the south side by 8 A.M. By then, the clouds had given way to a bright, hot sun. A Confederate battery opened fire on the crossing area just as Williams's men were partly over the creek but did little harm.[26]

The division marched obliquely to the right as it tried to fill the gap between Geary and the Fourteenth Corps to the west. Williams "followed a farm road along a wooded ridge" that intersected the road south from Howell's Mill at the plantation of Hiram Embry. Confederate skirmishers were dug in to cover this intersection, so Hooker ordered Williams to stop 600 yards short of the junction where some "deserted houses" were scattered along the farm road. Williams placed Brig. Gen. Joseph F. Knipe's brigade on the right of the road and Col. James S. Robinson's brigade to the left. He also moved Brig. Gen. Thomas H. Ruger's brigade toward the right in an attempt to make contact with the left flank of the Fourteenth Corps. Most of the ascending terrain around Williams's position was wooded and broken up into ravines.[27]

There was no sense of urgency, so Williams massed his brigades, and the men stacked their muskets to rest. Knipe's brigade, for example, formed a frontage of only 250 feet according to Rice C. Bull of the 123rd New York. Hooker and Williams stopped at Knipe's brigade to eat their midday meal under the trees. The men did likewise. "We made our little fires," recalled Bull, "fried our pork, boiled our coffee, and ate our hardtack." Then the men rested in the increasing heat of the early afternoon. "Some were soon sleeping, others reading books or papers, a good many were having a friendly game of cards using the greasy pack that always was handy when we halted." Irving Bronson of the 107th New York caught a glimpse of Hooker "under the shade of a small tree with his hat, coat, and boots off, receiving and sending out orders."[28]

This was the atmosphere at Twentieth Corps headquarters that lazy afternoon. "No orders were given to put our Brigade in position to defend itself in case of attack," complained Bull in his memoirs. "During the campaign we had never been so massed while in the presence of the enemy unless a line of troops was deployed in our front and we were where we had time to form in line in case of emergency. But on this day, everyone from our Corps Commander to private soldier seemed certain that the enemy would make no stand until behind the entrenchments at Atlanta; so there was no need for placing our Brigade in line of battle. Our officers must have thought it unnecessary to use even the most ordinary precautions for the skirmish line was not advanced as far in front as usual. We were finally informed we would camp for the night as we were."[29]

This attitude certainly was not justified by either Thomas's or Sherman's instructions for the day. Neither Howard nor Palmer shared this lackadaisical attitude that Hooker imparted to his subordinates. It is true that no one thought the enemy would immediately attack the Army of the Cumberland on July 20; but as Bull indicated, the modus operandi during the course of the campaign was to be prepared for anything even if trouble was not anticipated, and Hooker was letting his guard down in a dangerous way on July 20.

For about three hours, Ward's and Williams's men lounged about in positions not suited for defense against a sudden attack from the enemy. They had plenty of time to advance their lines forward to high ground but received no encouragement, much less orders, from Hooker to do so. For those men who happened to be in open ground, the sun grew uncomfortably hot. Some of Williams's troops also heard the plopping of long-range overshooting by Confederate skirmishers some distance ahead as occasional bullets fell among them.[30]

The only activity was to Hooker's rear as efforts were made to construct more bridges to support the corps south of Peach Tree Creek. The high banks and muddy bottom of the stream made fording impossible; artillery and wagons needed bridges, and those had to be improvised out of whatever timber could readily be had near the bridge site. Capt. William Merrell of the 141st New York was given the job of managing a work detail to construct one such bridge for Williams's division. Merrell had worked in the lumber business before the war and had some knowledge of how to do this. The division pioneers were exhausted, so he detailed men from the ranks to help him. They cut timber and hauled it half a mile to the creek. Merrell measured the stream and found it was seventy-two feet wide and the water seven and a half feet deep in the middle. He used pine trunks to make a log crib work six by eight feet in dimension to be placed in the center of the stream. Because the bottom proved to be uneven, the crib work had to be more than twelve feet tall. Merrell's work detail then cut tall straight pine trees for stringers, laying them from the bank to the crib work. They were almost too long to be rigid under the weight of wagons and artillery, but Merrell had received a note of urgency from Williams to get the bridge finished soon and he decided to risk it. Fence rails were laid across the stringers to serve as the bridge roadway. Willow sprouts with a layer of dirt filled in the uneven parts. Merrell was barely finished with this improvised structure by midafternoon.[31]

Moving Ward and Williams to the south side of Peach Tree Creek was only the first step in Thomas's plan. After that, the entire Twentieth Corps was to move south in conjunction with Newton's division and Palmer's Fourteenth Corps. As we have seen, Newton did not wait for Ward to move up his main line and form a tight connection; he moved forward as soon as Ward established his skirmish line. Palmer nervously waited for Williams to establish a forward position, but Geary did not wait. His division had been on the south side since the day before, and it was ready to move forward at the first opportunity. As soon as Ward and Williams were on the south side, Geary was ready to go forward, even though neither division came up to support him. Hooker's lazy attitude toward corps operations that day did not rub off on Geary.

At 10 A.M., soon after Ward and Williams completed their crossing, Geary moved forward. He advanced a strong skirmish line supported by Col. Charles Candy's brigade with Col. Patrick H. Jones's brigade to its rear and Col. David Ireland's brigade behind Jones. The Federals pushed Confederate skirmishers from two ridges in their front and secured yet a third ridge that seemed to be the best ground in the area. It was on a line with the final position Newton's division assumed early that afternoon as well. By noon Candy's men were on that ridge and collecting fence rails to make an improvised breastwork. Unfortunately, Williams's division still lounged several hundred yards to the right rear of Ireland's flank. Geary was now about half a mile south of Peach Tree Creek, and both of his flanks were exposed because Hooker had not bothered to push forward either Ward or Williams.[32]

Geary's men also managed to eat something after assuming their new position. In fact, commissary wagons rolled up the hill to distribute rations to Ireland's brigade. The sun was burning hot by now, and there was little shade on the ridge top for Geary's troops.[33]

The tendency of all alert, ambitious commanders was to find the next good bit of ground in the direction of the enemy, and Geary was keen on seizing it. He quickly sent forward skirmishers after securing the ridge top to find out what lay ahead. Those skirmishers crossed "a swampy rivulet about 300 yards in front of my main line" and came to rest with their left wing in an open field and their right wing occupying "a high, narrow, timbered hill in front of my right." Geary decided he must secure that hill to protect his right wing and serve as staging ground for the next push forward. He ordered Jones to send a strong regiment forward to occupy it and prepare the ground for the placement of a battery.[34]

Jones selected Lieut. Col. Enos Fourat's 33rd New Jersey and accompanied it on the forward move. Marching in line, the regiment soon ascended the tree-covered slope and took position on the crest. It was evident to every-one that the hill was an isolated and vulnerable position. Fourat sent out his own skirmish line for added protection. Geary personally went forward a few minutes behind the 33rd New Jersey. Along the way he conversed with three captured Rebel skirmishers. "They were quite communicative, saying that there were no large bodies of their troops within two miles." This in-formation, plus what Fourat called "the feeble opposition made to our skir-mishers," led the division leader to assume that no trouble need be antici-pated.[35]

Still, the atmosphere on that hill was disturbing. Lieut. Stephen Pierson, adjutant of the 33rd New Jersey, recalled that the forest "was ominously still; even the birds seemed to have stopped singing." Geary had ordered a supporting regiment to the hill, and Lieut. Col. Allan H. Jackson's 134th New York began to move forward. As Pierson made his way back to the main line on an errand, he met Jackson in transit. Jackson caught the ominous mood of the place and extended his hand while saying "'Good-bye Adjutant.' I laughed at him, but he said: 'There'll be trouble out there.'" Back on the iso-lated hill Geary personally marked out the location for the 33rd New Jersey line, and the men started to gather logs to make a breastwork.[36]

While Geary aggressively pushed forward, Palmer focused on complet-ing the crossing of Peach Tree Creek by his Fourteenth Corps early on the morning of July 20 and then waited for Hooker to move before sending his men forward. Only two brigades of Davis's division managed to lodge on the south side by the evening of July 19, but Baird's division got over by mid-night. Baird took a position to the left of Davis's division and advanced half a mile south of the stream to secure "an important range of wooded hills."[37]

Johnson's men had made additional bridges to facilitate their crossing of Peach Tree Creek. As soon as those bridges were ready, the division began moving over the stream at 3 A.M. of July 20. Johnson moved forward to fill the gap between Baird's division and Hooker's corps, pushing Confederate skirmishers back in the early dawn of that day.[38]

Palmer felt frustrated by lack of activity on Hooker's part. His instructions were to advance farther south in conjunction with the Twentieth Corps, but Williams's division seemed content to lounge about rather than take up formation and connect firmly with Johnson. "Captain [Joel P.] Watson has been gone some time on the hunt for information as to General Hooker's purposes and movements," Palmer informed Johnson, "but has not yet re-turned. Do you know when General H. will be ready to advance?" Johnson was as much in the dark on that question as everyone else in the Fourteenth Corps. His division extended Baird's line eastward, but a considerable gap existed to the left where Williams's division should have been located. Johnson's men formed two lines at about 10 A.M. and started to build fortifications but were soon told to stop work because their officers expected an advance at any moment.[39]

Davis experienced great delay in bringing his last brigade over Peach Tree Creek; in fact, that brigade was the last of Palmer's Fourteenth Corps to move over the stream. James D. Morgan managed to cross five companies of the 60th Illinois early on the morning of July 20, bypassing the Confederates who still held the high bluff opposite Howell's Mill. It was not enough to compel the enemy to retire; in fact, heavy skirmishing resumed that morning near the mill as the Confederates stubbornly held on to the bluff. Late in the evening of July 20 the enemy seemed to have left, and Morgan pushed the 10th Michigan over the creek at 6:30 P.M., followed by three other regiments after dark.[40]

Earlier that day, Dilworth's brigade managed to get artillery up to the line it had established and held against Reynolds's counterattack of July 19. Capt. George Q. Gardner's 5th Wisconsin Battery had to be manhandled by the gunners into position because of the close proximity of Reynolds's skirmish line. The pieces delivered destructive fire and compelled the Rebel skirmishers to fall back on July 20. To Dilworth's right, Mitchell's brigade encountered stiff resistance near the junction of Peach Tree Creek and the Chattahoochee River. Confederate skirmishers fought stubbornly and compelled the Federals to keep part of the brigade on the north side of the creek as a reserve in case they had to retire across the stream. "The enemy cling with great obstinacy to [their position on] our right," Palmer informed Thomas's headquarters. This was the left anchor of Hood's Peach Tree Creek Line.[41]

By noon, Thomas had finished a ride along his line and sent a complete report to Sherman. He noted the heavy resistance to Palmer's right wing and informed his superior that all his troops were on the south side of Peach Tree Creek. After mulling over the evidence, Thomas concluded that Confederate attention "is fully occupied by us, and I am in hopes Generals McPherson, Schofield, and Howard will be able to fall upon his rear without any very great difficulty."[42]

Thomas, of course, was wrong. Hood's attention was almost fully on the Army of the Cumberland, and he actually was ill-informed of Schofield and McPherson's movements. Army of Tennessee headquarters was alive with preparations to attack Thomas that afternoon. "Feeling it impossible to hold Atlanta without giving battle," Hood reported, "I determined to strike the enemy while attempting to cross this stream."[43]

Hood called another conference of his major subordinates on the morning of July 20 to finalize details of the attack plan. He set 1 P.M. as the start of the assault to be conducted by Hardee's Corps and Stewart's Army of Mississippi, with Cheatham's Corps to be held as a reserve. Hood put together an unnecessarily elaborate battle plan. Rather than a simple frontal attack, he wanted the divisions to maneuver so as to herd the retreating enemy and trap them in the area near the junction of Peach Tree Creek and the Chattahoochee River. To do so, the rightmost division of Hardee was to start, followed by the next in line to the left after the first had gone 200 yards. After hitting the Federals, each division was to veer left to accomplish Hood's goal. This was an attack in echelon and something of an oblique movement as well. Any Civil War army would have found it difficult, and the Army of Tennessee did not have a sterling record of complicated movements on the battlefield. Yet Hood felt that Peach Tree Creek was a major terrain feature that could inhibit Thomas's retreat; he wanted to use the creek as an obstacle to pin the enemy and damage him more severely than if he had a chance simply to fall back northward. He told Hardee and Stewart to hold back a division each as a reserve.[44]

As soon as instructions filtered down the chain of command, Hardee's and Stewart's men began to prepare for battle. They filled canteens and received an additional twenty rounds of small-arms ammunition per man. Stewart made a special effort to ensure his division commanders fully understood the details of the operation. He also told them to thoroughly examine the terrain in front of the Peach Tree Creek Line so there would be no surprises when the assault began. There was still time for other things that morning. Albert T. Goodloe of the 35th Alabama met with his bible class "as usual, and had a good time studying the Scriptures" before they were called into line.[45]

By about midmorning, disturbing news from Wheeler indicated that Schofield and McPherson were looming as a more potent threat than Hood had previously thought. The Confederate cavalry had not served army headquarters well for the past few days; Wheeler had failed to station sufficient troops far enough east of Atlanta to detect and accurately report on Sherman's success in snipping the Georgia Railroad as early as July 18. The only explanation for this failure lies in Wheeler's preoccupation with opposing Thomas's advance north of Atlanta and his failure to station Kelly's cavalry division far enough from the city's east side to know what was happening near Decatur.

That failure of intelligence hampered Hood's plans severely. Now, on the threshold of his first attack as army commander, he had to worry about a new threat.

A flurry of dispatches emanating from army headquarters to Wheeler began to appear by 10:20 A.M. of July 20. Through his staff members, Hood urged Wheeler to hold back McPherson as long as possible while he sent an additional cavalry force from Jackson's Division to help. He also told Wheeler that he had decided to extend Cheatham's Corps line all the way down to the Georgia Railroad. He also counted on the Georgia Militia to help secure the position east of Atlanta. By early afternoon William W. Mackall sent an urgent message to Wheeler asking him to report on the latest developments. Mackall wanted to know if he had fallen back much and how many Federals confronted him. Such inquiries clearly indicate that Wheeler was not in close, regular contact with Hood, increasing the sense of uncertainty about the planned assault on Thomas, which already was delayed by the time Mackall sent that dispatch to Wheeler.[46]

During the hours just before his attack, Hood increasingly was in the fog about major issues associated with the operation. He had pitifully few details about the threat posed by Schofield and McPherson and had authorized a shift in his army's line of battle before the attack could begin. In Hood's mind, this would involve a relatively minor movement. He wanted Cheatham to shift right so as to reach the Georgia Railroad with his right flank, but he apparently had no idea how far Cheatham would have to move to do this.[47]

To make matters more complicated, there actually were two movements discussed that morning, not just one. Cheatham had been complaining that ever since he moved Brown's Division south of the Peach Tree Creek Line to begin forming the new Confederate position facing east on the evening of July 19, the rest of his corps (still on the Peach Tree Creek Line facing north) was stretched too thin. His other two divisions there had to hold the same sector as the three divisions had formerly held, and Cheatham could do that only by thinning his line to one rank in the center of that two-division sector. On the morning of July 20, Hood authorized Cheatham to make up for this by shifting Hardee and Stewart to the right the equivalent of one division frontage. He divided up the responsibility; both Hardee and Stewart were to shift right the equivalent of half a division. This would make the north-facing Peach Tree Creek Line compact and fully manned along its entire length.[48]

This minor adjustment in the Confederate position really had nothing to do with the other shift, the effort to move Cheatham all the way down to the Georgia Railroad. But for reasons that are not fully clear, Hood confused the two shifts in his mind. He seems to have assumed that Cheatham merely needed to shift the length of one division to reach the railroad and never kept the two shifts clear in his thinking or in his orders to subordinates. When the shift began, Cheatham intended to move all the way to the railroad, a distance of about one and a half miles (or about a two-division frontage), but Hardee and Stewart understood that they were only to move about half a division frontage in order to keep pace with Cheatham.[49]

Who was primarily responsible for this mix-up in the Army of Tennessee? Historians have generally, and rightfully, placed blame on Cheatham. He was new to corps command and admittedly not well suited for the job. Handling three divisions was very different from handling one, and Cheatham was not up to his enlarged duties. He held the fundamental responsibility for informing army headquarters of his position and needs, and he failed to do so. But Hood cannot be held blameless. Such a basic misunderstanding of the army's position never occurred when Johnston held command. He used his staff effectively to keep tabs on unit positions and always knew where they were and what sectors they needed to fill. Hood's mobility was severely restricted by his physical infirmities (a major reason why he should not have been placed in command of the army), but he also does not seem to have used his staff well to serve as his eyes and ears. There is no indication that army-level staff members rode along the line to inspect unit locations on July 20. Hood still had much to learn about managing an army.[50]

As usual, Hood completely ignored this problem in his official report and in his memoirs. In the former, Hood argued that Cheatham's new position, with most of his corps facing east, could serve a purpose in the proposed attack on Thomas. If Cheatham's left could hold firm at the angle in the north-facing and east-facing Rebel position (near the junction of Pea Vine Creek and Peach Tree Creek), that would help to separate Schofield from Thomas and make the Army of the Cumberland more vulnerable to Hardee's and Stewart's assault.[51]

Cheatham began to shift his corps to the south at about 10 A.M. and did so in stages rather than in one movement. Once settled in their new position, his men hurried to dig earthworks. The left flank of the corps rested at Jones' Mill on Clear Creek, and it still faced north. Then the line extended east for one and a half miles before heading south another two miles to reach the Georgia Railroad. Cheatham's new position was in general well chosen to take advantage of the terrain. It conformed to the high ground east of Lull-water Creek, a tributary of Pea Vine Creek. But some units of Henry D. Clayton's Division found their line commanded by a high ridge. That afternoon elements of Wood's Federal division occupied the ridge, set up artillery, and punished the Confederates. Clayton had no artillery immediately available to counter this fire, so his men counted on improving their fortifications to endure it. Clayton also contended with aggressive Union skirmishing that afternoon but managed to hold the blue-coated skirmishers on their side of no-man's land.[52]

Cheatham's stage-by-stage shift of one and a half miles caused a great deal of confusion for Hardee, who was told by army headquarters that all he would have to do was move right the equivalent of half a division. According to Hood's specific instructions, Hardee posted Maj. Samuel L. Black, one of his staff members, in a good place to superintend this shift. Black stationed himself where Hardee's left flank was supposed to stop to accomplish the shift and showed one of Stewart's staff officers the spot so the right flank of the Army of Mississippi could rest there too. But, when Hardee realized that Cheatham was moving much farther away, he had to make a quick decision as to his own course. As Hardee correctly noted in his report, if Hood had been in the field rather than at his headquarters, he could have consulted with the army commander. But there was no time for that. Hardee correctly decided to continue shifting in order to maintain contact with Cheatham's left flank; considering that the enemy was in heavy force within striking distance, it was safer to keep a connected line.[53]

Black also was confused when he saw the left flank of Hardee's line disappear from the spot where it was supposed to stop. He asked the leftmost brigade commander and was told orders had been issued to continue moving. Half an hour later, the right flank of Stewart's command neared the spot. Black explained the situation to Stewart's rightmost brigade commander and then rode to consult with Hardee, who told him of his decision to keep touch with Cheatham. "I know that General Hardee expressed his impatience at the delay," Black recalled after the war, "and his annoyance at the repeated movements to the right." Expecting to attack, it came as an odd diversion for most members of Hardee's Corps to suddenly be called on to move so far in line to the right. This also meant that most units that had deployed skirmishers also had to move their skirmish lines to the right as well.[54]

Stewart was as surprised and annoyed by the continued shifting as Hardee. In fact, when he realized that Hardee was moving farther than the expected half a mile, Stewart stopped his men and sent word to army headquarters suggesting that the shift be canceled so the troops could attack near the 1 P.M. start time for the assault. Stewart implied that Hood mandated he keep contact with Hardee, which actually was the only course of action to take. Hardee and Stewart could not attack without firm connection.[55]

William W. Loring, who commanded the rightmost division of Stewart's Army of Mississippi, later reported that Samuel Black informed him Hardee suggested that Stewart rest his right flank where it was originally intended, only half a division front to the right. Skirmishers could fill the gap between Stewart's and Hardee's commands. But Loring must have misunderstood, for Black never implied in his postwar letter that he said anything of the kind. Moreover, Hardee never implied it either, and it would make little sense to do this if the intention was to attack as soon as the shift was completed. When Stewart instructed Loring to keep going, the division continued moving east.[56]

Loring's subordinates were irritated by the continued shifting. Winfield S. Featherston, whose brigade led Loring's movement, was astonished to be pushed farther east onto ground that was completely new to him. He had spent hours reconnoitering the lay of the land before his former position one and a half miles to the west on July 19, and all that time and energy was now wasted. Brig. Gen. Thomas M. Scott moved his brigade behind Featherston, followed by the rest of Stewart's army. In some ways the shift was beneficial for the Confederates. They had massed quite a bit on the far left, nervous about keeping touch with the river near the railroad bridge. Now Stewart thinned out his left wing, but the unexpectedly long shift served to stretch his line almost too thinly. Samuel G. French's small division, which held the far left, had to cover most of the Fourteenth Corps front.[57]

Fighting his new command for the first time, Stewart was extremely careful to convey exact instructions to his subordinates. He not only fully explained the attack plan early that morning, but he repeated the instructions by personally talking with his division commanders after the shift ended. His thoroughness paid off in that no one in the corps was confused about what to do. Division level staff officers spoke to brigade commanders, who in turn conveyed the exact meaning and spirit of the attack orders to their regimental officers. As Featherston put it three days later, "The fight was to be a general one along our lines, and the victory to be made as decisive as possible." Stewart also gave an impromptu speech to Scott's Brigade after the shift, explaining the battle plan to them. In his instructions to division commanders, Stewart emphasized a point Hood made; if the men encountered earthworks, they were to attack vigorously and carry the fortifications. There is no evidence that Hardee exerted himself to explain the battle plan or encourage his men as did Stewart.[58]

Hood believed he had done everything to set the army in motion for the first Confederate attack of the campaign that approached the nature of a general assault. Late that morning, he spoke to Felix G. De Fontaine, a newspaper correspondent of the *Savannah Republican*, while leaning on a crutch in the doorway of his headquarters house. "At one I attack the ... enemy. He has pressed our lines until he is within a short distance of Atlanta, and

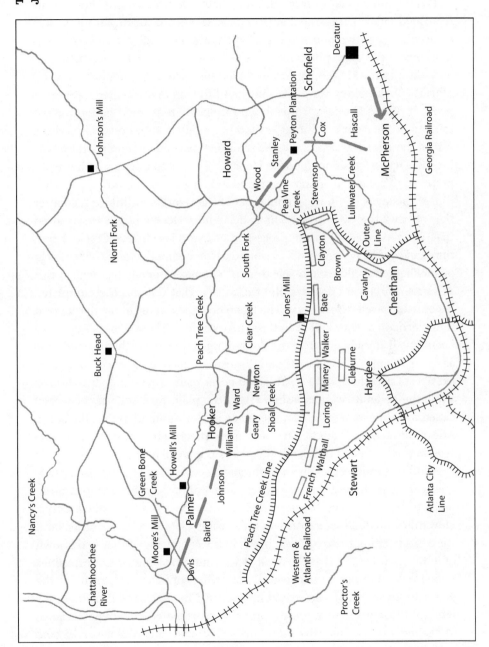

Three p.m.,
July 20

I must fight or evacuate. I am going to fight. The odds are against us, but I leave the issue with the God of Battles." Then Hood and his staff rode to Stewart's headquarters to observe the fight.[59]

Did the unplanned shift of one and a half miles to the right seriously affect Hood's plans? It is true that the attack, instead of starting at 1 P.M., was delayed at least two hours and perhaps three, depending on whose testimony one relies on to pinpoint the exact time of starting. It is also true that virtually all attacking units now occupied new ground, unfamiliar to their officers. But in many ways the shift had little effect on Confederate prospects. It placed Hardee's Corps in a position where it could have exploited the gap in Sherman's line that existed between Newton's division and the rest of the Fourth Corps. Stewart's strongest division, commanded by Loring, now was in position opposite Hooker's Twentieth Corps, which was ill-prepared to receive an attack compared to Palmer's command.[60]

But Gustavus W. Smith, commander of the Georgia Militia, argued after the war that the two-or-three-hour delay hurt Hood's plans. He believed that Thomas was still in the process of crossing Peach Tree Creek at that time and could have suffered a "serious disaster before the forces of Schofield or McPherson could have reached him." Thomas Connelly has echoed this assessment in recent decades. But the truth is that Thomas had completed his crossings well before 1 P.M. His troop positions were almost the same at midafternoon as they had been three hours before. There really would have been little if any advantage to the Confederates to strike at the planned time as far as Thomas's movements and dispositions were concerned. Moreover, as Albert Castel has pointed out, Hood never really intended to hit Thomas while the Federals were crossing. His battle plan, for better or for worse, called for a movement to trap the Army of the Cumberland on the south side of the stream. It might have been more effective to hit exactly when the crossings were taking place, but the plan did not call for it.[61]

Another serious breakdown of intelligence at Army of Tennessee headquarters lay in the fact that no one was aware of the significant gap in Sherman's position between Newton's division and the rest of the Fourth Corps. Howard estimated that gap as two miles wide. Cheatham and Hardee both were in a position to exploit that break in the enemy line if they had known of it. Cox pointed out that the angle where the two Confederate corps lines joined "would interpose between the two wings of Sherman's army" as the Federals advanced. Hardee could have moved his right and Cheatham his left into the gap. Such an assault probably represented Hood's best chance of dealing a serious blow to Sherman's grand plan; it certainly would have called on all the resources of grit and stamina the Federals possessed, even though the rugged, brush-engulfed terrain would have posed a difficult problem for the Confederates.[62]

Sherman did not worry about the gap. While visiting Howard's headquarters at 2 P.M. on July 20, he expressed the conviction that Hood would strike Schofield and McPherson because the left wing of his army group was tearing up a vital line of communications into Atlanta. The lack of apparent concern for the gap among Federal generals would have accentuated the effect of a major Confederate assault into that area.[63]

But the Army of Tennessee would not conduct a surgical strike into the gap. It would move straight ahead and to the left in an effort to beat, trap, and demolish the Army of the Cumberland, its most common opponent on the battlefields of the Western Theater. Estimating the number of men on the opposing sides depends on which source one uses. Abstracts of returns dated July 10, 1864, place the strength of the Army of Tennessee at 45,500 men. Albert Castel believes Hood inherited 55,000 troops from Johnston on July 18, but Johnston claimed the number was 51,000. It is certain that not all of them would take part in the battle of Peach Tree Creek; only Hardee and Stewart were slated to conduct that assault. Henry Stone, one of Thomas's staff officers, estimated the opposing forces on July 20 at 30,000 Confederates and 20,000 Federals, and the abstracts of returns dated July 10 support Stone's estimate of Rebel strength that day. Richard McMurry believes the number of troops Hood threw at Thomas was closer to 23,000 men, divided into five divisions with two more divisions as support. McMurry accepts Stone's estimate of 20,000 Federals divided into four divisions, with a brigade of Fourteenth Corps men involved as well. Stone also estimated Sherman's overall strength as 45,000 men in the left wing of the army group and 30,000 men in the right wing.[64]

Whichever way one tilts the numbers, Hood managed to create a flawed but viable scenario for his first attack as army commander. "By a mixture of boldness and good luck," Richard McMurry has concluded, "Hood had brought a superior force to the point of battle." The numerical superiority was by no means overwhelming, but the Rebel commander at least had some justification for hope as his troops finished their shifting and turned their faces northward toward the enemy.[65]

Here they come, boys! By God, a million of them.
—unidentified Federal skirmisher

Never was I under a heavier fire than there. . . . I thought I
would certainly see my 'Valhalla' that day.—J. Cooper Nisbet

I gave them 75 rounds for Chickamauga.—Day Elmore

Hardee versus Newton

According to Hood's plan, Hardee was to lead off the Confederate attack on Thomas's army that afternoon with an assault by divisions en echelon. By the end of his shift to the right, Hardee found that the right flank of his corps ended up near the valley of Clear Creek. This placed his entire command squarely opposite the position of Newton's Fourth Corps division. Maj. Gen. William B. Bate's Division held the right and was opposite the sector east of Newton's men; in other words, Bate faced the gap between Newton and Wood. W. H. T. Walker's Division held Hardee's center and confronted Newton's left wing. Cheatham's Division, now led by Brig. Gen. George E. Maney, occupied Hardee's left and confronted Newton's right wing, extending a bit beyond it toward the west. Maj. Gen. Patrick R. Cleburne's Division was held in reserve behind Walker and Maney.[1]

The strength of the opposing forces on this part of the battlefield has been variously estimated. According to historians, Hardee had perhaps 15,000 men on the field. Abstracts of returns dated July 10 indicate that his corps contained 16,567 men present for duty that day, but the number undoubtedly dropped by July 20. Newton initially reported that he had 3,200 men in his division but later downgraded that number to 2,700 troops. One thing is certain; Hardee brought overwhelming strength to the field compared to his opponent. Never before and never since would the Army of Tennessee enjoy such an astounding advantage of numbers (as much as five to one) against an opponent.[2]

The exact time at which the battle began is debatable. While Sherman and latter day historians have generally agreed that it started at 4 P.M., a careful screening of the many reports by Union and Confederate participants provide different times for the beginning of the battle. More observers cited 3 P.M. as the actual start of the fight than any other time.[3]

John Newton was ready for anything that afternoon. Like Thomas a Virginian by birth and a graduate of West Point, he served as an engineer before the war and participated as a brigade, division, or corps commander in all the major campaigns of the East from the Peninsula to Gettysburg. He was one of several officers transferred to the West in time for the Atlanta campaign, and Sherman found room for them in his large Military Division of the Mississippi. Newton took over Philip Sheridan's division, one of the best in the Western Federal armies. It suffered enormously in the failed June 27 attack on Johnston's line at Kennesaw Mountain. Though reduced in numbers, the survivors of that attack were tough fighters who could not easily be cowed, and their commander was vigilant and resourceful. "John Newton could never be surprised," Howard proudly wrote of his subordinate.[4]

Observers noted with interest that Newton's formation consisted of a capital T, with two brigades in line at the front forming the cross bar and a third in column to the rear forming the stem. Kimball's brigade deployed to the right of the Buck Head and Atlanta Road, except that the 88th Illinois lay east of the thoroughfare, and Scovill placed four guns of his Ohio battery in the roadway. Blake's brigade deployed east of the road and to the left of the 88th Illinois. Bradley's brigade formed a column of regiments along the road to the rear of this line. "I call this whole formation 'Newton's Cross,'" wrote Howard after the war.[5]

Newton's men had just begun to construct breastworks a few minutes before the Confederates attacked. Some units put together fairly substantial works, while others had little if any shelter. Several observers noted that the breastworks were "half finished," but even a slight barricade offered some degree of safety and emotional security in battle. There were no trenches, no head logs, no abatis to trip up an attacker. Hardee's men had the comparatively rare advantage of avoiding the kind of serious impediments to an assault that had become common features on battlefields of the Atlanta campaign.[6]

Whether the Confederates could capitalize on their many advantages in

John Newton, whose Fourth Corps division anchored the stout Union defense on the afternoon of July 20. (Library of Congress, LC-DIG-cwpb-05201)

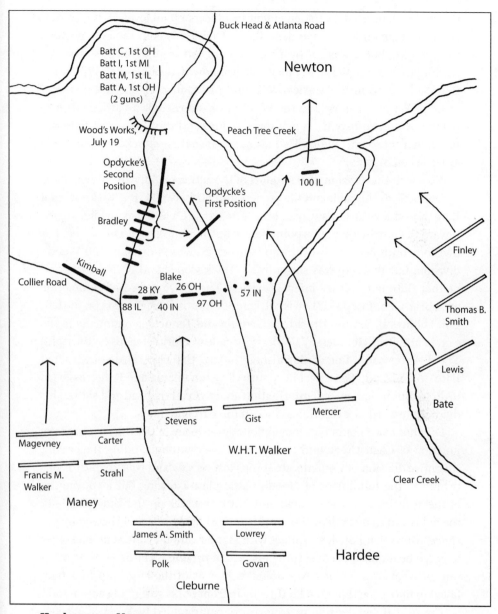

Buck Head & Atlanta Road

Batt C, 1st OH
Batt I, 1st MI
Batt M, 1st IL
Batt A, 1st OH
(2 guns)

Newton

Wood's Works,
July 19

Peach Tree Creek

Opdycke's
Second
Position

Opdycke's
First Position

100 IL

Bradley

Finley

Kimball

Collier Road

Blake
28 KY   26 OH
88 IL   40 IN   97 OH

57 IN

Thomas B.
Smith

Lewis

Stevens

Gist

Mercer

Bate

Magevney   Carter

W.H.T. Walker

Clear Creek

Francis M.   Strahl
Walker

Maney

James A. Smith   Lowrey

Polk   Govan

Hardee

Cleburne

Hardee versus Newton

this sector depended on management by officers on all levels, from Hardee down to regimental commanders. Bate's Division was in the best position to capitalize, but it was led by a career politician from Tennessee who, according to many critics, had failed to learn how to be a general. William B. Bate had served in the Mexican War and had gained extensive experience in Civil War engagements in the West, but his record as a battlefield commander was at best spotty. A newspaper editor and state legislator, Bate was far from a thorough soldier. He had mismanaged an attack by his division at Dallas on May 28.[7]

No one in the division filed a report of the action on July 20, and personal accounts from the rank and file are few and far between. But we know that Bate moved forward in a way to take him across Clear Creek, which angled toward the northwest at this point before flowing into Peach Tree Creek. His division continued toward the gap between Newton's division and Wood's division, but that gap was shrouded by thick woods and underbrush, and neither Bate nor Hardee knew it existed. The division formed in one line with Brig. Gen. Joseph H. Lewis's Brigade of Kentucky regiments on the left, Col. Thomas B. Smith's Brigade of Georgia and Tennessee regiments in the center, and Brig. Gen. Jesse J. Finley's Brigade of Florida troops on the right. The division had a line of skirmishers to lead the way. Hardee instructed Bate "to find, and, if practicable, to turn" Newton's flank, and Bate tried hard to do so. But he had no real information about what lay ahead and shoved his division forward in a reconnaissance in force to find out.[8]

For about two hours Bate's men floundered away in the thickets near the junction of Clear Creek and Peach Tree Creek without finding the enemy. An entire division of Confederate troops lost its way and was unable to contribute to the fulfillment of Hood's battle plan. Nothing but a contingent of the 57th Indiana was located east of Clear Creek on the Federal side of the field, and that small group quickly retired at the onset of the enemy advance. Moreover, Bate lost contact with Hardee and failed to send messages to corps headquarters concerning his lack of progress. Hardee was as ignorant of what that division was doing as he was of the large gap that Bate failed to find, even though it lay directly in front of his struggling command.[9]

The next Rebel division to go forward, commanded by W. H. T. Walker, was positioned to the left of Bate and just to the east of the Buck Head and Atlanta Road. Walker was one of the most experienced officers in the Army of Tennessee, having served in the Second Seminole War and in Mexico. For most of the sectional conflict combat had eluded him, but now his division occupied the center of Hardee's line in Hood's first strike to defend Atlanta. He advanced after Bate began to move forward through the brush to his

William J. Hardee, whose corps enjoyed an enormous numerical superiority over Newton's embattled division but failed to capitalize on it. (Library of Congress, LC-USZC4–7972)

right and before Maney's Division started to his left. As far as the Federals were concerned, the sudden appearance of Walker's troops signaled a surprise attack by the enemy. "With lightning-like speed," wrote a newspaper correspondent, "heavy columns of rebels appeared in front of, or rather tumbled out of, the forests, their columns seeming to be endless." A Federal skirmisher who scampered back to Newton's main position graphically alerted his comrades by shouting "Here they come, boys! By God, a million of them."[10]

Walker arrayed his division in one line with Brig. Gen. Clement H. Stevens's Brigade on the left, its left flank touching the Buck Head and Atlanta Road. Brig. Gen. States R. Gist's Brigade held the center of the division formation, and Brig. Gen. Hugh W. Mercer's Brigade anchored the right. The division was nestled in the largely open area between the Buck Head and Atlanta Road on the west and the winding course of Clear Creek on the east. In fact, Mercer's men crossed that shallow, meandering stream at least twice as they advanced, slowing their progress until Gist to their left lost touch with Mercer's flank and surged ahead.[11]

The two brigades constituting Walker's center and right advanced into the gap between Newton and Clear Creek. Gist and Mercer were opposed in this assault only by the 57th Indiana, which formed a skirmish line linking Blake's brigade with Clear Creek, and the 100th Illinois, which occupied ground near the junction of Clear Creek and Peach Tree Creek. Just before Gist and Mercer appeared, Lieut. Col. Willis Blanch detailed ten men to go south of his skirmish line and find out what lay ahead. Blanch led them personally. The group had proceeded a few hundred yards and captured a Confederate picket who refused to divulge any information. Just then, Rebel troops could be clearly seen moving forward. Blanch and the scouts ran back to the regiment, and the 57th Indiana conducted a fighting retreat northward. The Indianans stopped now and then to fire at the approaching Rebels, taking cover in the abandoned Confederate rifle pits held prior to Wood's crossing of the creek on July 19. They had to give up those pits as well and found themselves in the area where Clear Creek joined Peach Tree Creek. There was no recourse but to wade the deep stream as best they could, although a sharp bend in the creek prevented one wing of the regiment from crossing. As Blanch reported, half of his men rallied on the north bank while the rest stayed in a comparatively secure spot on the south side. Both wings continued to deliver fire on the approaching Rebel troops.[12]

Maj. Charles M. Hammond's 100th Illinois was caught up in this unexpected rush. Hammond also ordered his men to cross to the north side of Peach Tree and most of them were able to do so. The Federals who escaped to the north side did good service. Later, when small groups of Confederates tried to move over Peach Tree Creek, they were able to repel them and protect the rear area of Thomas's line.[13]

The rapid advance of Gist's and Mercer's Brigades inspired a corresponding rush of noncombatants from Newton's division. Hundreds of ambulance drivers, handlers of pack mules, and personal servants took fright and ran north along the Buck Head and Atlanta Road toward the bridge over Peach Tree Creek. Armed guards were quickly placed at the bridge to stop any combatants from rushing to the rear, but observers proudly reported that there were none in the crowd. Members of Bradley's brigade had the best view of these stragglers. They saw "a road full of fugitives fleeing as though their lives depended on their haste." Bradley and other officers tried to calm them but had no luck. The armed guards at the bridge allowed these men to pass by and clear the way for battle.[14]

Gist's and Mercer's sudden appearance disconcerted some of the fighting men in Newton's division, at least initially. A few Federals assumed the Confederates had been lying in wait for some time and intended to ambush Newton's division if it continued to advance. When it stopped to dig in, in their view, Hardee now opted for a sudden attack. The enemy "came down upon us like a thunderbolt," wrote Maj. Frederick A. Atwater of the 42nd Illinois. Bradley told his sister that "the rebels burst upon us in a perfect storm,... expecting to carry our position with a rush."[15]

As the Confederates bypassed the left flank of Newton's line, pushing back the 57th Indiana along the way, Blake held his position firmly. It was up to Bradley to do something about the Confederates who threatened to engulf Newton's left flank. Bradley reacted quickly by putting Col. Emerson Opdycke in charge of four of his regiments (the 3rd Kentucky, 64th Ohio, 65th Ohio, and 125th Ohio), and telling him to screen the road and bridge. Opdycke formed a line obliquely toward the east and north (facing southeast) only a few minutes before the Confederates came near. But Bradley soon thought better of the position and ordered Opdycke to fall back. The men did so hastily and, Opdycke admitted, "*in not very good order.*" He now formed the four regiments in line facing due east. The left flank reached almost to the bridge over Peach Tree Creek. The four regiments were in a good spot to fire into Gist's and Mercer's flanks as soon as the Confederates came within close range.[16]

Opdycke took up this position just in time, for the enemy neared within minutes. The Federals waited until the Rebels were within 100 yards before opening fire. The Confederates staggered and hesitated; Opdycke could see that their officers "exerted themselves to rally and charge again, but did not succeed." As the Federals fired at least five volleys, it seemed to Ralsa C. Rice of the 125th Ohio that a massacre was taking place in the Confederate line. "We were evening up matters with June 27 in mind," Rice later boasted.[17]

As Opdycke acknowledged, Federal artillery came into play to help him stop the enemy. Newton had positioned two guns of Scovill's Battery A, 1st Ohio Light Artillery on the Buck Head and Atlanta Road where Wood had constructed his first line of works the day before. This placed the guns about a quarter of a mile south of Peach Tree Creek. The rest of Scovill's pieces were on Newton's line three-quarters of a mile south of the creek. The two detached guns at Wood's old line were in a good position to pound Gist's and Mercer's men as they neared the bridge.[18]

But Thomas also became personally involved in saving the bridge. An artilleryman in the prewar U.S. Army, he rounded up guns to fire on the gray-clad infantrymen. A heavy-set man with a stoic, ponderous manner, Thomas "could move quickly enough when duty demanded it," as Howard gently put it. Thomas ordered Capt. Marco B. Gary's Battery C, 1st Ohio Light Artillery and Capt. Luther R. Smith's Battery I, 1st Michigan Light Artillery from the Twentieth Corps artillery reserve to move to a point near the bridge. Members of Wood's brigade, Ward's division, saw Thomas riding about in unusual haste and then slapping the artillery horse's flank with his sword to speed them on the way. The two batteries hurried across the bridge and took position next to the two guns Scovill had posted at Wood's July 19 fortifications. Capt. George W. Spencer's Battery M, 1st Illinois Light Artillery, a Fourth Corps unit, also added its guns to this concentration. All told the Federals used twenty pieces to pound Gist and Mercer, and those guns contributed greatly to the repulse of the Confederates. As Howard recalled Thomas's words after the battle, "It relieved the hitch."[19]

The effect of the combined fire of Opdycke's infantry and the artillery was too much for the Rebels. William D. Hynes of the 42nd Illinois may have exaggerated a bit when he described the "terrible hail of canister, literally mowing them down." From Hynes's perspective, the Confederates halted "a few minutes" and then, seized by panic, "fled like a flock of sheep."[20]

Bradley reported that the repulse of Gist and Mercer consumed little more than half an hour's time. He characterized it as "a sharp fight" and could have added that it was a close call as well.[21] The Confederates had come close to reaching the bridge over Peach Tree Creek that Newton depended upon as his lifeline to the north. But the combined weight of Opdycke's infantry fire and Thomas's artillery fire, both delivered into the Confederates' left flank and front, stopped their attack.

As Gist and Mercer plowed into the open space east of Newton's division,

George H. Thomas, who temporarily set aside his stolid demeanor to rush artillery units into a position from which the guns could play an important role in repelling Hardee's attack. (Library of Congress, LC-DIG-cwpb-00679)

Brig. Gen. Clement H. Stevens's Brigade advanced on the left of Walker's formation. He directly confronted Blake's brigade on Newton's left. Born in Connecticut, Stevens was living in South Carolina when the war broke out and sided with the Confederacy. After recovering from a wound received at First Manassas, Stevens was elected colonel of the 24th South Carolina but saw relatively little combat before the Atlanta campaign.[22]

Blake's men had just begun fortifying when the Confederates appeared. Many members of the 40th Indiana were to the rear collecting material for breastworks. Blake rushed forward his reserve regiment, the 28th Kentucky, as quickly as possible. Brigade pioneers dropped their tools and formed a skirmish line extending south from Blake's left flank. The brigade barely was ready for Walker when the Confederates began closing in on its position.[23]

Col. J. Cooper Nisbet's 66th Georgia was the leftmost regiment in Stevens's Brigade, with its left flank resting at the Buck Head and Atlanta Road. "We were told that the enemy had just crossed Peachtree Creek that morning," recalled Nisbet after the war, "and were unfortified." But Nisbet was worried that he had no connection with George Maney's Division to the left. "I protested against advancing until this gap was filled, but the order was given—and the line went in with a rush." In the ranks of the 88th Illinois, positioned just east of the Buck Head and Atlanta Road, Richard Realf saw Stevens's men approach. "With muskets at a right-shoulder shift they moved in the confidence of expected triumph, hoping to find our lines unformed."[24]

As Stevens's men moved forward, the Union skirmishers commanded by Joseph Conrad gave way. Most of the Federals turned and fired as they retreated amid shouts from the Confederates to surrender. Half of the 15th Missouri fell back to Blake's line, and the other half moved through the Union position along the Buck Head and Atlanta Road, allowing the four guns of Scovill's Ohio battery to open fire as soon as it passed by. The 73rd Illinois with the 24th Wisconsin fell back to the right flank of Newton's division line.[25]

After pushing Conrad's men away, Stevens halted at the captured Union skirmish line. The fire coming from the front was heavy, and Nisbet reported slightly enfilading fire from the left where Kimball's brigade was located. Kimball could deliver this fire because, according to Hood's instructions to advance in echelon by divisions, Maney had not yet come forward to support Stevens's left flank. Nisbet and Stevens acted as if they had no idea that Maney was supposed to delay his advance, for the brigade leader rode his horse to Nisbet's location and began to order him to fall back. The volume of fire coming from the front was increased by the fact that the 40th Indiana and 28th Kentucky of Blake's brigade were armed with Spencer repeating rifles. One observer indicated that the men fired from 80 to 100 rounds during the course of the battle at Peach Tree Creek, taking full advantage of the rapid-firing capabilities of this advanced weapon. The four guns of Battery A, 1st Ohio Light Artillery that Scovill placed on the road within Kimball's left wing also pounded the Confederates with both canister and shell. Stevens's men returned the fire as best they could, inflicting some casualties on Blake's command.[26]

At the height of this firefight Stevens became a victim. His horse was shot and killed, compelling him to rapidly dismount. Just as he turned his side to the Federals a bullet smashed into his head behind the right ear. He was still alive as his aides carried him off the field; two of them were wounded along the way. The front and enfilade fire increased in intensity, striking Nisbet as unusually severe. "Never was I under a heavier fire than there—for a brief time." He lost one-fourth of his men to it and fully expected to be numbered among the slain. "I thought I would certainly see my 'Valhalla' that day," Nisbet later wrote.[27]

Nisbet survived this fire, but Stevens did not. Surgeons removed the bullet, and his staff arranged to transport him to Vineville, near Macon, but the general died there on July 25. His body was shipped to Charleston for burial. Stevens's death caused widespread regret. Members of his command "severely felt" his loss, and Arthur M. Manigault, who led a brigade in Brown's Division of Hood's old corps, called Stevens "one of the best officers in our army." After the battle, soldiers of the 40th Indiana took the saddle and holsters from his dead horse on the field.[28]

The Federals opposing Stevens's Brigade were concerned about the security of Blake's left flank. Bradley therefore sent the 42nd Illinois to bolster that flank and support Col. John Q. Lane's 97th Ohio at the left end of Blake's line. Lane also commanded the brigade pioneers who had strung out in a skirmish line eastward from his flank. The added weight enabled Blake's left wing to hold firmly in place.[29]

With their leader down and faced with furious fire from Newton's immovable line, the troops of Stevens's Brigade held for a while at the captured Federal skirmish position before retiring. "Well we saw a hot time yesterday you may be shore," reported a solder of the 29th Georgia to his father. Other members of the 29th as well as of the 1st Georgia (Confederate) reported that their regiments received less fire and suffered fewer casualties than other units, such as Nisbet's 66th Georgia.[30]

Lieut. Col. Morgan Rawls detailed three companies from his 54th Georgia in Mercer's Brigade to deploy as skirmishers. Lieut. Hamilton Branch of the 54th Georgia was among them. Branch saw some men building breast-

Clement H. Stevens, who pushed his brigade forward just east of the Buck Head and Atlanta Road only to become the highest-ranking Confederate casualty at Peach Tree Creek. (Library of Congress, LC-USZ62–113171)

works forward of the main Union position and accompanied a few scouts to see who they were. He was surprised to discover they were Federals re-establishing a skirmish line. In fact, Branch stared at a Yankee who was just as surprised as he was at a distance of no more than fifty yards. The staring contest lasted "for a full minute," he told his mother. "I then jumped behind a tree" and started for the Confederate line before it was too late. Confederate and Union skirmishers continued to fire at each other for most of the evening. Mercer's Brigade suffered a loss of twenty-three men that day; losses in Gist's Brigade and Stevens's command were not reported.[31]

Walker failed to press his considerable weight in numbers on Blake's brigade. Col. Charles H. Olmstead of the 1st Georgia (Volunteer) in Mercer's Brigade accurately evaluated the performance in his memoirs. "Indeed we never got fairly into action as the attack had failed in other parts of the field and the Division was withdrawn before it reached a point of close touch with the enemy." It seemed to B. Benjamin Smith, one of Gist's staff officers, as if Stevens conducted "a feeble attack." Mercer's son, who served on his brigade staff, also concluded that "nothing important was accomplished" by Walker's command that day.[32]

Blake's brigade stood like a rock, even though two Confederate brigades completely outflanked its left and a third approached its front. While Blake never filed a report of the battle, Brig. Gen. George D. Wagner, the usual commander of the brigade who was on sick leave in late July, praised his men for their accomplishments on July 20. Each one "stood nobly to his work" in that trying hour. Their steadiness was a key factor in Newton's ability to hold his position; indeed, Blake's men were literally the left anchor of Thomas's entire line along Peach Tree Creek. With the aid of the brigade pioneers, the 42nd Illinois from Bradley's brigade, the support of the rest of Bradley's regiments, and Thomas's artillery concentration, the Union left flank held firm and prevented Walker from achieving a battle-winning victory.[33]

Blake's brigade suffered only thirty-eight casualties in the battle of Peach Tree Creek. The 26th Ohio lost but three men wounded. Such a short list of killed and wounded was remarkable considering the weight of enemy power brought against the command and the significance of its stout defense of Newton's position. Whenever possible during the fight, Blake's men continued to work on their breastworks and by evening they had ample protection.[34]

To the left of Walker, George Maney led Cheatham's old division against Kimball's brigade west of the Buck Head and Atlanta Road. A Tennessee native with experience in the Mexican War, Maney was a lawyer who became colonel of the 1st Tennessee before taking control of a brigade in the main western army of the Confederacy. Maney organized his division in two lines. He placed Vaughan's Brigade, now under Col. Michael Magevney Jr. on the left and Col. John C. Carter's Brigade on the right of the first line; his old brigade under Col. Francis M. Walker on the left and Brig. Gen. Otho F. Strahl's Brigade on the right in the second line. Three companies of the 5th Tennessee from Strahl's Brigade deployed as skirmishers to front the division.[35]

Maney waited a few minutes following the start of Walker's advance to conform to Hood's echelon plan. Then the division set out. "The boys at first did not like the idea of going outside the breastworks," admitted Martin Van Buren Oldham of the 9th Tennessee, "but few failed to go." Lieut. J. W. Howard led one of the skirmishing companies with spirit, waving his cap in the air to encourage the men. Conrad's Federal skirmishers had already evacuated their position by that time, having fallen back when Walker first advanced, and the Rebel skirmishers took possession of the Union skirmish line.[36]

Maney did not stop at the Federal position but pressed forward. His small force of Tennessee skirmishers advanced under heavy artillery and rifle fire until it reached a shallow ravine a bit less than 100 yards short of Newton's line. Here they took shelter behind the scattered trees and waited for Maney's main line to approach. When the division reached the slight shelter of the ravine, it halted and took cover behind trees, the lay of the land, and any other natural feature that offered itself. Here the division stayed for some time, trading shots with the Federals. Edwin Rennolds of the 5th Tennessee in Strahl's Brigade later commented that "all the efforts of their officers failed to induce them to go farther." This static firefight produced significant casualties in Magevney's Brigade. Col. William M. Watkins's consolidated 12th and 47th Tennessee suffered fifty-two casualties on July 20; Company A of the 12th lost twelve men. Lieut. Col. John M. Dawson's 154th Tennessee suffered forty-five losses.[37]

The view of Maney's assault from the Union position was impressive. Kimball's men had barely started to construct breastworks when the Tennessee skirmishers made their appearance. Indiana born, a schoolteacher and medical doctor before the war, Kimball had gained considerable experience as a regimental, brigade, and division commander in the Eastern and Western theaters before the Atlanta campaign. He could see that Maney was deployed in two lines and that the Rebels were "charging with great confidence with a rapidity and an absence of confusion I have never seen equaled."[38]

The echelon formation of Hood's army allowed the Federals to deal with each division in turn. By the time Maney's troops settled in the ravine, it was possible for other Union brigade commanders to send help to Kimball. Blake dispatched the 28th Kentucky and 97th Ohio from his left flank to Kimball's line, and Bradley sent the 51st Illinois to the location of the 88th Illinois. Kimball's men delivered a steady fire at Maney's troops. Day Elmore of the 36th Illinois told his parents that "I gave them 75 rounds for Chickamauga." The slight shelter of the ravine enabled Maney to stay put for the rest of the evening. Capt. James I. Hall's Company C, 9th Tennessee lay down on the second line in Walker's Brigade until a pine tree directly in front was almost cut in two by a Federal artillery round. As the top part of the trunk hung down, attached to the rest only by a splinter, he worried that it would fall on his men. Within a couple of minutes after moving the company back twenty paces, another round plowed the ground his troops had just vacated. "The warning given by the broken tree top saved the lives of many if not all the company," Hall later concluded. It was indeed "a remarkable Providence." Maney held his division in place until 10 P.M. then retired to the starting point of his advance.[39]

Hardee's artillery tried to support the infantry that afternoon but with scant success. Capt. Cuthbert H. Slocomb's Fifth Company, Washington Artillery of New Orleans, took position along the Buck Head and Atlanta Road near a tobacco barn, where it fought an unequal duel with Union artillery pieces. The Federal guns nearly decimated Slocomb's command, and the unit was ready to retire from its exposed position when Oscar Legare called on his comrades to fire a parting shot. While readying the piece, a Parrot shell exploded in the middle of the crew. The blast shredded the upper bodies of Legare and another man behind him. "The two boys were torn to pieces from the waist up," recalled Philip Daingerfield Stephenson. "We found long strips of flesh high up on the trees behind them." The two were carried to the rear suffering terribly and died soon after.[40]

When Slocomb pulled his guns back, Stephenson noticed sights that demoralized him. "Evidences of strife were all about us, dead and wounded men and horses, upturned limber chests, etc. One sight caught my eye—an artillery horse jammed head foremost against a tree, the head twisted far under the neck and the body squatting. Stone dead—as though, having torn back, frantic from wounds and blind with pain and fear from the front and run all tilt against the tree."[41]

Hardee's command suffered all the trials of heavy combat without experiencing the thrill of success. Newton estimated that the initial assault of Hardee's Corps lasted only thirty minutes. In short, within a half hour, Bate, Walker, and Maney had stalled in their attempt to fulfill Hood's battle plan. Newton asserted that from this point on the Confederates "made frequent attacks on my line, though none so severe as the first, and a constant fire had to be kept up along my lines until dark." It is true that Confederate sources confirm the keeping up of steady fire until dusk on some parts of the line, especially Maney's Division. But there is no evidence from the Rebel side that any more attempts to attack took place beyond the repulse of the first advance. Newton was guilty of some exaggeration when he reported to corps headquarters the next day that the enemy assaults were "so rapid that I could not keep account of them." It is possible Newton counted each individual brigade's advance as a separate Confederate assault for they came on within a few minutes of the previous advance. Maney's Division maintained its position at high tide longer than any other of Hardee's units. The firefight west of the Buck Head and Atlanta Road therefore lasted several hours. In fact, it lasted so long that some of Kimball's men continued to fire even after the Rebels retired because of the pent-up excitement of the day.[42]

Hardee began to make plans to renew his assault with the only reserve available. Cleburne had positioned his troops so their formation straddled the Buck Head and Atlanta Road. Brig. Gen. James A. Smith's Brigade of Texas regiments was on the first line and west of the road, while Brig. Gen. Mark P. Lowrey's Brigade of Alabama and Mississippi units held the first line east of the road. Brig. Gen. Lucius E. Polk's Brigade of Alabama, Mississippi, and Confederate units anchored the second line west of the road, while Brig. Gen. Daniel C. Govan's Brigade of Arkansas troops held the second line east of it.[43]

Cleburne was positioned close enough to receive much long-range artillery fire. At one point in the engagement Hardee, Cleburne, and their staff members rode north along the Buck Head and Atlanta Road as a battery targeted the group, killing a member of Cleburne's escort who rode very near the division leader. The Union pieces delivered a disconcerting amount of fire on Cleburne's formation. Lieut. Robert M. Collins of the 15th Texas Cavalry (dismounted) thought it made "a fellow feel like he was very small game to be shot at with such guns."[44]

The fire took effect. Complaining after the war that they "were catching all the cannon balls," Charles A. Leuschner of the 6th Texas Infantry watched as an artillery round flew within three feet of his body, killed four comrades, and cut off another man's leg. There was such a spray of blood that Leuschner and four other men were splattered with it. Hardee was close enough to witness the incident and expressed a good deal of concern about the exposure of his troops. Regimental losses in Smith's Brigade at Peach Tree

Creek ranged from two in the consolidated 17th and 18th Texas Cavalry (dismounted) to seventeen in the consolidated 6th and 15th Texas Cavalry (dismounted).[45]

Lieutenant Collins suffered a serious wound from this fire. A shell exploded directly in front of him, injuring several men and lodging "an ounce ball" in his left thigh. Collins remembered grabbing the wound to stop the bleeding "and thereby hold on to life long enough to give our past history a hasty going over and to repeat all the prayers we knew." As four men with a litter transported him to the rear, the group had to run a gauntlet of artillery fire. When Collins asked one of the men if he was still bleeding, the man replied in a thick Irish accent, "Not a drap of the rudy current to be seen, Lieutenant." This report so encouraged Collins that he thought about not only surviving the wound but enjoying a leave of absence based on it. He was even further encouraged by a surgeon who quickly examined the injury. The doctor proclaimed "it an ugly one, but not necessarily fatal. We thanked him from the bottom of our heart for these words."[46]

As Collins was taken to the rear, Lowrey held his command to the rear of Walker's troops and saw that Stevens's Brigade failed to close in on the enemy position. When what was left of Stevens's men fell back under Nisbet's control, the two officers met each other. Nisbet recalled feeling that Lowrey's presence had been wasted. "If they had come up sooner, we could have held our captured works" on the Union skirmish line. Nisbet briefly filled Lowrey in on the situation, but the latter did not believe there were obstacles in the way. "'Colonel, you must be mistaken about the enemy being fortified,' Lowrey told him. 'General Hood informed me that they had just crossed the creek.'" Nisbet offered to prove it by sending one of his regiments forward just enough to allow Lowrey a view of the position. After his personal examination, Lowrey admitted that it would be a useless sacrifice of life to launch another assault. Even so, Lowrey reported losing forty-five men of his brigade to Union artillery fire that day.[47]

The officers in Cleburne's second line had far less opportunity to see what was happening on the battlefield. "Did not engage the enemy," reported Capt. Aaron A. Cox of the 5th Confederate in Polk's Brigade. "Enemy's force not known; did not see him."[48]

By about 6 P.M., Hardee not only planned to use Cleburne but made efforts to get Bate's Division more fruitfully involved in the fight. Col. W. D. Pickett of his staff rode about to locate Bate and, when he found him, discovered that the division commander was searching for the Union left flank. "He is now moving slowly onward," Pickett reported to Hardee, "but it is necessarily slow, as the undergrowth is in places dense. I fear he will not be able to strike the enemy's flank much before dark." In fact, Bate never found much less struck that flank even after dusk descended on the battlefield.[49]

Cheatham's Corps played a very small role in Bate's attack. Brig. Gen. Randall L. Gibson's Brigade, the leftmost unit in Clayton's Division, held the Confederate line east of Bate's position. The entire brigade moved forward when Bate began his assault. Gibson did not go very far, even though he inadvertently faced the two-mile gap in Sherman's position. Gibson, Clayton, and Cheatham had no idea such a gap existed and made no attempt to exploit it.[50]

Not hearing the sound of small-arms fire from Bate, Hardee issued orders for Maney to resume his advance and for Cleburne to go into action and support him. The decision was supported by a message from Stewart, whose command had also tried and failed in its first attack by this time. Loring had assured Stewart that if Hardee could renew the assault he would make a second try as well.[51]

Hardee had established his headquarters in a grove of trees near the Buck Head and Atlanta Road and just to the rear of Cleburne's second line. There Cleburne reported his division ready to go in and received Hardee's order to attack. According to staff members who were present, the two generals talked for only "a few seconds" before Cleburne rode off to get his men started. Cleburne selected staff members to go to each brigade commander with the necessary instructions. But before they left, a staff officer from Hardee's headquarters galloped up with orders to cancel the attack. Hood had just instructed Hardee to send a division to help Wheeler contend with Schofield and McPherson, and Cleburne's Division was the only choice for this assignment. "Five minutes more would have been too late, and would have found this command heavily engaged," Irving A. Buck reported after the war.[52]

In fact, Smith's Brigade had already begun to prepare for a forward move by the time the recall was sounded. It moved forward to a point just behind Maney's two lines to be ready to support them. Capt. Thomas J. Key personally scouted forward to see if he could advance the guns of his Arkansas battery between the lines and fire at close range to support the infantry attack. According to Irving A. Buck, the combined forces of Maney and Cleburne had only to cross a relatively narrow space of ground before engaging Kimball's and Blake's commands in close-range fighting. If pressed vigorously, it might have been too much for Newton's lone division.[53]

It is possible that McPherson's approach saved Newton that day, although the Fourth Corps troops had many advantages that also could have spelled success for the Federals even in the face of a concentrated attack by a force twice as large as Newton's command. By the early afternoon, Wheeler fell back so much that he caused alarm at Army of Tennessee headquarters. By late afternoon, that alarm had grown so far as to cause Hood to divert troops from the battle taking place north of Atlanta. The order reached Hardee's headquarters probably about 7 P.M., arriving "at a critical moment" in Jacob Cox's words. Hood's order was "imperative," in Hardee's estimation, and the quick departure of Cleburne's Division spelled the end of his efforts that day. Bate was not in position to help much; Maney and Walker alone could not be counted on for success in the renewal of an action in which they had already failed to produce results. Besides, dusk was fast approaching. It is questionable, as Albert Castel has pointed out, whether Cleburne could have exploited any success he may have achieved given the late hour at which the attack would have started.[54]

The troops of Cleburne's Division left their reserve position immediately upon receiving the order from Hardee's headquarters. They marched south along the Buck Head and Atlanta Road past the Peach Tree Creek Line and to the Atlanta City Line defenses, arriving well past dusk. Bivouacking there for the night, the division wound up not supporting Wheeler at all until the next morning. Ironically, one of the best divisions at Hood's disposal neither contributed to the effort at Peach Tree Creek nor helped Wheeler hold back McPherson on July 20, providing another example of the limited sense of good timing, foresight, and planning at Hood's headquarters.[55]

Rumors of fighting at Peach Tree Creek circulated among the rank and file in the Army of Tennessee before day's end. The fact that Walker and Maney captured the Union skirmish line highlighted verbal reports and gave the impression that the Confederates had won a significant victory. When word arrived that the main Union line held firm, the news of Hood's order for the diversion of Cleburne seemed to be a handy excuse for the failure. By 10 P.M. Andrew Jackson Neal of Capt. Thomas J. Perry's Florida Battery more accurately told his father what had happened. "I had heard of some success but most places we failed to accomplish anything."[56]

Neal pinpointed the essential truth. Despite the fact that he outnumbered Newton five to one, Hardee had utterly failed to bring his strength against the enemy. Peach Tree Creek witnessed the most dismal battlefield perfor-mance of Hardee's career. Col. Charles H. Olmstead of the 1st Georgia (Vol-unteer) in Mercer's Brigade evaluated the result accurately. Hardee's attack "was delivered in a half-hearted, hap-hazard dis-jointed way," he wrote after the war. "It lacked resolution and likewise proper dispositions for the mutual support of the Divisions and Brigades engaged." Hardee's biographer has argued that Hardee should not have shifted so far to the right before the attack, as timing was essential for success.[57]

As noted earlier, the timing of the shift was not really the key failure, for the Federals were as ready in the late afternoon as they were in the early part of the day. More importantly, Hardee handled his corps as if he was brand new to that command level rather than the most experienced corps leader in the Army of Tennessee. Hood's insistence on an advance in echelon also contributed to failure; Newton's troops therefore could deal with each Confederate division in turn rather than as an overwhelming whole. Given the situation, much depended on the initiative and determination of brigade and division commanders and it has to be admitted that none of them exhibited much energy or grit on July 20. Bate, Walker, and Maney failed to deliver results at Peach Tree Creek, and it is not easy to explain these failures. For example, no one in Maney's Division spelled out why the troops simply stopped short of the Union position rather than continue their advance. Bate never explained why he floundered through the thickets all afternoon, and Walker, noted as a fiery Southern patriot, remained silent on why his division could not do more than capture the Union skirmish line. The entire corps shared responsibility for Hardee's dismal performance.

At Hood's headquarters, an idea already was germinating to explain that dismal performance. Thomas B. Mackall, who acted as an aide for his uncle, the army's chief of staff, noted in his journal that "Hardee does not think proper to attck eny's strong works." Hardee's biographer discounts the idea that the general failed to push his attack. But soon after the battle, Hood came to believe that a fear of charging Union earthworks (a breakdown in morale) was the chief reason Hardee failed to exploit his advantages on July 20.[58]

Howard understandably was overjoyed by the success of Newton's embattled command at Peach Tree Creek. "The division made a gallant fight and deserves unqualified praise," he reported to Thomas's headquarters the next day. "The position held was vital," Howard argued, "securing, as it did, the Buck Head and Atlanta Road, and constituting the left of our right wing, while the army was divided." Howard also accepted Newton's exaggerated report that the Confederates launched several assaults, and Thomas even stated in a circular that Newton repelled a total of seven attacks on his position. A newspaper correspondent saw how the defensive victory affected the division commander. "'Wasn't it dusty,' exclaimed Gen. Newton, as he came riding back, his face aglow with triumph, and his horse laboring for breath." One can forgive Newton for exaggerating the number of attacks his men repulsed, for continually pointing out the importance of the position he defended, and for making sure everyone understood that his troops stopped cold an elite corps of Hood's army.[59]

Newton's fight was largely on open and high ground within sight of thousands of Union and Confederate soldiers. The Federals often emphasized that their works were so immature that it was almost like an open field fight as well. Maj. Frederick Atwater wrote of his men in the 42nd Illinois that "at no time had they any works to fight behind with the exception of an occasional tree that had been felled for the purpose of building works." Unlike many previous confrontations in the Atlanta campaign, there were no trenches, abatis, chevaux-de-frise, or traverses to offer maximum protection. The slight rail and log barricades served a purpose, in the view of most observers, but they were limited in scope, calling on the grit and determination of all Union troops behind them to repel the enemy.[60]

The Federals also marveled at the relatively light casualties Newton suffered on July 20, despite the slim protection of their works. Luther Bradley thought success carried a "cheap" price. Newton reported only 102 casualties in his division and attributed it to "the partial protection of the rail barricades, and the fine natural position." He could also have noted that Hardee failed to bring to bear his artillery in an important way to pound that position, for the slim rail works would have offered little protection against such fire. The fact that no Confederate unit closed in on Newton's line also must account for the light casualties in Federal ranks. Kimball reported losing only 34 men out of a total of 1,400 engaged in his brigade. The 24th Wisconsin in Kimball's command suffered two casualties. Bradley's brigade lost twenty-four men while the 42nd Illinois in that brigade counted only two men wounded that afternoon.[61]

Hardee never estimated the losses in his corps, nor did any of his subordinates report their casualties. No doubt on the basis of reports fed him by officers in Newton's division, Howard estimated that Hardee suffered losses of 1,500 men. This probably is about right considering that total Confederate casualties in Hardee's and Stewart's commands are estimated at 2,500 men.[62]

As the day waned, and Maney's and Walker's troops remained relatively close to the scene of action, a number of Confederates who were isolated between the lines worked their way toward the enemy. They had gotten into positions of danger and hid behind trees or undulations of the ground until drumming up enough courage to show themselves. When this happened the Federals on that part of the field stopped firing and yelled, "Come on Johnny, you shan't be hurt." As John Wesley Marshall of the 97th Ohio reported, a given Confederate often would begin to come into Union lines, but some other Federal a short distance away "would yell at him to come there, thus completely bewildering him." As Marshall put it, every Yankee wanted "to have the fun of taking him in."[63]

In this way the Federals of Newton's division celebrated and enjoyed their surprising defensive victory of the day. In this way, some bewildered Confederates put an end to Hardee's surprising and dismal failure.

I waited till they came close enough, & then without any orders from any one, I ordered my Brigade to charge.
—Benjamin Harrison

A victory snatched from the trembling balance of battle.
—John Coburn

Featherston versus Ward

Unlike Hardee, Stewart prepared energetically to lead his Army of Mississippi into battle on July 20. He disseminated detailed information about the attack plan, gave inspirational talks to the troops, and injected an air of optimism and opportunity for his command. He would face far tougher odds than Hardee. Returns dated July 10 indicate Stewart had 13,354 men present for duty, but historians have estimated his troop strength as significantly lower ten days later. Thomas Robson Hay believes Stewart led 11,000 men on July 20, while the four Union divisions opposing his sector mustered 16,682 troops. Confederate dispositions had inadvertently massed too many men on one sector and not enough on another; better planning could have evened out this differential if Hood had more time and experience to plan the battle.[1]

The contest between Stewart and Hooker played out on a rugged battlefield along the high ground just south of Peach Tree Creek. Geary's division and the skirmish lines of Ward's division and Williams's division ran along the second ridge south of the creek, the highest ground in the area. Collier Road also ran along that ridge connecting to the Buck Head and Atlanta Road on the east, near the right flank of Newton's division, and to Howell's Mill Road on the west, at the location of Hiram H. Embry's plantation. Collier Road had once been a section of the old Montgomery Ferry Road that linked Decatur with the Chattahoochee River. Andrew J. Collier's gristmill was situated on a stream that drained northward into Peach Tree Creek about halfway between the Buck Head and Atlanta Road and Howell's Mill Road. It was variously called Shoal Creek, or Early Creek, or Tanyard Branch.[2]

Williams's division, after crossing Peach Tree Creek early on July 20, had moved along a small country road toward the southwest before stopping part way up the high ground at a collection of buildings. If Williams had continued, he would have reached Embry's plantation and the junction of Collier Road with Howell's Mill Road. Ward had also crossed Peach Tree Creek early on July 20 and, like Williams, had been told by Hooker to rest his men near the creek. Due to Hooker's nonchalance that morning, there were two gaps in his corps line to either side of Geary, covered only by skirmishers.[3]

The key to Hooker's position was the second rise of ground that his skirmishers and Geary held. On Ward's sector, the left of the Twentieth Corps position, the ground rose as one moved southward from the Peach Tree Creek bottomland until reaching the first rise, which had a covering of small pine trees. Then the landscape descended into a ravine that drained westward into Shoal Creek. Collier's Mill was located at the junction of these two streams. The ground once again ascended to the second rise, which was a bit higher than the first and largely clear of trees. Here Collier Road was sunk in places and had rail fences on both sides of the roadway—a pretty good defensive position. The ground was largely open in front of Ward's division with patches of timber especially within the ravine, which lay about 350 yards from Ward's resting troops. The ravine at its deepest had slopes some thirty feet high. It was another 200 yards at least from the ravine to Collier Road. John Coburn estimated that the ground rose some seventy feet in 400 yards as one walked south from the Peach Tree Creek bottomland.[4]

Lieut. Col. Edward Bloodgood's 22nd Wisconsin skirmished forward to the second ridge on Ward's sector. After establishing his men along Collier Road, Bloodgood saw a thick belt of timber half a mile across the open ground in front. Within that timber signs of Confederate activity could be detected; the enemy appeared to be "massing preparatory to a charge."[5]

The Confederates were indeed preparing to attack. After taking command of the Army of Mississippi on July 7, Stewart had yet to lead it into battle, and he was determined to do all he could to make the charge a success. Loring's Division held the right, Walthall's Division the center, and French's Division the left of the Army of Mississippi line. Each division had

Alexander P. Stewart, fighting his new command, the Army of Mississippi, for the first time on July 20. (Library of Congress, LC-DIG-ppmsca-20282)

detached a brigade to hold Hood's left flank near the Western and Atlantic Railroad and the Chattahoochee River; therefore, each division commander could use only two remaining brigades against their opponents.[6]

On Loring's sector, Brig. Gen. Winfield Scott Featherston's Brigade of Mississippi troops held the right connecting with Maney's Division of Hardee's Corps. Featherston had only 1,230 men available for the assault. He had left 200 of his troops on picket duty along the sector his brigade held before the grand shift to the right earlier that day. Born in Tennessee, "Old Swet," as Featherston was called, had served in the United States Congress and worked as a lawyer in Holly Springs, Mississippi. Featherston commanded the 17th Mississippi in Virginia before transfer to the West and elevation to a brigade command.[7]

"The plan of the battle was fully explained to me by Genl Loring," Featherston told Hood after the war. He understood that an interval of 300 yards was required in the echelon formation and that all units were "to oblique to the left, and sweep down the creek." Perhaps more importantly, Loring imparted an air of urgency to the operation. "My orders were to fix bayonets and charge their works when we reached them, to stop for no obstacle, however formidable, but to make the attack a desperate one." Featherston imparted these instructions accurately to his regimental officers. Loring told Featherston that only part of Thomas's army was yet across Peach Tree Creek and was vulnerable to a vigorous, determined assault.[8]

In order to reach a point where such an assault could be delivered, Featherston had to worm his command through a thick belt of timber that fronted the Peach Tree Creek Line. His men moved forward by the right flank by companies, the easiest way to deal with a forest. The regiments resumed their normal line upon reaching the Confederate skirmish position at the northern edge of this timber. The brigade assembled there with the 40th Mississippi on the left, then the 31st, 22nd, 3rd, and 33rd Mississippi in succession to the right. The 1st Mississippi Battalion of Sharpshooters acted as skirmishers for the brigade, supported by a company each from the 22nd and 40th Mississippi. Some 600 to 700 yards north, across open ground, lay Collier Road and the Union skirmish line held by Bloodgood's Wisconsin regiment.[9]

Featherston was ready by about 3 P.M. according to his watch, but he had to wait at least ten minutes for Maney's Division to move forward 300 yards. Then he gave the order for his Mississippians to move out. "I was struck with surprise at the time we moved to the front," Featherston told Hood after the war, "that no guns, either artillery or small arms were heard on our right save a feeble skirmish." Featherston assumed this meant that Maney found no

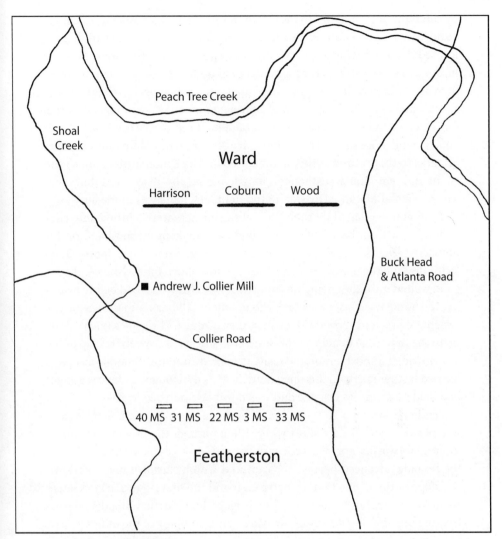

Peach Tree Creek

Shoal
Creek

Ward

Harrison   Coburn   Wood

Buck Head
& Atlanta Road

■ Andrew J. Collier Mill

Collier Road

40 MS 31 MS 22 MS 3 MS 33 MS

Featherston

Featherston versus Ward

Union troops in his front. He could not imagine, given the sense of urgency imparted by Stewart and Loring, that Hardee's men would have failed to find and drive any blue-coated opponents before them.[10]

Featherston's men advanced "with eagerness and rapidity" at the double-quick. "Troops never marched into the field of conflict with more determination, coolness & courage than my command did on this occasion," he told Loring. "The charge was made in gallant style." Some parts of the brigade moved through patches of woods, and the entire line came upon a marshy swale 300 yards from Collier Road. Several regiments once again moved by the right of companies to negotiate this obstacle. Maj. Martin A. Oatis's 22nd Mississippi endured "a murderous enfilade fire" from Union guns located in the left wing of Geary's division while crossing the swale. Massing his men to move through the footpaths civilians had made through the swale increased his casualties to this fire. "In effecting the passage of this marsh I lost many of my bravest and best officers and men," Oatis sadly admitted. Once across the swale, Featherston's men endured direct fire from Bloodgood's 22nd Wisconsin. The Federals had no hope of holding off an entire brigade, so they retired as the enemy closed in. The Union fortifications were slight and temporary, Featherston noted, and he also discovered that there was no sign of Maney's Division to the right. His flank was in the air.[11]

Featherston gloated that the Federal skirmishers were "thrown into confusion and driven back," but Bloodgood actually kept a good hand on his men. As soon as the Mississippi brigade emerged into view, approaching "with the true rebel yell," he sent a message to Coburn for assistance. Bloodgood waited until the enemy was only thirty feet from the road before ordering the 22nd Wisconsin to retire. The regiment fell back into the ravine between the first and second ridges. Just then, Coburn's brigade came rushing up to the first ridge to help, and Featherston's Brigade crowded on top of the second ridge almost simultaneously. It looked to many Federal observers located farther north on this open battlefield as if Bloodgood's lone regiment had held off an entire brigade and was now hotly pursued.[12]

Featherston's men stopped at Collier Road, seeing it as a good defensive position, and fired a short while. Then parts of the brigade continued to move forward. Capt. Moses Jackson's 33rd Mississippi on the far right of the brigade advanced beyond the captured Union skirmish line and down the slope of the ravine that lay between it and the first ridge. Part of Oatis's 22nd Mississippi in the center of the brigade line pursued Bloodgood's retreating men for about forty or fifty yards until stopping at the military crest of the ridge, if one looked north. The fortified Union skirmish line, of course, looked south and found more advantageous ground where Collier Road was located on the natural crest of the ridge top. In short, unlike the men of the 33rd Mississippi, some of the 22nd Mississippi troops did not go down into the ravine between the two ridges. All of Capt. Charles A. Huddleston's 40th Mississippi on the far left of the brigade advanced forty yards beyond the captured Union skirmish line and stopped. It received a great deal of Federal artillery fire from Geary's division to the left. This fire "decimated the ranks to a very considerable extent," reported Huddleston. Col. Thomas A. Mellon's 3rd Mississippi also remained on the crest of the ridge rather than advance into the ravine.[13]

No one in Featherston's Brigade clearly explained why only part of the command advanced beyond the captured Union skirmish line. On the basis of Confederate reports, the 31st and 33rd Mississippi moved down into the ravine separating the two ridges. Part of the 22nd Mississippi also moved into the ravine, and the 1st Mississippi Battalion of Sharpshooters apparently was in a position to contribute to the Confederate forward movement. The 3rd and 40th Mississippi remained on the second ridge near Collier Road. At best, it can be said that four of the six units in Featherston's Brigade moved beyond the second ridge and toward the hole in Hooker's position. The entire brigade took 1,230 men into action, which means that at most 820 of them advanced while 410 remained on the crest of the second ridge near the captured Federal skirmish works. There is no indication that Featherston personally advanced beyond those captured works as well; apparently, he remained near Collier Road.[14]

Those 820 Confederates thrust themselves toward Ward's division of the Twentieth Corps, some 4,000 men strong. Featherston's situation mirrored Hardee's in reverse; his troops were outnumbered more than four to one as they tried to extend the brigade's advance down the ridge and into the ravine.[15]

Their opponent was less than a stellar battlefield leader. Like Thomas a Virginian by birth, Ward grew up in Kentucky, fought in the Mexican War, and served in the state legislature as well as the United States House of Representatives. His Civil War career consisted mostly of garrison duty until called on to lead a brigade in the Third Division of the Twentieth Corps that was composed mostly of western regiments. He took command of the division when Daniel Butterfield went on sick leave part way through the Atlanta campaign. Ward had handled the division poorly on July 3 during the follow up to Johnston's evacuation of the Kennesaw Mountain Line, exposing Coburn's brigade by pushing it too far forward from its supporting units. "Hooker gave it to Ward for being so rash as to lead one brigade alone into such a place," reported John H. Roberts of the 22nd Wisconsin.[16]

Fortunately, Ward's division received early warning of the Confederate advance from an unlikely source. Pvt. Henry Crist of Company I, 33rd Indiana had wandered southward past the Union skirmish line looking for blackberries. As he stopped in a ravine, the glint of sunlight on burnished steel caught his attention, and he saw Featherston's Brigade preparing to advance. Rushing back, he not only told the Federal skirmishers but raced to John Coburn with the news. Coburn took the report seriously. He immediately ordered his brigade to fall in and then told Benjamin Harrison of the report, suggesting that their two brigades form and move south at

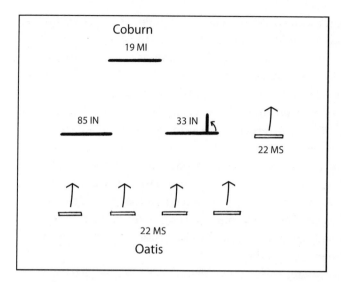

Coburn

19 MI

85 IN   33 IN

22 MS

22 MS

Oatis

least to the first ridge to meet the enemy. Harrison agreed to the plan, as Coburn rushed off to get Ward's approval. The division commander hesitated. Hooker had not authorized a move south, and there was yet no confirmation of a Rebel advance. But Ward was willing to act if Coburn could ride forward and see for himself that action was justified.[17]

Coburn wasted no time in riding up the slope to the Union skirmish line. From there he watched as the Confederates emerged from the timber and began their advance across open ground. Coburn galloped his horse back to the bottomland, shouting *"Harrison they are coming"* as he rode by on the way to his own men. "I never shall forget Colonel Coburn's voice as it rang out 'forward 2nd Brigade,'" recalled Jefferson E. Brant of the 85th Indiana. Learning the news, Ward finally issued orders for all three of his brigades to push forward. "The division moved at once in splendid order," he reported.[18]

Coburn's brigade occupied the center position of Ward's division, with the 33rd Indiana on the left, the 85th Indiana on the right, and the 19th Michigan to the rear as a reserve. It took 1,315 men into action that afternoon. Just before reaching the crest of the first ridge, Coburn's men encountered the Union skirmishers retiring from their fortified position near Collier Road. Bloodgood brought his 22nd Wisconsin through the ranks of Coburn's troops and reformed the regiment in rear of Ward's division.[19]

Maj. Levin T. Miller's 33rd Indiana encountered some difficulty working through a dense patch of pine and oak trees on the slope of the first ridge before it stopped on the crest. Here Coburn ordered his line forward into the ravine between the first and second ridges. He first told Miller to go forward, and the 33rd Indiana found that the tree cover extended down into the ravine in front of the left wing, which crossed the small stream in the bottom of the ravine before the right wing got close enough to cross. Miller reformed his ranks at the foot of the opposite slope and waited for orders.[20]

To the right, Lieut. Col. Alexander B. Crane stopped the 85th Indiana on the crest of the first ravine. Then he saw Coburn's assistant adjutant general, Lieut. Francis C. Crawford, motioning to him to continue moving forward into it. Because he knew Crawford was positioned to see what the 33rd Indiana was doing, he trusted his judgment and ordered the men forward. Just as the 85th Indiana reached the stream at the bottom of the ravine, Crane could see Oatis's 22nd Mississippi of Featherston's Brigade begin marching down the opposite slope into the ravine as well.[21]

As his men were moving down into the ravine, Coburn realized that the Confederates were threatening to flank his left as well as approaching his front. Wood's brigade had lagged behind his own in forming and moving forward, and the way was clear for Featherston's Confederates to advance south in that sector. Coburn rode fast to Wood's brigade and urged its commander to hurry forward before he returned to his own command in time for the confrontation with the 22nd Mississippi. Harrison's brigade to the right was a bit behind Coburn's pace also, but it soon came forward and began to advance beyond his position, engaging the enemy at about the same time as Coburn's brigade.[22]

The members of Coburn's command remembered the opening of the battle vividly. Crane's 85th Indiana crossed the small stream inside the ravine and used the shallow bank as cover when they took aim at the Confederates descending the slope. They "poured a deadly and continuous fire into the enemy, who were within fifty feet of the front of the regiment," as Crane put it. Oatis's men seemed to be "in a large unorganized mass, pushing forward, and were evidently surprised to find our lines so near them."[23]

Miller's 33rd Indiana also "poured a rapid and well-directed fire" into the Rebels who came down the ravine slope. Featherston's men extended farther west than Miller's line and threatened to turn his left flank. The Union officer refused the two left companies of his regimental line "as quick as possible." Those two companies fired heavily enough to discourage any flanking movement. Crane worried about the right wing of his 85th Indiana, however, which had lagged a bit behind the left. But Francis Crawford once again helped the brigade by urging on the right wing. Crane "heard a shout and knew then that" his right wing had crossed the stream and was connecting with the left. He then ordered the entire regiment to advance while firing up the ravine slope, and his men did so with a loud yell that could be heard above the musketry.[24]

Coburn's brigade not only stopped the Confederate advance in its front but counterattacked up the ravine slope, the 33rd Indiana and 19th Michigan joining in the movement. The 22nd Mississippi was disorganized and retreated in what Ward described as the "wildest confusion." Some Rebels lagged behind and were taken prisoner—200 of them if Coburn's estimate is reliable. Harvey Reid of the 22nd Wisconsin saw the fight from a distance, having been detailed to commissary work with the brigade wagon train. Coburn's men moved steadily up the ravine slope firing as they went, and the broken enemy dotted "that bare slope" until they made it look like "an ant hill swarming with dark objects hurrying back to the cover of the woods."[25]

On the way up the ravine slope, the Federals encountered abandoned Confederate flags. Pvt. Thomas J. Williamson of Company A, 85th Indiana initially picked one up and waved it a few times but then threw the color down. When asked later, he said "he could not carry it and fire his gun." Someone else retrieved the flag and undoubtedly received credit for "capturing" it, even though Crane did his best to document that Williamson was the first Federal to lay hands on it. A group of men from the 33rd Indiana and 19th Michigan picked up a Confederate flag and gave it to an officer they did not know, asking him to take care of it for them. They only recalled that the officer served on Ward's division staff, but they never received credit for the flag.[26]

By the time Coburn's brigade neared the top of the second ridge, where Collier Road and the Union breastworks were located, the men were mingled up. The 19th Michigan merged in many places with both the 33rd and 85th Indiana. A few members of the 22nd Wisconsin had also elected to go in with Miller's 33rd Indiana rather than fall back to the rear of the division, and they thus participated in the unique uphill attack that afternoon. Featherston's men fell back farther south, and Coburn occupied the roadbed, but his men quickly restored order by forming two lines to secure the crest.[27]

As yet, Wood still had not moved forward fast enough to keep pace with Coburn and there was no support to the east. To the west, Harrison's brigade was only a few minutes behind Coburn's fast-paced advance to the second ridge. Harrison, who would be elected president of the United States twenty-four years later, faced the most trying day of his military service. After Coburn alerted him, Harrison rode up to the left flank of Geary's division line and from there saw the Confederates emerge from the woods at

Benjamin Harrison, a future president, who enjoyed the best day of his Civil War career while leading his brigade forward in an effort to stop Featherston's Brigade. (Library of Congress, LC-DIG-cwphb-03891)

Shoal Creek

Harrison

105 IL

70 IN

102 IL

79 OH

129 IL

31 MS

31 MS

Drane

the start of their attack. He quickly rode back to his command, receiving Coburn's hurried cry that the Rebels were on their way.[28]

Harrison's men had been lounging on the bottomland of Peach Tree Creek before the first indication of trouble, but now they already were formed in line and ready to respond to their commander's order to move up to the crest of the first ridge. A sense of urgency was readily apparent. Men who had straggled forward before the first alarm came rushing back from the front saying, "O God, boys, they are out of their works! We've got 'em now!" Capt. Howard Dunlevy, Harrison's assistant adjutant general, rode along the brigade line shouting "Forward! They are driving us on the right and left!"[29]

Harrison's brigade formed in two lines straddling the narrow valley of Shoal Creek. The 129th Illinois held the left end of the first line with the 79th Ohio in the middle and the 102nd Illinois on the far right and west of Shoal Creek. In the second line, the 70th Indiana lay east of the creek and the 105th Illinois west of it. The creek interfered with Harrison's ability to maneuver and handle his regiments, but he had to overcome those difficulties in order to fill the gap between Coburn's brigade and Geary's division.[30]

The men encountered no opposition as they struggled up the slope. Some units worked their way through thickets and blackberry bushes before the brigade reached the ridge crest with its covering of pine trees. By this time Harrison had ridden back to the left flank of Geary's division line, the best observation post he could find on the battlefield. From there he saw the

Confederates coming down the ravine slope. Geary's guns were pounding them, and 100 men Harrison had contributed to the skirmish line, before the battle, were retreating. From his perspective, Harrison saw that the Rebels were becoming disorganized by all these factors. He even reported seeing some Confederates who plopped to the ground, refusing to continue although their officers "with drawn swords, were trying to steady their lines and push them forward." The enemy advance seemed to stall about 100 yards from his brigade's position on the first ridge top.[31]

Like Coburn, Harrison quickly realized that he had to advance beyond the first crest and drive the enemy back. He sent Dunlevy to urge forward the three regiments east of Shoal Creek, while he personally moved forward the two regiments west of the stream. As of yet no Confederates fronted the two right regiments; Harrison saw this as an opportunity to connect with Geary's left flank and gain the crest of the second ridge before his left wing could fight its way up the slope.[32]

Believing from the looks of things that the enemy "greatly outnumbered me," Harrison proudly told his wife about his decision to move forward from the first ridge crest. "I waited till they came close enough, & then without any orders *from any* one, I ordered my Brigade to *charge* which they did in *splendid style*." Ward also took a great deal of pride in what Harrison's brigade did that afternoon, for it was his old command before taking over the division from Butterfield. George F. Cram of the 105th Illinois described Ward as the division's "worthless but doting general," yet the men treated his weaknesses with amused tolerance, calling him "'Old Stoughten-bottle,' and 'Jack of Clubs'" because of his fondness for liquor. The general rode a white horse and wore "tremendous gloves," habitually pulling them when agitated. "He was greatly excited," related John L. Ketcham of the 70th Indiana, who was a member of Ward's staff, "and jerking first at one glove, then the other, he called out to his aid, Lieutenant [Samuel K.] Harryman of our regiment, 'Ha'yman, Ha'yman, come hea. Look how the First Brigade, my old brigade, goes in!'"[33]

The main Confederate force, Lieut. Col. J. W. Drane's 31st Mississippi, approached Harrison's left wing. That wing consisted of Col. Henry Case's 129th Illinois and Capt. Samuel A. West's 79th Ohio, with Lieut. Col. Samuel Merrill's 70th Indiana to the rear as a reserve. Case pushed his regiment forward into the ravine and began to ascend the opposite slope. Part way up he received "a galling fire" from Drane's Confederates in front of the regiment's left wing and off to the left as well. His men were temporarily stunned but began to return the fire and then resumed their forward movement. The left wing soon ground to a halt in the face of stiffening resistance by Feather-

William T. Ward, the doughty commander of the Twentieth Corps division that opposed Featherston. He wisely allowed his brigade leaders to handle their men without interference. (Library of Congress, LC-DIG-cwpbh-03168)

ston's men, but the right wing had little in its front and began to slowly wheel to the left.[34]

At this point, the ground to Case's left was filled only with Confederate soldiers of the 22nd Mississippi. Although starting later than Coburn, Harrison's brigade had surged ahead of him by this time. Case had the unenviable job of dealing with a heavy concentration of enemy troops in his front, enfilade fire from the left, and the uncertainty of not knowing when Coburn's men would come forward to cover his flank. Rather than hesitate, he simply pushed his command forward and trusted Coburn would soon come up.[35]

Harrison was keenly aware of Case's problems and responded by pushing his two reserve regiments obliquely to the left to extend the brigade line left of the 129th Illinois. Merrill was eager to bring his Indiana men into action. As soon as the 129th Illinois began to leave the first ridge crest and descend into the ravine, the 70th Indiana fired its first volley at the Rebels over the heads of Case's troops. Then it followed Case, moving "through the sassafras bushes, over a gully some four feet wide and seven feet deep," and then began ascending the opposite slope. On the way up, as the 129th Illinois slowed and stalled, the 70th Indiana obliqued left according to orders. Lieut. Col. Everell L. Dutton's 105th Illinois crossed Shoal Creek and followed Merrill's regiment in the oblique movement. When the two regiments ended their slide to the left, the 70th Indiana was some distance to the left of the 129th Illinois but not far enough to allow all of the 105th Illinois regimental line to fill the gap between the two units. The four companies on the right of Dutton's line overlapped the left wing of Case's 129th Illinois, but the two units had done well to extend Harrison's brigade line and support Case's hard-pressed regiment.[36]

Before the 70th Indiana and 105th Illinois arrived, and before the right wing of Case's regiment completed its wheeling movement, the left wing of the 129th Illinois had a tough fight. Hand-to-hand combat broke out at one point, as the Confederates stubbornly held on in some timber on the ravine slope. Pvt. George A. Newton recalled that Lieut. Col. Thomas H. Flynn, a veteran of the Mexican War, became so wrapped up in the close-range fighting that he emptied his revolver at the Confederates and then managed to grab a few of them by their arms, "gave them a kick, and, with language more forcible than polite, ordered them to the rear."[37]

While Case later reported that the enemy greatly outnumbered him, the fact was that relatively few of Featherston's men opposed Harrison's brigade in its uphill struggle. After a few minutes the combined effect of fierce hand-to-hand fighting, the wheeling movement of his right wing, and the support of the 70th Indiana and 105th Illinois had its desired effect. Confederate resistance in front of the left wing of the 129th Illinois weakened until the enemy fled precipitately. The Federals followed them up by continuing their upward movement, the 105th Illinois taking prisoners and a Confederate flag along the way.[38]

Harrison's right wing contributed to the forward movement of the brigade. Not fronted by resistance, the 102nd Illinois occupied high ground west of Shoal Creek that enabled the men to see much of the action on the brigade's left wing. Capt. William A. Wilson advanced the regiment until his men could partially wheel left and then deliver long-range fire at the Confederates with their Spencer repeating rifles. West's 79th Ohio contributed to this oblique fire until Confederate resistance in front of the 129th Illinois broke.[39]

The brigade fought its way up to the crest of the second ridge in this way. As the right wing of the 129th Illinois continued to wheel, it reached the top before any other unit in the brigade. Featherston's men gave way from the crest as the right wing advanced a bit toward the east, compelling other Confederates farther down the slope to hurriedly retreat from the front of Harrison's extreme left wing. Case was then able to advance his regimental left wing up to Collier Road, followed by the 70th Indiana and 105th Illinois to the left and the 102nd Illinois and 70th Ohio to the right. The Federals took some losses even upon claiming the ridge top. One of George Newton's mess mates was shot through the body by a Confederate as he reached the fence rail breastworks along Collier Road.[40]

"Our advance, though desperately resisted by the enemy, was steady and unfaltering," wrote Harrison in his official report, "the fighting was hand to hand, and step by step; the enemy was pushed back over the crest in our front and the key-point of the battle-field won." Rather than continue, he decided to plant his men along Collier Road and stay there. A short time later, Harrison noted signs of trouble in Geary's division to the right. One of Geary's officers told Harrison that the division's right flank had been broken. This brought yet another point of crisis, but Harrison still was determined to maintain his hard-won position on the ridge crest. There was no possibility of retreating across Peach Tree Creek for the stream was too much of an obstacle to be easily crossed. It was either fight or die along Collier Road as Harrison trusted "to the brave troops on our right to recover their ground."[41]

Although Harrison tried to keep the trouble affecting Geary's division secret, other men in his brigade learned of it as well. An unidentified officer, supposed to have been one of Harrison's staff members, approached Wilson and told him he had better retire the 102nd Illinois from the ridge or face the possibility of being outflanked when Geary fell back. Wilson told him he "didn't see it" and held his position. In fact, Wilson directed the fire of his men obliquely to the right to give Geary some assistance.[42]

Harrison reached the crest of the second ridge a short time before Coburn, and Ward's remaining brigade reached it a bit after Coburn's men secured their position on the top. James Wood Jr. had received signals from several directions that the Confederates were preparing to advance. Lieut. Col. Frederick C. Winkler, who had sent some companies of his 26th Wis-

consin to reinforce the 22nd Wisconsin on the skirmish line, told Wood of
signs that the enemy might be massing in Ward's front. Coburn did not give
Wood any warning, but the sound of musketry to the left where Newton's
division was located, the rush of noncombatants from Newton's position
toward Peach Tree Creek, and the firing of Ward's skirmish line provided
ample proof that a battle was heading his way.[43]

Wood quickly assembled his brigade in two lines with the 20th Connecticut on the left and the 26th Wisconsin on the right in the first line. Behind those two units, Wood positioned the 55th Ohio on the left and the
73rd Ohio on the right. The 33rd Massachusetts had been detached to guard
Ward's wagon trains and did not take part in the battle. Four companies of
the 136th New York were engaged in the fight, but the rest of the regiment
was held back as a reserve.[44]

Like Coburn and Harrison, Wood ordered his brigade to advance at least
to the first ridge crest, and the men set out after the other two brigades
had already started. Upon reaching that crest, it became apparent that the
Federal skirmishers were retiring, and Col. Jabez L. Drake's 33rd Mississippi was following them. Wood pushed his men down the slope into the
bottom of the ravine where at least the first line lay prone and allowed the
Union skirmishers to pass through its ranks. The bottom of the ravine was
lined with trees and underbrush, affording some degree of cover for Wood's
troops as they waited for Drake's men to descend the opposite slope and
then opened fire at close range, only ten paces according to George Hoenig

of the 26th Wisconsin. Samuel H. Hurst of the 73rd Ohio saw and heard that first Union fire—"a most murderous volley," he called it—which stunned the Confederates and brought down many men.[45]

The ravine slope in front of Winkler's 26th Wisconsin was open, but off to the left a thick patch of trees allowed many members of Drake's regiment to take cover and lay down an oblique fire on Winkler's regiment at a range of only sixty yards. As yet, the 20th Connecticut had not advanced far enough to offer Winkler any assistance. Confederate troops in front of the 26th Wisconsin also steeled their nerves and moved closer. "For a time the conflict was desperate," Winkler reported. "I took every man who could be spared on the right to re-enforce the left." Drake's men gained a point as close as fifteen paces from Winkler's line. "Our men loaded & fired as rapidly as possible & with the aid of officers, who exerted their utmost to spy & point out the points to fire at, made the fire very effective."[46]

This sharp firefight lasted only a few minutes. Drake's Mississippi regiment came closer to stopping the Federals than any other in Featherston's Brigade, but it could not stand the intense firing from Winkler's troops. The Confederates broke and retreated with the Wisconsin boys pushing as rapidly as they could up the ravine slope after them. Drake's color-bearer fell wounded, and Capt. William John Fuchs of the 26th Wisconsin was the first to grab the flag. Drake also was killed on the battlefield during the retreat of his regiment up the slope. Winkler later counted a total of thirty-four Confederate dead and seventy wounded Rebels on the ground encompassing his fight with Drake. Winkler had 260 men involved in this battle and probably slightly outnumbered the 33rd Mississippi. He suffered forty-five casualties, a loss ratio of 17.3 percent, in the brief fight.[47]

Winkler's 26th Wisconsin had to bear the brunt of fighting much of Drake's 33rd Mississippi. The 20th Connecticut failed to make enough headway to help it, and the second line apparently did not get involved in the fight. Wood praised the Wisconsin regiment highly. "The brave, skillful, and determined manner in which it met this attack, rolled back the onset, pressed forward in a countercharge, and drove back the enemy, could not be excelled by the troops in this or any other army."[48]

When the 26th reached the crest of the second ridge, its position remained insecure for some time. Confederates still lurking in the thick woods on the left obtained an enfilade fire on the regiment until, some fifteen minutes later, the 20th Connecticut finally reached the crest and drove them away. By this time Winkler's men were exhausted and almost out of ammunition. He asked Wood for help, and the brigade leader ordered the 73rd Ohio to relieve his regiment.[49]

"The intense exertion & excitement together with the scorching heat of the sun had utterly exhausted my men," Winkler reported a few days later. "One officer was sun struck, & a number of others had to be helped to the rear though not wounded." He allowed most of his troops to go back into the ravine to rest a few minutes in the shade and then reformed his regimental line forty yards behind the 73rd Ohio. Winkler now had an opportunity to replenish his ammunition supply, which essentially was exhausted. The 26th Wisconsin had fired so intensely that it had to scrounge among the dead and wounded to find more cartridges. Many muskets were so fouled as to require cleaning as well. The advance up the slope in pursuit of Drake's men had been so rapid that about forty Confederates who fell into Winkler's hands were bypassed. The Wisconsin men had no time to take possession of them and trusted to the second line to take care of the prisoners.[50]

Lieut. Col. Philo B. Buckingham's 20th Connecticut had a good excuse for not keeping pace with Winkler during the advance up the two ridges. It had to contend with a deep penetration of the Union position by the right companies of Drake's 33rd Mississippi. That penetration also threatened the right flank of Kimball's brigade in Newton's Fourth Corps. Newton estimated that Featherston's Brigade attacked about fifteen minutes after Maney's Division of Hardee's Corps advanced toward Kimball's front. When elements of Drake's 33rd Mississippi bypassed Kimball's right flank, Kimball created a refused line with the 73rd Illinois to fire in their direction.[51]

But Buckingham's 20th Connecticut bore the primary responsibility for ejecting those Confederates from the gap that existed between Kimball's right and Winkler's advancing 26th Wisconsin. Buckingham had advanced to the first ridge crest when the Confederates penetrated the space between his regiment and the Fourth Corps position. From his perspective, it seemed as if Kimball's brigade fell back, but in reality Kimball merely formed a refused line at his right flank. Drake's men managed to go so far as to threaten Buckingham's left flank as well, so the Connecticut officer refused his left wing and fired into them. "For a short time," wrote John W. Storrs of the 20th Connecticut, "the regiment was in an extremely critical situation." But the fire of the refused left wing drove the Confederates back.[52]

The way was now clear for Buckingham to swing the left wing back into alignment with the right and push his regiment forward. Wood ordered him to cross the ravine and take position on the crest of the second ridge. He encountered no more resistance in this forward move before taking position along Collier Road on the ridge top. But Buckingham noted that a gap of 125 yards still existed between his left flank and Kimball's brigade. To cover that gap, he once again created a refused flank by forming his two left companies to face east. Wood detected signs of instability in Kimball's ranks and worried about the area off to Buckingham's left as well. He held his two reserve regiments in the second line for a while in case they were needed in that direction but soon realized Kimball was in no danger. He then authorized the 73rd Ohio to relieve Winkler's 26th Wisconsin and the 55th Ohio to fill the gap between Buckingham and Kimball.[53]

Finally, Ward's division line was in place where it should have been since early morning, connected and firmly facing the foe. Wood found that Collier Road "was a well-traveled highway, on the south side of which was an ordinary fence of rails, partly standing and partly thrown down. The men took position behind this fence and kept a constant and continuous fire upon the enemy." Featherston's Confederates were withdrawing toward the timber that shielded the Peach Tree Creek Line farther south.[54]

"This ended this severely contested engagement," Wood proudly reported of his brigade's part in the battle of Peach Tree Creek. "To us it was a brilliant feat of arms. We encountered the enemy in superior numbers in the open field. We met his offensive attack with an offensive return; his charge with a countercharge. The victory was complete and decisive." Buckingham echoed this praise in his own report. He also asserted that his men had fired 150 rounds each, which seems an exaggeration considering the relatively short duration of the fighting. The 20th Connecticut lost fifty-five men. Wounded Rebel officers left on the field told the Federals they lost more troops in this battle than in any previous engagement. By sundown, the 136th New York relieved the 20th Connecticut, which fell back to occupy the second line of Wood's brigade formation.[55]

Ward's division had indeed responded to the appearance of Featherston's Brigade with vigor, determination, and an aggressive forward drive that saved the field that afternoon, but Ward personally had little to do with it. The real work was done by Coburn, Harrison, and Wood and the officers and men under their command. Other than cheering the troops on, Ward's only contribution to the fight was in refusing Thomas's request to send a brigade from his division to help Newton. Ward correctly told Thomas that it was impossible. When Thomas then asked for just two regiments, Ward continued to refuse. The only reserve available to him consisted of six companies of the 136th New York. Pulling away any units "would have made a gap in my line that would probably have proved fatal to my division, if not the entire corps." In the end, Newton did not need the reinforcement. Ward had at least one artillery unit in action, Lieut. Jerome B. Stephens's Battery C, 1st Ohio Light Artillery, which fired over the heads of his troops for at least

Joseph Hooker on the battlefield. This inaccurate view of the battle of Peach Tree Creek contains little in the way of reliable information about the actual course of the engagement. The battle lines were not formed so near the creek, and Hooker was on the farther side of the stream with his staff during the engagement. Theodore R. Davis, the field artist who sketched the original image, also unfairly focused public attention on Hooker's personal leadership as a central feature of the day's events. (Hood, "Defense of Atlanta," 4:336)

part of the battle, but generally the Union artillery played little role in the division's countercharge.[56]

Despite its initial success at capturing the Federal skirmish line, Featherston's Brigade was decisively defeated on the afternoon of July 20. At most only two-thirds of Featherston's men advanced beyond the crest of the second ridge into the ravine to engage Ward's division, and they were outnumbered four to one by the Federals. Moreover, the Confederates who ventured beyond the captured Union skirmish line only loosely coordinated their advance.

Yet, the Rebels who tried to exploit Featherston's initial success gave a good account of themselves. In the center of the Confederate line, three color-bearers were shot down carrying the flag of Oatis's 22nd Mississippi by the time Featherston had driven the Federal skirmishers away from the second ridge. Then the regimental adjutant, Lieut. C. V. H. Davis, took the flag and encouraged the men to move down into the ravine only to be shot when the regiment confronted Coburn's brigade.[57]

On Featherston's left, Drane's 31st Mississippi confronted the left wing of Harrison's brigade in the ravine. Drane ordered his men to fall back just before he was badly wounded. Maj. F. M. Gillespie was injured soon after but, unlike Drane, was left on the field as the regiment retired. Adjutant William J. Van de Graaff also was wounded as he held the regimental colors following the loss of three color-bearers before him. Van de Graaff was left behind during the retreat to the crest of the second ridge. Every company commander was shot during the short engagement with Harrison's men until 1st Lieut. William B. Shaw of Company G took command of the regiment.[58]

Drake's 33rd Mississippi on Featherston's right confronted Wood's brigade in some of the most intense fighting on Ward's division sector. Drake was killed while waving his sword to encourage the men. Capt. Moses Jackson, who took command of the regiment, led it during the fall back toward the second ridge crest. The regiment lost its flag during the retreat. At least one color-bearer was shot, and "others attempted to get the colors and were wounded," reported Matthew Andrew Dunn, but it was left on the ground for the enemy to pick up. Dunn put it well when he wrote, "we were badly cut to pieces" in this "very bloody affair."[59]

While the 22nd, 31st, and 33rd Mississippi advanced northward into the ravine, with at least some support from the 1st Mississippi Battalion Sharpshooters, Featherston and the 3rd and 40th Mississippi remained on the second ridge crest near Collier Road. Exactly why has never clearly been explained. Capt. Charles A. Huddleston reported that the 40th Mississippi halted only forty yards north of the captured Union skirmish line but still on top of the ridge crest. "It was discovered that the regiment was very much depleted in numbers," Huddleston wrote to imply the reason for its failure to move farther north. Lieut. Col. George P. Wallace was wounded and lost an arm, while Maj. W. McD. Gibbens was killed. The regiment held on the ridge for twenty-five minutes before the units that had advanced into the ravine fought and fell back to the captured Union skirmish line. Then the 40th Mississippi retired from the ridge. Mellon's 3rd Mississippi also remained near Collier Road "partially protected by a rail fence." Mellon was wounded soon after it reached the crest, and Lieut. Col. Samuel M. Dyer took charge of the regiment. He was content to hold it behind the slim rail breastwork for about twenty minutes before the other regiments retreated out of the ravine.

Part of Oatis's 22nd Mississippi remained on the ridge too, taking shelter behind the captured Union skirmish works, which "afforded us partial protection." Oatis's men merely moved the rails from one side of the road where the Federals had placed them to the other side to better suit their notion of how to defend the position.[60]

Featherston's Brigade fell back soon after the retreat from the ravine brought out everyone who could escape the battle. The Confederates made their way over the largely open ground to the south of the Union skirmish position under what Oatis called a "murderous fire." Featherston restored his line about 300 yards south of Collier Road partially in a strip of woods as Maj. James M. Stigler reformed his 1st Mississippi Battalion Sharpshooters into a skirmish line to protect the brigade's new position.[61]

For the Federals who climbed the ridge to the top, seeing the enemy retreat was a moment of supreme exultation. "Then up went the Cry they are going back," wrote Lysander Wheeler of the 105th Illinois. "Contrary as ever they walked off not hurrying much which gave our boys lots of Chance to pepper them which they improved with glee." Andrew Jackson Johnson joined his comrades of the 70th Indiana in plopping down along Collier Road and firing as fast as he could "into their retreating colums [sic]." The musketry fire combined with oblique Union artillery fire from Geary's position produced quite a few casualties. The next day, Federal troops who examined the ground just south of the Union skirmish line found many bodies lying in gullies and ravines.[62]

Harrison, who rode his horse during the entire battle, worried about the heavy expenditure of ammunition by his men and wondered if they would run out. He sent an aide and his assistant adjutant general to find more. Not only did they secure some boxes from Union ordnance wagons, but several men worked to gather cartridges from dead Confederate soldiers lying just south of Collier Road and distribute them along the brigade line.[63]

According to Federal accounts, the Rebels lost several regimental flags during their retreat from the second ridge crest. Either they were dropped or, in one case, a color-bearer had planted the staff in the ground. A Federal who ventured out to retrieve one of the flags was killed before he got back to his regiment, but another flag reportedly was taken by other Union soldiers under cover of darkness that night.[64]

Ward's men secured control of the second ridge crest by increasing the height of the rail breastworks, which by now had changed hands twice. The work of fortifying the line along Collier Road continued after darkness fell. Men roamed the rear area to find fence rails or anything else to carry up the ridge because entrenching tools were not yet available to dig trenches on the crest.[65]

Many of Ward's men counted themselves lucky for surviving near misses or slight injuries. A captain in the 70th Indiana saw three bullet holes in his hat after the battle, and a ball passed through the coat sleeve of Samuel Merrill. Andrew Jackson Johnson of the same regiment recalled an incident wherein one Confederate bullet hit him and two comrades while all three were lying down on top of the second ridge. It glanced off Red Garrison's knapsack and "Struck the back part of my left thigh[,] passed on and Struck Newt [Adams]." All Johnson had to contend with was "a black spot on my thigh" that was "quite sore. I must be very lucky as it Seems as though the Johnny balls cannot enter," Johnson concluded.[66]

The warm, humid weather played a role in the battle, according to many Confederate officers. They tended to cite this factor when explaining their defeat on the afternoon of July 20. "The heat was very oppressive," argued Oatis, "and some of the men exhausted by the charge fell almost fainting at the enemy's works." Oatis implied that this was a reason some of his regiment failed to advance beyond the captured Union works. But even officers who led their troops into the ravine cited the heat as impeding their ability to resist Ward's advance. Jackson thought his men of the 33rd Mississippi "were so completely exhausted and overcome with heat it was difficult for them to load and fire their pieces." Loring and Stewart not only accepted this partial explanation for Featherston's defeat but also cited the lack of support by Maney's Division to the right.[67]

But Loring was willing to make a second effort after the repulse of Featherston's men. He informed Stewart that if a fresh brigade could be found and Hardee could cooperate, his division would try again. Nothing came of this idea, and the Confederates merely skirmished for several hours from their position at the former Confederate skirmish line located along the edge of the tree cover a few hundred yards north of the Peach Tree Creek Line. Several Federal officers reported that Featherston attempted to attack again more than once, but there is no evidence to support such a contention.[68]

Out of 1,230 men engaged, Featherston lost exactly half, or 626. The 31st and 33rd Mississippi combined accounted for half of Featherston's losses, testifying to the fierce fight they conducted with Ward's division in the ravine. In fact, 164 men out of 215 in the 31st Mississippi were lost, amounting to 76.7 percent of the total engaged.[69]

Two hundred troops Featherston had left behind on picket duty before shifting to the right that day returned after the attack had failed, and it is likely these relatively fresh reinforcements were primarily responsible for keeping up a steady skirmish fire at the Federals that evening. John Adams's Brigade reached Loring's Division from its picket duty along the Chatta-hoochee River late that evening as well, but it was too late to take part in the battle.[70]

Ward's division suffered a total of 551 casualties, significantly fewer than the Confederate brigade it fought that day. Roughly 4,000 Federals opposed Featherston's Brigade and 13.7 percent were lost. Coburn took 1,315 men into action and lost 216 of them, amounting to 16.4 percent. Harrison's bri-gade suffered 181 casualties, amounting to 13.7 percent if his troop strength was similar to Coburn's. Wood lost 143 men of his brigade or 10.8 percent if he had as many men as Coburn.[71]

The Federals on Ward's sector claimed to have captured seven Confeder-ate colors plus twenty-five officer swords. They secured 114 Rebel prisoners in addition to taking in 132 wounded Confederates left on the field. Levin Miller's 33rd Indiana picked up 152 Confederate small arms and turned them over to Ward's ordnance officer.[72]

Featherston insisted that his men had done all they could to carry out Hood's order and did so with enthusiasm. "No numbers were too large for them to attack," he wrote to Hood after the war, "and no works too strong for them to charge. I cannot employ language sufficiently expressive of their courage and spirit displayed on this occasion." He consistently blamed Maney's Division to the right for not supporting his advance.[73]

But the Confederate brigade commander ignored the fact that at least one-third of his men did not advance into the ravine to support the other two-thirds who moved forward to engage the enemy. The brigade com-mander also did not personally go down into the ravine with those regi-ments. If one judged by casualties, the 31st and 33rd Mississippi bore the brunt of Featherston's battle. While the Mississippians of his brigade ini-tially advanced with good spirit to capture the Union skirmish line, the spirit went out of many of them as soon as they planted themselves on the second ridge crest along Collier Road. "They lost their organization," as Jacob Cox generously phrased it, and some regiments continued forward in piecemeal fashion. Featherston did not have any artillery support to buck up his men's courage or weaken Union resistance.[74]

The Federals had every reason to crow about their success that afternoon. Coburn called it "a victory snatched from the trembling balance of battle." Many Federal participants were proud of the fact that they had fought and won an open field engagement without the aid of fortifications.[75]

For the men of Coburn's brigade, the victory at Peach Tree Creek called to mind their terrible defeat at Thompson's Station on March 5, 1863. A few miles south of Franklin, Tennessee, the brigade engaged in an unequal contest with a numerically superior force of Confederate cavalry, was defeated, and largely captured. "We remembered Thompson's Station and were even," wrote Jefferson E. Brant of the 85th Indiana.[76]

Perhaps Coburn also had Thompson's Station in mind when he reacted so quickly and decisively to the first news of a Rebel approach on July 20. To Coburn belongs the lion's share of the credit for the success of Ward's division. Levin Miller of the 33rd Indiana put it well when he wrote that, "unless we had met the rebels just as we did and at the place we did, defeat and rout, I think, would most certainly have occurred." Thanks to Hooker's negligence, the division was lounging where it "had no position at all to stand and resist the large force and rapidly advancing attack that was being made by the enemy." It was an uphill fight for all of Ward's men, but they won it and established their line on top of the second ridge where they could not be moved.[77]

Ward received no credit from his own men. They were convinced the division would have suffered ignominious defeat if he had been responsible for its actions that afternoon. "Genl W. will get great credit I suppose," Benjamin Harrison told his wife, "when the literal truth is his Div never heard from him during the fight." Harrison did not see Ward or any of his staff members during the battle.[78]

Coburn's men certainly saw their own commander as the hero of Peach Tree Creek. He made himself conspicuous by riding to every part of the brigade, cheering the men. Even Harrison's troops gave Coburn his due. "I have always held that he saved the Army of the Cumberland that day," wrote Capt. William M. Meredith of the 70th Indiana. "Had it not been for his promptness, our brigade would have been surprised and driven into the creek."[79]

Coburn, Harrison, and Wood, in addition to the subordinate officers and the rank and file, deserved enormous credit for how they handled the crisis presented by the attack of Featherston's Brigade. But it is worth pointing out that the Confederates moved no more than about 820 men into the ravine to engage Ward's division, which outnumbered them by more than four to one. The normal advantage of occupying higher ground did not avail the Confederates on July 20; the Federals, attacking uphill, stopped them and threw them back with heavy Rebel losses. Numbers, spirit, superior leadership, and unit cohesion decided the contest on Ward's division front.

We raised the old Rebel yell and rushed on the works.
—J. P. Cannon

For three hours the fury of the battle along our entire
line could not be surpassed.—John W. Geary

Scott versus Geary

John W. Geary's division was already positioned in as good a
spot as possible to receive an enemy assault, and soon after
Featherston hit Ward's sector that attack came rolling forward. Having taken post on the Collier Road ridge crest earlier
that day, Hooker's Second Division contained a bit fewer than
3,000 men. Born in Pennsylvania, Geary had been a teacher,
lawyer, and surveyor before taking command of a Pennsylvania regiment in the Mexican War. He had also served as governor of strife-torn Kansas Territory in 1856–57. His Civil War
service spanned many battles in Virginia and the West.[1]

The formation Geary adopted for his division on July 20
both helped and hindered his ability to make a stand on the
second ridge crest. He stacked his three brigades in a column
formation, one a short distance behind the other. Largely this
was done because of the terrain. The ridge top was heavily timbered on Geary's sector, and the ground to his right was cut
up by ravines. To the left the ground was largely open and the
responsibility of Ward's division, with Shoal Creek only about
eighty yards from Geary's left flank. Geary placed his main
line even with the skirmish line of Ward's command and advanced his skirmishers and the 33rd New Jersey a few hundred yards farther south.[2]

Geary decided to form his division on a narrow front of only one brigade but to place the two supporting brigades close enough to the first to
be readily available. Col. Charles Candy's brigade formed the first line on
the ridge crest with Col. Ario Pardee Jr.'s 147th Pennsylvania anchoring the
left. Next Candy placed Lieut. Thomas E. Sloan's Battery E, Pennsylvania
Light Artillery with Capt. Robert Kirkup's 5th Ohio to its right. Capt. Henry
Bundy's 13th New York Light Artillery was positioned to the right of the
5th Ohio. A shallow dry ravine drained southward to the right of Bundy's
battery, and on the west side of it stood Capt. Myron T. Wright's 29th Ohio.
Then Lieut. Col. John Flynn's 28th Pennsylvania extended the line, and
Lieut. Col. Eugene Powell's 66th Ohio anchored the brigade's right flank. To
Powell's right lay rugged ground that as yet was uncovered by a Federal line
of battle. Candy's men had time to pile up fence rails for a slight breastwork
along their position, which was a few yards north of Collier Road.[3]

Behind Candy and at the foot of the first decline in terrain north of his
position lay Col. Patrick H. Jones's brigade. The 73rd Pennsylvania held the
left flank, followed to the right by the 119th New York and, on the west side
of the shallow ravine, the 134th New York. Jones formed a second line with
his remaining available units, placing the 109th Pennsylvania on the left
and east of the ravine with the 154th New York on the right and west of
the ravine. He had already sent his 33rd New Jersey forward to occupy an
advanced position on Geary's skirmish line before the Confederate attack.
Although relatively close to Candy, all regiments of Jones's brigade would
have to move up a fairly steep and timbered slope to reach the first line of
the division.[4]

Geary held Col. David Ireland's brigade in a column of regiments about
100 yards behind Jones's command. Here it would be in position to rush
forward in case of trouble. The division's formation enabled Geary to mass
strength on a narrow front, but he in essence abdicated responsibility for the
cut-up terrain to his right, relying on Alpheus Williams's division to cover
that sector. But Williams, under Hooker's direct order, had stationed his
men only part way from Peach Tree Creek up to the second ridge crest. There
they lounged around for several hours before the Confederate attack. That
cut-up sector was not adequately defended and posed an enormous advantage to the enemy's approach. A gap of 200 to 300 yards existed between
Ireland's brigade and Williams's division thanks to Hooker's unaccountable
lack of concern about positioning the Twentieth Corps that afternoon.[5]

The weakness of Geary's position lay in the fact that he as yet had no
support to right or left. Toward the east, Ward's division had largely open
ground, and thus it was possible to see the Confederates approach and pos-

John W. Geary, who commanded the only Twentieth Corps division to be ready for the Confederate attack on July 20. (Library of Congress, LC-DIG-cwpb-07246)

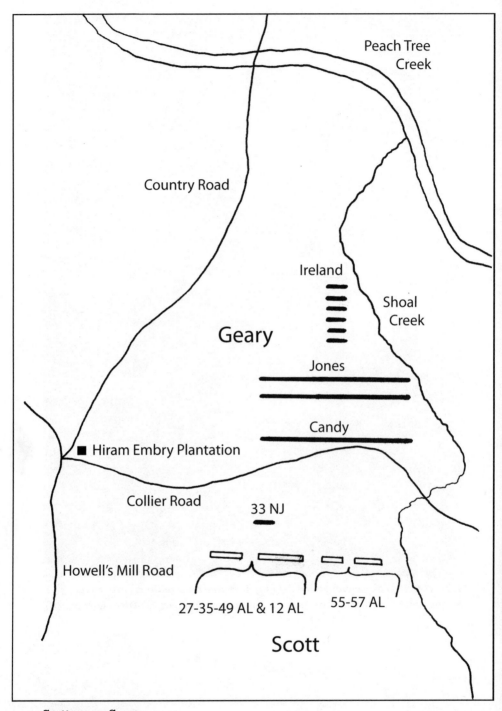

Peach Tree Creek

Country Road

Ireland

Shoal Creek

Geary

Jones

Candy

■ Hiram Embry Plantation

Collier Road

33 NJ

Howell's Mill Road

27-35-49 AL & 12 AL

55-57 AL

Scott

Scott versus Geary

sible for Ward's men to move quickly up slope to meet them, which is exactly what happened. To the west, the timbered ravine next to Geary's right flank offered a covered approach for the Confederates, allowing them to get close in to the division before being seen and inhibiting the reaction of the defending Unionists. Fortunately, Williams's division was not far away and in a position to front the enemy, but the terrain and Geary's formation both allowed the Rebels an opportunity to create more trouble than was necessary if Williams had been placed forward before the battle.

Williams's sector was located opposite division lines of authority on the Confederate side. While Brig. Gen. Thomas M. Scott's Brigade of Loring's Division fronted Geary, Col. Edward A. O'Neal's Brigade of Maj. Gen. Edward C. Walthall's Division fronted Williams. O'Neal's command was often referred to as Cantey's Brigade after a previous commander. A native of Georgia, Scott had been a farmer in Louisiana before commanding the 12th Louisiana early in the war. He led a brigade in the Vicksburg campaign and achieved promotion to brigadier general by May 1864.[6]

Scott took 1,320 men into battle, if one averages his troop strength according to the fact that 330 men served in the 57th Alabama of his brigade. That is likely a high average, because only 318 men filled the ranks of the 12th Louisiana. The brigade advanced from the Peach Tree Creek Line by the right of companies to negotiate the tangled terrain just north of that fortification. J. P. Cannon in the 27th Alabama recalled the forest in his memoirs. "It was a heavy-timbered section and the trees had been felled, lapped and crossed until they presented an almost impassable barrier, but we finally made our way through the worst of it and were then halted and wheeled by the left flank into line-of-battle." By this time, Union skirmishes were already firing at them.[7]

According to Cannon, the Confederates were well aware of the risks attending this assault. "It is a fearful thing to charge an enemy in his works, especially when outnumbered two or three to one, but feeling that it had to be done we nerved ourselves up to this point to do our whole duty." Cannon felt his comrades "were ready" for the attack when Scott ordered the brigade to "fix bayonets, forward, double-quick, march." Scott's men moved out with courage. "We raised the old Rebel yell and rushed on the works, but the yell was soon drowned by the roar of musketry and thunder of cannon, canister, and minie-balls."[8]

While Scott outnumbered the Federal skirmishers, he had no artillery support to contend with the fire issuing from Sloan's and Bundy's guns. A portion of his line opposite Candy's left wing, advancing in largely open ground, faltered under this fire until Scott personally led the 55th and 57th

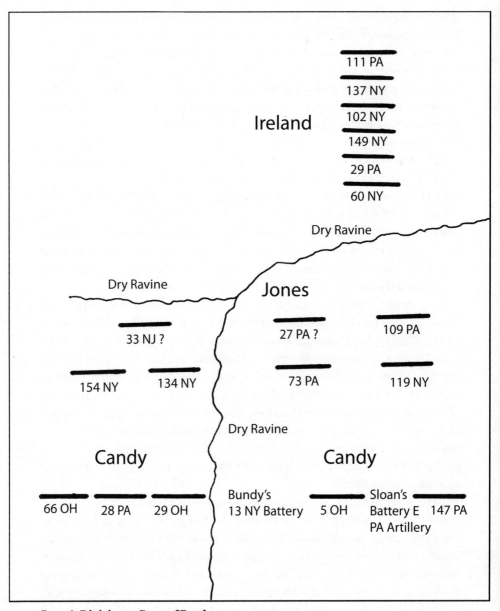

111 PA

137 NY

102 NY

149 NY

29 PA

60 NY

Ireland

Dry Ravine

Dry Ravine

Jones

33 NJ ?

27 PA ?

109 PA

154 NY

134 NY

73 PA

119 NY

Dry Ravine

Candy

Candy

66 OH

28 PA

29 OH

Bundy's
13 NY Battery

5 OH

Sloan's
Battery E
PA Artillery

147 PA

Geary's Division at Start of Battle

Alabama in a renewal of the advance that finally took the Union skirmish line. Ironically, some of the Federal skirmishers who were taken prisoner and rushed south were killed and wounded by the fire of Union artillery descending on the rear areas behind Scott's advancing men.[9]

Similar wavering took place on Scott's left wing as well before the gray line continued advancing northward, but here the Federal skirmish line had heavy reinforcements. Before Scott began his advance, Geary had sent forward Col. Enos Fourat's 33rd New Jersey from Jones's brigade to occupy a ridge more than 300 yards in front of the right wing of Candy's brigade. His skirmish line occupied the ridge too, which was a short feature in the timbered landscape, and a swampy stream lay between the ridge and the main Federal line. Geary also ordered forward the 134th New York from Jones's brigade to support the Jerseymen, and it had barely started moving forward when the enemy approached.[10]

Scott's left wing, consisting of Col. Noel L. Nelson's 12th Louisiana and the consolidated 27th, 35th, and 49th Alabama under Col. Samuel S. Ives, approached the Union skirmish line anchored by the 33rd New Jersey on the ridge. The Confederates were able to advance through the timber before they engaged the Federal skirmishers only seventy-five yards from Fourat's Jersey line. For a few minutes the opposing sides held static as Fourat sent his adjutant, Lieut. Stephen Pierson, to the left to see what was happening. Pierson went far enough to be able to look into the open ground fronting Candy's left wing and saw Scott's right wing approach the Federal skirmishers. "I stopped but a few moments to take it all in, and then rode back to report," Pierson remembered. By the time he returned, Scott's left wing was pressing forward. "How the bullets did come in from the front!," Pierson marveled.[11]

Fourat's men held firm and returned the fire, stalling the Confederates even though the Federals did not yet have breastworks. Not until Scott's left began to wrap around Fourat's right did the Union position crumble. Fourat refused his two right companies, but they could not stop the Confederates from continuing to flank that end of the regiment. To make matters worse, Scott's troops began to flank the left end of the New Jersey line as well. As Fourat put it, "to stand longer was madness, and I reluctantly gave the order to retire fighting." With the enemy closing in rapidly from three sides, the bearer of the regiment's state flag fell, and several members of the color guard also were hit. There was no time to recover the flag, and it fell into Rebel hands as the regiment barely had time to escape. Ives credited John E. Abernethy of the 27th Alabama with capturing those state colors, although an unidentified correspondent of the *Augusta Daily Constitutionalist* claimed they were taken by Pvt. John H. Badgett of the same regiment.[12]

Charles Candy, whose brigade anchored Geary's position along Collier Road on the best high ground to be had by the Federals south of Peach Tree Creek. (Library of Congress, LC-DIG-cwpb-04609)

Stephen Pierson remembered the frenzied retreat of the 33rd New Jersey back to Geary's main line that afternoon. As he crossed the swampy stream, he marveled at the sight of bullets plopping into the mud and water. Some Confederates followed up the retreat quite closely. The Federals came across Lieut. Col. Allan Jackson's 134th New York still on its way forward. "Where are they, Adjutant?" Jackson called to Pierson. "Deploy quickly, Colonel, they are right here," was the answer, but Jackson was wounded before he could give any orders. As a result, the 134th was swept up with the retreating 33rd New Jersey. Both regiments fell back through Candy's line and tried to regroup behind Jones's position. Here the men met Hooker who was riding forward, "magnificent in appearance," according to Pierson. The corps commander told them, "Boys, I guess we will stop here."[13]

Fourat was frantic with concern about the fact that his regiment not only retired in disorder but lost one of its flags. Three days later, he wrote a full report of the incident to the adjutant general of the state of New Jersey, assuring him that Geary and Jones placed no blame on his men. Hooker told Fourat, "Colonel, it is no disgrace to lose your colors under such circumstances; I only wonder that a man of you escaped capture." Fourat stated that his troops were proud "of their blue banner," but "it was an impossibility" to save it from falling into enemy hands.[14]

Geary had been with the 33rd New Jersey for a time just before the Confederate attack and rushed back when the gray tide began to roll forward. According to Henry E. Clarke, a 29th Ohio man detailed to Bundy's battery, Geary crossed the thin breastwork of Candy's line yelling, "A general engagement! A general engagement! Men, hold your ground. I will send support to you." Geary came back in time to cancel the forward movement of another regiment instructed to go forward and support the 33rd New Jersey. Col. John T. Lockman's 119th New York had started from Jones's position and reached the breastworks of Candy's brigade when the New Jersey unit and the 134th New York came rushing back. Geary told Lockman to stay just behind Candy's men and support them when needed.[15]

Very soon after the 33rd New Jersey and 134th New York returned to Geary's position, the Confederates began to flank the Federals. The temporary resistance offered by the 33rd New Jersey caused Scott's Brigade to break into two wings separated by at least 100 yards. Both wings kept advancing without being able to support each other. The left wing took full advantage of the timbered ravine immediately to Geary's right and bypassed the Federal flank. Nelson's 12th Louisiana and Ives's consolidated 27th, 35th, and 49th Alabama participated in this flanking movement, throwing an entire division of Union troops into confusion and near catastrophe.

Nelson and Ives were able to accomplish more for their limited numbers than any other Confederate commanders at Peach Tree Creek. If properly supported by additional men, they might have been able to break open Hooker's position at a key point.[16]

Scott's right wing failed to support this advantage. Geary witnessed the approach of the 55th Alabama and 57th Alabama across the open ground against Candy's left wing, coming from the woods "in immense brown and gray masses ... with flags and banners, many of them new and beautiful." Pardee ordered his 147th Pennsylvania to open fire as Sloan's and Bundy's gunners trained their sights on the two Alabama regiments. "The lines of the enemy were broken and they were soon compelled to seek cover in the woods," Pardee reported.[17]

But Scott's left wing quickly produced trouble for the Federals. The first regiment to feel the pressure as enemy troops circled round the right flank in the woods was Lieut. Col. Eugene Powell's 66th Ohio, which retreated in some haste. Then Col. John Flynn's 28th Pennsylvania peeled out of line. The 29th Ohio, under Capt. Myron T. Wright, stood its ground for a while and fired at the Rebels in front. The thick woods hid the enemy in front and on the flank, and soon it became apparent that Confederate troops were to the rear as well. A member of Wright's command named Ike recalled that his comrades could hear the Rebels yell "surrender you yankey sons of bitches but we could not see it in that line as long as thare was one hole left to git out of so we lit out." The 29th Ohio fell back about 200 yards "in some disorder" according to Wright and reformed at the foot of the slope behind Jones's brigade. "One half minet later and we would of lost the hole regt," concluded Ike.[18]

Within a short while, the right flank of Candy's brigade crumbled and retreated in disorder. In falling back, it affected several other regiments that had rushed forward to its support. As soon as trouble became apparent, Jones moved his 134th and 154th New York forward and obliquely to the right until the right flank of those two regiments was roughly even with the right flank of the 66th Ohio. The men lay down just behind Candy's line, but very soon that forward line broke. As each regiment fell back it passed over Jones's two regiments and brought them back too. Maj. Lewis D. Warner admitted that some degree of panic affected his 154th New York as Candy's troops trampled over them. "I could say that it was a race for life," reported William Harper of the 154th New York, "the minnies pelting the ground like so much hail."[19]

Scott's left wing disrupted and forced back five Union regiments thus far, clearing Federal troops from Candy's line west of the dry ravine and exposing the right flank of Bundy's battery. At the same time that Scott's left wing met and drove Candy's right wing, Geary and his subordinates were rushing more help to Candy from Jones's and Ireland's brigades. The 109th Pennsylvania held the left end of Jones's second line and, at the first sign of a Rebel attack, was moved forward to support Pardee's 147th Pennsylvania. As soon as it arrived, trouble became apparent on the right of Candy's line so the 109th was moved in that direction. The Pennsylvanians met the 29th Ohio as it retreated "in a confused mass," according to Fergus Elliott of the 109th. Elliott saw the color-bearer of the 29th Ohio and called on him to stop and rally the troops, but he refused. Just then Elliott saw Serg. Samuel Gourd fall. "Gourd was a staunch friend of mine," Elliott remembered more than thirty years later, "and his death seemed to nerve me to do what I had first intended doing—make a stand." Elliott grabbed the colors of the 29th Ohio from the reluctant flag bearer and waved them while shouting. Two of his comrades understood and encouraged him. "That's right, Ferg, stand where you are, we'll stand with you." Elliott played an inspiring role in bringing order out of chaos at the foot of the slope behind Candy's line.[20]

Federal officers could not hide the fact that five regiments fell back in so much disorder as to nearly constitute a panic, but Candy's left wing held firm in the chaos. "The disorganized masses of men as they rushed by the right of my line told a fearful tale," reported Ario Pardee. "The men seemed to be panic-stricken and I regret to say that there was manifested a lack of energy, coolness, and determination on the part of the officers which was truly deplorable." It was impossible to stop them, and, as Pardee put it, "one might conclude that destruction and defeat were inevitable." Samuel Ives of the consolidated 27th, 35th, and 49th Alabama agreed with Pardee. "The enemy offered but feeble resistance," he wrote, "and in their precipitous flight threw away their knapsacks, guns, and accouterments."[21]

But fresh regiments and cool heads came into the picture to slow the retreat and stop the enemy. From Jones's brigade, Maj. Charles C. Cresson led his 73rd Pennsylvania up to a position behind Pardee's regiment. When receiving Rebel fire from the right, Cresson retired his regiment about eighty yards, faced it to the right, and advanced a short distance to an advantageous spot for defense. Here the 73rd Pennsylvania stayed and delivered fire at the enemy. Col. John T. Lockman also moved his 119th New York of Jones's brigade to help Cresson, positioning it to the right of the 73rd Pennsylvania.[22]

Ireland also sent units from his brigade column to the rear of Jones. Col. Abel Godard led the 60th New York forward from the head of the column and encountered the Confederates on his way. Godard reacted calmly and effectively to the threat. He "faced his regiment by the rear rank, and made an oblique change of front forward on first company" before giving the order to fire. With the stout defense offered by the 73rd Pennsylvania and 119th New York a short distance away, Godard contributed well to stemming the Rebel tide.[23]

At the same time, Capt. John H. Goldsmith led the 29th Pennsylvania forward from its position as the second regiment in Ireland's brigade column. He encountered refugees of the retreating right wing of Candy's brigade while moving forward. One of Ireland's staff members brought word to head for Bundy's battery and support it. While Goldsmith continued moving forward, he encountered a group of Confederates who responded to his call to surrender by opening fire. Goldsmith ordered his right company to return the fire (it was the only part of his regiment able to reach the group) until the shooting died down, when he moved forward toward the endangered battery.[24]

Ireland moved the last four regiments of his brigade forward but with only limited success. Formed in column at the start, each regiment had to deploy into line. Ireland assigned his assistant inspector general, Capt. Michael Nolan, to superintend the deployment. The first regiment was to advance immediately after deploying to be followed by the next en echelon, with each regiment to the right of the previous one. It was a complicated maneuver to conduct under fire, in the woods, and on uneven terrain.[25]

Col. Henry A. Barnum moved the 149th New York forward after deploying but in crossing the ravine that lay at the foot of the slope received heavy Confederate fire. As Barnum put it, the regiment "was not in a position to inflict much damage upon the enemy." The 149th New York lost thirty-five men "almost in an instant," including Lieut. Col. Charles B. Randall and Capt. David J. Lindsay, who were killed. Nearly the entire color guard was shot down, and nearby Confederates called on Color Sergeant William Crosier to give up the flag. "I cried to them to take it, if they could, and, swiftly tearing the flag off the staff, stuffed it under my shirt and retreated, leaving my flagstaff behind." The 149th New York then retired in disorder.[26]

Col. Herbert von Hammerstein's 102nd New York moved out next and lost sight of the 149th New York very quickly. Suddenly it received heavy fire from the right as it crossed the ravine. With this punishment added to the confusion in the area, Hammerstein's men broke and fell back. The 102nd New York lost fifty-five troops in its brief exposure to battle at Peach Tree Creek. Next, Lieut. Col. Koert S. Van Voorhis moved his 137th New York forward after Hammerstein left and encountered similarly heavy fire. Van Voorhis managed to control his men and stop them briefly to make a stand, but his right flank ended inside the ravine, and the line was enfiladed with no good prospects for refusing it to meet the enemy. The 137th New York therefore retreated some 300 yards to reform.[27]

Lastly, Col. George A. Cobham Jr. moved forward his 111th Pennsylvania and managed to get it through the ravine and at least part way up the slope toward the location of Candy's embattled brigade. But it received an increasingly heavy fire from Scott's men that brought down many Pennsylvanians. According to John Richards Boyle, "some of the wounded were rolling down the steep declivity." Boyle initially thought men of Williams's division were mistakenly firing on Ireland's brigade, but when the enemy troops came within fifty yards of the regiment, they began to call on the Yankees to surrender. Cobham ordered his men to change front and meet this threat when he was shot through the lungs while waving his sword in the air. He died later that night. "In an instant," wrote Boyle, "the regiment had dissolved to the left rear and rallied on its colors in a new and corrected line."[28]

Lieut. Col. Thomas M. Walker took charge of the 111th Pennsylvania and commanded it for the rest of the battle. The men were out of immediate danger but faced with what Boyle called a torrent of fire from the ravine. The terrain and vegetation accentuated the sound and impression of this fire. "Trees were clipped of their branches, bushes were cut away as by knives, and rails with which the swale was bridged were splintered. The clothing of many of the men who were not wounded was perforated. The coat and trousers of one of the officers were in shreds from the musket balls that barely missed his person." According to Boyle, the ravine "was a throat of death," the worst experience of the war for the 111th Pennsylvania. For half an hour it endured this fire and lost 74 men out of about 200 engaged. Thirty-two of the casualties were missing, captured by the Confederates during the pull-out from the ravine.[29]

Ireland's four regiments reformed near the scene of their repulse in and around the ravine with the 149th New York on the left and the 102nd New York on the right. The 137th New York and 111th Pennsylvania formed behind those two regiments. Eventually, Barnum and Hammerstein moved the 149th and 102nd New York back to the other two so that all four regiments were now together in one line. At this point in the fight, Hooker rode up to show himself and received "stirring cheers" from the troops.[30]

It had been a remarkable occurrence; half a Confederate brigade disrupted the attempt of four Union regiments to form and participate in the battle. Scott's men had the advantage of terrain and tree cover, but most importantly they were well in hand and hit Ireland's units exactly when the Federals were vulnerable, moving forward individually and not suspecting

111th Pennsylvania at Peach Tree Creek. A dramatic visual representation of the fierce fight experienced by the regiment as it met Scott's Confederates in and near the ravine behind Candy's brigade. (Boyle, *Soldiers True*, 234)

a threat to their right. But the Unionists recovered quickly and reformed a short distance away to shore up the developing line of resistance that would hold for the rest of the engagement.

Despite the chaotic way in which it deployed, Ireland's brigade managed to blunt the further progress of Scott's left wing down the ravine behind Candy's position. Added to regiments of Jones's brigade, the developing Union line behind Candy managed to hold ground and prevent further danger to Geary's division. How far the comparatively small number of Confederates might have penetrated is an open question, but their attack ground to a halt in the rugged terrain somewhere to the rear of Geary's front line.

While Ireland and Jones dealt with the rear areas, an intense and deadly fight occurred for the ground occupied by Bundy's 13th New York Battery in Candy's line. The 66th Ohio, 28th Pennsylvania, and 29th Ohio peeled away to expose the right flank of the battery. According to Capt. Robert Kirkup of the 5th Ohio, positioned to the left of Bundy's command, the Federals "gave way and retreated in confusion." Kirkup however was determined that his men would stay and support the guns. Ario Pardee, from his position in the 147th Pennsylvania to the left of the 5th Ohio, had nothing but praise for Kirkup's cool conduct and success in holding the Ohio men to their work.[31]

Capt. Henry Bundy also worked hard to hold his gunners in their place. When Featherston's Confederates initially hit Ward's sector to the left of Geary's division, Bundy directed his fire at them. A few minutes later, Scott's Brigade appeared in front of Candy's line and Bundy redirected his fire to the front. Soon after, the Confederates began to wrap around Candy's right flank, and the three infantry regiments fell away.[32]

The heaviest pressure fell on Bundy's right section of two guns, led by Lieut. Henry Muller. The crews continued to work their pieces even though they were subjected to heavy fire. Within minutes six cannoneers were wounded. A noncommissioned officer at one gun received nine bullets, and another at the other gun was hit eight times. Twenty horses fell in this hail of rifle fire from Scott's men. The surviving men at the two pieces gave up and fled, abandoning their guns. Elements of Samuel Ives's consolidated 27th, 35th, and 49th Alabama did this damage to Bundy's battery.[33]

Henry E. Clarke of the 29th Ohio, who had been detailed to help Bundy's men serve the guns, vividly recalled being captured in the confusion as the two pieces were abandoned. "Give the d-d Yanks no quarter!" he heard the Confederates yell, but no one killed them in cold blood. Instead, Clarke was taken prisoner and hurried south from the battlefield. When reaching the tree cover behind the Confederate skirmish line under guard, Clarke saw the effect of the fight on his enemy. "The woods were full of wounded rebels, who were getting off the field in the best manner they could."[34]

Clarke was captured at Scott's high tide, but effective work by Candy's left wing now blunted Confederate progress. Bundy redirected the fire of his other four pieces toward the right to keep the enemy away from the two abandoned guns, firing canister at short range. Pardee refused the right wing of his 147th Pennsylvania to fire in that direction too, behind the 5th Ohio to his right. Two of Ireland's regiments came forward to help as well. Maj. John A. Reynolds, Hooker's chief of artillery, was on the scene and came upon Godard's 60th New York. He asked Godard to move up and join the refused right flank of Pardee's Pennsylvania regiment. One of Ireland's staff officers had earlier ordered Goldsmith's 29th Pennsylvania forward to support Bundy, but Goldsmith was delayed by encountering elements of Scott's left wing on the way. After dealing with those Confederates, Goldsmith continued forward and aligned to the right of the 60th New York in the new position. These regiments—Candy's 147th Pennsylvania and 5th Ohio, plus Ireland's 60th New York and 29th Pennsylvania—provided immediate support for Bundy's battery at the same time that the rest of Jones's and Ireland's brigades blocked the other Confederates circling round through the ravine.[35]

Bundy's two abandoned pieces remained for a few minutes in no-man's land, isolated between the opposing lines. Pardee saw them and told Capt. Jacob P. Kreider of Company F, 147th Pennsylvania to retrieve the guns. Kreider called for volunteers, and several of his own men plus some from Company A came forward. A number of Bundy's men and troops from Kirkup's 5th Ohio also joined the group. As these Federals moved forward to secure the guns, parts of the 109th Pennsylvania also joined them and helped to turn the cannon around so as to fire toward the right and rear of Candy's line.[36]

Bundy took charge of those two abandoned guns and directed their fire. Everyone was full of praise for the 13th New York Battery men. The stand of Bundy's four remaining guns proved to be the key to stopping Confederate progress along the ridge top where Candy held his line. Supported by the work of numerous infantry regiments to the left and rear, Scott's attack was blunted. Bundy lost eleven men. Sloan's Battery E, Pennsylvania Light Artillery, positioned between Pardee's 147th Pennsylvania and Kirkup's 5th Ohio, was not threatened. It fired a total of 530 rounds to the front and obliquely to the left. Sloan lost five men and fourteen horses.[37]

The fight for the ridge top occupied by Candy's brigade was short but intense. This spot "was the key position of the entire battle," Geary asserted, and "once gained by the enemy the day was lost." It had been a very emotional experience for the men of Bundy's battery. They almost lost their guns and narrowly averted a humiliating defeat. A lieutenant of the battery broke into tears when he thanked the men of the 109th Pennsylvania for helping to recover the two abandoned pieces.[38]

Stephen Pierson of the 33rd New Jersey visited Bundy's battery soon after the fight and saw that the spokes of some wheels were nearly cut in pieces by musketry. One of Bundy's sergeants, "still black and grimy from the fight," leaned against one of the guns while "patting it affectionately with his hand, as a mother might pat her child who had been in great danger, but had been saved." The New Jersey soldiers had a habit, when their cartridges became damp, of taking the minie balls out and filling old socks, which they then gave to Bundy's gunners. Bundy had used those *stocking legs*," as the sergeant called them, that afternoon. They served as improvised canister rounds, effective at short range.[39]

The sketchy reports written by regimental commanders in Scott's left wing agree that the Confederate units received "very heavy fire" and that the wing was unsupported to right and left. Unit commanders also united in reporting that the hot, humid weather was a problem. "Owing to the rapidity of the advance and the ruggedness of the ground," reported Colonel Nelson of the 12th Louisiana, "my men were very much exhausted." A company clerk of the 12th noted in the unit's record of events that "many fell, completely exhausted."[40]

Scott apparently remained with the right wing of his brigade, consisting of the 55th and 57th Alabama, which had been repulsed in the first attempt to strike at Pardee's and Kirkup's Union regiments. The left wing of Scott's Brigade receded from its high tide and fell back, compelling Scott to order the right wing to retire as well. Federal observers noted the time of the Rebel fall back as about 6 P.M.[41]

Geary's division reacted to the unexpected with commendable alacrity and intelligence. In a sometimes chaotic process, brigade and regimental commanders adjusted their positions under extreme pressure to form a long refused line from the left wing of Candy's brigade toward the position of Williams's division to the right and rear of Geary's location. Eventually, that refused line connected with Williams's left flank to form a solid barrier to any Confederate advance. The 33rd New Jersey of Jones's brigade formed on the extreme right of this refused line and connected with Williams. The process of forming the refused line saved Geary's division. Hooker personally helped to establish this refused line by pointing out the best places for some of the regiments to take position and ordering the Federals to construct breastworks to more securely hold the new line.[42]

Despite their repulse, Scott's men achieved a remarkable feat. With scarcely two-thirds of a brigade, the Confederates disrupted and threw into confusion the majority of three Union brigades. They came closer than one could have expected to breaking through Geary's position. Only because Geary had depth in his formation were the Federals able to respond quickly enough to meet this threat.

When he fell back, Scott left skirmishers near the skirt of timber that shielded the Peach Tree Creek Line. These Confederates kept up a sporadic fire on Geary's division until after dusk. Ward's division, now positioned on the ridge top to the left of Geary's line, contributed its fire to keep this Rebel skirmishing down to a manageable level.[43]

"I have never seen more heroic fighting," Geary reported of the engagement at Peach Tree Creek. "For three hours the fury of the battle along our entire line could not be surpassed." Looking at the field afterward, noting how the musketry scored trees and brush, Geary was reminded of the great battle at Gettysburg more than a year before. He saw Peach Tree Creek "as

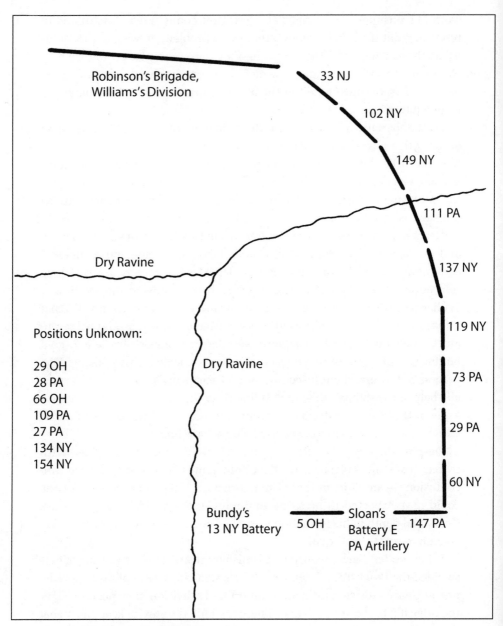

Robinson's Brigade,
Williams's Division

33 NJ

102 NY

149 NY

111 PA

Dry Ravine

137 NY

119 NY

Positions Unknown:

29 OH
28 PA
66 OH
109 PA
27 PA
134 NY
154 NY

Dry Ravine

73 PA

29 PA

60 NY

Bundy's
13 NY Battery

5 OH

Sloan's
Battery E
PA Artillery

147 PA

Geary's Division at End of Battle

a test of the discipline and valor of our troops, and as the first defeat of the newly appointed commander of the rebel army." The battle "was glorious in its results."[44]

Geary's division lost 476 men, constituting 15.8 percent of the somewhat less than 3,000 troops involved. Ireland's brigade suffered 233 casualties, roughly half the division losses, while forming the new refused line. Regimental casualties varied among Geary's units. The 109th Pennsylvania suffered sixteen losses and the 154th New York only seven, even though its Companies D and E fired an average of eighty rounds per man during the battle.[45]

Scott lost 390 men out of 1,320 engaged on July 20. That amounted to a loss rate of 29.5 percent. The 55th and 57th Alabama in Scott's right wing suffered the most. Their combined casualties totaled 284 troops, or 72.8 percent of the brigade casualties. These regiments attacked Pardee and Kirkup across open ground and suffered enormously for it. Ironically, the regiments of Scott's left wing, which operated mostly on cut-up, timbered ground, achieved far more than the right wing and lost comparatively fewer troops.[46]

Capt. Augustus L. Milligan reported that the 57th Alabama suffered the loss of two field officers, one staff officer, and fifteen line officers. One of the latter was Capt. Bailey M. Talbot of Company H. Talbot "acted imprudently, in the charge," reported Joel Dyer Murphree to his wife. He advanced ahead of his men in the forward movement and lagged behind in the retreat. When last seen, Talbot was moving slowly back across open ground at the rear of the regiment. "He may have laid down behind something to protect him and was captured," Murphree surmised. Talbot died on the field at age twenty-nine instead. The day before the battle he wrote to his young son Riley. "Should I fall fighting for what history will tell you, my boy, avenge the blood of your father." Milligan wrote a eulogy for his fallen men. "The long list of casualties in this regiment in the engagement of the 20th instant will be sufficient evidence of its deep devotion to the cause of Southern liberty and independence," he asserted.[47]

Scott's men supported Milligan's effort to portray the battle of Peach Tree Creek as evidence of devotion to duty. J. P. Cannon argued after the war that the troops "literally obeyed" Stewart's order to attack regardless of obstacles. He blamed Hardee's Corps for not supporting Stewart's efforts. Troops of the Army of Mississippi "could have driven the enemy across Peach Tree Creek" if they had had proper help to the right and left. Milligan of the 57th Alabama praised Scott for showing himself "in the midst of danger cheering the men with his presence and cool determination," but failed to note that the brigade's left wing went behind Candy's line without his guidance.[48]

Loring used only two of his brigades in the attack on July 20 and lost 1,016 men in the process. With a combined total of 2,550 men, Loring lost 39.8 percent of his strength in the attack on Ward's and Geary's divisions. He believed his troops had taken out of action 2,500 Federals, but that was an exaggerated estimate. Ward's and Geary's combined losses totaled 1,027 men out of about 7,000 engaged, or 14.6 percent. The number of Union and Confederate casualties on this part of the battlefield was almost equal, but the percentage lost was dramatically worse for the Confederates (39.8 percent compared to 14.6 percent). Stewart noted in his report to Army of Tennessee headquarters that Loring lost more heavily than his other division commanders. The result of this bloodletting was a failed effort to break Hooker's line.[49]

Boys, don't shoot until you see them—there's a bully place
to bury them out there.—Joseph Hooker

The clouds of smoke . . . poured down on us to hide everything
but the flash of the enemy's guns.—Rice C. Bull

Thus we had made a desperate charge, lost many of the best men
in our Corps and accomplished nothing.—Robert H. Dacus

8

O'Neal versus Williams and
Reynolds versus McCook

Loring's troops were in action only a short while before
Stewart threw another division of his Army of Mississippi into
the attack. Commanded by Maj. Gen. Edward C. Walthall, it
fronted Williams's division and the left end of Palmer's Fourteenth Corps line. Born in Virginia, Walthall lived most of his
life at Holly Springs, Mississippi, where he practiced law and
entered the war by joining the 15th Mississippi. He served in
the Western Theater, rising to brigade and then division command by 1863. Walthall led only two brigades into action on
July 20. He positioned Cantey's Brigade, now commanded by
Col. Edward A. O'Neal, on his right connecting with the left
of Scott's Brigade of Loring's Division. On the left, Walthall
placed Brig. Gen. Daniel H. Reynolds's Brigade. His other
unit, led by Brig. Gen. William A. Quarles, was left in reserve.
Stewart accompanied Walthall's Division to observe its progress that day.[1]

Like Loring, Walthall ordered his regimental commanders to advance from the Peach Tree Creek Line by the right
of companies so they could negotiate the heavy timber that
fronted the position. When the troops reached the northern

edge of that timber, at the location of the Confederate skirmish line, they fronted once more into line. Waiting a few minutes for Loring to go in, as he was instructed, Walthall found that Hood's complicated plan of maneuver had fallen by the wayside. The troops to his right seemed to be guiding right, as they should have done, but they were not then wheeling to the left as Hood instructed. From nearly the start of the battle on Hardee's sector, the attack was devolving into a simple, straightforward advance. In fact, Walthall found that he had to move farther to the right than anticipated in an attempt to keep his right flank somewhere near Loring's left flank. As a result, the right wing of his command, O'Neal's Brigade, landed up east of Howell's Mill Road and confronted Williams's division. The left wing, Reynolds's Brigade, remained west of the road and attacked the far-left end of Palmer's corps line.[2]

But the shift to the right enabled Walthall to more directly hit the space between Geary's division and Palmer's corps, which was covered only by a blue-coated skirmish line. O'Neal's Confederates swept across Hiram Embry's plantation near the junction of Collier Road and Howell's Mill Road, driving back the Federal skirmishers and moving into the rugged and timbered ground that fronted Williams.[3]

O'Neal had a rather checkered history of service in the Civil War. Born in Alabama and a college graduate, he worked as a lawyer before securing a commission as colonel of the 26th Alabama in Virginia. He did well in several major battles as a brigade commander until Gettysburg, when his performance did not match Lee's expectations. Transfer to the West with his old regiment led to his elevation to brigade command once more. Brig. Gen. James Cantey had fallen ill and was out of service since mid-May, 1864, so O'Neal took over the brigade. He aligned his command with the 37th Mississippi on the right, followed by the 17th Alabama, then the 26th Alabama, and the brigade sharpshooter battalion next, with the 29th Alabama on the far left. A member of the 37th Mississippi reported his regiment had 210 men in the attack. If that was an average for all, then O'Neal took 1,050 troops into action.[4]

Like other units before it, the brigade advanced by the right of companies to negotiate the tangled vegetation fronting the Peach Tree Creek Line. Then O'Neal ordered his officers to front their regiments about 300 yards from the Federal skirmish line. O'Neal then urged his men to "drive every obstacle before them." They charged with a yell and forced back the Union skirmishers. Col. Orlando S. Holland proudly reported that the color-bearer of his 37th Mississippi was the first to plant a flag on the captured Union breastworks. Serg. Samuel W. Jones, who had been a member of the regimental

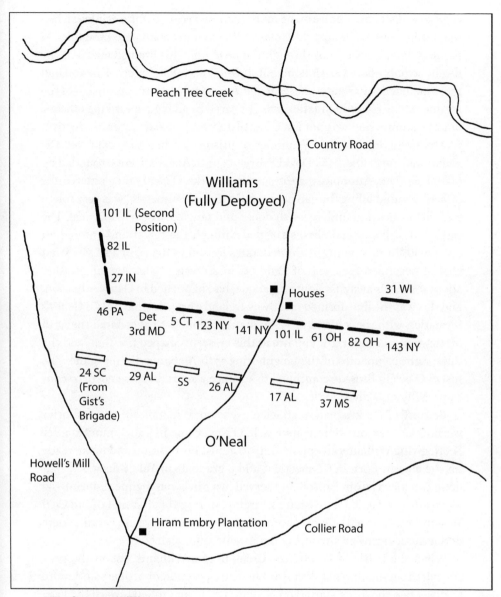

Peach Tree Creek

Country Road

**Williams
(Fully Deployed)**

101 IL (Second
Position)

82 IL

27 IN

46 PA   Det
         3rd MD   5 CT 123 NY 141 NY 101 IL 61 OH 82 OH 143 NY

Houses   31 WI

24 SC
(From
Gist's
Brigade)   29 AL   SS   26 AL   17 AL   37 MS

O'Neal

Howell's Mill
Road

Hiram Embry Plantation   Collier Road

O'Neal versus Williams

color guard since his enlistment more than two years before, accomplished the deed. Jones excitedly told Holland "Colonel my colors are here first." A moment later he was shot through the head and "his brains bedaubed the flag he so nobly bore," as Holland put it. Only two weeks before, Holland had recommended the twenty-one-year-old Jones for promotion to ensign of the regiment. The recommendation was approved by all higher-ranking officers, but the commission was not issued until July 22, two days after his death.[5]

The Confederates took a number of prisoners when they captured the Federal skirmish line. Maj. David F. Bryan's 26th Alabama alone rounded up fifteen captives. After passing the skirmish works, O'Neal's men entered the difficult ground filling the gap between Geary and Palmer. It "was very rough and the bushes and undergrowth dense and tangled," reported O'Neal. The right end of his brigade line struggled through the forest and entered an open field. At this point the Confederates looked to the right and saw what O'Neal described as a line of Federals in a crescent shape configuration about 100 yards away. By now a great deal had happened in Geary's division, and this was the line, formed mostly by Ireland's brigade, that linked Geary's formation with the left end of Williams's division. O'Neal ordered the 37th Mississippi to wheel right and fire at this crescent-shaped position, and the three right companies of the neighboring 17th Alabama did the same. The rest of O'Neal's Brigade continued to advance a short distance north to confront Williams's division.[6]

Because of Hood's plan to attack en echelon, Williams already had prior warning of the Confederate approach. O'Neal came in a few minutes after Scott, giving Williams an opportunity to adjust his position and make ready for the enemy. Born in Connecticut and a graduate of Yale University, Williams practiced law in Detroit and served in a Michigan regiment during the Mexican War. He led a division in Virginia during the first half of the Civil War and was one of the most thoroughly experienced division commanders in Sherman's army group during the Atlanta campaign.[7]

When the battle of Peach Tree Creek began, Williams was in the process of strengthening his skirmish line with a section of artillery and more troops. Then the firing started on Newton's front and rolled toward the Federal right. Williams firmed up his position to get ready for trouble. Earlier that day he had advanced from the bottomland skirting Peach Tree Creek along a country road that angled toward the southeast and joined Howell's Mill Road at the Hiram Embry plantation, stopping his division about 600 yards short of the Embry place where a straggling group of deserted houses was located. Williams had assigned Brig. Gen. Joseph F. Knipe's brigade to take position to the right of the road, while Col. James F. Robinson's brigade

Alpheus S. Williams, a stalwart division leader in Sherman's army group whose men expertly handled themselves to deal with the unexpected Confederate attack. (Library of Congress, LC-DIG-cwpb-07269)

took post to the left. Brig. Gen. Thomas H. Ruger's brigade remained to the rear of Knipe as a reserve. Given Hooker's lack of concern about hurrying things forward, the division lounged about for hours before the Confederate advance without maintaining proper formations or planning to move forward. It needed advanced warning of trouble and, thanks to Hood's plan to attack en echelon, received it.[8]

The terrain constricted Williams's deployment. A rugged ravine covered his left flank, the same ravine used by the left wing of Scott's Brigade to cause so much trouble for Geary. Another ravine separated Williams's right flank from the left end of Palmer's Fourteenth Corps line. Robinson and Knipe occupied the higher ground between these two ravines, the division line bisected by the country road. Williams immediately ordered Knipe and Robinson to form their men properly. Sections of Lieut. Charles E. Winegar's Battery I, 1st New York Light Artillery and Capt. John D. Woodbury's Battery M, 1st New York Light Artillery were positioned where possible to cover the high ground and the ravines.[9]

Williams ordered Ruger to move his brigade to the right a bit where one of Palmer's units was positioned. Brig. Gen. Richard W. Johnson, who commanded the division on Palmer's extreme left, had earlier placed Col. Marshall F. Moore's brigade west of the ravine separating the two corps. Moore faced his men east and started to construct breastworks to protect Palmer's left flank. Williams now wanted that ground for his own division, and relieving Moore allowed the Fourteenth Corps troops to rejoin their parent division west of the ravine. Ruger relieved Moore quickly and formed his brigade in a line behind Robinson and Knipe.[10]

In the midst of all this excited preparation, Hooker was shaken out of his lethargy. The fire of battle seemed to awaken him. Always a keen proponent of elan under stress, Hooker rode along Williams's developing line and encouraged the troops. "Boys, don't shoot until you see them—there's a bully place to bury them out there," he yelled.[11]

Ohio-born James S. Robinson, a volunteer soldier who had worked as a newspaper publisher and state politician, commanded the 82nd Ohio in Virginia before coming west with Hooker's command in the fall of 1863. Like Williams, Robinson heard the initial roll of musketry on Newton's front and observed its progress toward Hooker's right. He barely got his brigade deployed from column into line before O'Neal's men approached through the timber in front and started to fire. "The battle at once grew fierce and bloody," Robinson reported, "a portion of my troops becoming mingled with those of the enemy in an almost hand-to-hand conflict." Robinson had the 143rd New York on his extreme left, then the 82nd Ohio, 61st Ohio, and

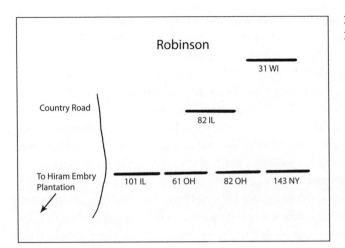

Robinson

31 WI

Country Road

82 IL

To Hiram Embry
Plantation

101 IL   61 OH   82 OH   143 NY

101st Illinois on the extreme right at the country road. The 82nd Illinois was held a few yards to the rear as a reserve. Hovering about in the rear of Williams's developing line was the 31st Wisconsin, which had only recently joined Sherman's army group and had not yet been assigned to a brigade.[12]

Col. Horace Boughton's 143rd New York received its first fire as it deployed from column into line, but Boughton held the men firmly to their duty. He obeyed Robinson's order to move forward and make connection with Ireland's brigade to the left. Going ahead a few yards, it soon became clear that Ireland had fallen back and could not make connection. Moreover, the 82nd Ohio to Boughton's right failed to advance as far as he did, so the 143rd New York was unsupported on both flanks. But the New York men were sheltered by thick woods; as O'Neal's troops advanced within twenty yards of their position, they poured in a disciplined fire that forced the Confederates to retire. Boughton credited the success to his men's skill at musketry, "which was done with such precision and effect." Boughton felt uncomfortable holding his advanced position and immediately retired about forty yards to rejoin the rest of Robinson's brigade.[13]

Col. Stephen J. McGroarty's 61st Ohio, positioned to the right of the 82nd Ohio, also advanced nearly as far forward as Boughton's New Yorkers. McGroarty's men held firm and fired their rifles well enough to stop O'Neal's first attack, with some Confederates falling within ten feet of the Ohio line. The Federals also took heavy casualties in this fight. McGroarty was wounded along with four other officers and more than seventy men. The 61st Ohio fell back to the rest of the brigade line at about the same time as Boughton's New York regiment.[14]

In the lull between O'Neal's first and second attacks, Robinson's men fired left oblique into the ravine separating them from Ireland's embattled troops. In this way the infantrymen and artillery gunners of Williams's division aided Geary's efforts to a limited degree.[15]

Robinson's brigade held firm for the rest of the battle, anchoring Williams's left flank near enough to Geary so that eventually Ireland could establish contact with it. In the meanwhile, the experiences of individuals in Robinson's brigade told the story of Peach Tree Creek in personal ways. Lieut. George Young, a member of Robinson's staff, was shot while riding across a field to deliver a message, the bullet entering the lower part of his left leg. Young endured many operations over the coming years that never completely took away the recurring pain until his death in 1909. Within the ranks of the 82nd Ohio, which lost sixty-two men on July 20, Dewitt C. Foos encountered trouble when he left the ranks after O'Neal's first attack. Foos later claimed he helped a wounded comrade to the rear, but his officers testified that he had no permission to do so. Once to the rear, a provost marshal ordered him to escort some prisoners to the rear. By the time he returned to his company, Foos was branded as a deserter in the face of the enemy. He was tried by a general court-martial, found guilty, and sentenced to stand on a barrel two hours per day for twenty days "with a placard in his back in letters three inches long 'I skulked before the enemy.'" Williams approved the findings, and Foos apparently learned a lesson about leaving ranks without explicit permission of his officers.[16]

Williams's right wing was led by Joseph F. Knipe, a former shoemaker from Philadelphia and Mexican War veteran who had worked for the Pennsylvania Railroad before the Civil War. As colonel of the 46th Pennsylvania and leader of a brigade, Knipe gained experience in several Virginia battles. Many men of Williams's skirmish line were drawn from his command on July 20, giving a good account of themselves in their fighting retreat from Walthall's advance.[17]

Knipe's men were resting in column when the fighting started, and the first shots came as a surprise to them. According to Rice C. Bull of the 123rd New York, everyone knew how disastrous it would be if the enemy hit them while the brigade was still massed in column. As a result, everything moved in quick time as the men marched south before deploying lines, first Col. William K. Logie's 141st New York and then Lieut. Col. James C. Rogers's 123rd New York. Logie's men went no more than 200 yards before they met the retiring Federal skirmishers and, behind them, O'Neal's men. The 141st New York "ran head-on into them," as Bull put it, in the woods. The first few minutes of firing brought down many troops, including Logie, who was killed, and Andrew J. McNett, his lieutenant colonel, who was wounded.

Joseph F. Knipe, the excitable brigade leader who played a large role in stopping O'Neal's Confederates but who still could take time to share his chewing tobacco with his men. (Library of Congress, LC-DIG-cwpb-05077)

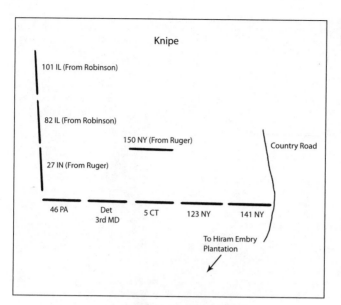

Knipe

101 IL (From Robinson)

82 IL (From Robinson)

150 NY (From Ruger)

27 IN (From Ruger)

Country Road

46 PA

Det
3rd MD

5 CT

123 NY

141 NY

To Hiram Embry
Plantation

**Knipe's
Brigade**

Nevertheless, the regiment managed to come into line and hold firm, as Rogers brought the 123rd New York up to its right in the same fashion. Rogers also lost several men while coming into line. The 5th Connecticut and a detachment of the 3rd Maryland next came into line to the right of the 123rd New York, with Col. James L. Selfridge's 46th Pennsylvania anchoring Knipe's right flank.[18]

The reaction of Knipe's men to the sudden Confederate attack led Rice Bull to contemplate the nature of his comrades. "No brigade was ever in a more dangerous position to receive an attack," he wrote, and only because it consisted of "experienced veteran soldiers, men who knew what to do under the most adverse and changing conditions," the situation was saved in the nick of time. Bull had further reason to contemplate human nature under trial when he recalled seeing a Federal skirmisher belonging, according to the insignia on his cap, to the 27th Indiana of Ruger's brigade. "He was a straight young fellow at least six feet tall and looked every inch a soldier." The man stopped a moment when he reached the line of the 123rd New York to take one more shot at the Rebels but was instantly killed by a bullet that slammed so hard into his forehead it made a loud noise. Gunners of Winegar's New York battery had to move his body out of the way as they maneuvered a section of guns into position. Bull never knew the name of this brave man; he was buried anonymously with the dead of Knipe's brigade, and his family probably never learned the details of his fate.[19]

The quick response of Logie and Rogers brought their regiments into line in time to blunt O'Neal's first attack. The ground sloped downward in front of Knipe's position and was covered with trees but little underbrush. From Rice Bull's perspective, the enemy was shrouded by a cloud of musket smoke, but "their loud yells could be heard above the roar of their guns." When the firing slacked off, Rogers told the men in his rear rank to go back and tear down the deserted houses to obtain wood for a breastwork. There was one old log building "loosely put together" with surrounding buildings also made of logs. The New Yorkers managed to make a barricade up to their knees by loosely piling this old timber in a line along their position before O'Neal launched his second attack of the day.[20]

O'Neal's first advance was blunted by the 143rd New York and 61st Ohio of Robinson's brigade and by the 141st and 123rd New York of Knipe's brigade. O'Neal regrouped his men and soon made a second effort, which bore more heavily than the first, especially upon Knipe's men. Before pressing forward once again, O'Neal discovered that his brigade line had become extended. Despite the rugged, timbered ground, his line had been "well formed and advanced in good order" during the first attack, except that the 29th Alabama on the extreme left had misunderstood orders and guided left instead of right. This compelled the sharpshooters and the 26th Alabama to extend "almost to a skirmish line." While O'Neal worried about the weak spot in his left center, the mistake actually benefited his second attack by elongating the brigade line enough to threaten Knipe's right flank.[21]

Before beginning his second drive, O'Neal received another regiment to extend his line even further. Col. Ellison Capers led the 24th South Carolina of Gist's Brigade, Walker's Division, Hardee's Corps. The regiment had been left on picket duty along Howell's Mill Road when the Army of Tennessee shifted to the right earlier that day. Reynolds's Brigade swept past the South Carolina regiment when it advanced that afternoon. Capers had no orders to join the assault, so he began to pull his men back in order to find his own brigade. But Stewart saw the regiment and stopped it because Walthall had told him he needed more troops. Stewart sent Capers to Walthall, who temporarily assigned his regiment to O'Neal's Brigade. Just as the Carolinians came under fire, Capers was slightly wounded, and Lieut. Col. Jesse S. Jones took command. O'Neal placed the 24th on the far left of his line in time for the second attack, and it played a large role in the effort.[22]

The second attack on Williams's division pressed along the entire Union line. On the left, Horace Boughton's 143rd New York of Robinson's brigade intensified its fire. Some Confederates were shot down only thirty yards from the Union line. Farther to the right, Rogers's 123rd New York of Knipe's brigade stood behind their quickly improvised breastwork of building timber and delivered heavy fire at the Rebels emerging from the woods. "The boys loaded and fired with such rapidity," recalled Henry C. Morhous, "that their guns became so heated that they could not hold their hand on the barrel." When John Smith's rifle went off before he finished loading it, shooting out the ramrod, Smith had to look for a spare before he could resume firing.[23]

The Confederates exerted great pressure on Knipe's right flank, compelling a rush of reinforcements to that threatened sector. Williams ordered Ruger to send help, and Ruger dispatched Col. John H. Ketcham's 150th New York from his brigade. Ketcham led the regiment forward but could not find sufficient room for all his men. Only three companies managed to worm into the center of Knipe's line and opened a heavy fire at the Confederates. While Maj. Alfred B. Smith directed these three companies, Ketcham lined up the other seven companies a short distance behind to act as a reserve. "Some of the men loaded and fired so fast that their rifles became overheated," recalled Edward O. Bartlett. As occurred with Rogers's 123rd New York, the barrels became so hot they could not be touched.[24]

Farther to the left, Knipe stood behind the 123rd New York to observe its heavy fire on O'Neal's men. As Rogers walked toward him, Knipe excitedly blurted "Colonel, the best d-d regiment in my brigade!" When Knipe saw three men skulk from the ranks, he personally caught and forced them back into line, telling regimental officers to shoot them if they ran again.[25]

Sensing the intensity of the fight, Col. Francis H. West wanted to do something with his 31st Wisconsin. Not yet assigned to a brigade, West nervously held his men as a general reserve behind Williams's division until moving forward toward the 123rd New York. The Wisconsin regiment was relatively new and as yet inexperienced. The veterans had subjected it to a lot of nagging ever since the regiment joined Sherman's army group only a few days before. Now the stout men of the 123rd New York called out "Go back we don't want you! We can hold this line without help. Go where you are needed, you can't relieve us." West got the message and moved his regiment away.[26]

The Federals were indeed putting up a good fight with a sustained and well-delivered fire that echoed across the rugged landscape and filled the woods with smoke. In the 123rd New York, Rice Bull fired seventy rounds that day and reported that some of his comrades shot off 100 rounds. While some regiments had to be resupplied twice with cartridges, the men of Selfridge's 46th Pennsylvania also had to replenish their cartridge boxes once during the fight.[27]

To deliver such prodigious amounts of fire, the Federals continued shooting almost without stopping. There were brief lulls as they took time to let the barrels cool or to swab them in order to remove powder residue. Rice

Bull saw more than one musket prematurely discharge as the new cartridge was placed in the overheated barrels. When this happened to one of Bull's comrades, the man was very much taken by surprise, especially because the premature explosion threw away his ramrod, and he could not immediately continue firing. But the man was so worked up emotionally that he shook his fist in the direction of the enemy and yelled "Take that you _____ and see how you like it."[28]

The rapid firing produced a thick cloud of powder smoke that covered the battlefield, made worse by the rapid firing of Winegar's guns close to the line of the 123rd New York. "The clouds of smoke … poured down on us to hide everything but the flash of the enemy's guns that gave us their position," commented Bull. The smoke colored the men's skin. By the end of the battle "we presented a strange appearance, smoke and powder stains had covered our faces and made them look as blue as indigo. The day had been hot and we were as wet as though we had been in the water." Some of the New York infantrymen were little more than twenty feet from the artillery, and the loud thumping of the cannon affected their ears. "For two days our hearing was almost gone," Bull reported, and "it was several days before it was again normal."[29]

While some men of the 123rd New York had tried to shirk their duty, most stayed in line and contributed to the regiment's sterling performance on the hot afternoon of July 20. Many slightly wounded officers and enlisted men refused to seek medical aid in the rear. Henry Morhous recalled the story of Pvt. Henry Chapman of Company I, who had enlisted early in 1864 and was shot in the left breast at Peach Tree Creek. He had enough strength to give his rifle and equipment to Capt. O. S. Hall and told him he knew he would "have no further use for them, for I have fought my last fight." Chapman thanked Hall for being kind to him and then walked a short distance to the rear and lay down. He died less than two hours later.[30]

Morhous recalled another affecting story of loss at Peach Tree Creek. Capt. Henry O. Wiley of Company K had purchased a bottle of wine while on recruiting service but kept it through the Atlanta campaign. Early on the morning of July 20, he sensed the need to share it with his comrades. Four other officers joined him in drinking the contents at breakfast that day. "We may never all be together again, so I think we had better drink it," Wiley commented. By the end of the day, two of the party, including Wiley, lay dead, and another was in the hospital badly wounded.[31]

The noise of Knipe's battle echoed across the valley of Peach Tree Creek as the Federals stood firm against O'Neal's second attack. Bull credited the improvised breastworks made of timber from the deserted houses as playing a key role in his brigade's stand. It protected many men from the return fire delivered by the Alabama and South Carolina troops engaged on this part of the battlefield, much of that fire delivered at ranges of twenty-five yards according to Rogers of the 123rd New York.[32]

Col. James L. Selfridge had placed his 46th Pennsylvania on the far right of Knipe's line with its right flank resting on a little knoll. While the regiment was positioned in the open, a thick cover of timber shielded the ground west of the road. Through this timber, the troops of Jones's 24th South Carolina began to turn Selfridge's flank. The left flank of Palmer's Fourteenth Corps was too far to the right and rear to protect him. When enfilade fire began to descend on the Pennsylvania men, Selfridge refused his right wing, capturing three Carolina Rebels in the process as an indication of how far Jones had managed to creep around the right end of the Union line. Selfridge asked Knipe for help, and Knipe asked Williams to loan him a regiment.[33]

Ruger's brigade supplied the reinforcement. Already occupying the partially fortified spot just vacated by Moore's brigade of Johnson's division, Ruger's men were busy working on the breastworks when the call for help arrived. Knipe personally chose the regiment from Ruger's command. According to Edmund Randolph Brown of the 27th Indiana, Knipe "was a mercurial, demonstrative little man always; but now he was wrought up more than common. He was frantic." He spoke with "loud, impassioned tones, and with many vigorous gesticulations." Hooker happened to be nearby and saw the commotion. Riding over, the corps commander pointed to a regiment in Ruger's line. "No-o, no-o, I don't' want that one," Knipe replied loudly and started to walk away. Hooker sent a staff officer to retrieve the excited brigadier and pointed to the 27th Indiana. "All right!" said Knipe, "I'll take that one.'" He placed himself before the regiment and called out "Twenty-seventh Indiana, I want you. This old brigade never has been whipped, and it never will be whipped."[34]

Col. Silas Colgrove moved the regiment forward seventy-five yards, running forward with Knipe ahead of his men so the two officers could point out the position it was to occupy along a dilapidated fence that bordered a ravine. To the left lay the open ground where the 46th Pennsylvania was located and to the right and front "a jungle of trees and bushes." The ravine lay to the right of Colgrove's position, and a branch of it covered the regiment's front. The 24th South Carolina approached through that jungle and settled near its edge to deliver heavy fire on Colgrove's men, who returned it even though they could hardly see human targets.[35]

One of the heaviest firefights of the battle at Peach Tree Creek now erupted. Federals who crowded behind the first rank at the old fence reloaded muskets for their comrades in front, as many of the Indiana men fired more than 100 rounds that afternoon. Colgrove became an early casualty of the fight. While lying on his side just behind the regimental line, an unexploded shell hit a tree limb and deflected straight for his position. It hit the ground just under his body and "lifted him up several feet and whirled him over and over," recalled Edmund Randolph Brown. "It was strange that he was not killed, but he was hurt more seriously than the first examination indicated." Colgrove suffered a major injury to his arm and a serious contusion to his side. His sword was "bent and twisted like a piece of tin or scrap-iron that has passed through hot fire." Colgrove was so badly hurt he never commanded the regiment again. Lieut. Col. John R. Fesler took charge of the 27th Indiana.[36]

Knipe excitedly paced up and down behind the regiment for some time, encouraging the men in their heated exchange with the 24th South Carolina. An Indiana sergeant saw him and interjected an element of humor in the tense situation. "General, have you any chewing tobacco?" he called. Knipe stopped, pulled out a small plug, and gave to the sergeant, who gazed upon it as if deciding whether to take all or nothing. Knipe noticed his expression and "in a perfectly natural, though plaintive, tone,—all of his strained, keyed-up condition entirely gone,—'That's all I've got.'" The men within hearing laughed as the sergeant produced a pocket knife and cut a small piece off. Knipe retrieved the rest and continued his pacing.[37]

Williams brought more reinforcements to Knipe's aid, ordering Robinson to send two regiments from his brigade. Robinson dispatched one of his reserve units, Lieut. Col. Edward S. Salomon's 82nd Illinois, and detached Lieut. Col. John B. Le Sage's 101st Illinois from his main formation. Both regiments headed to the far right of Knipe's line to support the 46th Pennsylvania and 27th Indiana, which were resisting the most serious pressure of any units in the division.[38]

Salomon moved his men on the double-quick, losing several of them along the way to enemy fire. By the time he reached the vicinity of the 27th Indiana, the Confederates were only thirty-five yards away. Salomon's troops opened a heavy fire, which, according to Max Schlund, "had a terrific effect" on them. But O'Neal's men continued to press forward until they were in places only ten steps from the blazing Federal line. When the Rebels fell back, many men of the 82nd Illinois, worked up by the excitement of battle, called out, "Come on Johnny, you coward Southerner!"[39]

Salomon estimated that the men of his 82nd Illinois fired up to 140 rounds each over a space of three hours during the battle of Peach Tree Creek. If true, that amounted to one round every one and a quarter minutes, which is consistent with rapid firing rates in other Civil War battles. Max Schlund estimated the regiment fired 200 rounds per man.[40]

Thomas H. Ruger, whose brigade supplied Knipe the 27th Indiana, had graduated from West Point but entered the law profession before becoming colonel of the 3rd Wisconsin. He had already sent the 150th New York forward before dispatching the 27th Indiana. The rest of his brigade remained in place waiting for the call to go into action. The 3rd Wisconsin held Ruger's right flank fairly close to the left flank of Johnson's division, Palmer's corps. In fact, a few of the right companies of the 3rd Wisconsin fired obliquely to help Fourteenth Corps troops when Daniel H. Reynolds's Arkansas brigade attacked them soon after O'Neal's men moved against Williams. Although not really engaged, the 3rd Wisconsin was exposed to much random fire and lost three men in the battle of Peach Tree Creek. The story was much the same for the other regiments in Ruger's brigade, with some suffering the loss of several men even though they were not really part of the fight.[41]

Capt. William Merrell of the 141st New York of Knipe's brigade had been working diligently on making a bridge over Peach Tree Creek when O'Neal initially struck the Federal line. Suddenly a flood of refugees from the division, "camp followers, pack mules, darkey servants, and some of the skirmish line" came rushing toward the creek. Most of Merrell's pioneers got caught up in this rush and went north of the stream with it, leaving him only three men on the south side, who tried to run away, too. Merrell managed to get in front of these men and physically force them to remain. "I suppose they thought it another Bull Run for Washington," Merrell wryly commented in his memoirs. Just then an ordnance officer appeared and asked if he could cross his wagons over the bridge. Merrell allowed him and was hugely relieved to see that the long stringers he had used as the main supports held under the weight of three loaded wagons and their six-mule teams.[42]

An order arrived that Merrell should form a line and stop all stragglers from crossing to the north side of the creek, but he also learned that the 141st New York was heavily engaged. Anxious to help, he left another officer in charge of the bridge and made his way forward to Knipe's position. He arrived to find that Capt. Elisha G. Baldwin's 141st was short of ammunition. Merrell volunteered to procure more, carrying an ammunition box to the regiment, breaking it open, and distributing the cartridges along the line. He then took an abandoned musket and contributed to the regiment's fire. When he had time to contemplate the effects of Peach Tree Creek on the 141st New York, Merrell was stunned. Colonel Logie, "a young lawyer from Gorning, N.Y., a graduate from a military school and a strict disciplinarian, was riddled with Minnie balls. Our lieutenant colonel [McNett] lost his right arm close to the shoulder. Our major [C. W. Clanharty] was shot through the thigh and our adjutant was shot through both thighs, only myself and Captain Baldwin left of the line officers for duty."[43]

Williams's division had indeed fought one of the hottest fights in the battle of Peach Tree Creek. O'Neal's Brigade drove deep into the Union formation and held in the woods for some time while punishing the 141st New York, 27th Indiana, and several other Federal regiments. The Confederates could not push Williams's men away, but they held at high tide and did all they could.[44]

Washington Bryan Crumpton and a handful of his comrades in the 37th Mississippi had also tried their best that afternoon. After O'Neal ordered the regiment to wheel and face the enemy soon after crossing the Union skirmish line, Crumpton and his mates fired rapidly for what seemed like an hour. They scrounged ammunition from the dead and wounded and adopted a quick-loading plan—striking the butt of their muskets on the ground rather than using a rammer to push the charge home. "It was almost like a repeating rifle," Crumpton later reported.[45]

When the pressure grew too much, Crumpton and his comrades fell back, firing at a line of Yankees that had taken position to the north, and soon came across Walthall. The division leader told them to take post on Howell's Mill Road, and he rounded up more stragglers until nearly 500 men had gathered. An unidentified colonel showed up, "drunk as a fool," Crumpton insisted, and led them in an advance on the enemy. Crumpton guided the group forward toward the same position he and his comrades had vacated, but by then Federal troops barred the way, and many in the improvised unit fell under close-range rifle fire and retired. Crumpton's story demonstrated the finality of Confederate defeat. Regimental commanders reported that they had no support to right or left by this stage of the fight and decided that retiring was the best course of action. O'Neal confirmed that decision, as his scattered men retreated by about 7 P.M., according to most Union observers.[46]

The Federal survivors of O'Neal's attacks were proud of their reaction to the sudden appearance of the enemy, their stout defense of an uncomfortable position, and their eventual victory on July 20. The Confederates "charged our hole [sic] line in sollade column," reported William H. Carrier of the 3rd Wisconsin to his wife, and they "tried to brake our lines but could not come it." James Robinson praised his brigade highly in his official report. "Never was the hardihood and temper of my entire command more completely and thoroughly tested. The battle was sprung upon it at an unexpected moment, and with a fury not hitherto exceeded in the annals of the campaign." Williams echoed the praise of his subordinates by noting that, "Not a regiment was broken or shaken, but without cover and in a fair field a little over two-thirds of my command received and rolled back the repeated assaults."[47]

Williams had some artillery support from Winegar's and Woodbury's New York batteries. Winegar fired a total of eighty-four rounds and lost four men and six horses, while Woodbury fired 178 rounds. Neither battery played a key role in defending Williams's position. The rugged, wooded terrain inhibited gunners' ability to locate and reach the enemy, but at least the big guns added some degree of reassurance to the harried Union infantrymen.[48]

Williams never reported his troop strength, but the combined total of men in Geary's and Ward's divisions amounted to about 7,000. If that is a guide, then about 3,500 men fought in Williams's ranks. He lost 580 of them, or 16.5 percent. Knipe suffered very heavily. With a little more than 1,000 men, he counted casualties of 288 troops, or 28.8 percent. In fact, Knipe accounted for nearly half the losses of Williams's division. Selfridge's 46th Pennsylvania lost 113 men, while the 123rd New York suffered forty-seven casualties, nearly one-third of all its losses during the four-month long campaign for Atlanta. The 141st New York lost seventy-eight men, including its colonel, lieutenant colonel, major, and adjutant. Col. Warren W. Packer's 5th Connecticut lost sixty-four men, which was the second highest loss rate it suffered in the entire war (next to the battle of Cedar Mountain). According to William T. Shimp, one company of sixteen men lost eleven killed and wounded that afternoon.[49]

O'Neal's Brigade suffered, too, in accomplishing this damage to Williams. Out of 1,050 men engaged, he lost 279 or 26.5 percent. Holland's 37th Mississippi took 210 men into the battle and lost forty-eight of them, amounting to 22.8 percent. The deep penetration of the Federal position and the fact, as reported by O'Neal, that his brigade took 293 prisoners allowed some Confederates to view the attack as a victory of sorts. "We whipped them in the fight the other day," Robert W. Banks of the 37th Mississippi told his father. O'Neal also put the best face on his effort. "We drove the enemy nearly a mile, captured some of his works, and had punished him severely, and were executing the order of the major-general to kill or capture everything in our front" when, due to lack of support to right and left, the brigade was compelled to retire.[50]

Daniel H. Reynolds led the other brigade of Walthall's Division that participated in the battle of Peach Tree Creek. Born in Ohio and educated to be a lawyer, Reynolds practiced in Arkansas before deciding to serve the Confederacy at the outset of the war. He led the 1st Arkansas Mounted Rifles and eventually rose to brigade command. Reynolds's small Arkansas brigade had done heavy picket duty along Peach Tree Creek for days before the battle, fighting a fierce engagement on July 19 with Dilworth's brigade of Davis's division, Fourteenth Corps. Early the next morning, Quarles's Brigade of Walthall's Division relieved Reynolds, and the Arkansas troops took their place in the division line. Because Reynolds did not have the services of his 9th Arkansas, which remained on picket duty and then joined Quarles's Brigade later in the day, he took only 540 men into action on July 20.[51]

Reynolds moved out from the Peach Tree Creek Line at midafternoon, guiding his right flank along Howell's Mill Road. His regiments marched by the right of companies for up to 500 yards in order to negotiate the heavy timber north of the line. Like all Confederate units that preceded it, the brigade reformed at the Confederate skirmish pits. While waiting to allow for the echelon maneuver, a comforting rumor circulated through the ranks. As Robert H. Dacus of the 1st Arkansas Mounted Rifles (dismounted) put it, "word was passed down the line that General Johnston was in command for that evening. This was done in order to stimulate the men and give them confidence in the move." Dacus implied that he did not necessarily believe the rumor, but it did no harm to the men's morale. Walthall had intended Quarles's Brigade to form to the rear of his other two brigades as a reserve, but Quarles was still too far west to do so. Hood's major shift of the Army of Tennessee to the right just before the attack took the division a good distance east of Quarles, and there was no possibility of retrieving the brigade soon.[52]

When Reynolds advanced, keeping west of Howell's Mill Road, his Arkansas men handily captured the Federal skirmish line like all other Confederate units before them. The Union skirmish pits were located in "a dense thicket of small oaks and undergrowth," according to Col. Henry G. Bunn, whose 4th Arkansas was on Reynolds's extreme left. Continuing north, the advance became more problematic. Reynolds's right wing slowed down with some men staying in the captured Union works and others moving forward, but the left wing moved on in greater unity and zeal.[53]

Reynolds's Brigade mostly confronted the left wing of Anson McCook's brigade of Johnson's division, Fourteenth Corps. McCook's left flank barely extended a short distance east of Howell's Mill Road. Johnson had been waiting all day for Hooker to advance Williams's division so he could also move forward, but that was not to be. He had placed Moore's brigade entirely east of Howell's Mill Road to cover his left flank and ordered McCook to postpone constructing fortifications, anticipating an imminent move forward. When the Confederate attack began, Ruger relieved Moore and allowed the latter to take place in Johnson's line just to the right of McCook.

Ruger's men now were within firing range of McCook and about even with McCook's flank.[54]

McCook's men were taken by surprise and with only half-finished breastworks. The brigade had formed two lines, but irregularities in the ground compelled one regiment to be separated from the rest. Lieut. Col. Douglas Hapeman's 104th Illinois held the left flank of the first line just west of Howell's Mill Road. A ravine passed by his right flank and curved a bit toward the rear of the regiment. McCook's first line continued with the 15th Kentucky, which was positioned 125 yards to the right rear of Hapeman's regiment. The 42nd Indiana lay to the right of the 15th Kentucky, and the 88th Indiana anchored the right of McCook's first line. Behind and some distance from Hapeman's command lay the 10th Wisconsin, the only regiment of the brigade positioned east of Howell's Mill Road, with the 21st Wisconsin behind the 15th Kentucky, the 94th Ohio to the right of the Wisconsin men, and the 33rd Ohio anchoring the right of McCook's second line. To Hapeman's front, the underbrush lay thick among the trees, making it difficult to gauge the approach of an enemy.[55]

Hapeman recalled that the Confederates made an appearance only a few minutes after the sound of gunfire could be heard on Hooker's Twentieth Corps front. Opening fire as much by sound as by sight, the 104th Illinois let loose a volley into the trees. It stopped the Arkansans in their tracks. Lieut. Col. Morton G. Galloway's 1st Arkansas Mounted Rifles (dismounted), located on the extreme right of Reynolds's line and just west of Howell's Mill Road, settled down to exchange rounds with McCook's troops. But the rest of Reynolds's Brigade moved by the left flank into the ravine and then marched forward to approach the right flank of Hapeman's regimental line. The left wing of Reynolds's Brigade "attacked the regiment square on the right flank," Hapeman reported. The Confederates had found and exploited the 125-yard gap between the 104th Illinois and the rest of McCook's command. "They poured a terrible fire along the rear of [the] rude works," Hapeman continued. He struggled to refuse the regiment's position, moving Companies A, B, and C so as to form a new line perpendicular to the other companies. As these companies evacuated their works, the Arkansans occupied up to 100 yards of the abandoned fortifications.[56]

After refusing his flank, Hapeman looked for support from the rest of the brigade. The men of the 15th Kentucky and 42nd Indiana offered aid by firing their muskets at comparatively long range to disorient the Confederates and compel them to stop for a time, but the Rebels continued to fire toward the Illinois regiment. Hapeman had asked McCook for support even

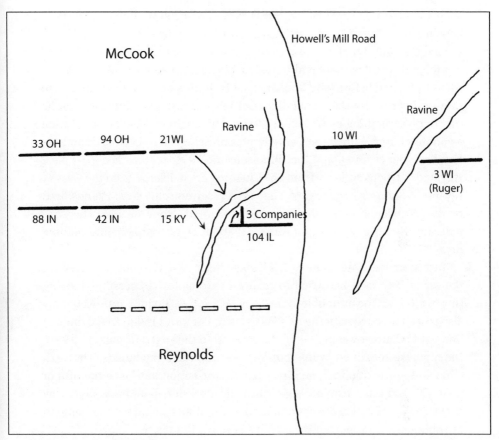

Reynolds versus McCook

before the enemy appeared in his front, and now McCook was beginning to bring it forward.[57]

Before help arrived, Hapeman's troops suffered a great deal. His left wing was comparatively sheltered from the fire to his right because the ground crested slightly about midway along the regimental line, but the right wing was punished severely by the Confederate fire. William Wirt Calkins believed up to half of the men in the regimental right wing fell in this fire. Hapeman's adjutant was shot through the head while rallying the troops and Capt. William Strawn of Company F later concluded that the veteran coolness of the men was the only thing that saved the regiment. As Calkins put it, they "took it for granted that to simply obey orders was the surest way to come out all right."[58]

McCook could bring many more men into this fight than Reynolds, and soon the blue tide came rolling forward. Capt. Jacob W. Roby's 10th Wisconsin moved forward from its position anchoring the left end of McCook's second line, but it took position to the left and rear of Hapeman's embattled regiment where it was not really needed. Hapeman asked again for help, but to his right, and before long Maj. Michael H. Fitch's 21st Wisconsin began to move forward from the second line. But before it arrived, Hapeman felt he had to do something extraordinary to save his regiment. He personally led a countercharge against the Confederates pressing his right wing. Hand-to-hand combat erupted, and the Illinoisans took a Rebel flag. For their part, Reynolds's troops suffered from an enfilading fire delivered from the west by several of McCook's regiments. They even received some stray rounds fired by the 1st Arkansas Mounted Rifles (dismounted) from the east. The Confederates finally gave way and retreated about eighty yards before holding firm.[59]

Just after the Confederates fell back, Fitch's 21st Wisconsin arrived on the scene. The men had tried to rush forward as fast as possible, moving through the ravine at double-quick. Col. Marion C. Taylor's 15th Kentucky also moved forward with the 21st Wisconsin. The 42nd Indiana remained in line but had already contributed its fire to help the 104th Illinois. The 88th Indiana also remained in line but lost four men to stray bullets. The 94th Ohio and 33rd Ohio took no direct part in the action but lost a handful of men. The 3rd Wisconsin of Ruger's brigade also contributed in a small way to the saving of McCook's command. Several of its companies were able to fire obliquely in support of the embattled 104th Illinois.[60]

As soon as the Confederates gave way, McCook reestablished his skirmish line, and Hapeman's men began to collect abandoned muskets from the battlefield. In his report of the campaign, filed in early September 1864, Hapeman claimed the 104th Illinois lost thirty men, all of them from the right wing. But he set the losses at forty-six in his diary entry made the same day of the battle. "The losses were appalling for so small a command," asserted Calkins, "and cast a shadow of gloom over the Regiment." Capt. William Strawn consoled his friend Capt. John S. H. Doty, one of three company commanders lost in the brief but vicious fight with Reynolds. Doty was hit by five bullets and asked Strawn to pray for him. "His blood saturating my clothing," recalled Strawn, "I held him until he was carried to the rear on a stretcher." While burying the dead of the regiment, several bodies were found to be pierced by bayonets.[61]

Everyone praised Hapeman's conduct during the fight. A modest, unassuming man, Hapeman did not mention his personal leadership of the countercharge that finally broke Rebel resistance in his official report. Three decades later, his men decided that his action should be rewarded. They wrote to the War Department and secured a Medal of Honor for Hapeman in 1897.[62]

Many members of the 104th Illinois criticized McCook for leaving them exposed and unconnected to the rest of the brigade. William Wirt Calkins nursed his feelings quietly for a few days after the battle until an account appeared in a Cincinnati newspaper praising McCook's handling of his command. "Bah!," Calkins wrote in the regimental history. "The Brigade having been placed in an awkward position and made to believe there was no enemy within striking distance, when the time came, handled itself!"[63]

Despite the problems of unit placement, McCook reacted well enough to support Hapeman's heroic stand, and the left end of Johnson's division held firm. There are no casualty statistics for the 15th Kentucky, 10th Wisconsin, or 42nd Indiana, but the other five regiments in McCook's brigade lost a total of sixty-seven men. The 104th Illinois accounted for 68.6 percent of the brigade losses. Hapeman's regiment did most of the fighting for the brigade that day and understandably felt proud of its achievement in repelling Reynolds's Brigade.[64]

In contrast, gloom pervaded the ranks of Reynolds's command. "Thus we had made a desperate charge," wrote Robert H. Dacus, "lost many of the best men in our corps and accomplished nothing." The brigade could do little more than hang on near McCook's position and fire at the Yankees. Members of the 1st Arkansas Mounted Rifles (dismounted) fired up to 100 rounds each during the course of the battle. At 5 P.M., several regiments in the brigade unaccountably fell back. When Galloway inquired, he was told it was by order of Reynolds, so he pulled the 1st Arkansas Mounted Rifles back as well. When Reynolds realized what was going on, he stopped the retrograde movement, claiming to have issued no such order. The regiments moved back to their close position and stayed there. Galloway was keenly aware that O'Neal's Brigade east of the Howell's Mill Road was nowhere to be seen. He posted pickets along the roadway to screen his exposed right flank until Reynolds pulled the entire brigade back to the Peach Tree Creek Line by 9 P.M. Reynolds reported losses of 67 of the 540 men he took into battle, or 12.4 percent.[65]

Walthall tried to bring Quarles's Brigade into action, but it proved impossible. He sent a message for the men to hurry over to Howell's Mill Road, creating an air of crisis in the ranks that spurred the troops to march as fast as possible. Arriving about dusk, just when O'Neal and Reynolds fell back, Quarles's men prepared to attack, but the order was never issued.[66]

Ending the battle at dusk, Walthall felt his men had done all they could

Anson G. McCook, whose brigade repelled Reynolds's Arkansas troops even though the 104th Illinois was in a detached position from the rest. Many of his men blamed him for the positioning that endangered the Illinois regiment. (Library of Congress, LC-DIG-cwpbh-03858)

that day, and Stewart supported that view in his official report. Walthall noted that his two brigades captured the enemy skirmish line and pressed hard against the main Union position near Peach Tree Creek. He blamed their failure to capture that position on lack of support from neighboring units, a common complaint among Rebel commanders. "If the whole of our line had pressed forward with the same energy and determination which the troops of this division did," argued O'Neal, "we would have carried the day and driven the enemy in confusion across the creek."[67]

Stewart's Army of Mississippi had not yet expended all efforts that day. His artillery came into play and pummeled the opposing line for some time. Maj. William C. Preston, who commanded one of four artillery battalions assigned to Stewart's Army of Mississippi, brought the guns of Selden's Alabama Battery, now under Lieut. Charles W. Lovelace, into action. Preston placed them just west of Howell's Mill Road and behind Reynolds's Brigade after the Arkansas troops had moved forward for the attack. Lovelace had the disadvantage of being in an open field on a descending slope and was heavily damaged as a result, but his gunners returned fire with vigor. Preston personally directed some of this fire until he was killed by an artillery round. He was the son of Brig. Gen. John S. Preston and the brother of Sally Buchanan Campbell Preston, who was widely believed to have been the intended fiancée of John Bell Hood.[68]

The men of Selden's Battery experienced what Lovelace called "the first serious engagement in which the battery had ever been engaged, and the ordeal was a severe one." But the Alabama gunners "behaved with a courage and coolness which could not have been surpassed." They continued firing until running out of ammunition. Maj. John D. Myrick's Battalion of Stewart's Army of Mississippi provided relief for Lovelace's hard-pressed men. The Lookout Battery of Tennessee under Lieut. Richard L. Watkins rolled forward to relieve Selden's Battery. The more experienced gunners of the Lookout Battery delivered a scorching fire at Federal guns that posed the greatest threat to their position. Watkins directed the fire of his four Napoleons with precision, largely silencing the Union guns in about half an hour. He continued to pound the Federal position until a bit after sunset, putting up with Federal skirmish fire the entire time. Watkins fired a total of 260 rounds, or sixty-five projectiles from each gun. He lost fifteen men wounded, two horses killed and one horse wounded on July 20.[69]

Lovelace and Watkins primarily fired at the position held by Marshall F. Moore's brigade of Johnson's division. In fact, Moore reported his men endured a "terrific fire" of enemy artillery that afternoon. He suffered thirty-seven losses both from the artillery and in skirmishing, even though the brigade was not attacked by Rebel infantry. Lieut. Ben Park Dewey of the 38th Indiana was reading a novel while the regiment waited in Moore's brigade line. A shell fragment hit his hand, but Dewey was convinced the novel deflected most of its destructive force. The only real injury was a broken forefinger.[70]

Federal guns went into action to counter this heavy Confederate fire. Capt. Hubert Dilger advanced his Battery I, 1st Ohio Light Artillery well forward of the main Union line. According to Richard W. Johnson, Dilger violated orders prohibiting the unnecessary exposure of his gun crews. Known as Leather Breeches because of his habit of wearing buckskin clothing, Dilger lost some men to Confederate skirmish fire. When Johnson remonstrated with him about it after the battle, Dilger claimed he lost no men. Johnson pressed him again, and Dilger finally understood what his division commander meant. "Oh, yes, with dem leetle balls; none by artillery." Dilger "did not count a man killed unless he was killed by a cannon ball or shell," Johnson explained in his memoirs. "He was a fearless fellow and had a splendid battery, and was never so happy as when engaged with the enemy."[71]

In addition to artillery, Stewart tried to engage his reserve division in the battle of Peach Tree Creek. Commanded by Maj. Gen. Samuel G. French, it anchored the left end of Hood's Peach Tree Creek Line. Born in New Jersey and a graduate of West Point, French had served in the Mexican War and had married into the plantation aristocracy of Mississippi before the outbreak of the Civil War. He had largely been in various backwaters of that conflict until thrust into the Atlanta campaign in charge of a division.[72]

At 4 P.M., French received word from Stewart's headquarters "to move forward and attack the enemy, looking well to your left." He was told to maintain an interval of 300 to 400 yards with Walthall's Division to the right and instructed clearly as to Hood's overall plan to strike the enemy and then drive him left toward the Chattahoochee River. French could use only two of his three brigades. Brig. Gen. Claudius W. Sears's Brigade was his largest, but it was responsible for holding the Western and Atlantic Railroad near its crossing of the Chattahoochee River. Sears also strung out pickets along the south bank of the river and the southern bluffs of Peach Tree Creek. Cockrell's Missouri Brigade, now led by Col. Elijah Gates, was positioned with its left flank on the road between Marietta and Atlanta, and Brig. Gen. Matthew D. Ector's Brigade lay to Gates's right. French issued orders for Gates and Ector to move by the right flank until they neared Howell's Mill Road. Together, the two small brigades numbered only 1,500 men. Upon completing this maneuver the troops fronted north and then moved through the timber north of the Peach Tree Creek Line by the right flank of compa-

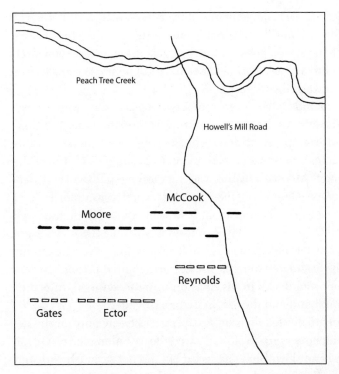

Peach Tree Creek

Howell's Mill Road

McCook

Moore

Reynolds

Gates   Ector

nies. They finally reformed a battle line at 5 P.M. just south of the location of Selden's Battery.[73]

French took the order to watch well to the left seriously. He felt more comfortable stopping Ector at this location behind Selden's Battery and ordering Gates to move forward alone. As Gates advanced until he was stopped by a large mill pond about 300 yards from Moore's brigade of Johnson's division, French personally scouted the ground to the west. He found that a large open field was in the area and came to the conclusion that the Federals were making no moves to flank his division. French therefore ordered Ector to move toward Gates's position through a skirt of trees to mask his movement from the enemy, and Ector did so, closing up with Gates and reinforcing the static position assumed by French's two little brigades.[74]

French also joined the two brigades and, upon examining their position more closely, became worried. He noticed that a ridge to the left could command his position. By this time Stewart had ridden to the place occupied by Ector and Gates as well. When French told him of his worry, Stewart ordered French to place some artillery on that ridge and support it with Sears's Brigade. French told Ector to take charge of Gates's Brigade as well as his own and rode off to make these arrangements. Stewart remained with Ector and Gates to observe events, but it was already late in the day. French was able to do little more than select a position for the guns on the ridge. Soon after, the battle dwindled to a close. Darkness began to fall before the artillery or Sears could move toward the ridge.[75]

Meanwhile, Ector and Gates simply remained in place, sometimes showing their men at the edge of the timber fronting Moore's brigade. The Confederates made no attempt to advance and challenge the Federals on this part of Johnson's line. It was just as well. Lieut. Col. Daniel F. Griffin of the 38th Indiana thought Moore's position was very strong and the Confederates "dared not try us." Gates's regiments endured pretty accurate Federal artillery fire for some time that afternoon. It "was heavy, and their guns well handled," admitted Capt. Joseph Boyce of the 1st Missouri (CS). "They got our range in short order, but the shells burst just as they passed over our position, and as the fragments were blown forward, injured no one." Nevertheless, French reported losses in his division of nineteen men, fifteen of them in Gates's command and the rest in Ector's Brigade.[76]

Johnson was fortunate; his division was pressed heavily only on the extreme left where Hapeman's 104th Illinois saved the day. Along the rest of his line, Rebel artillery and skirmishers harassed but did not seriously threaten his position. Johnson's division lost 125 men on July 20. McCook's brigade accounted for 53.6 percent of the division casualties. Surg. Charles W. Jones, who served as Johnson's chief medical officer, transported the wounded to Vining's Station north of the Chattahoochee River for treatment.[77]

Palmer's other two divisions were not attacked by the Confederates on July 20, but Absalom Baird's command, immediately to the right of Johnson, received a good deal of artillery fire from Selden's Battery and the Lookout Battery. In fact, Baird characterized the artillery fire "as constant and as terrible as any that I have ever witnessed." He argued that the loss to his division was "considerable" although he did not provide statistics. James A. Connolly, one of Baird's staff officers, claimed the division lost only twenty men. Connolly also was convinced that the troops would have handily repulsed any advance by Confederate infantry because they "had worked all the night before building strong breastworks, and so were better prepared for the attack than many other Divisions."[78]

Davis's division, to Baird's right, also received some of the Confederate artillery fire and returned it with a few guns. For Davis's men, the battle of Peach Tree Creek played out on other parts of the long Union line. "I could see the smoke rise" off to the left and hear the sound of heavy musketry, wrote John J. Mercer of the 78th Illinois in his diary. Davis maintained a heavy skirmish line that fired at the enemy pickets, adding to the noise and smoke but contributing little to the progress of events that day.[79]

In an effort to find help for hard-pressed parts of his line, Thomas sent a message to Palmer asking for a brigade to be sent to Newton "at once." Two brigades or even a division would be better, the note read. Even though the message was sent at 5 P.M. and received later than that at Fourteenth Corps headquarters, Palmer did not respond to it. He could have spared troops but did not know what lay ahead in the Confederate attack plan. Playing it safe, Palmer retained his men, and Newton, as it turned out, needed no help.[80]

This business of approaching prepared parapets, from the rough nature of this wooded country, was perplexing and dangerous.
—Oliver O. Howard

All your troops should push hard for Atlanta, sweeping everything before them.—William T. Sherman

Rest of Day, July 20

While the Twentieth Corps and elements of the Fourth and Fourteenth Corps battled it out with Hardee and Stewart, the rest of Sherman's army group continued to advance cautiously along its planned route. Even though within relatively short range of the battle, no one recognized the sound of a heavy fight taking place to the west. News of the Confederate attack did not filter through the rest of Sherman's command until late in the night of July 20. Thomas's men fought their great battle with virtually no one outside the engaged divisions knowing that a battle was taking place.[1]

John Schofield continued to maneuver his Twenty-Third Corps in the intermediate space between Thomas's command and McPherson's Army of the Tennessee, mostly traversing the heavily timbered ground in the area of the South Fork of Peach Tree Creek. Jacob Cox's division had reached the area of Peyton's Plantation just south of the South Fork by the evening of July 19, close to where the road he used crossed Pea Vine Creek. Cox deployed his main line on the morning of July 20 to face the Confederate Outer Line, putting three brigades in position and holding one in reserve.[2]

Late in the afternoon, Milo Hascall brought his division forward and deployed it to the left of Cox. On Schofield's urging, Hascall then detached a brigade commanded by Col. William E. Hobson and sent it to Cox's right. Hobson sent the 111th Ohio and two companies of the 13th Kentucky forward as a heavy skirmish line. The troops captured a ridge "with some loss," driving back the Confederate skirmishers. When the Rebels counterattacked a bit later, they were repulsed. Hobson then extended Cox's line to the west. Meanwhile, to Cox's left, Col. Silas A. Strickland's brigade also advanced and drove Confederate skirmishers with "a hell of a whoop," as Lieut. Col. Thomas B. Waller of the 20th Kentucky put it. Strickland's men pushed the opposing skirmishers back to the Confederate Outer Line and firmed up their position extending from the left flank of Cox's division.[3]

Sherman traveled with Schofield's Army of the Ohio all day, expecting that Hood, if he attacked, would do so against either the Twenty-Third Corps or McPherson's command. By 6:10 P.M., when the battle of Peach Tree Creek was winding down, the latest word to reach Sherman's headquarters from Thomas was a dispatch written at noon, three hours before the battle began. It is unclear why there was such a long time lag between the sending of this dispatch and its delivery only a few miles away, but the delay kept Sherman in the dark as to developments on his right wing. For much of the time Sherman kept close to Strickland's brigade, and according to Col. George W. Gallup of the 14th Kentucky, he "often exposed himself to fire." One of Sherman's staff officers had his horse killed while close to the commander.[4]

The arduous task of David Stanley's and Thomas Wood's divisions of Howard's Fourth Corps was to keep pace with Schofield and try to cover the yawning gap between Sherman's right and left wings. Fortunately for the Federals, that gap existed in the cut-up and timbered ground between the North and South Forks of Peach Tree Creek, and the Confederates knew nothing about it. But Stanley and Wood were incapable of adequately covering the hole; in fact, they found it difficult to maneuver their brigades along the narrow roads so as to find Schofield and create the semblance of a line.

Stanley led the way with Wood following and Howard along with the column. The Federals crossed the South Fork of Peach Tree Creek on the morning of July 20, moving Col. Jacob E. Taylor's brigade across the stream. Taylor established a line to cover the pioneers as they rebuilt the burned bridge, and then he used artillery to support his infantry's push against Confederate skirmishers on a commanding ridge nearby. After taking the position, Taylor formed his brigade on the ridge and prepared to deal with the next high ground, the last Confederate skirmish line before the Rebel Peach Tree Creek Line and the Outer Line. Assembling eighteen guns, the Federals mounted a major push against this position. Taylor advanced about 3:30 P.M. and forced the Rebel skirmishers away. He stopped his main line about 100 yards beyond the captured position and sent a skirmish line forward, which advanced so close to the Rebel main position that the 21st Kentucky found it too dangerous to dig in while it was still daylight. Col. William Grose's brigade took position to Taylor's right, with his skirmishers also advancing within thirty yards of the Confederate line. Col. Isaac M. Kirby's brigade took position to the left of Taylor's brigade, with skirmishers also well advanced close to the enemy position.[5]

The Confederates who held this part of Hood's position mounted a serious effort to push the Union skirmishers back. They advanced a heavy skirmish line in the afternoon along Stanley's division sector. The Confederates came on with energy, but the Federals held their ground. The 101st Ohio of Kirby's brigade had no breastworks, and "for the first time in the campaign two forces met, without works, in an open field," commented William Lewis English. The regiment lost thirty-five men that day in a spirited but little-noticed fight. It was an "impulsive effort," Howard thought, but his men met it with steadiness.[6]

The Federals had another success late in the evening when Taylor energetically pushed his skirmishers forward once again to clear out Confederate troops who had not fully retreated from their earlier attempt to drive his men back. Lieut. Robert F. Drullinger of the 9th Indiana led this effort, which nabbed forty-three Confederate soldiers in the gathering dusk. The 30th Indiana supported this advance to Drullinger's right. The Federals lost no men in this push, which allowed them to properly form a well-connected skirmish screen before Stanley's division.[7]

Stanley opened communication with Schofield's headquarters on the morning of July 20 and by late evening extended his skirmish line to the left far enough to connect with the right flank of the Twenty-Third Corps. But to the right the huge gap still existed. Grose detached the 36th Indiana and 59th Illinois to screen that gap as far as they could until Wood's division made its appearance at about dark. Wood placed Col. Frederick Knefler's brigade to the right of Stanley's division and Col. William H. Gibson's brigade to Knefler's right, holding Brig. Gen. William B. Hazen's brigade in reserve on the north side of the South Fork of Peach Tree Creek. Wood extended his division line to cover as much of the gap as possible. Knefler and Gibson put every regiment they had in one line "with considerable intervals between, . . . leaving a large interval between the divisions, occupied only with a skirmish line." According to Howard's brother and staff member, this enabled the Fourth Corps troops to place Gibson's right flank close to the junction of the two forks of Peach Tree Creek. That still left about a mile and a half of ground uncovered between Wood and Newton. Wood's division was not engaged in skirmishing on July 20.[8]

"This business of approaching prepared parapets, from the rough nature of this wooded country, was perplexing and dangerous," Howard later wrote of his advance on July 20. Stanley and Wood accomplished all that was reasonably possible, just as Schofield had done. Neither force could have accomplished more given the terrain and the presence of a full Confederate line in their front that was protected by earthworks. By midafternoon, the Army of Tennessee had shifted dramatically to the right so that Stevenson's Division faced east, its left flank resting at the sharp angle where the north-facing Peach Tree Creek Line met the east-facing Outer Line. Cox's division of the Twenty-Third Corps and Stanley's division of the Fourth Corps faced Stevenson. Brown's Division extended the east-facing Outer Line to Stevenson's right in an effort to support the Confederate cavalry opposing McPherson's tentative advance toward Atlanta. To Stevenson's left, occupying the right end of the north-facing Peach Tree Creek Line, Clayton's Division opposed part of Stanley's division and all of Wood's deployed division. The left wing of Clayton's Division and Bate's Division of Hardee's Corps faced the gap of one and a half miles in the Union position.[9]

McPherson faced less opposition than did Schofield or Howard, yet he made slow, uncertain progress. Ironically, he worried his opposing Rebel commander so much that Joseph Wheeler called loudly for help, prompting a major and unexpected change in Hood's battle plans for July 20 at the last minute, a change that prevented Hardee from launching what might have been a promising second attack by his corps against Newton's embattled division.

Yet one wonders at the fact that McPherson, who controlled 25,000 men and was opposed by only 3,500 Rebel cavalry supported by 700 Georgia Militia, allowed himself to advance at a snail's pace on July 20. Albert Castel has estimated that both McPherson and Schofield advanced that day at a rate of one mile in three hours. The terrain accounted for Schofield's and Howard's slow pace, but McPherson had good roads and more open country to traverse. He missed a good opportunity; an aggressive advance that pushed Wheeler away and turned Brown's flank would have been disastrous for the Army of Tennessee, with most of its strength arrayed against Thomas along Peach Tree Creek.[10]

Wheeler failed to keep Army of Tennessee headquarters fully informed of developments on his front. He did request reinforcements at midmorning of July 20 but imparted no sense of emergency in his dispatches until late in the afternoon. As Castel has written, Hood's battle plan for July 20 was based on the assumption that he had time to deal with Thomas before McPherson approached close enough to Atlanta to pose a threat. Wheeler's late afternoon dispatches destroyed that assumption and forced Hood to call on Hardee for a division, and the only division Hardee could send was the one he was about to launch in an attack on Newton.[11]

McPherson therefore accomplished something on July 20, but it was a small part of what it might have been possible for him to do that day. As it was, the Army of the Tennessee got within long artillery range of Atlanta by that evening. Capt. Francis De Gress fired three shells from his Battery H, 1st Illinois Light Artillery at a range of two and a half miles. The 20-pounder Parrott rifles became the first to hurl artillery rounds into the city. McPherson positioned his infantry so as to be ready for striking the Confederate Outer Line the next day.[12]

At the end of the day's operations, McPherson informed Sherman that nothing but cavalry had been in his way and that he was near the main Rebel position fronting Atlanta. Sherman was disappointed, having expected more from his friend and favorite subordinate. At 1 A.M. of July 21, he responded to McPherson's report and softly criticized him for failing to capitalize on his opportunities.[13]

The Federals who rebuffed Hood's first attempt to save Atlanta spent the hot, humid evening of July 20 consolidating the positions they defended. Their commanders advanced skirmish lines as the Confederates fell back from the edge of the tree cover fronting the Peach Tree Creek Line. Amid sounds of moaning coming from the scattered enemy wounded, the Yankees moved entrenching tools forward to their main line and continued to strengthen the position along Collier Road with improved breastworks. In Newton's division, most work on the fortifications ended by about midnight so the men could catch some much-needed sleep, even though the sounds of pain from the wounded could be heard all night. The 97th Ohio in Blake's brigade kept one-third of its men awake and on duty to guard against a surprise attack, but the enemy had no intention of trying Newton's strong position once again.[14]

Many members of Newton's division tried to offer help to the wounded on the night of July 20. Confederate details had gathered some of their own injured wherever possible, but still many remained unattended on the battlefield. Ralsa C. Rice of the 125th Ohio established a picket line near the edge of the tree cover fronting the left wing of Newton's sector and then took time to track down some of the Confederate casualties before darkness ended the effort. "Dead and dying rebels lay strewn over the ground," he wrote after the war, "a harrowing, pitiful sight. The dead did not have that angry look which we ascribe to men fighting for their lives, but rather a sorrowful, frightful one of death by violence. I followed a trail of blood through the weeds to the creek. Here I found a young man in the agonies of death; grapeshot had torn across the body, disemboweling him. In his pain he had sought the creek and let himself down into the water. Poor fellow, I could do nothing to help him."[15]

When a Federal picket heard sounds coming from a nearby ravine, Rice investigated and found a seventeen-year-old Confederate badly wounded by a bullet through the leg. "We gave him hot coffee and food," Rice recalled, and he took down the man's name and address. The Rebel died in a Union hospital not long after, but Rice felt comforted in his old age to know "that he had been treated with the utmost kindness on our part." Rice also struck up a correspondence with the man's family after the war so they would know what happened to him. Another wounded Confederate taken in that evening was "a mere boy" according to Wilbur F. Hinman. He cried when the Federals treated him gently. "They told us that you-all would kill us if you took us prisoners," Hinman recalled the boy's words. "I didn't think you'd be so kind to me!"[16]

On the sector held by Ward's division of the Twentieth Corps, work proceeded that night on the breastworks even though the men were exhausted by the battle and the heat of the afternoon. "We worked all night, and a tireder and lamer set of men I never saw," wrote Hamlin Coe of the 19th Michigan in his diary. "I never suffered so from heat before. My clothes were as wet as though I had been in water." George A. Newton of the 129th Illinois also had his clothes soaked with perspiration but was told to go on picket duty for the night. He had no opportunity to change or dry his clothes, and the temperature became cool during the night. Newton was "almost chilled to the bones" until a comrade managed to obtain a canteen full of whisky and pass it around. The liquor revived and warmed Newton, and it "possibly was the means of saving my life" he recalled years later.[17]

While some Federals stood picket, others built earthworks, issued rations, and tended to wounded soldiers on the night of July 20. Benjamin Harrison did not sleep at all after exerting himself strenuously during the battle. His men took care to construct an impressive line of works on the second ridge, in some sectors laying them out in zig-zag fashion so as to fire obliquely at an approaching enemy. In most units men were detailed to work on the defenses while their comrades slept, so that at least some members of each unit would be relatively fresh in case of trouble.[18]

Still other members of Ward's division exerted themselves to find and recover wounded Rebels from the field. The moon eventually rose in a cloudless sky to offer some help to these men, who tried all night to aid the unfortunate enemy. Others worked to bury Rebel dead, and still others found a few live and uninjured Confederates on the battlefield. When a Federal picket heard voices coming from a ravine, he called on those who were talking to come out and surrender. An officer and thirteen Rebels emerged. They had gotten into a position late in the battle from which it would have been dangerous to retire in daylight and had hidden in the ravine for hours. When hailed by the picket, they were making preparations to rejoin their regiment but decided to give up instead. Ward's men also received much needed rations during the night, for it was now safe for commissary wagons to advance within close range of the main line and unload food for each unit.[19]

The story was much the same for Geary's and Williams's divisions. The Confederates fell back late in the evening, taking along all the wounded they could reach. The Yankees' spirit ran high because of their successful battle as they established a strong picket line in front of the main position along Collier Road. The Confederate pickets fronting the Peach Tree Creek Line stood about 600 yards in front of the Federal pickets. The troops of Geary and Williams also worked hard to strengthen their earthworks that night.[20]

With most of the battlefield in Union hands, it became possible for the Federals to help the wounded and discover sights never to be forgotten. William Merrell instructed a group of Federals in tearing down a building on the Hiram Embry Plantation, which had been behind O'Neal's and Reynolds's positions at the height of the battle. They were surprised to discover a number of dead and wounded Confederates under the building. One man had been shot in the back and had "died in extreme agony. His head clear back between his shoulders, and such an expression of extreme suffering on his countenance, one which I never can forget, though I should like to.... His limbs were drawn up and in his death struggle he had clutched the ground with each hand, in which he was holding with death grip, dirt, sticks, etc."[21]

Henry C. Morhous of the 123rd New York recalled the story of a wounded Federal skirmisher belonging to the 5th Connecticut who, after the battle, crawled back to the Union line. He was soon followed by a wounded Confederate, but the Federal recognized him, claiming he was the man who shot him. The wounded Yankee became enraged and wanted to kill the Rebel, but Knipe prevented him from doing so.[22]

To the right of Williams's position, Richard W. Johnson used some of his men to reinforce other parts of the line. He sent regular troops from Brig. Gen. John J. King's brigade to help Newton that night and to support Anson McCook's brigade. Farther to the right of Johnson's position, the rest of Palmer's Fourteenth Corps saw little change in their situation from afternoon to night. Davis's men kept up a lively skirmish fire with the Confederates opposing them all afternoon and evening, and in places the main Union line was close enough to add its fire to that of the skirmishers. The 78th Illinois fired 17,000 rounds that day even though it was not positioned on the skirmish line.[23]

At Army of the Cumberland headquarters, Thomas finally found time to inform Sherman that a major battle had taken place. Writing at 6:15 P.M. he reported that Hood "attacked me in full force about 4 P.M., and has persisted until now, attacking very fiercely, but he was repulsed handsomely by the troops all along my line." Thomas hoped that Schofield, Howard, and McPherson would make fast progress in their advance so as to hit Hood's right flank at an opportune time that day, but it was not to be. The Federals had to be satisfied with a decisive repulse of the attacks—or, as one of Thomas's staff members put it, "the enemy has been gloriously thrashed."[24]

Thomas was a bit late in telling Sherman that a battle was under way, and then, as we have seen, it took some time for that news to reach his superior. While Howard's headquarters received word of the battle at 8:30 P.M., it was not until about midnight that Sherman received Thomas's 6:15 dispatch. Before then, Sherman was largely in the dark as to developments on his right wing. At 3:25 P.M., just before or after Hood's attack began, Sherman told Thomas that Schofield, Howard, and McPherson were within a couple of miles of the target city. "All your troops should push hard for Atlanta, sweeping everything before them," he wrote.[25]

By 6:10 P.M., when the battle was winding down, Sherman already was thinking about shifting troops to the west and south of Atlanta. McPherson had broken the Georgia Railroad east of the city, and the only remaining line of communications feeding Hood's army lay to the south of Atlanta. If Thomas could advance and contract his line, Sherman could detach troops to swing around the west side of the place. Given the stiff resistance fronting Schofield, Howard, and McPherson, Sherman hoped Thomas faced little opposition and could move south to prevent the Confederates from digging a new line of earthworks north of the city. As yet he had no information about the Peach Tree Creek Line.[26]

At 8 P.M., still without word of the battle that had already ended, Sherman continued to urge Thomas to be aggressive in pushing forward the next day. "If we cannot break in, we must move by the right flank and interpose between the river and Atlanta, and operate against the road south. If you can advance your whole line, say to within three miles of Atlanta, I can throw a force around your rear to East Point."[27]

Thomas's 6:15 P.M. dispatch was still not in Sherman's hands when he made his almost daily report to Henry Halleck in Washington, D.C. at 9 P.M. "The enemy still clings to his intrenchments," he wrote, while reporting several small-scale Confederate attacks on Schofield and Howard. He also informed Halleck of his idea to swing part of the Union army group west of Atlanta to hit the railroad. John C. Van Duzer, in charge of Sherman's telegraph service, also sent daily reports of the campaign to his superior in Washington, who in turn had Secretary of War Edwin M. Stanton's ear. Van Duzer repeated the essence of Sherman's report at 10 P.M. No one in Washington or at Sherman's headquarters knew of the battle of Peach Tree Creek before midnight of July 20.[28]

Hood learned of the outcome of his first strike to defend Atlanta that evening and confirmed the orders of his subordinates to pull away from the battlefield. His men fell back all along the line at about dusk and retired to the Peach Tree Creek fortifications. Some of them received rations upon arrival but were too exhausted to cook and eat. In Maney's Division the Confederate skirmish line remained within 100 yards of Kimball's brigade until 10 P.M., when everyone fell back to the Peach Tree Creek Line "silently and in good order," reported Edwin Hansford Rennolds of the 5th Tennessee.[29]

For a time, before falling back to the entrenchments, rumors circulated through Mercer's Brigade of Walker's Division that a night attack would soon be attempted. Mercer's men prepared for it. The rumor had at least some validity, for Thomas B. Mackall, serving at Army of Tennessee headquarters, noted in his journal: "At night determined to 'pierce eny's centre.'" Col. Charles H. Olmstead of the 1st Georgia lay with his men waiting for the attack order until early in the morning hours of July 21 when the project was canceled. "I must confess to having felt a great sense of relief when the order came for the plan seemed to me to promise nothing but grave disaster," Olmstead recalled years later. No one outside Mercer's Brigade mentioned this projected night assault, and the entire program remains somewhat mysterious.[30]

Stewart had hoped to mount a second attempt at the enemy late in the evening and sent a request to Hardee for Maney's cooperation with the effort. Before anything could be arranged, an officer from Hood's headquarters arrived with an order to give up the fight and retire to the Peach Tree Creek Line. Stewart instructed Loring and Walthall to gather all the dead and wounded possible. By 9 P.M., that melancholy task had been done as far as the location of the existing Confederate skirmish line permitted. Earlier than that, at about dusk, John Adams's Brigade rejoined Loring's Division from picket duty along the Chattahoochee River. Three companies of the 3rd

Mississippi in Featherston's Brigade had also been detached to Adams for picket duty and now rejoined their regiment.[31]

Loring ordered his men to fall back from their position at the edge of the timbered ground that fronted the Peach Tree Creek Line where they had held since late afternoon. Leaving that position at 9 P.M., they kept their skirmish line intact until 11 P.M., when the entire division evacuated the battlefield of Peach Tree Creek. During the night, the men were able to recover a number of muskets abandoned on the field by their comrades.[32]

Walthall had also tried to bring his last brigade into the battle but failed to do so. At 5 P.M., William A. Quarles received an order to move to the support of O'Neal and Reynolds, but it meant disengaging the troops from a picket line that in places was quite close to Palmer's Fourteenth Corps skirmishers. Delay ensued before that could be accomplished, and then the brigade had to move some distance to reach the scene of action. By the time Quarles arrived, the fighting was largely over, and dusk was rapidly descending. He formed a skirmish line to cover the withdrawal of O'Neal and Reynolds to the Peach Tree Creek Line. They retired much earlier than had Featherston and Scott of Loring's Division. Although not actively engaged, Quarles lost twenty-four men that day.[33]

At 7 P.M. French received Stewart's order to collect the dead and wounded before pulling away from the battlefield. After doing all he could, the division fell back to its former position. While leaving a skirmish line to cover his withdrawal, French marched Ector and Cockrell to a point near the Marietta and Atlanta Road.[34]

Cheatham had a much different mission on the afternoon of July 20 than that accorded Hardee and Stewart. His job was to hold the east end of the Peach Tree Creek Line and the newly created Outer Line to secure Hood's right wing and the approaches to Atlanta from the northeast and east. Arthur M. Manigault, a brigade commander in Brown's Division on the far right of Cheatham's line, was located about three miles from the scene of combat but knew something was going on because it was possible to "see the smoke rising from the battlefield, and hear the discharges of musketry and artillery."[35]

To Brown's front, the Confederates began to skirmish as soon as Schofield and McPherson approached closely enough for contact to be made that afternoon. To Brown's left, Stevenson's Division faced the brunt of Schofield's and Howard's push toward the Outer Line. Troops of this division aggressively skirmished with the Federals but could not prevent them from lodging securely within a short distance of the main Rebel earthworks. To Stevenson's left, Clayton's Division held the right end of the Peach Tree Creek Line and faced north. Clayton advanced Randall L. Gibson's Brigade to support Bate's attack that afternoon. Even though there were no enemy troops in his front, Gibson advanced a short distance into the tangled brush where the two forks of Peach Tree Creek joined and then flowed to the junction of Clear Creek, an area where the vegetation and terrain hid the fact that a gap of one and a half miles separated Sherman's wings. Gibson remained forward of the Confederate earthworks until midnight before retiring, but his brigade did nothing while out there.[36]

Hood's cavalry had a tough assignment in holding back the Federal Army of the Tennessee all day. Joseph Wheeler eventually led 3,500 men after receiving some reinforcements, but he was heavily outnumbered by the cautious McPherson. In addition to his own command, Wheeler cooperated with Brig. Gen. Samuel W. Ferguson's Brigade of Brig. Gen. William H. Jackson's Division. Together, Wheeler and Ferguson slowed McPherson's advance to a crawl and barely covered the vulnerable eastern approach to Atlanta, operating to the right of Cheatham's Corps line.[37]

Wheeler's repeated calls for help in the late afternoon of July 20 were the first indications to Hood that trouble was brewing on the right flank. Cheatham received similar messages from Wheeler. Reacting to one such dispatch at 5:30 P.M., the newly appointed corps commander told Wheeler that his own line was extended to the point that he had only a single rank of troops along a 1,000-yard sector located in the center of the corps, and he already had his leftmost brigade (Gibson's) in action. Hood's headquarters told Wheeler to retire, if necessary, to the Outer Line, where Smith's Georgia Militia and some reserve artillery batteries could support his cavalrymen. By 6:45 P.M. Cheatham wrote with an air of crisis to Wheeler about his own situation. The Federals were pressing him near the angle in the Confederate line pretty hard where his own line was thin. "I am afraid it will not sustain itself. I have weakened my entire line" to extend the corps position southward toward the Georgia Railroad. Cheatham felt he could not do anything more for Wheeler, despite the fact that Hood's headquarters had instructed him to detach a brigade to help the cavalry.[38]

This is the situation that compelled Hood to ask Hardee for an entire division to shore up his right flank. That order arrived just in time to prevent Hardee from renewing the attack on Newton and in turn prevented Hardee from arranging cooperative movement between Maney's Division and Stewart's Army of Mississippi. Whether there was any real hope that a renewal of the assault could have succeeded so late in the day and after the Federals were in the flush of triumph is highly questionable, but the reality was that another round of assaults was not even possible.

Cleburne's Division was ready to strike when Hood's order arrived, and Hardee immediately ordered it instead to move toward Atlanta. The troops initially retired to the Peach Tree Creek Line to rest a bit and after dark marched south. They moved to the center of the city and then directed their feet eastward, bivouacking at the edge of town along the Georgia Railroad. Cleburne was unable to help Wheeler on July 20 but was in position to offer assistance the next morning.[39]

At 11 P.M., Hood informed the Richmond authorities of the day's occurrences by telegraph, but he kept the report to a minimum, glossed over the details, and tried to put the best possible face on reality. "At 3 o'clock to-day a portion of Hardee's and Stewart's corps drove the enemy into his breast-works, but did not gain possession of them. Our loss slight." Hood admitted that Clement Stevens was badly wounded, but he reported that Wheeler's cavalry "handsomely repulsed" the Federals advancing from the east of Atlanta. This was the best spin he could put on the day's frustrating events, the inauguration of his grand effort to save Atlanta with a new style of leadership to take the war to the heart of the invading foe.[40]

I have never seen the dead rebels lie so thickly strewn upon the ground, since the battle of Shiloh.—Emerson Opdycke

Found a female dressed in mens clothes & a cartradge box on her side when we picked her up. She was shot in the breast & through the thy & was still alive and as gritty as any reb I ever saw.
—Judson L. Austin

10

Cleaning Up

The battle of Peach Tree Creek left behind a landscape littered with dead, wounded, and the debris dropped by men under extreme pressure of events. The Federals controlled this shattered ground by the end of July 20 and upon them fell the job of cleaning it up. The first order of business was to take care of the human toll of combat and then to secure trophies in the form of abandoned enemy flags and weapons. Burying the dead was a comparatively quick task but taking care of the Union and Confederate wounded seemed never ending. It took weeks, months, even years for men to heal or eventually to succumb to their battlefield injuries. The legacy of Hood's first strike at Atlanta lived on for many participants until the end of their long, suffering lives.

Many Federals walked across the battlefield on July 21 and saw sights that stunned them. John W. Houtz of the 66th Ohio counted eighty Confederate dead lying on the slope north of the position Ward's division occupied on top of the Collier Road ridge, and he was fully aware that this was only one portion of the battlefield. It was easier to see sights of the dead on the Twentieth Corps sector because the enemy had driven beyond the ridge line, and thus their fallen lay scattered behind

Hooker's entire position. To some observers, the sight was very impressive. "The field was literaly [*sic*] covered with dead and wounded rebs," reported Charles Laforest Dunham of the 129th Illinois. Another man, John March Cate of the 33rd Massachusetts, thought the "ground was piled in heaps of dead and wounded," and reports indicated that on Williams's sector bodies "frequently lay across each other." Confederate dead lay close to Williams's line. "It was a terrible sight to see their mangled limbs," thought Alfred H. Trego of the 102nd Illinois. "I never saw the dead men lay so thick," concluded another man in Harrison's brigade.[1]

On Newton's sector, the Federals found enemy dead lying between the main line on the ridge and the Union skirmish position farther south. Some lay only a few yards from the breastworks. After riding along both Newton's and Hooker's line, Emerson Opdycke thought, "I never have seen the dead rebels lie so thickly strewn upon the ground, since the battle of Shiloh." Several men found the dead piled in heaps on Newton's front as well as Hooker's, and blood stained the ground where Confederates had been hit and then crawled away. In fact, Hamlin A. Coe of the 19th Michigan discovered "several places where the blood has run in streams down the hillside, and go where you will, there are pools of blood. It is a sickening and horrid sight such as I never wish to see again."[2]

Many men paid special attention to the facial expressions of the Confederate fallen. For a soldier in the 70th Indiana who signed himself as Bode when writing a letter to the *Indianapolis Daily Journal*, some of them had smiles, and others looked horrid with blood streaked across their features. The body of Col. Jabez L. Drake of the 33rd Mississippi drew a good deal of attention. He was the highest-ranking Confederate officer left on the field and appeared to George Hoenig of the 26th Wisconsin to be "a huge guy with a red beard." According to Maj. Charles P. Wickham of the 55th Ohio, Drake died partially in the pose of battle. The Rebel officer's "tall form was still in death," Wickham reported to Hartwell Osborn, "but with extended arm, sword in hand, had an air of resolution and defiance." John March Cate reported that more than twenty Confederate dead were found "killed by blows on the head," indicating the intensity of hand-to-hand combat on Ward's sector.[3]

Soldiers also noticed that the battle of Peach Tree Creek scarred the natural landscape. Harry Stanley of the 20th Connecticut reported that the trees suffered enormously on parts of the battlefield. An artillery projectile bored a hole clean through a live oak tree three feet in diameter "as though it had been a straw. Other trees of smaller diameter were cut in two and their shattered limbs lay scattered in every direction. Every shrub and bush was cut and scarred by musket balls while the trunks of the larger trees had some times as many as 50 & 60 balls in the rough bark."[4]

Most Federal and Confederate soldiers who participated in the battle of Peach Tree Creek were veterans of many engagements. There was little that they had not already seen in the form of human destruction on the battle-field. Their descriptions of the dead at Peach Tree Creek tended to report on the appearance of just another scene of death in a matter-of-fact way.

The task of tallying the numbers lost on both sides at Peach Tree Creek now began. Thomas started by issuing a circular from his headquarters on July 25 announcing that 6,000 Confederates had fallen. That circular was widely read by the troops and carried considerable weight in many men's eyes. Thomas's estimate was supported by John Coburn, who reported a total of 500 Confederate losses on his brigade front. If one extrapolated that figure for the entire Union force engaged in the battle, it would mean Hood lost 6,500 men.[5]

Thomas's and Coburn's estimates rang true for many Federal observers. While George W. Balloch, Hooker's chief commissary, supported it, other officers thought the number was too low. Douglas Hapeman of the 104th Illinois placed enemy losses at 8,000, as did a soldier in the 70th Indiana of Harrison's brigade. Two men in Newton's division thought it could run as high as 10,000. Jacob Cox noted that Hood did not dispute Sherman's estimate of less than 5,000 Confederate casualties, even though he had the chance to do so after the war, but Cox also believed Thomas's 6,000 figure was closer to the mark.[6]

But many other Union officers estimated enemy losses as significantly lower. Sherman placed it at 4,796, while Henry Stone, the assistant adjutant general on Thomas's staff, put it at 2,800 or 3,300 depending on which of the two figures he concocted after the war. Estimates varied but normally ran from about 3,000 to 5,000.[7]

Federal losses were far easier to establish, and Thomas's circular put it at 1,733 men. A month later, for unexplained reasons, Thomas reduced that number to 1,600 men. Henry Stone put it at 1,950 and 1,968 in two postwar publications, but unofficial estimates of Union casualties normally cited fig-ures between 1,500 and 2,000. Historian Albert Castel places the number as 1,900 men.[8]

Not surprisingly, Confederate observers typically reported their own casualties as much lighter than did the Federals. Rebel estimates of their own loss ranged from only 1,000 to 1,700 men. Returns filed in the Army of Tennessee on July 10 and 31 bracket the time period of Hood's three battles for Atlanta. Hardee and Stewart combined had 4,752 fewer men on July 31 compared to July 10. Hardee also fought heavily on July 22, and one division of Stewart was deeply engaged at Ezra Church on July 28. Splitting the number of troops lost by both corps from July 10 to 31 indicates that Hardee and Stewart could have suffered combined casualties of roughly 2,376 men on July 20. Historian Albert Castel has placed Confederate casualties at Peach Tree Creek at 2,500 men, and other historians have accepted that figure as official.[9]

It was far easier for the Federals to count the number of Confederate dead they buried on the battlefield than to estimate total Rebel casualties. Thomas reported that Newton's men buried 200 bodies of the enemy on their division front. Thirteen of them lay before the 26th Ohio according to Lyman Gardner of Blake's brigade. Three wounded Confederates also lay so close to the brigade's line that their comrades could not retrieve them during the night.[10]

In Ward's division, official counts of Confederate dead included thirty-eight "found behind and near our advanced line of battle" for Wood's brigade, although wild reports of up to 400 Confederates buried on Wood's sector alone exist. Drake's burial attracted much attention. He was interred near where he fell along with several dozen of his men. Someone erected a sign that read "Col. Drake, 33 Miss., and 34 men."[11]

As burial details began their work on Coburn's sector, they first gathered the dead and placed them in rows, while other Federals dug burial trenches nearby. The sight of these bodies impressed a man in the 22nd Wisconsin. "I counted in front of our brigade 128 rebels, lying stark and stiff, in winrows, [sic] ready for the burial party." The details continued to bring in the dead all through the day of July 21 in driblets, accumulating them so that as many as fifty-three could be interred in one long trench. Each regiment of Harrison's brigade sent out details to collect and bury the enemy, totaling about 150 Confederates on the brigade sector. Thirty-four of them lay before the 70th Indiana, and forty-three in front of the 105th Illinois. The Indiana men dug trenches six feet wide and twenty feet long for the fallen enemy.[12]

For Geary's troops, the task of interring Confederate dead on the division front meant digging graves for 409 bodies. But Williams had to admit that his men failed to keep accurate count of the number they interred. Some regimental parties in Williams's division reported the number; for example, the 123rd New York buried sixteen Confederates. Farther west, in Johnson's division of the Fourteenth Corps, Douglas Hapeman reported that his men buried five Confederate dead on the 104th Illinois sector, but Hapeman also noted that the Confederates had taken most of their dead away in the night.[13]

Peach Tree Creek Battlefield. This well-known photograph, exposed by George Barnard a few months after the engagement, is difficult to place. One can discern at least ten graves with wood taken from a nearby board fence serving as markers. At least two markers have writing on them; one appears to be "A sergeant of . . ." The fact that most of the graves are lined with fence rails to protect them from roving animals indicates they must be the graves of Union soldiers. Because none of the terrain features can be linked to the topography of the battlefield, we have to rely on Barnard's note that this is the Peach Tree Creek field. (Library of Congress, LC-DIG-ppmsca-32828)

There was no danger involved in collecting the enemy dead behind the main Union line on the second ridge, but forward of that line it was a different matter. When Harrison sent details forward to find all they could, Confederate skirmishers opened fire on them. "After this exhibition of bad faith," Harrison reported, "I made no further effort to reach the rebel dead that could be seen between our lines."[14]

The result of all Union burial efforts from July 21 to 25 amounted to 563 Confederate bodies recovered and interred by the victors of Peach Tree Creek. Thomas estimated Hood's men also were able to recover 250 more of the fallen. If he was correct, then the Confederates left at least 813 of their dead and mortally wounded on the field when they broke off the engagement on the evening of July 20.[15]

There were a number of Federal dead to be buried on July 21 as well. Details collected them separately from the Rebel bodies but also lined them up in rows prior to interment. Joseph B. Newbury of the 79th Ohio counted 214 Union dead in the sector held by Ward's division. For some of the fallen, comrades fashioned a headboard out of available wood and even scribbled name and unit with a lead pencil on it. When possible, the Federals covered their own dead with some ceremony. A chaplain officiated over the trench wherein fifty-one men of Harrison's brigade were buried. "I can never forget the solemn and impressive scene," recalled Edwin H. Conger of the 102nd Illinois, "as, standing around that hallowed trench," the chaplain said "'*Many in one*' is the motto borne proudly on our Nation's banner. *Many in one grave* our fallen brothers rest, and is not the coincidence a fitting one?"[16]

The bodies of prominent Federal officers received special treatment. Col. George A. Cobham Jr. of the 111th Pennsylvania was among the highest-ranking Union casualties of the battle; his body was preserved for shipment to his home in Warren, Pennsylvania, where it was buried. Lieut. Col. Charles B. Randall of the 149th New York received the same treatment. "Our Lt Col looks just as natural as life," commented E. P. Failing, a hospital attendant belonging to the regiment. "The expression is that of entire satisfaction just as tho he was hugely pleased, he died instantly." For those Federal officers not sent home, burial on the battlefield became an exercise in individualism. No mass graves for them, but a separate burial spot carefully marked so that the family could find it later. Benjamin Harrison wrote to Malcolm A. Lowes and gave him this information so he could recover the body of his son, Lieut. Josiah Lowes of the 70th Indiana, who had been killed at Peach Tree Creek. Trusted staff officers also received special treatment when possible. One of Geary's aides was killed on July 20. Burial details located the body and brought it to Geary's headquarters. The general could not help but cry on seeing the remains of this member of his military family.[17]

Hooker made a show of riding along the lines on July 21 to congratulate his men and observe the burial of the dead. "Boys, we have whipped them again," he told the troops. The men greeted him with cheers when he reached one unit after another. "He stopped a while" at the 129th Illinois "and looked at the staring dead, and was soon surrounded by our men. He could not, however, control his feelings, tears came in his eyes, and he rode off." But at least one officer in Ward's division rejected postbattle reports implying that Hooker saved the day on July 20. "The boast about his rallying his running soldiers on the day of the fight is sickening," commented John McWilliams.[18]

Working hard on July 21, the burial details managed to find and inter the overwhelming majority of the dead, both Union and Confederate. But the woods covering part of the battlefield hid other bodies for days to come. By July 23, the Federals had stumbled across many decaying remains of their enemy in the brush. By then "the bodies are loathsome and appear fit emblems of their Confederacy," thought William A. Brand of the 66th Ohio. Roaming through the woods to find blackberries, George Loyd of the 149th New York came across the bodies of sixteen Confederates on July 24. Two days later, nearly a week after the battle, the problem still had not been solved. Two squads of volunteers from the 73rd Ohio went out through the woods to find all they could, and no more complaints about overlooked remains were heard after that.[19]

The battlefield of Peach Tree Creek was littered not only with the fallen but with thousands of articles of war ranging from muskets to the personal equipment of hundreds of Union and Confederate soldiers. The most prominent and sought-after articles were the unit flags dropped by Rebel color-bearers as they were shot or stumbled in retreat. According to Thomas's circular of July 25, the Federals recovered seven Confederate flags on July 20. Detailed accounts filed by staff members indicate that two sergeants of the 105th Illinois secured the flag of the 12th Louisiana after its bearer was shot by other regimental members, but the 12th Louisiana participated in the action against Geary's right wing, not opposite Harrison's brigade. Reports also indicated that Pvt. Dennis Buckley of the 136th New York took the flag of Drake's 31st Mississippi after he "knocked down color bearer with musket and wrenched colors from him." Buckley later received a Medal of Honor for the deed. The 26th Wisconsin was credited with the capture of the flag belonging to the 33rd Mississippi.[20]

But one must read official accounts of flag captures with caution. Enemy colors were the most prominent trophies of the battlefield, and most of them were actually dropped by their bearers and abandoned rather than literally captured by victorious troops. Moreover, exactly who "captured" a particular flag often was clouded by controversy. For example, Pvt. Thomas J. Williamson of the 85th Indiana recovered a Rebel flag while the regiment was advancing with Coburn's brigade, but he left it on the ground and continued moving forward "as he could not carry the flag and shoot at the same time." The flag was later picked up by someone else who undoubtedly claimed it as a captured trophy. An unnamed private of Company C, 22nd Wisconsin also picked up a Confederate color but left it on the ground. It was later claimed by a man in the 26th Wisconsin. Lieut. Col. Edward Bloodgood tried to retrieve the flag on July 21 so it could be credited to his 22nd Wisconsin, but the officers of the 26th refused to give it up. Capt. John Speed, Ward's assistant adjutant general, broke up the heated discussion about the issue by consoling Bloodgood. "Colonel, you needn't care for the flag; the 22d Wisconsin have enough to cover themselves with glory."[21]

While flags were a scarce and sought-after commodity on the battlefield, there was a host of minor trophies lying about. Hooker's headquarters compiled a list of them to indicate which regiment recovered the more prominent of these smaller symbols of victory. The list was focused mostly on officers' swords and scabbards, with one trophy reportedly wrenched from the hands of its owner by Capt. Samuel T. Walkley of the 129th Illinois. Individual Union soldiers recovered trophies that were not officially reported, becoming the personal property of the man who took possession of them. Charles Harding Cox of the 70th Indiana obtained an officer's sword and a Confederate canteen made of cedar wood, in addition to a haversack. Many Federals ransacked the dead before burial to find watches and other valuables. One man recovered nine gold pieces worth twenty dollars each from a dead Confederate officer. "Quite an amount of 'green backs' was found upon the persons of the rebels," reported Charles A. Booth of the 22nd Wisconsin.[22]

The Confederates had no opportunity to recover trophies from the battlefield. Having retreated from the ground, they had to content themselves with the praise of their comrades and officers. The Richmond government had earlier allowed badges of honor to be awarded individual soldiers based on the votes of their comrades as a way to reward valor on the battlefield. Several men in the 2nd Arkansas Mounted Rifles (dismounted) were voted such badges by their fellow soldiers, "but we never received them," complained Pvt. John W. Leeper of Company G. He was not alone; virtually all Confederate soldiers voted to appear on the Confederacy's Roll of Honor failed to receive their awards. The Richmond government did not find the time or money to fulfill its promise to the soldiers.[23]

In addition to trophies, the Federals finished cleaning up the battlefield by collecting abandoned weapons and equipment. Dropped by fallen soldiers and sometimes by retreating Confederates who were not injured, rifle muskets littered the ground. The guns were piled up for collection by ordnance officers, who also gathered all other government property left on the field. Blake's brigade of Newton's division collected more than seventy-five muskets on its sector. Samuel Merrill's 70th Indiana collected 168 abandoned small arms for Harrison's ordnance officer from July 21 to 23. Altogether, the Army of the Cumberland recovered 794 weapons during the month of July 1864.[24]

The capture of enemy soldiers also was seen as a major sign of victory on the battlefield, and Thomas reported 360 prisoners taken on July 20. Of that number, 122 (or exactly one-third of the total number) had been wounded before they were taken captive. This was a comparatively small proportion of the 2,722 prisoners and deserters received by the Army of the Cumberland during the month of July 1864. The fact that only 13.2 percent of the month's haul of Confederate personnel resulted from the battle of Peach Tree Creek (the only battle Thomas's men fought in July) indicates that a large number of deserters had given themselves up to Thomas's troops during that pivotal month of the Atlanta campaign.[25]

Many of the captured Confederates were eager to talk to the Federals about any number of topics. They spoke freely of Hood's battle plan to drive Thomas's army toward the Chattahoochee River and revealed that Hood made it clear to everyone he intended to fight "with 'guns instead of spades and picks.'" A Rebel officer told Joseph B. Newbury of the 79th Ohio that his comrades "thought they would come out … and gather a few Acorns," referring to the corps badge of Palmer's Fourteenth Corps. But the Rebels hit Hooker's Twentieth Corps instead. While these conversations relayed mostly accurate views from the Confederate side of the contending lines, other prisoners reported nothing but rumors. The idea that Hood personally led the attack at Peach Tree Creek and was killed "leading a charge" was widespread among the Rebel prisoners. It probably says more about what many Confederate soldiers wished had happened than anything else.[26]

The wounded men who littered the field at Peach Tree Creek became an object of dedicated work for many Federal surgeons and attendants. Details used blankets as well as stretchers to collect them from the ground and transport them to field hospitals behind Union lines. Some of those hospitals were close by and others some distance away. Geary's division hospital was located two and a half miles from the fight because his chief surgeon, H. Earnest Goodman, had to take care of many sick soldiers. Goodman did position one section of his hospital only half a mile from the battlefield where the most severe cases were treated. He ran six operating tables altogether in the two sections of his hospital, and they were used constantly until 1 A.M. of July 21. In Williams's division, surgeons took possession of the vacant cabins located near the Union line to treat the injured. The three division hospitals in Hooker's Twentieth Corps admitted a total of 1,051 Federal wounded and 106 Confederate wounded during and after the battle of Peach Tree Creek. Of that number, 169 (or 16.0 percent) received amputations. An unknown number of Union soldiers were so slightly injured that they did not bother to report to a hospital for treatment. Andrew Jackson Johnson of the 70th Indiana "was struck by a spent ball on the thigh, making a very sore place," but he nursed it privately.[27]

Given that most of the Federal hospitals were from one to two miles from the scene of conflict, orders went out to move them closer. Surg. William Harrison Githins of the 78th Illinois in Davis's division had his hands full with caring for the numerous wounded resulting from Dilworth's battle with Reynolds on July 19. But he received orders to move his hospital closer to the division late on July 20. It proved impossible to do so that day, so preparations were begun before dawn of July 21. Githins and another surgeon worked nearly all day dressing the wounds of 160 men, then supervised their loading onto ambulances and sent them forward "load after load until late in the night" of July 21. They moved the hospital equipment and supplies the next day. Githins was stressed and exhausted: "How we long for the slaughter to stop," he wrote his wife, "just think of the wagon loads of arms and legs we have had to take off."[28]

Githins's experience was not unique, for many field hospitals in the Army of the Cumberland were on the move in an effort to snuggle the care facilities closer to the fighting line. In addition, as soon as wounded men were able to travel, they were shipped northward. Thomas's Department of the Cumberland operated a general field hospital at Vinings' Station near Marietta, and that was the arrival point of these injured men for a temporary stay until they were either transported farther north in the hospital system or returned to duty.[29]

For several days following the battle, these field hospitals gave the appearance not only of individual suffering but of general chaos as thousands of needy men crowded a small and overworked medical staff. Henry Perrin Mann, a teamster who wandered into a Twentieth Corps field hospital, was stunned by the experience. "The sights I saw I never want to see again," he confided to his diary, "the ground for nearly half an acre was covered thick with wounded waiting for their turn to have their wounds dressed." Rice C. Bull visited his comrades of the 123rd New York in Williams's division hospital to find that some 500 men were lying injured on the ground waiting for attention. Rufus Mead of the 5th Connecticut, another teamster whose train was located near a hospital, reported that some of the many wounded men waiting for the doctor were "crazy & raving and other[s] suffering all that mortals can." The surgeons worked as fast as they could, and the pile of amputated limbs began to grow, according to Mead. He noticed a terrible odor as well. "Flies were flying around in swarms and maggots were crawling in wounds before the Drs could get time to dress them." Mead thought this was the worst exhibition of human suffering he ever witnessed in the army.[30]

The quality of care offered by Federal surgeons created a small controversy. It was true that, not anticipating a battle, the doctors of Ward's division were unprepared for the influx of wounded men. Surg. William Grinstead had only one section of the division hospital near the battlefield because the other sections were still located at Buck Head, where 250 sick men had to be attended. Even so, the section near Ward's division was taken by surprise when the firing started. For Surg. John W. Foye, Hooker's medical director, "the want of system was painfully apparent" in Grinstead's establishment. Somehow surgeons in Newton's division heard of the trouble and offered their help. Foye was grateful, as was Grinstead, but it was obvious to Foye that "much suffering would have ensued" if not for that timely assistance. The other sections of Ward's division hospital reached the battlefield area on July 21, enabling Grinstead to put all of his wounded under shelter.[31]

As far as the infantry was concerned, the battle of Peach Tree Creek was fought at close range, and the wounded suffered "generally severe" injuries as a result. But the medical staff saved the overwhelming majority of the troops brought in to their hospitals. Grinstead and Goodman reported that only about 6 percent of the wounded entrusted to their care in Ward's and Geary's division hospitals died of their injuries. Including the wounded of July 20, Geary's medical staff treated a total of 295 men for combat injuries during the month of July. Of that number, sixteen (5.4 percent) died of their wounds. Surg. Edwin Hutchinson of the 137th New York thought the wounded of Peach Tree Creek "were better and more quickly cared for than at any Battle heretofore."[32]

The Confederate wounded also were retrieved from the battlefield, although some reports indicate that many of them received secondary attention. A man in the 70th Indiana wrote that some of the Rebels lay on the field all night before stretcher details could get them into the hospitals. A man of the 3rd Wisconsin wandered through the woods on July 27 looking for blackberries and came across two Confederates who had lain in the brush for a week. One was dead and the other barely alive with maggots crawling in his wounds. The sufferer "was so near gon that he did not know eney thing," wrote William H. Carrier. The close-range firing created many severe injuries. In fact, Grinstead reported that the Rebel wounded he treated in Ward's division hospital mostly had multiple bullet wounds, and six of them died within hours of admission, while another thirty died before he could transport them farther north. It is true that those Confederates who could not get away from the field tended to be the ones most severely injured; their rate of recovery was far lower than that of only slightly wounded men.[33]

A remarkable discovery was in store for many Federals as they gathered and tended wounded Confederates. Judson L. Austin of the 19th Michigan was a member of one detail scouring the battlefield when he "found a female dressed in mens clothes & a cartradge [sic] box on her side when we picked her up. She was shot in the breast & through the thy & was still alive and as gritty as any reb I ever saw." When later telling the story to his wife in a letter, Austin admonished her never to think of doing such a thing. "I hope our women will never be so foolish as to go to war or get to fighting," he told her.[34]

Stories about women soldiers circulated freely through Federal ranks after the battle. Watson C. Hitchcock of the 20th Connecticut heard that not one but three women "all dressed in soger clothes" were found injured on the battlefield and had been brought into Geary's, Ward's, and Newton's division hospitals. The woman that Ward's staff treated had her leg amputated and later died, but the others apparently survived. Stephen F. Fleharty of the 102nd Illinois relayed a rumor that one female soldier, who endured the pain of a broken ankle with heroism, admitted she had been in the field for twenty-eight months "and was not sorry that she had enlisted." Another report circulated that a woman soldier had been found dead on the field, while yet more rumors indicated that two women soldiers were captured by the Federals at Peach Tree Creek.[35]

Many of Hooker's medical personnel devoted superb attention to the wounded found on the battlefield. Andrew J. Gilson, assistant surgeon of the 5th Connecticut, stayed on the field during the battle to dress the wounds of regimental members before they were taken to the field hospital. He was widely known to be the only surgeon in Knipe's brigade to do so, and his admirers wrote a letter to their hometown newspaper a few days later to sing his praises. Surg. Jesse Brock of the 66th Ohio suffered an injury while operating on wounded in the field hospitals. He accidently pricked his finger "on some exposed bone." When it became gangrenous it had to be amputated.[36]

Surgeons relied heavily on attendants to support their work in the field hospitals, and normally they were simply detailed from the regiments to this duty. Edward P. Failing of the 149th New York took this assignment seriously as he worked to administer anesthetics to the wounded of Peach Tree Creek. "Have been busy giving chloroform," he confided to his diary on July 21. "Administered chor to a rebel, had his leg taken off, dressed another who had his head badly used." Failing worked "very hard" for ten hours on the evening and night of July 20; his duties continued without let up on the 21st, but he took a break the next day to compile a list of casualties in the regiment and "then commenced dressing the wounded," a daily chore for the hospital attendants.[37]

Some of the medical attendants preferred to work on the battlefield. Marcus Daniels of the 19th Michigan had normally helped Surg. George Martin Trowbridge in previous engagements, but on July 20 he wanted to stay on the field because both the regimental surgeons were busy in the hospitals. Trowbridge allowed him to do this, but Daniels paid for his dedication with a serious bullet wound in the foot.[38]

Trowbridge left behind a detailed record of his actions, thoughts, and feelings in a series of letters to his wife. Soon after the opening shots were fired, he reported to Ward's division hospital, and by dusk he was helping to care for 250 men. "Used the knife till 3½ am this morn," he wrote on July 21, "then only rested for a little to give attendants time to rest. Tis enough to make the heart ache to see the mangled bodies."[39]

Trowbridge devoted the morning of July 22 mostly to operating on the Confederate wounded, and "I of course enjoyed thinking when amputating a leg had finished the soldiering of a reb." He was struck by the seriousness of the wounds suffered by the captured Confederates and feared they would have less chance of survival than the more lightly wounded Federals he saw. Trowbridge continued to work away at his operating table all day of July 22 and into the night to nearly complete the procedures necessary on all the Union and Confederate wounded in his hospital. He had about 110 severe cases to worry about. Moreover, "the filth, flies & maggots tis terrible, 24 hours is sufficient to have a wound filled with life."[40]

Under the stress of these days Trowbridge both enjoyed his work and was appalled by it. He considered standing for hours at an operating table and then wading through dirt and maggots as "a military necessity." Throughout it all he was expected "to be jovial & happy; cheering the suffering, sustaining the weak, healing the wounded." Privately he worried because all the men he worked on would soon be shifted north, and there would be no way he could learn what role his care played in their recovery. While Trowbridge thought his colleagues had performed prodigious feats to care for the hundreds of injured men so well and so quickly, he was left with a sense of emptiness because there was no opportunity to follow through with subsequent care to bring the torn body back to health.[41]

Trowbridge had ample opportunity to observe the enemy in his hospital, and his observations began with a captured Confederate surgeon who was told to care for his own wounded. The doctor did not impress Trowbridge, who considered him "rather an inferior appearing man." He had a more generous appraisal of the Rebel rank and file as they filtered into his hospital and endured operations on the table. Trowbridge noted that their wounds tended to be more severe, that they usually were taken off the field later than the Federal wounded, and that flies had infested their open flesh far more thoroughly than that of the Union men in the hospital. They seemed to have been living better than Sherman's men because of shorter supply lines and more ready access to home. Trowbridge saw no indications of scurvy among the wounded Rebels, while he was well aware that the condition, brought on by a deficiency of vitamin C, was evident in many units of Sherman's army group. "There is a general healthy fresh appearance" among the Confederates, "indicative of plenty & good variety of food, & all say have plenty: & are well clothed with homespun quality of course linen made by the *pilgrim mothers*; more durable & better for summer than our dress." Trowbridge was, in short, impressed by many aspects of the enemy's condition in the summer of 1864.[42]

Trowbridge's junior colleague in the 19th Michigan was Asst. Surg. John Bennitt, who also kept his wife informed of developments in the hospitals of Ward's division. Five days after the fight at Peach Tree Creek, Bennitt had his fill of Civil War combat. "A Battle is a terrific affair, and may God grant that it be not my lot to be under the necessity of participating in any manner in another." When the engagement started, Bennitt was searching for a suitable place to establish a hospital as close as possible to Hooker's line. He therefore set up a temporary aid station "behind a bank that was sheltered from their bullets." He finally moved everyone back to the division hospital, where he also amputated the mangled limbs of several captured enemy soldiers.[43]

Confederate medical personnel were busy with their own injured troops on July 20 and for days after the battle. Seventy men of Gist's Brigade in Maney's Division were treated in a hospital located between the battlefield and Atlanta, while at least some houses inside the city were taken over by Confederate doctors. The home of Annie Robson was chosen, and one of her neighbors, Sarah Conley Clayton, remembered for the rest of her life the horrible groans coming from the operating tables set up on the front porch and in the yard.[44]

In Loring's Division hospital, Dr. P. F. Whitehead slaved away with the wounded all night of July 20. He stopped for a break at 6 A.M. the next day to drink coffee and scribble a short letter to his friend Irene Cowan. "The wounded are still being brought in from the field," he reported before taking up the scalpel once again. Surg. James Madison Brannock of the 4th and 5th Tennessee in Strahl's Brigade, Maney's Division also worked all night of July 20. At dawn the next day three wounded Federal officers arrived at his hospital, and Brannock took good care of them. One struck him as "a handsome young Lieutenant with his leg badly shattered." The Federal officer joked with Brannock. "Well, Doctor, I have got to Atlanta at last! ... But how differently from what I expected! I little thought to reach here only to die!" Brannock amputated his leg on July 21, and the next day the lieutenant passed away.[45]

Brannock compiled a detailed account of the wounds suffered by members of the 12th and 47th Tennessee in Vaughan's Brigade (commanded by Col. Michael Magevney Jr.) of Maney's Division. Of twenty-seven men, five (18.5 percent) suffered amputation of limbs and two (7.4 percent) died of their injuries. One man, Pvt. Robert F. Brown, displayed four slight wounds on different parts of his body. While twelve men (44.4 percent) were listed as having severe wounds, only five (18.5 percent) had slight injuries. This proportion seems atypical; normally the number of slight injuries heavily outnumbered the serious wounds. In fact, if those statistics were reversed, they would seem to be more in keeping with the norm.[46]

On both sides of the battle lines around Atlanta, concerned comrades visited field hospitals after the engagement to check on friends and regimental associates and to inform their families what had happened to them. Many men fully understood the anxiety of hometown residents and tried to ease their tension with quick, accurate reports of who was lost and who survived. "After a fight, matters are reported worse than they really are," admitted Col. Patrick Jones to a hometown newspaper editor. "God knows it is bad enough as it is." One of Rice C. Bull's comrades in the 123rd New York asked him not only to write his family but "to be sure and say, 'We licked them well.'" William Salter, a U. S. Christian Commission worker traveling with Sherman's army group, performed a similar favor for wounded men in Twenty-Third Corps hospitals during the days following the battle at Peach Tree Creek, for Schofield's men had also suffered some injuries in the skirmishing of July 20.[47]

James K. Murphree took the pains to compile a list of eighty men in the 57th Alabama who were killed, wounded, and missing on July 20. In part he traversed the hospitals to do so but admitted he had missed a few men who had been sent to hospitals farther afield. The list was not only essential for the regimental commander but of great interest to the families at home. James Madison Brannock also took time to send a list of casualties in the 4th and 5th Tennessee to his wife so she could inform the relatives of the wounded men.[48]

As news spread concerning who was hit and lying in hospital, the human dimensions of combat at Peach Tree Creek filtered through civilian society and became more personal. Quite a few men left behind their own accounts or their personal stories were told by friends, or those stories were encapsulated by medical personnel in reports eventually published in the multivolume *Medical and Surgical History of the Civil War*. These personal stories vividly told of suffering, uncertainty, and fate in blue and in gray.

Joseph Leassions of the 123rd New York was squatting down during the battle when a Confederate ball slightly injured his hand before smashing into his face. It "entered near his left eye and lodged back of the ear," according to Albert M. Cook. Fortunately, the bone did not fracture, and Leassions was expected to recover. Peter Helmreich of the 44th Illinois in Newton's division was hit in the head with a ball and spent months in various hospitals as a result. Initial treatment in the division field hospital was followed by transfer to the general field hospital of the corps and a trip to Cumberland Hospital at Nashville by July 27. Helmreich later wound up in hospitals at Mound City and Quincy, Illinois. All this time "the wound was discharging, and he had occasional headache." Helmreich finally was released from the army on June 10, 1865, having spent the remainder of his term of service in hospitals because of the bullet that found his head on July 20.[49]

A brief mention of Henry Welch's injury at Peach Tree Creek appeared in the *Salem Press* of his home community in upstate New York on August 2, 1864. It merely mentioned that the twenty-year-old corporal, who served in Company K, 123rd New York had been hurt in the hand. The report failed to reveal the entire story, for Welch lost the small and ring fingers of his left hand. It is quite possible his family did not worry unduly, for Henry wrote a letter from his Chattanooga hospital bed on July 29 telling them he was doing well. "I am treated first rate here and plenty to eat. When I get where I am to remain long enough for you to answer my letter I will let you know."[50]

The family of Henry Welch of the 123rd New York could count its blessings, for another man named Henry Welch who served in the same regiment was mortally wounded at Peach Tree Creek. This twenty-five-year-old private in Company G was badly injured during the engagement. His brother Charles S. Welch enlisted the help of John Law Marshall to carry Henry to the regimental surgeon. Marshall also found some water for the unfortunate man, and Henry implored him "to see that his parents did not suffer & spoke of it several times & after he was taken to the Division Hospital he told charley to take good care of his folks, this seemed his chief anxiety." Henry seemed convinced from the moment he was hit that he could not survive. In fact, he fell into Marshall's arms on the battle line and "said God forgive me, Good bye boys & we then carried him back." Welch indeed passed away at 1 A.M. of July 21.[51]

The color sergeant of the 123rd New York also fell to Confederate fire at Peach Tree Creek. William Hutton Jr. was a close friend and tentmate of Serg. Henry C. Morhous. When he was hit by a bullet in the back, Hutton gave up the flag and was transported to the division hospital. Morhous received permission to visit him on the morning of July 21 and found Hutton resting on rubber and woolen blankets on the ground inside a tent. He gathered some leaves to provide a cushion for him and learned that the surgeon had tried but could not find the bullet. Hutton's case did not seem mortal at the time, but when writing to his sister, Morhous told her he had been only slightly wounded. Hutton then gave Morhous a book of poetry to remember him by, a volume that Morhous kept for the rest of his life. He returned to the hospital on July 22 expecting to find his friend better but was shocked to see several fresh graves near the tent and a board marking one that read "William Hutton, Jr., died July 21." Richard Terrill, another member of the 123rd, told him what happened. At forty-four years of age, Terrill was literally twice the age of both Hutton and Morhous and thus was detailed to hospital duty. Hutton had asked Terrill to fetch Morhous during the night but that was impossible; there were too many wounded to care for, so Hutton died alone. At least Terrill was able to oversee the erection of the headboard. Morhous never forgot his friend Hutton and told the sergeant's story in a book of reminiscences published fifteen years after his death.[52]

There are many individual stories of Federal soldiers badly wounded at Peach Tree Creek who survived despite the tremendous pain and stress on their bodies. Serg. William V. Taylor of the 66th Ohio had already been wounded at Antietam and Gettysburg, but his Peach Tree injuries were more serious. He was shot in the hand, arm, and shoulder; surgeons cut out two and a half inches of bone but the man healed well enough to be discharged in December 1864 and sent home with a pension. A few months later, Dr. B. B. Leonard of West Liberty, Ohio, took Taylor into his care, probed the shoulder wound, and found half a minie ball. When Leonard extracted it, Taylor healed quite readily and lived a good life despite the hail of Confederate fire that descended on him in three battles.[53]

Taylor represented a comparatively unusual case. More common are stories of Union soldiers badly injured who barely survived the war and often led lives of limited opportunities. Serg. Cyrus Shade of the 46th Pennsylvania was twenty-three years old when a ball injured his left ankle. Simple dressings were all that were needed before he returned to duty August 13, and in fact he received promotion to lieutenant before leaving the army in the summer of 1865. But Shade suffered from "pain, weakness, and swelling on over-exertion" and received a pension as well. Corp. John H. Jaycox of the 143rd New York endured several operations to resection bones in his arm before leaving the army in June 1865. He also received a pension because, despite the surgical procedures, the arm often swelled up and became useless as far as his ability to make a living was concerned. Nineteen-year-old Pvt. Thomas Donohue of the 123rd New York also endured several operations for his shoulder wound and was shifted to Nashville, Louisville, and eventually New York by May 1865. Although surviving this ordeal and returning to civilian life, Donohue could not use his arm or shoulder and came to rely on a government pension.[54]

Shade, Jaycox, and Donohue represented men whose bodies were impaired enough by Peach Tree wounds to alter their lives forever, but others suffered emotional and mental trauma as well as physical pain and disfigurement because of what happened to them on July 20. Pvt. Asbell A. Webster of the 19th Michigan was badly wounded in the head and "was insensible or delirious for a considerable time," according to the compilers of the *Medical and Surgical History*. A surgeon at Nashville extracted several pieces of bone from the wound, one of which was three-quarters of an inch long, and when gangrene set in, it sloughed off a considerable portion of the scalp. But the wound eventually healed, and Webster was transported to Michigan to be discharged in January 1865. "His mental faculties, especially his memory, were somewhat impaired, and the eyesight was, to some extent, weakened." For these conditions, Webster was granted a pension four years after Peach Tree Creek. For all that, Webster suffered less than Lieut. James P. Conn of the 66th Ohio. Hit on the head by a sword in the fight, "he continued to complain of the pain" and "eventually became mentally unbalanced and ended his days in the Cleveland Hospital for the Insane."[55]

Capt. Ezra Dickerman was called on by fate to endure more than most Federal wounded of Peach Tree Creek. Commanding Company I, 20th Connecticut, the twenty-three-year-old officer was badly wounded in the head and lay "in an insensible condition" for "several days." Overworked surgeons in the field hospital tried but could not locate the bullet. By the time Dickerman was transported to Chattanooga, he began to awaken although in tremendous pain and delirious much of the time. In the Officer's Hospital at Nashville by July 31, he begged the surgeons to continue trying to find the bullet. One of them was successful; it had imbedded into a bone. While two assistants held Dickerman's head, the surgeon wrenched the ball out with a forceps. He "was obliged to pull with all his strength," according to reports, but managed to get it out. Dickerman left for his home a week later.[56]

After several months of recuperation, Dickerman was well enough to return to light duty and rejoined his regiment in time for muster out in June 1865, but his condition was not good. The captain had suffered "complete loss of sight and smell of left side, and the hearing was much impaired." Moreover, Dickerman labored under a "general want of intellectual vigor" and lost some of his memory capacity. It was almost a miracle that he could do any duty at all, and his condition worsened after the war. Anytime he worked in the sun or tried to use his cognitive abilities, he suffered from headaches and even vertigo. By the summer of 1866 epileptic convulsions set in which often lasted fifteen minutes. During his third attack of epilepsy, in December 1867, "rigidity and unconsciousness lasted about half an hour. Foaming at the mouth and a dull heavy pain at the forehead." It was the last episode of Dickerman's life. After three days of this, he slipped into a coma and died December 22, 1867. An autopsy revealed that an abscess had developed at the site of the wound caused by the bullet before it had been extracted.[57]

The case of Lieut. George Young of the 143rd New York was not as severe as Dickerman's but also illustrates how a Peach Tree Creek wound could alter and cloud someone's life. Young served as provost marshal for Robinson's brigade of Williams's division when he was shot while taking a message across the battlefield. The bullet killed his horse and badly injured his right leg. The ball splintered two bones and lodged in the leg. Surgeons extracted it, and Young was sent to his New York home by the fall of 1864, where he was discharged from the army. Young lived a productive life. He partly owned a paper mill at Napanock, New York, got married, and fathered two sons. He even served as sheriff of his county for a couple of years before moving to his hometown of Ellenville.[58]

But this cheery summary of Young's life hid the fact that his Peach Tree Creek wound never really healed. In 1884 Young endured two operations to relieve his suffering. In the first, attended by three local doctors, it was found that part of the bone had diseased and needed to be chipped away. Puss from an abscess was scraped, and the wound was dressed, but an opening was maintained to allow pus to flow out. The half-hour operation gave him some relief, but a second operation was required five months later to clean away more bone particles that had become diseased. As he aged, the leg bothered Young a great deal. In fact, the attending doctor listed the Peach Tree Creek wound as the prime cause of his death on March 31, 1909. One can admire Young's persistence at living a normal life despite the problem, but it has to be admitted that one bullet could cause an enormous amount of never-ending suffering even for those who survived battle.[59]

There are fewer examples of Confederate soldiers who endured long suf-fering because of their wounds at Peach Tree Creek, only because the South never compiled a medical history of its war effort. But Federal authorities had access to some Confederate medical data and included it in the *Medical and Surgical History*. Pvt. E. Collins of the 33rd Mississippi was hit on the battlefield, the ball badly injuring his right ankle. It fell into Collins's shoe after doing the damage, but the wound never really healed. Despite stays in several hospitals, the hole remained so big one could insert a finger into it, and it drained and swelled. On June 8, 1865, surgeons finally decided to amputate the leg. The operation proceeded without problems, and Collins was sent home the next month.[60]

Federal authorities also knew of the case involving James Palmer of the 40th Mississippi, who was hit in the right hand, the projectile cutting the stock of his musket in two as well. He spent one night in Loring's Division hospital before leaving Atlanta on July 21 for Macon by railroad. After two days there, Palmer traveled to Columbus, Georgia, where he spent four days. He was well enough to be furloughed for sixty days and used a combination of railroad, wagon, and steamboat to reach Meridian, Mississippi, in five days. Here Palmer had his wound dressed again before he set out by rail and on horseback to reach his home near Shuqualak, Mississippi. His relatively light injury did not prevent him from taking a rather long and trying jour-ney home, and he parceled out his sixty-day furlough into a stay of seven months before he joined a cavalry regiment rather than return to the 40th Mississippi.[61]

The strange case of Serg. Oscar Bowen of the 3rd Mississippi indicates how wrong a wounded soldier could be concerning his fate. Badly wounded on July 20, a surgeon predicted his death in two hours. Bowen asked his comrades to dress him for the grave, but they transported him to the depot at Atlanta instead. There he had a spasm while waiting for the train. When he came to consciousness, Bowen realized he was on his way to Macon and begged to be let out of the train, but no one paid attention to him.[62]

Bowen was left at Barnesville, Georgia, and taken to the hospital where surgeons once again predicted he would die soon. He had enough presence of mind to make arrangements, dictating a last letter to his nurse, selected a coffin from among several he could see from his hospital bed, and inquired about local cemeteries. Despite all this, Bowen did not die. He suffered more spasms, and soon his father arrived at Barnesville to find him alive. Bowen's first sight of him was to see his father "looking into my face with dumb silence, the tears ran down his cheeks." He took his son home as soon as he was able to travel. The war was over for Bowen; he not only survived but became a Baptist minister at Handsboro, Mississippi, after Appomattox.[63]

A Confederate officer who survived a shell wound in his left thigh later wrote an engaging description of how he recovered from it. Lieut. Robert M. Collins of the 15th Texas made his way to Atlanta in a decrepit ambulance and was deposited at City Hall. The grounds around the building were filled with wounded and studded with operating tables. In fact, the lawn had "been turned into a carving pen," in Collins's words. When it came his turn, he was placed on "a big broad pine table" as four men held down each limb because the surgeon did not want to use chloroform on any but the most serious cases. Two surgeons probed the wound and found an ounce ball from the projectile had pushed against the femoral artery. They were able to extricate it without damaging the artery.[64]

Collins was now placed on a cot inside a tent set up on the lawn of the Trout House near City Hall where he spent a comfortable night before riding the train to Forsyth on July 21. He stayed in a good hotel in Forsyth, dining on chicken, coffee, and fresh butter. Collins even began to stump around a bit but then "break-bone wounded man's fever set up." The wound began to suppurate, and the matter in passing pressed on a major nerve that caused excruciating pain. Red matter oozed out of the wound seemingly without let up, and Collins could endure the pain only with constant doses of morphine for eighteen days. He complained so much about it that a doctor tried to "burn it off" as Collins put it by shoving "the sharp corners of a chunk of bluestone" into the wound. It was extremely painful. When the surgeon also stopped the morphine, he gave Collins a quart of "Confederate whiskey" instead. Collins was in a foul mood about everything; relying on the morphine, his first reaction to its absence was to throw the whiskey bottle at the surgeon. His mood changed when a local planter took him to his home on the Chattahoochee River to recuperate for a few weeks. Here he lived very comfortably until he was well enough to return to the hospital at Forsyth and continue healing under the care of army surgeons.[65]

Many Union and Confederate soldiers who were wounded at Peach Tree Creek struggled with death and won, while others did not. Capt. Oliver R.

Post of the 20th Connecticut was wounded on July 20 and died the next day. He had edited the *Hartford Post* and was noted for "the cool, cutting and sarcastic yet eloquent writings from his pen," according to Harry Stanley. "He had fine talents and a good education and never was at a loss to find words to most eloquently express his meaning." Post also left a wife and three children behind.[66]

John Potter deeply remembered the story of his close friend, William C. Young. Both men served in the 101st Illinois, and Young confided to Potter a short while before the battle of Peach Tree Creek that he was sure he would die soon. The thought of never seeing his beloved wife Tilly caused deep anguish. Young was hit on July 20 and remained convinced the bad wound in his abdomen would end his life. Potter tried to buoy his spirits. "John, I don't want to die yet!," Young told him. "O, it is so dark before me; everything is so dark! So dark!" Not long after their last meeting, Young died in the hospital at Marietta and was buried there. Potter had a chance to visit Tilly soon after the regiment was discharged in 1865. She was distraught that her husband "had to be left down there" in Georgia. Potter learned that Tilly was so sickened by her loss that she died a few years after the war ended.[67]

Unlike Tilly, the wife of Pvt. John Hart of Company E, 149th New York had accompanied her husband in the field and was with the wagon train during the fight of July 20. Hart was killed during the engagement, and his comrades buried him that night. Only the next morning did Mrs. Hart learn of his fate and rush to the field, desperate to see the body. The men felt so sympathetic they began to dig, but Mrs. Hart jumped into the hole just before they reached him and frantically used her hands to finish uncovering his face. That brought forth "the most excruciating cries of agonized grief" the men had ever heard. The cries brought tears to many eyes as she continued to grieve for him before Hart's comrades finally had to physically remove her from the grave of her husband.[68]

Soldiers met death in numerous ways at Peach Tree Creek, and for years after the battle as well, because of battlefield injuries suffered in Hood's first attack at Atlanta. None met it with more resignation and acceptance than William Allen of the 123rd New York. He had taken a load of canteens to the creek and was bringing them back to the regiment when a bullet struck. Taken to a hospital, the surgeon told him bluntly he would die soon. "Well, here she goes," Allen said, according to Henry C. Morhous, "and turning over on his side died soon after without uttering another word."[69]

We have fought the battle of this campaign.—Charles Harding Cox

**I think we will have Atlanta in a few days if nothing gits rong.
—Henry H. Maley**

**I have every reason to believe that our attack would have been
successful had my order been executed.—John Bell Hood**

11

July 21–22

Beginning on July 21, the men who survived the battle of Peach Tree Creek began a long process of coping in various ways with the experience of combat. For the Federals, the process was largely a joyous celebration that they had been taken by surprise and yet triumphed over Hood's first attempt to crush Sherman's advancing army. For the Confederates, the process was largely a painful exercise in justifying their failure or coping with the terrible truth that they had frittered away many advantages on the field. The men of both armies informed their loved ones what had happened, evaluated their commanders, themselves, and their enemy, and prepared for further movements and possibly another battle.

There was a good deal of crowing to be done on the Union side of the contested field. "We have fought *the* battle of this campaign" exulted Charles Harding Cox of the 70th Indiana in a letter to his sister, "and given the enemy the soundest thrashing they have yet had." For participants, the battle seemed enormously long, desperate, and "one glorious victory," as John Marsh Cate of the 33rd Massachusetts phrased it. William D. Hynes of the 42nd Illinois conducted a quick survey of the position held by Newton's division and drew an elaborate map for his brother back home so he could better understand the accomplishment of Newton's veterans.[1]

Not surprisingly, Federal troops praised their comrades enormously in letters home. "Our boys never done better," asserted Lysander Wheeler of the 105th Illinois. They fired so effectively that slain Confederates were left in piles on the battlefield. The men of Coburn's brigade in Ward's division were especially exhilarated by their victory. After suffering the painful emotions of defeat and capture at the battle of Thompson's Station more than a year before, their determined advance up the creek bluffs on the afternoon of July 20 seemed to erase all shame. In fact, someone wrote an eight-stanza poem about the brigade's part in the battle. The author compensated for lack of artistic merit with an innocent fervency, including the casualties and naming each regiment in the brigade as part of its tortured wording.[2]

Federal soldiers were not just reporters of the news; they were friends, brothers, and fathers of the recipients of it. They often inserted personal touches in their missives home. Judson L. Austin of the 19th Michigan apologized for the paper he used when penning a letter to his wife. She had sent it to him much earlier, but Austin had kept it in his cartridge box, and as a result it was quite messy. "Don't look at the dirt but just read it over & imagen how I must look" as he sat down "under a bush on the leaves with men on every side doing almost every sort of business" while writing.[3]

When Philo Beecher Buckingham penned a report of the 20th Connecticut's role in the battle of Peach Tree Creek to be filed with the adjutant general's office of his home state, he sent a copy of it to his wife so she could better understand what happened. The copy was written hurriedly under artillery fire, so Buckingham urged her to have their son George gain penmanship practice by writing it out again in a plain hand. He also wanted his wife to give a copy to his father, sharing this official document surreptitiously with many family members.[4]

There was a limit to reporting news of the battle. Samuel Merrill described it well to his wife up to a certain point but then stopped before illustrating the more horrid sights to be seen. "I can't bear to write about such things any more than you could bear to think of the battle field if you had ever been on one," he told his wife. Those bloody sights led more than one Federal survivor of the battle to thank God he had been spared injury or death. They also thanked what Benjamin Harrison called "a good Providence" that they had won the awful contest.[5]

For Harrison, there also was an opportunity to brag about his personal role in the victory. Hooker rode along the line and praised Ward's division for saving the day. He stopped at Harrison's headquarters to shake his hand

and tell him, "Harrison you did gloriously. I will make you a Brig Genl if my influence can do it." But for the unassuming Hoosier this kind of praise "was satisfaction enough for me."[6]

Several Federal soldiers wrote letters to their hometown newspapers to spread the word of the battle. They generally wrote the same things they expressed in personal letters, emphasizing the suddenness of the Confederate attack and the crushing defeat suffered by Hood's men. They portrayed Peach Tree Creek as a "bloody and terrific" battle and the assault of Hardee's and Stewart's men as "the most reckless, massive, and headlong charge of the war." In general, Civil War soldiers did not trust the writing of newspaper correspondents to be fair and balanced, which was one reason they often wrote letters for newspaper publication. But Charles Harding Cox referred his sister to the pages of the *Cincinnati Commercial* for accurate information about the battle of Peach Tree Creek because, once started in describing the particulars, "10 pages would not contain what I would like to say."[7]

Confederate survivors of the battle tended to report the news far less than did their counterparts in blue, and when they did, it often was tinted by strenuous efforts to put the best face on the event. F. Halsey Wigfall on Hood's staff emphasized in letters home that Hardee and Stewart "drove the enemy back to their works," even if they failed to accomplish anything more than that. Robert W. Banks of the 37th Mississippi asserted to his father that the Army of Tennessee was in good heart and fully confident in its new general. "The grief for the loss of General Johnston was painfully borne by the troops in silence," he wrote. But Maj. Thomas McGuire of Scott's Brigade in Loring's Division offered a very different view of the battle. "It was a shocking loss of life, without any results. We miss Gen Johnston so much. He would have retreated to Macon, rather than make such a sacrifice."[8]

Southern newspapers also spread the word of the battle less fulsomely than did northern sheets. The first news of Peach Tree Creek appeared in the *Augusta Daily Constitutionalist* by July 22. The tenor of the report reflected the view from Hood's headquarters, echoing what Halsey Wigfall had written privately to his family. The Confederates attacked Sherman's right wing, drove the Federals to their works, and captured several hundred prisoners. The report contained no word about the ultimate failure of the assault or the loss of life.[9]

No one could know better the result of the battle than the men in blue and gray who survived it, and the Federals continued to praise themselves for a long time to come that they had finally met the enemy in a large battle. "It was an open, 'square stand-up fight of give and take' without cover or defense on either side," proclaimed Edwin E. Marvin of the 5th Connecticut long after the war. Hood's men were "driven back by downright hard fighting." They often worded their description of this fight as "fair," and thus a better test of manliness and battlefield prowess than one fought from behind breastworks. "This will ever be a memorable day in the History of this Rebellion," concluded Alanson B. Cone of the 123rd New York.[10]

Sherman evaluated the battle accurately in his official report of the Atlanta campaign, noting that the Confederate attack "was sudden and somewhat unexpected." While Newton and McCook were protected by works, most of Hooker's command, which bore the brunt of the engagement, was in the open. The most important fact, as expressed by Sherman's chief engineer Orlando Poe, was that the Rebel effort "was completely foiled."[11]

After the war Sherman saw Peach Tree Creek from a broader perspective. "We had . . . met successfully a bold sally," he wrote in his memoirs, "had repelled it handsomely, and were also put on our guard; and the event illustrated the future tactics of our enemy." On one level these new tactics played into Sherman's plans. He preferred to fight the Army of Tennessee in the open on favorable terms rather than "being forced to run up against prepared intrenchments." Yet on another level the Confederates had some advantages in this phase of the campaign. Using the defense line around Atlanta as a base, Hood could "mass a superior force on our weakest points. Therefore, we had to be constantly ready for sallies." As long as his men were indeed ready for those sallies, Sherman felt he possessed the advantage, for they brought his enemy out in the open.[12]

For the men who had repelled Hood's first sally, however, the battle of Peach Tree Creek demonstrated the futility of the new Confederate mode of operations at Atlanta. "This grand charge was Hood's inaugural," commented John W. Geary, "and his army came upon us that day full of high hope, confident that the small force in their front could not withstand them, but their ardor and confidence were soon shaken." Every Federal commentator saw Peach Tree Creek as proof of Hood's failure. The Confederate commander "thought to rip the federal army all to pieces by the way he dashed into us," announced Miletus Tuttle of the 111th Pennsylvania, "but how handsomely he has failed." The fact that much of the battle took place in the open field accentuated Hood's failure in the view of most Federals, for it demonstrated that even without the aid of fieldworks the Yankees were a match for the Rebels in any type of fighting. They took away from the engagement of July 20 a conviction that Hood definitely was a fighter compared to Johnston, but it did not daunt Union courage or faith in Sherman's ability to handle the new man.[13]

Union troops evaluated the rank and file of their enemy with respect for the courage they displayed in the attack of July 20. As Geary put it, they "seemed to rush forward with more than customary nerve and heartiness," and John Marsh Cate reported the enemy "fought like very Devils." Of course, praising the Confederates for fighting hard simply emphasized the victory achieved by the Federals. John Potter of the 101st Illinois noted that Northern endurance won out over Southern enthusiasm. "Our men in this bloody battle certainly outwinded the Confederates," he concluded.[14]

One Federal soldier, however, believed that Southern enthusiasm had been bolstered by liquor. Albert M. Cook of the 123rd New York surveyed the battlefield soon after the firing ended and found "several whiskey bottles which show what gave them the courage to attack." Cook asserted that many Rebel prisoners appeared to be drunk, but there is no corroborating evidence for his assertion that whiskey played a role in the Confederate attack on July 20.[15]

The Rebels seem to have bolstered their courage with reports that the Yankees were out in the open with no breastworks for protection. Prisoners frankly told their captors this point after the battle. Their officers had assured them that "it would be easy to drive us into the creek and then they could shoot us down at their leisure," reported Harry Stanley of the 20th Connecticut. When they found some Federal units such as Newton's division behind works, the realization "astonished" the Confederates.[16]

When the Union soldiers evaluated their own commanders, Sherman of course came off very well, even though he had no direct, personal connection with the battle of Peach Tree Creek. Some men, such as Emerson Opdycke in Newton's division, thought Sherman could have reaped the benefits of the victory on July 20 more fully by taking the offensive against the Confederates, but he was content to know that his commander preferred to move slowly and surely.[17]

Even though Hooker had dallied too long in placing Williams and Ward before the battle, thus endangering the corps position, his troops overwhelmingly loved him as their commander. "When there was anything going on he was there at the head of his men," wrote John H. Roberts to his sister, "while other Generals were back in the rear. . . . Every one that knows old fighting Joe as *all* of the boys call him like him." Hooker's praise was sounded by most men of the Twentieth Corps, but the western regiments of Ward's division tended to be more enthusiastic than the easterners who had experienced Hooker's great fiasco at Chancellorsville more than a year before the battle of Peach Tree Creek.[18]

Ordinary Federal soldiers evaluated their own performance in the battle in overwhelmingly positive tones. "Everybody seems pleased that everything appears to have gone right yesterday," wrote John Wesley Marshall of the 97th Ohio, "and nothing but encomiums and congratulations are heard on every side." The men of Newton's division saw it as payback for their bloody repulse at Kennesaw Mountain on June 27. Many viewed the battle as proof that "'Yankee pluck' was more than a match for 'Southern dash.'" Despite the surprise attack, the Federals were able to respond quickly and effectively. "It is not over-praise of the National Army to say that its veterans were panic-poof," concluded Jacob D. Cox after the war, "and its well-tried courage was so intelligent and quick-witted that the smallest detachments could be relied upon to do a wise and bold thing in almost any juncture."[19]

The Unionists took away from Peach Tree Creek a deepened confidence in themselves that strengthened Sherman's prospects in the campaign. "I think we will have Atlanta in a few days if nothing gits rong," asserted Henry H. Maley of the 84th Illinois on July 21. The reason for this self-confidence was not difficult to see. James A. Connolly of Baird's division staff was sure the toughest fighting of the campaign "would take place between the river and the city." The battle of Peach Tree Creek seemed to prove him right, and it also proved that the Federals could handle the increased danger and still beat Hood's army. "We are like the big boy, 'too big to be whipped,'" Connolly wrote.[20]

When Confederates evaluated the battle of Peach Tree Creek, the tone of their writings contrasted starkly with that of their enemy. For L. D. Young, who served in the Kentucky Brigade of Bate's Division, the engagement did not even seem like an engagement. It was "a straggling, haphazard kind of hide and seek affair, magnified into a battle." For J. Cooper Nisbet of Stevens's Brigade in Walker's Division, the attack was "a miserable affair ... from start to finish. For the want of concert of action, the army lost many valuable lives and accomplished nothing of benefit." Rebel survivors tended to blame Hood for the failure, although some of them argued that the rank and file attacked with spirit even though depressed by the loss of their beloved Johnston.[21]

Convinced that Johnston had already planned to attack Sherman at Peach Tree Creek and that Hood had inherited the scheme, Charles H. Olmstead of the 1st Georgia (Volunteer) in Mercer's Brigade summed up his view of the battle in his memoirs. "A man of only moderate intellectual power, suddenly called to execute the plans of a military genius, with an army of disappointed discontented men without confidence in their leader, under changed conditions from those upon which those plans were based, was not the one to command success."[22]

But some Confederate soldiers looked sympathetically upon Hood, noting that with time his popularity increased among the rank and file. Some also recognized the context within which Hood tried to exercise command and saw the many difficulties he had to face. Higher-level officers tended to be more positive about Hood. Winfield S. Featherston, whose brigade lost its contest with Ward's division on July 20, retained faith in Hood's battle plan even after the war ended. In a long letter to Hood, Featherston praised the concept of the battle, argued that many other officers felt the same way he did, and blamed the failure on Hardee's Corps. "Had the attack been vigorously made by all the troops on our right," Featherston wrote in 1866, "and the plan of the battle been strictly carried out, I then believed and still believe the victory would have been a brilliant one, and the Federal forces on the South Side of Peach Tree creek, would have been all either killed, wounded, or captured."[23]

Featherston's letter must have encouraged Hood tremendously because it reinforced his own view that Hardee was the chief culprit of July 20. In his official report of the Atlanta campaign, written in February 1865, Hood began a long process of officially attaching blame on Hardee for not vigorously pressing the attack and thereby making it impossible for Stewart to achieve success. "I have every reason to believe that our attack would have been successful had my order been executed," he stated in this official document.[24]

When the report became public, Hardee was of course incensed at this slur. In his official response to it, Hardee admitted that he had not wanted to serve under Hood. He felt the young man "unequal in both experience and natural ability to so important a command" as the Army of Tennessee. When his request to be transferred was denied, Hardee remained and "gave to the commanding general an honest and cordial support." Hood never indicated that he had any ill feeling toward him until the publication of the official report "with its astonishing statements and insinuations."[25]

Hood could not leave bad enough alone. In his memoirs, published one year after his death due to yellow fever in 1879, he again slammed Hardee for not serving the cause well at Peach Tree Creek. Hardee's men did little more than skirmish on July 20, in his view, and many of them, "when they discovered that they had come into contact with breastworks, lay down and, consequently, this attempt at pitched battle proved abortive." Hood also blamed Hardee for the fact that the attack took place much later than planned, apparently still ignorant of the mix-up of intelligence coming from Cheatham's headquarters concerning the length to which the army had to shift right in order to strengthen the Outer Line against McPherson and Schofield. Hood's own headquarters shared equal blame for that breakdown of information, something Hood never recognized or even seems to have understood.[26]

Although Hood admitted that even a late-starting attack should have succeeded, he wondered for two weeks after the battle why it had failed. According to his memoirs, Hood found the answer one day in early August 1864 when Patrick R. Cleburne visited army headquarters and told him that, while preparing his division for the attack, Hardee had warned him, in Hood's words, "to be on the lookout for breastworks." Hood attributed this action of Hardee to the temper instilled in the Army of Tennessee by Johnston's extreme caution and to Hardee's fear of Hood's reputation for rashness. His conclusion was that Hardee might have been willing to frustrate his plans, or "at least willing I should not achieve signal success."[27]

According to Hood's memoirs, other high-ranking officers in the Army of Tennessee shared his view that Hardee was the chief cause of failure on July 20. Samuel G. French certainly thought so, and Arthur M. Manigault, who commanded a brigade in Hood's old corps, reported that this view was widely bandied about among the officers as well. Hood contrasted Hardee's actions with those of Stewart, praising the latter for exhorting his men just before the attack to push on regardless of any kind of opposition. He dwelled on the important role high-level commanders could play in men's battle spirit by the content of their words and the manner in which they spoke them. "Every word, portending probable results, passes like an electric spark through the entire command," Hood wrote. "It is, therefore, in the power of an officer to inspirit his men, and incite them to deeds of valor in the hour of battle, as well as to depress and demoralize them by an expression of despondency, one word foreshadowing the possibility of defeat."[28]

Hardee died in 1873, seven years before this fresh attack on his character appeared in Hood's memoirs, and thus was unable to answer it. Thomas B. Roy, Hardee's faithful staff member and, in the postwar years, his son-in-law, took up the challenge. He wrote to many officers in Hardee's Corps to see if there was any truth to the accusation. "I have found no one who ever heard of the alleged warnings against breastworks except in and by this book," he concluded of Hood's memoirs. Not only were Hardee and Hood dead, but Cleburne had preceded each of them through his death at the battle of Franklin on November 30, 1864.[29]

Roy compiled the answers to his query in a long article concerning Hardee's conduct during the Atlanta campaign, and there were numerous letters by officers who roundly denied that Hardee ever cautioned Cleburne or anyone else about running up against breastworks at Peach Tree Creek. Walter L. Bragg, who commanded sharpshooters in Cleburne's Division, argued that everyone already knew the Federals might be ensconced behind earthworks and that not even a lowly lieutenant would have dared caution his men against them, much less the corps commander. No one contacted by Roy could believe the story, and Roy categorically denied it in his article, which was published in the *Southern Historical Society Papers* in 1880, soon after the appearance of Hood's memoirs.[30]

It is unclear whether Cleburne really made such a comment to Hood. We have nothing but Hood's word for it that the conversation took place. Cleburne was not only a loyal subordinate but a friend of Hardee's, and it is difficult to believe he would have said such a thing to Hood. The fact that all the principals involved in this had passed away by the time the accusation appeared in print made it impossible to have closure concerning it, but from the evidence available to us today there is every reason to believe Hood misunderstood some innocuous comment about the fight at Peach Tree Creek. While Hood wrote a great deal in his memoirs about duplicating Robert E. Lee's aggressive method of commanding troops in battle, he completely overlooked a key component of Lee's method when it came to dealing with his subordinates. Lee would never have publicly blamed one of his corps commanders for losing a major battle, especially upon such slim, hearsay evidence as Hood used to attack Hardee's reputation after Hardee had already gone to his reward.

In the end, the overwhelming majority of Confederate commentators on the battle of Peach Tree Creek found it easy to conclude the effort had been an abject failure. "Take it all together my opinion is we did not make it pay," wrote Capt. Alfred Tyler Fielder of the 12th Tennessee in Maney's Division. The perspective of someone who did not participate in the battle confirmed that the opinion was widespread throughout the Army of Tennessee. Arthur M. Manigault had missed the fight because his brigade was in Cheatham's command facing the twin threats posed by McPherson and Schofield, yet he accurately characterized the battle of Peach Tree Creek as "a complete failure. We lost more men than the enemy did, and gained no substantial advantage. It did not delay the enemy twelve hours, but only made him more cautious, and caused him to be in a better state of preparation for any occurrence of a like nature."[31]

The battle of Peach Tree Creek was one episode of a long campaign, and the flow of events barely paused for it. Sherman began thinking of his moves and prospects at 1 A.M. of July 21. Having digested the first reports of the battle, he informed McPherson what had happened to Thomas and characterized it as a vigorous thumping of the Confederates. The enemy had been "roughly handled" on July 20. "I would not be astonished to find him off in the morning, but I see no signs looking that way yet." If so, Sherman wanted a hot pursuit and expected the Army of Tennessee to move toward Macon. If Hood stayed, Sherman wanted Thomas to advance to shorten the Union line and gain more firm command of the Chattahoochee River. Sherman accurately predicted that Hood would reinforce his right to more strongly oppose McPherson and Schofield.[32]

Early on July 21, Thomas more clearly informed Sherman of the battle's characteristics, noting that it had involved some of the heaviest fighting of the campaign thus far but had produced comparatively light Union casualties. Thomas expressed little hope of advancing very far, assuming the Confederates were well fortified a short distance from his position. As a result, the Army of the Cumberland did relatively little on July 21, "a fearfully hot day" in Howard's view. The men of Newton's division rested, buried the dead, and strengthened their earthworks. Thomas told Newton not to advance until he could secure firm contact with Wood's division to the east, and that could only be done by Wood's advance.[33]

By 4 P.M., Newton sent two regiments from Blake's brigade forward to reconnoiter the area south of his position. Col. John Q. Lane led the units and skirmished heavily with the enemy before falling back and reporting what he discovered. Newton relayed the information to army headquarters, indicating that Lane had found the Rebel skirmish line heavily fortified and only 500 yards south of Newton's position. The works were strongly held, and there was no prospect of success if Newton launched an attack on them without heavy support to right and left. Thomas's staff officers replied that the commander had no idea of a major attack that day.[34]

If the annoying gap between Newton and Wood had to be filled on July 21, it was up to Wood and Stanley to do so. A glimmer of hope appeared when Union skirmishers reported at 5 A.M. that Confederate skirmishers in front of the two Fourth Corps divisions had fallen back to the main enemy line the night before. Howard immediately issued orders for the two divisions to move forward by wheeling left. Stanley's left brigade did not have to move at all for it already had assumed a position very close to the Confederate main line the evening before, but Wood's command, to Stanley's right, advanced a mile and a half to close up with the enemy's main line of works. By 11 A.M., both divisions were well within musket range of the Confederate Peach Tree Creek Line and the Outer Line.[35]

By 2 P.M., Howard received a note from Schofield asking for a Fourth Corps brigade to relieve one of his own brigades that barely filled a sizable gap in the Union line between Stanley's left flank and Schofield's right. The Twenty-Third Corps had to shift left to secure its contact with McPherson's right, and it would help Schofield a great deal to have Howard relieve that brigade. Unlike his usual helpful attitude, Howard refused to do so. "I have one small brigade in reserve," he explained to Schofield, "and there is quite a space between my right and Peach Tree Creek. Hood is great for attacking, and I feel that it is necessary for safety to retain this brigade in a movable condition. The enemy is in strong force throughout my entire front, also opposite the gap between Wood and Newton." In fact, Howard was busy with shifting units along the line held by Stanley and Wood to even out troop strength, and he issued orders to fill up a deep ravine that bisected the Fourth Corps position with timber to prevent the enemy from using it to split his command in two.[36]

On Wood rested the responsibility of holding Howard's right. Wood had started the day with Knefler's brigade on his left and Gibson's on his right, holding Hazen's brigade as a reserve behind the line. During the advance, Hazen brought his men up between Knefler and Gibson to extend Wood's line before it came to rest about 800 yards from the main Confederate position. For the rest of the day, Wood's troops busied themselves with digging earthworks and making their new position as secure as possible. For many men in Gibson's brigade, that meant cutting small timber and rolling the logs forward to reduce their exposure to enemy fire. When a Confederate deserter came into their lines that afternoon and warned that his former comrades were preparing to attack, the men of Knefler's brigade quickly dropped their entrenching tools and got ready for a battle that never took place. Heavy skirmishing however occurred all along the line that day.[37]

Gibson found that there still were no friendly troops near his right flank after the move forward so he stretched almost his entire brigade out in a single line as well as reinforced the skirmishers stationed off to his right. Signal officers in Hazen's brigade found a good pine tree and climbed it; from the top they could clearly see the streets of Atlanta. Despite the move forward, Wood was still unable to make contact with Newton. Howard told Thomas's headquarters that, by the end of the day, there was still a gap of half a mile between the two divisions. Brig. Gen. John H. King's brigade of regular troops, however, had been shifted from Johnson's Fourteenth Corps division to this sector on the evening of July 20. King now tried to cover the gap by positioning his men on the north side of Peach Tree Creek opposite the interval.[38]

Sherman was pleased with this incremental advance, even though it did not unite his entire command in one continuous line. The Confederates still held a conspicuous hill near where Stanley's left met Schofield's right, and there they "keep up an infernal clatter" of skirmish fire that could be heard some distance away. Schofield paid little attention to it, focusing most of his energy on securing his connection with McPherson instead. On his right flank, Col. William E. Hobson's brigade held a road junction linking the routes to Power's Ferry on the Chattahoochee River with a major road leading to Atlanta. Hobson was barely in touch with the extreme left flank of Stanley's division. His men skirmished very heavily with the Confederates who held the hill all day of July 21 without relief from the Fourth Corps. In fact, Schofield kept Hobson there all day of July 22 as well before letting him return to Hascall's division.[39]

Schofield was able to firm up his connection with McPherson on July 21 and, for most of his men, that day was characterized by heavy skirmishing along the Twenty-Third Corps line. The troops also could hear the railroad cars clanging away in Atlanta, and some were able to climb trees and catch a glimpse of the city.[40]

McPherson made greater progress than any other element in Sherman's army group on July 21, mostly because he had been farther behind the other armies during the preceding days. One of his divisions attacked a prominent hill and captured it in heavy fighting, breaking the far end of the Confederate Outer Line. His troops were thereafter held in place by the Rebels who fought to minimize the effect of this loss as Hood scrambled to mount a major attack on McPherson the next day.[41]

While Sherman's left wing inched forward, with McPherson's progress dramatically prompting plans for a renewed offensive by Hood, the Union right wing remained in place. Newton's division had already shown that little more than skirmishing and reconnoitering was possible for Thomas's men on July 21. While Thomas wanted Hooker to press forward and find out what the enemy was up to, there was little opportunity of doing more to help Sherman's overall plan. Brigade commanders along the Twentieth Corps line pressed their skirmishers forward and relayed the expected news that the Confederates were in force a short distance south of the corps line. In some Federal units, rumors of a second attack steeled the nerves of expectant Unionists, who were to realize by the end of the day that they were in fact merely rumors. For most men in the Twentieth Corps, July 21 was a day of burial, digging earthworks, and resting from the labors of the day before.[42]

Irving Bronson of the 107th New York had a fresh look at the aftermath of battle when he accompanied a skirmish line that moved forward according to Thomas's instructions. The line advanced far enough to catch a glimpse of a strongly fortified Confederate skirmish line through the pine trees. Along the way, Bronson also saw evidence of trauma from the battle of July 20. "There was blood, chunks of flesh, hair, and an arm and leg, besides torn clothes, four or five muskets, and lots of things that a soldier has to carry. Some one of our shells must have done terrible execution on that spot." Bronson estimated that six men had been killed here, and their remains moved away.[43]

The appearance of Hooker remained a highlight of July 21 for many men of the Twentieth Corps. Hooker was a master of bravado, and the western troops in Ward's division particularly loved him for it. "His face looked just like a sunbeam," wrote George F. Cram of the 105th Illinois. "When he came along to our regt. we brought out a battle flag which we captured, he stopped and coming up to us said, 'Boys what regt. is this?' The 105 Ill., we replied. Then said he, 'You did splendidly, splendidly but they did just as well on the right, the corps is all right.' We gave him cheer after cheer and it was carried from regt. to regt. all along the line as he rode on."[44]

When not cheering Hooker, members of the Twentieth Corps amused themselves by reading the letters and other material found on the bodies of dead Confederates in their sector. William T. Shimp of the 46th Pennsylvania called them "Love Letters," and he also found the words to a Southern patriotic song on the body of a slain enemy soldier. Lewis Dickinson of the 22nd Wisconsin found a bogus election ticket on the body of a dead Mississippi man that read "'Save the Union,' 'No civil war.'" The Federals who read it assumed it indicated the depth of resentment toward the Confederacy among at least some of the rank and file in the Confederate army.[45]

Thomas's instructions for Palmer's corps were much the same as for Hooker's command; advance as far as possible and entrench. Davis's division was farther behind than any other in the Army of the Cumberland, so his men had a special task: to mass their strength and move south far enough to come abreast of the other troops. Sherman strongly supported these instructions and urged Thomas to move his right flank so as to clear the entire south bank of the Chattahoochee River and make firm contact with the railroad between the stream and Atlanta.[46]

Johnson's division moved a reinforced skirmish line forward at midafternoon of July 21 and met heavy fire. Nevertheless, the line captured the Confederate skirmish position, having advanced in places from 300 yards to a half mile. Dozens of Rebels were captured in the process, but Johnson lost an equal number of men as well. To Johnson's right, Absalom Baird's division also moved south on July 21. The Confederates were unable to stop either Johnson or Baird from advancing their lines. "With a heavy force they succeeded in gaining a portion of the line of pits and compelled the retirement of the whole," reported William H. Young of Ector's Brigade in French's Division.[47]

Davis's division had never fully pushed back the enemy skirmish line in the area near Howell's Mill, but now it mounted a major effort to do so. James D. Morgan advanced the 10th Illinois of his brigade and captured the stubbornly held skirmish position that barred further progress. This freed up the entire division, and Davis was able to come up with Baird to his left. Davis also was able to push heavy skirmish lines toward the Marietta and Atlanta Road and the Western and Atlantic Railroad to his right. The Federals occupied a section of the former for a couple of hours before Confederate reinforcements pushed them back in a countermovement. Nevertheless, the main line of Davis's division was now in position to see more of the landscape to the south. Brigade commander John G. Mitchell reportedly was able, with the aid of a field glass, to see a clock tower in Atlanta and "told the boys what time it was."[48]

Thomas felt that his men had done all they could on July 21, and he was right. There only was room for moving opposing skirmish lines because the Confederate Peach Tree Creek Line was too strongly held to be profitably assaulted.[49]

Hood was busy planning a major strike against McPherson on July 21 to take place the next day. But for the men of Henry D. Clayton's Division, positioned on the far left of Cheatham's Corps facing north at the eastern end of the Peach Tree Creek Line, there was a momentary alert. An order to attack the Federals circulated through the chain of command at 10 A.M. on July 21. The troops got ready and waited until noon when the order was canceled. This "relieved our *feelings* not a little," commented Elbert D. Willett of the 40th Alabama. Who ordered this attack and why has never been explained, but Willett indicated it applied to the entire corps. Cheatham's men endured a good deal of skirmishing all day of July 21.[50]

In Loring's Division, Winfield S. Featherston tried to crack down on straggling in his brigade. Perhaps he was prompted by a realization that one-third of his command had failed to advance farther than the captured Union skirmish position the day before. On July 21, Featherston ordered all regimental commanders to retrieve their stragglers. "They will find out and report all cases of cowardice and stragling [*sic*] to the rear during the fight yesterday—also all cases of meritorious conduct."[51]

Sherman sent his first full report of the battle of Peach Tree Creek to Washington at 8:30 on the evening of July 21. It was an accurate accounting of the battle. "On the whole the result is most favorable to us," he told Halleck. At midmorning of July 21 Grant telegraphed the latest news gathered from the *Richmond Whig* edition of July 20, indicating that Hood had replaced Johnston and everyone expected severe fighting to result. Sherman's intelligence gathering as well as Hood's actions had already anticipated Grant's news.[52]

By the end of day on July 21, McPherson, Schofield, and Howard had advanced far enough to lay Atlanta under long-range artillery bombardment. Sherman wanted them to begin firing on the city the next day in earnest. Thomas was not close enough yet to do so, but Sherman wanted him to clear away remaining Confederate strength from the railroad south of the Chattahoochee River. "I do not believe the enemy will repeat his assaults," Sherman told Thomas, "as he had in that of yesterday his best troops and failed signally. Therefore I don't fear for your right flank. Still, it is well to be prudent."[53]

Hood's plan for the attack on McPherson involved giving up the entire Peach Tree Creek Line and the Outer Line on the night of July 21. He wanted to shorten his defensive perimeter by retiring to the City Line much closer to Atlanta. Cheatham, Hardee, and Stewart pulled their troops out of the trenches at 9 P.M. and moved back without detection by the Federals.[54]

"Somewhat to my surprise," Sherman admitted, reports filtered in during the early morning hours of July 22 that the works barring further progress toward the city were empty. "I confess I thought the enemy had resolved to give us Atlanta without further contest." He assumed too much and even issued orders for Schofield to take possession of the empty city while Thomas and McPherson pursued Hood south. Capt. Henry Stone, Thomas's assistant adjutant general, was no friend of Sherman's, but his postwar account of what happened next can be taken seriously. Stone reported that Lieut. Col. Charles Ewing of Sherman's staff (who also was Sherman's foster brother) rode breathlessly to Thomas's headquarters early on the morning of July 22 to announce that Atlanta was taken. He then rode away before anyone could question him about it. "The excitement was all his own, but the order was General Sherman's." In his memoirs, Sherman admitted that "for some moments I supposed the enemy intended to evacuate, and in person was on horseback at the head of Schofield's troops" until it became obvious upon moving forward that the City Line was full of Confederates. By then it was too late to stop Ewing and other staff members from spreading the erroneous report that the city lay at his feet.[55]

Howard received reports of the enemy evacuation by 3 A.M. of July 22, and Wood occupied the empty Confederate skirmish line two hours later. At 5:30 A.M., Howard received Sherman's order to pursue the enemy but to bypass Atlanta. Stanley and Wood moved out immediately, and many of their men, having heard the news, expected an easy march into the city. They scooped up nearly 100 Rebel stragglers before coming up against the City Line by late morning. All they could do was to develop another line fronting it. Amid heavy shelling and brisk skirmishing, the men of Stanley's and Wood's divisions dug in.[56]

In Newton's division, the men were so buoyant over their victory on July 20 that they readily believed rumors that Hood evacuated Atlanta. "You would laugh to heare the boys talk of what they are going to do when they git into town," wrote George W. Parsons of the 57th Indiana; "we hope that the Jonneys will leave us some tobaco if nothing else." The division moved out at 9 A.M. as many men passed by "a nice, large, bay horse, lying dead in the road," reportedly the mount which carried Clement Stevens when he was shot on July 20. Newton's progress south was impeded by Hooker, whose men also used the Buck Head and Atlanta Road leading toward Atlanta. Thomas's headquarters staff instructed Newton to wait until the Twentieth Corps had passed before resuming his march. Soon the unwelcome news that Atlanta was still in Confederate hands became known. Newton's men formed a new line opposite the Rebel works by midafternoon and began to dig in, as Howard issued orders for Fourth Corps artillery to open fire on Atlanta.[57]

The move forward finally enabled Howard to unite the Fourth Corps. As Newton's division moved south along the Buck Head and Atlanta Road, his left flank secured contact with the right flank of Wood's division. Howard also firmly connected the left flank of Stanley's division with Schofield's right flank. This was in a way a historic moment. Ever since the start of the Union offensive south of the Chattahoochee River on July 17, various gaps had been necessary in the moving Union position. None of them had been so long-lasting or potentially dangerous as the gap within Howard's corps line. Only because Hood did not know of that gap did it prove to be harmless. Now Sherman had a continuous, fully connected line of battle from one end of his massive army group to the other.[58]

Schofield also moved forward to follow up Cheatham's evacuation of the Outer Line in his front. He discovered the Rebel pull out by 3 A.M., and the Twenty-Third Corps moved forward three hours later. The news that Atlanta was an open city had also circulated through the ranks, for Sherman was with Schofield that morning. In fact, the men of Cox's division scrambled to be the first to enter. But they came up abruptly upon seeing the City Line. Most units in Schofield's command found good ground where the men were able to see Atlanta as artillery duels developed along the corps sector and the inevitable earthworks began to appear on the top of ridges and hills.[59]

McPherson spread Sherman's opinion that Hood had evacuated Atlanta to his corps commanders at 6 A.M. There was far less for the Army of the Tennessee to do that morning; it already had taken a portion of the Outer Line the day before and now merely had to adjust its position according to the new circumstances, which unfortunately for the Federals did not include a hot pursuit of the fleeing enemy toward Macon.[60]

Hooker also spread the word that the Confederates may have left Atlanta before his Twentieth Corps troops followed up the evacuation of the Peach Tree Creek Line, but he also warned them to be ready for another fight if the assumption proved wrong. The Twentieth Corps may need to defend itself once again or it may be the first Federals to enter Atlanta—that was the prospect he offered the troops early on the morning of July 22. As the men moved out, Ward's division managed to get onto the Buck Head and Atlanta Road before Newton's division, causing the Fourth Corps troops to wait some time before they could march south. Most of Ward's men assumed Atlanta would be open to them. "The bands were heard way off to our left playing," reported Maj. Levin T. Miller of the 33rd Indiana. "Officers and men were jubilant and in good spirits."[61]

As the Twentieth Corps moved south it crossed the Peach Tree Creek Line. The Federals were surprised at how well constructed the entrenchment appeared to be. Some men of Geary's division found a Confederate mail bag carelessly left behind, which included some letters detailing the heavy losses suffered two days before. A number of Confederate stragglers (or men who deliberately dallied to be taken prisoner) were scooped up by the advancing Federals. Some of these Rebels joked that "they were coming into the union" as they were taken to the rear. By early afternoon, after moving from two to three miles, Twentieth Corps troops came upon the City Line and realized it was full of Confederate soldiers. All they could do now was move off to right and left, select good ground, and begin the process of constructing works of their own under heavy artillery fire and the rattle of skirmishing.[62]

Along the way to this point many of Hooker's troops encountered scattered Confederate graves. Members of the 27th Indiana had come to know a few Georgia soldiers because they held informal truces while standing picket along the Chattahoochee River before Sherman crossed the stream on July 17. In fact, the Hoosiers had come to know some of their Georgia enemy by name. Now those Indianans found the graves of several of these same Confederates behind the Peach Tree Creek Line, and the realization struck them with a deep awareness of the tragedy of this war.[63]

Another burial site struck other Federals with an unexpected view of their enemy. Capt. Edward H. Newcomb served as aide-de-camp to Alpheus Williams when wounded on the picket line sometime on July 21 and was taken prisoner. He died in Confederate hands, and the Federals were surprised to find that Newcomb had been buried with care, and a headboard marked the site. Albert M. Cook of the 123rd New York considered it "very strange that the enemy should take so much pains to bury one of our officers and mark his grave." But the Federals had taken equal pains to inter Col. Jabez L. Drake of the 33rd Mississippi. Officers, especially those who were easily identified, tended to receive far more attention at burial time than enlisted men in both armies.[64]

With Ward's movement south, his medical staff received orders to move the field hospitals of the division south as well. George Martin Trowbridge was told to be ready for another battle on July 22. He took over a house along the Buck Head and Atlanta Road near the Peach Tree Creek Line, often referred to as the White House, a prominent landmark at a key location. "Am ready for another siege at operating table soon as fortunes of war furnish material," he told his family. He also shifted movable wounded from the July 20 battle by ambulance to Marietta. Some of the wounded Confederate prisoners were well enough by July 22 to feel their oats, bragging to their captors that Hood told them "he was not going to fight with picks & shovels but with guns" and that Confederate success was inevitable. But there was no resumption of fighting north of Atlanta. Stewart's troops remained on the defensive in the City Line. By July 24, Sherman wanted to use the White House on the Buck Head Road as his headquarters, so Trowbridge had to evacuate the place and rest his wounded under tents in the woods half a mile away.[65]

On Palmer's Fourteenth Corps front, Union skirmishers entered the abandoned Confederate works by 2 A.M. of July 22 and reported them to be in a very strong condition. Still the corps waited until 8 A.M. to allow the men to cook and eat breakfast before following up the Rebel withdrawal. Word circulated along the moving mass that Atlanta had been abandoned, and the mood of everyone soared to new heights of expectation. As the move continued, many Federals could see the church spires of the city "and all were joyous and happy at the thought that we would soon be there," admitted James M. Randall of the 21st Wisconsin. Before long they ran "smack against the same old foe, and him strongly fortified." It was a severe disappointment, "but a soldier becomes accustomed to this," mused Randall.[66]

Palmer's men now established a new line and started their earthworks, skirmishing heavily with the Confederates and enduring incoming rounds of artillery fire. Rather than an easy walk through Atlanta, they tended wounded and had more dead to bury on the evening of July 22. Now that the enemy had given up all the ground north of the City Line, Davis was able to move his division so as to secure the area along the south bank of the Chattahoochee River and the burned railroad bridge that took the Western and Atlantic Railroad across the stream. He rested his right flank at Proctor's Creek northwest of Atlanta. Federals who wandered about the abandoned Peach Tree Creek Line found places where Palmer's artillery had devastated parts of the works with concentrated fire. "To look at it and see the marks of shot and shell I don't see how any person could live in there," thought William Bluffton Miller of the 75th Indiana, "but the killed and wounded have all been removed." Fourteenth Corps artillery now began to fire shells into Atlanta itself.[67]

The Federals were now in complete control of the battle area and could plainly see the effect of their artillery fire on the trees fronting the Peach Tree Creek Line. "[I] counted 114 shotes in one tree 3 feate over," reported William Cline of the 73rd Ohio. In other places Cline noted that "the timber is literley moad off By grape and Shell ande the timber is cut to peaces Buy Hour mineyes." Similar scenes were reported by other observant Federals as well.[68]

By 11 A.M. it had become abundantly clear to Sherman that he was mistaken in believing Hood would evacuate Atlanta. Instead, "we again found him occupying in force a line of finished redoubts which had been prepared for more than a year, covering all the roads leading into Atlanta." The Confederates already were busy improving the basic line around the city, which had been constructed by Capt. Lemuel P. Grant beginning in the summer of 1863. Soon the City Line would be one of the most impressive semipermanent fortifications of the Civil War, laced with layers of obstructions to trip up an attacker and studded with redoubts heavily armed with artillery. Sherman's chief engineer, Orlando M. Poe, was impressed by the City Line and described it in detail in his report of the campaign. Poe also was fairly impressed by the Peach Tree Creek Line, although it was evident to him that it was not meant to serve as the main defense position of the city.[69]

Swallowing his disappointment, Sherman instructed Thomas "to press down close from the north and use artillery freely, converging in the town," and Thomas did as best he could on July 22. By the time the Army of the Cumberland came to rest at the end of the day, Thomas reported that no real fighting had taken place. He nabbed a few dozen prisoners and found good terrain for his new position. Earthworks were well begun and several points on this line offered Federal artillery the opportunity to bombard Atlanta. Thomas also moved a cavalry division under Edward McCook to screen his right by occupying a position along Proctor's Creek. Capt. John C. Van Du-

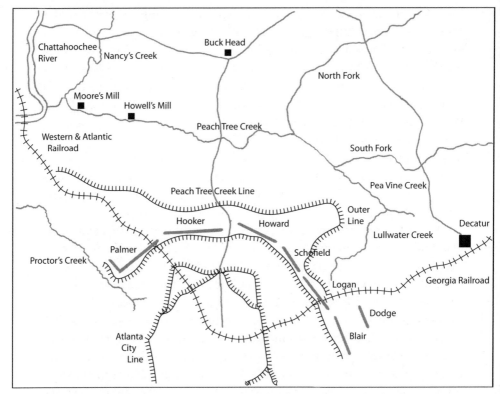

Midday, July 22

zer, who was in charge of Sherman's telegraph operations, began to stretch a wire along the railroad over the Chattahoochee River to a point within three-quarters of a mile of the City Line. From here Van Duzer stretched wires across the countryside right and left behind the new Union position to link Sherman with the headquarters of his chief subordinates. Here the Army of the Cumberland would stay for more than a month.[70]

Sherman's men had come a long way since the onset of the Atlanta campaign. "We have finally swept over all natural obstacles between Chattanooga and Atlanta," mused James A. Connolly of Baird's division staff to his wife. "The rivers are all crossed and the mountains all scaled, and nothing now remains between us and the doomed city but the ridges of red clay thrown up by the rebel army. We have crossed hundreds of such ridges between the Cumberland and the Chattahoochee, and the fair presumption is that we can cross those in our front now."[71]

Conclusion

· ·

Union and Confederate observers tended to judge the battle of Peach Tree Creek in clear and decided ways, reflecting a sense that the event had resulted in clear and decided victory or defeat on the tactical and strategic level. Unlike many major battles of the Civil War, the fight that took place on July 20 north of Atlanta tended to elicit unqualified praise from one side and frustrated disgust from the other.

"The engagement at Peach-tree was the turning-point for the overthrow and destruction of the rebel army of Georgia," asserted Asbury Kerwood of the 57th Indiana. His meaning was echoed by the judgment of Confederate artilleryman Philip Daingerfield Stephenson. "It was revealed in this very first move, that Hood was not able to handle great bodies of men for battle." Arthur M. Manigault, whose brigade missed the fight of July 20, also thought any possibility of victory that day had been wasted by "the unaccountable remissness or deficiency of our commanding officers [who] failed to take advantage" of opportunities.[1]

One such opportunity lay in the fact that the Federals were surprised by the assault and, on the Twentieth Corps sector, unprepared for it. A ready response and spirited fighting averted disaster on Hooker's line, but many Confederates admitted that their comrades did not engage the enemy with much enthusiasm on July 20. "The Peachtree fight was a tame and spiritless affair," complained Joseph B. Cumming, an officer on Walker's Division staff. "The fact is the army was dispirited by the removal of General Johnston and the assignment of General Hood. Nothing was accomplished by it." Many Federal veterans of the battle saw this too. "They don't fight with the courage and desperation that they formerly did," noticed Harry Stanley of the 20th Connecticut. "They seem to have lost all spirit and determination, though they still make some desperate attempts to retrieve their lost fortunes." In fact, according to Hooker, Loring confided to him after the war that if the Rebels had known the Twentieth Corps opposed them on July 20, "the attack would not have been made" in the first place.[2]

In contrast to the Confederate rank and file, the Federal armies opposing Hood were filled with men accustomed to winning on the battlefield. Edmund Randolph Brown of the 27th Indiana believed his comrades had become by this stage of the war immune to sudden attacks. "These Union soldiers would not give ground when properly commanded, and could not be forced to do so, unless they were fairly whipped . . . all that was needed was to give them a reasonable chance, and they would fight at one time, or facing in one direction, as well as another." Day Elmore of the 36th Illinois in Newton's division expressed this kind of confidence when he told his parents that Peach Tree Creek had been "a splendid open Field fight and we shipped them good."[3]

Evaluations of the battle's outcome gravitated toward assigning blame or credit. Stewart wrote a veiled criticism of Hardee when he asserted in his official report that "had the plan of the battle, as I understood it, been carried out fully, we would have achieved a great success." On the other hand, many Confederate and Union observers blamed Hood for mismanaging the affair. Henry Stone, one of Thomas's faithful staff officers, vigorously asserted that his commander saved the day, and Sherman did nothing to help the Federal cause on July 20. In contrast, Jacob Cox argued that Sherman played a key role because he carefully managed the entire movement of his three field armies in a coordinated way to force Hood to call off further attacks late in the battle.[4]

Latter-day historians have continued the fascinating task of evaluating the engagement and the men who commanded it, blaming Hardee for inexpertly handling his corps. Hood has come under extended criticism from historians for a variety of mistakes in conducting his first offensive as army commander. While Federal artillery played an important role in stopping Hardee, Confederate guns in contrast were ill-used on July 20. And historians have not ignored the fact that many Rebel soldiers failed to engage their enemy with spirit. "In brief," concluded Albert Castel, "where the Confederates had the advantage in strength, they did not fight well; and where they fought well, they were too weak. And because they did not fight well enough where they were strong enough, they lost. This in essence is the story of Peachtree Creek."[5]

The battle of Peach Tree Creek was the largest tactical offensive mounted by the Confederates thus far in the Atlanta campaign. At Resaca, Joseph E.

Johnston had attempted an attack on Sherman's left flank with one division and tried again at Cassville with one corps. Neither attempt resulted in major fighting. At Peach Tree Creek, Hood mounted an assault by two corps. He struck also with two corps on July 22, but the battle of Ezra Church witnessed futile attacks by only three divisions. Once again employing two corps on the first day of Jonesboro, the Confederates compiled a rather spotty record of organizing large-scale offensive operations during the four-month-long campaign.

Hood's first strike at Peach Tree Creek was a test, and the Army of Tennessee largely failed it. The army had good material in the rank and file and among a handful of its generals, but there is some truth to Hood's assertion that Johnston's persistent retreat from early May until July 17 had sapped some of the offensive spirit this army displayed under Braxton Bragg at Perryville, Stones River, and Chickamauga.

The corporate spirit of the Army of Tennessee had declined from its willingness to engage in fierce offensive tactics in previous battles to a decidedly defensive mind-set under Johnston's questionable tutelage. Never before did units of the army display such unwillingness to attack as occurred on July 20, 1864. Far more men made only a show of obeying orders to advance, stopping well short of pressing home the assault, than had ever done so before. Peach Tree Creek marked a new low in the Army of Tennessee's history of soldier morale.

Soldier reluctance was not the only reason for the poor Confederate performance on July 20; Hood's accession to army command, although not initially wanted by the young general, disrupted command and control from the top down and dispirited many men in the Army of Tennessee. Hood was utterly unprepared to take command, but circumstances demanded immediate action, and he was compelled to strike within two days after assuming charge of the army. He was woefully ill-informed of Schofield's and McPherson's movements, not even knowing that the Federals were on the Georgia Railroad until twenty-four hours after the fact. This was due mostly to Joseph Wheeler's failure to position troops far enough to the east to find out this important fact and also to his unexplained negligence in communicating with army headquarters. Hood also mismanaged the army's shifting to the right on the morning of July 20. This was due in part to Cheatham's unaccountable failure to fully inform him of his corps' needs and situation. That shifting had the effect of placing all Confederate units on unknown ground and under an imperative for Hardee and Stewart to attack immediately. But the shift also gave Hardee's Corps a wonderful advantage in terms of bringing a numerical superiority of four to one over its opponent,

Newton's lone division. Hardee could not capitalize on that advantage; it is doubtful he even knew he enjoyed such an advantage. The shift did not afford Stewart much advantage if any.

One cannot blame Hood fully for the troubles his army encountered during the first days of his tenure in command. He tried very hard to catch up with the flow of events but had every disadvantage to labor under in trying to do so. While Hood did not seem to know how to gather useful information, Sherman relied on a multiplicity of sources for his news. He had scouts roaming the area behind Confederate lines, he talked to civilians, and he read Southern newspapers and listened to his own cavalry reports. As a result, Federal headquarters personnel were remarkably up to date about developments in the enemy camp. There is no evidence that Hood drew on any source other than his cavalry for information as to Federal movements. He had infantry skirmishers fronting Thomas's approach to Peach Tree Creek, but there simply is no evidence that these skirmishers fed detailed and accurate information to army headquarters.

The Confederates also failed to push forward strong skirmish lines on July 20 just before and during their attacks. Because they relied heavily on battle lines, their advance resembled a reconnaissance in force as much as a real attack by infantry formations. All Rebel corps, division, and brigade commanders seem to have possessed little information about exactly what they could expect to find once they closed in on the enemy.

While Hood can be roundly criticized for undermining the administration's confidence in Johnston, he did so not out of a Machiavellian plan to replace the older man with himself; that appointment was a genuine surprise to Hood. But Hood was probably the worst choice Davis and Bragg could have made. Other than an aggressive, confident spirit, Hood held no other qualifications for such an important position.

Moreover, Hardee seems to have despised the young man and certainly did not handle his corps well on July 20, throwing away a surprising advantage over Newton's division in terms of numerical superiority. Most of Hardee's subordinates reflected their general's lack of enthusiasm for the attack, moving their units forward enough to give a show of attacking but failing to press home their advance. As a result, the best corps in the Army of Tennessee, which had by far the best opportunity of exploiting a one-and-a-half-mile gap in Sherman's line, flanking and overwhelming the only Federal division that stood in its way, accomplished nothing on July 20.

Stewart tried very hard to push his Army of Mississippi forward with spirit and determination, and much of that rubbed off on his division and brigade commanders. But Stewart's men faced considerable odds, outnumbered on their sector of the battlefield. Even though they had an advantage in Hooker's faulty placement of Twentieth Corps troops, the Federals were able to compensate for this disadvantage with impressive fighting and held their line securely.

It has also to be pointed out that even in Stewart's Army of Mississippi, many Confederates failed to press home their attack with determination. At least one-third of Featherston's Brigade elected to stay in the captured Union skirmish line along Collier Road rather than join their comrades in pushing down the ridge slope into the face of Ward's Twentieth Corps division.

The battle of Peach Tree Creek took place, out of necessity, during an interesting interim phase of the Army of Tennessee's history, when it was undergoing intense and emotional transitions in its leadership and the men were still mourning the loss of their most-beloved commander. Two of its three corps commanders had never led a corps in battle, and the third was miffed at having to serve under an officer he did not respect. Considering this context, it is not so surprising that the engagement ended in Confederate failure.

Could the outcome on July 20 have been different, and if so, what would have had to change to make it so? We can start at the top with the timing of Johnston's removal. Although it was pretty clear early on that Johnston was innately averse to offensive action, Davis waited too long before relieving him. That delay stemmed from his desire to give the commander every chance to prove his fears were misplaced, but Johnston was not the sort of man to change his stripes. He calmly retreated throughout the campaign, thinking there was nothing wrong with giving up territory while saving his troops. As a result, Davis relieved him at a crucial point in the campaign, exactly when Sherman crossed the Chattahoochee River and began bearing down on the city of Atlanta.

To make the consequences of this timing even worse, Davis selected one of the least prepared and qualified men to replace Johnston. Hood badly needed several days, even weeks, to learn how to become an effective army leader. He was hampered in this effort not only by his lack of experience at high-level command but by his dismal performance as a corps commander during the previous two months and by his limited intellectual and scholarly abilities. To a significant degree, commanding a field army demanded a certain degree of abstract thinking, a great deal of anticipation of wants and needs, and a habit of thorough study of a myriad of topics associated with logistics, geography, politics, and morale. Hood was at a disadvantage in all these areas. Selecting Hood merely because he talked and wrote confidently was one of the worst personnel decisions both Davis and Bragg ever made.

The timing of Johnston's removal and Hood's necessary transition phase into his new responsibilities altered everything about the battle of Peach Tree Creek. They prevented the Confederates from acting earlier and contributed to a near breakdown in the flow of detailed information coming into army headquarters. As a result, Hood was unaware of Schofield and McPherson's progress toward Atlanta, and he did not know that a potentially dangerous gap existed in the Union position to the northeast of Atlanta. One wonders if Johnston would have labored under these handicaps; his innate caution might have led him to hesitate before committing himself to battle until he knew exactly where Schofield and McPherson were located.

Hood also miscalculated the exact time when Thomas would be in the process of crossing Peach Tree Creek. Moreover, he spent too much effort trying to time his attack to hit Thomas when he thought the Federals would be most vulnerable. As Albert Castel has pointed out, Hood did not want to attack in the middle of Thomas's crossing but after most of the Federals were on the south side of the stream and before they could secure and fortify strong defensive positions. That was far too fine a point to focus on given the difficulty of ascertaining such a moment because Federal skirmish lines prevented the Confederates from close observation of Thomas's position.[6]

Hood also concocted an attack plan that was too elaborate and difficult to execute. Even an army that worked better than the Army of Tennessee would have found it very difficult to advance en echelon by divisions, wheeling left at the point of contact and trying to drive the enemy toward a common point as if they were a herd of sheep. A simpler and better plan would have been for the divisions to advance simultaneously straight ahead. While the Confederate divisions did advance en echelon, they were unable to wheel and simply acted as the circumstances seemed to demand at the moment. There was little else they could do given the complexity of Hood's orders.

Hood thought 1 P.M. would be the best time to launch the attack, but the sudden news that McPherson was nearing Atlanta forced him to postpone that start time and shift the Army of Tennessee far to the right. Anyone who tends to blame Confederate failure on this delay of about two to three hours should keep in mind a salient fact. The Army of the Cumberland had already crossed Peach Tree Creek by about dawn of July 20. Newton's division, Geary's division, and most of the Fourteenth Corps were already well in place on good defensive ground with some degree of fieldworks to protect them by late morning. Only Ward's division and Williams's division of the Twentieth Corps were not in line. If the Confederates had attacked at 1 P.M. there is no reason to believe they would have had any more success than later in the afternoon.

If the Confederates had attacked at dawn of July 20, especially with Cheatham's Corps as well as Hardee's and Stewart's commands, then Thomas could have been in serious trouble. He would have been much more vulnerable not only because several divisions had not yet secured positions south of the creek by dawn but also because Schofield and McPherson were taking longer than one could reasonably expect to close up on Atlanta from the east. That closing up was the key reason why Hood could not use Cheatham in striking at Thomas.

And yet, one wonders why Cheatham did not do more to help the cause on July 20, even within his primary role of protecting the eastern approach to Atlanta. His left flank was in a perfect position to explore forward and discover the one-and-a-half-mile gap in the Union line that separated Newton's division from Wood's division of the Fourth Corps. If anyone could have found and exploited that gap, it had to be Cheatham or his division commander on the spot, Henry D. Clayton. Yet nothing was done along these lines by anyone. No scouts were sent out, no skirmish lines pushed forward, and little was done even to support Bate's Division attack other than advancing Gibson's Brigade and keeping it idle in the woods all afternoon.

Could Joseph E. Johnston have conducted the attack better? We do not even know if Johnston was serious about conducting it at all, though there is a strong possibility that he did think about attacking Thomas when the Federals crossed Peach Tree Creek. Actually, such a scenario is highly reminiscent of Johnston's battle of Seven Pines more than two years before, when the Confederates assaulted the Army of the Potomac as it was engaged in a long drawn out crossing of the Chickahominy River during the Peninsula campaign. That attack was poorly coordinated, fell far short of decisive results, and resulted in Johnston's replacement as commander of the Army of Northern Virginia because of a serious wound suffered from the burst of a Federal artillery round.[7]

But simply thinking of attacking at Peach Tree Creek was not the same thing as actually doing it, and we will never know how strongly Johnston was committed to taking the offensive now that the enemy was knocking at the gates of Atlanta. But, if he had been able to drum up the moral stamina to order the attack at Peach Tree Creek, most likely the Army of Tennessee would have performed better than it actually did under Hood. Many of the problems associated with conducting the battle of July 20 stemmed from the relief of Johnston; if that relief had not taken place, presumably those problems would not have hampered the army's performance.

The Federals were not without fault on July 20. There is no explanation for Hooker's dereliction of duty in failing to put two of his three divisions properly in place to resist an enemy advance. While Geary's division was formed in a column of brigades near Collier Road, Ward's division and Williams's division were allowed to rest for hours to the rear, leaving two potentially dangerous gaps in the Twentieth Corps line. Hooker assumed there would be no trouble that day, and he communicated this belief to many of his subordinates. No such feeling existed in Newton's division, Geary's division, or the Fourteenth Corps, all of which were in place and ready for action when the first Rebel infantry appeared on the open ground to the south. The prompt and spirited response by brigade leaders and the rank and file saved the day for the Twentieth Corps. Hooker did little to compensate for his mistake; he did not even admit he had made one. The men of Ward's division tended to exaggerate the intensity of their battle with Featherston's Brigade, but it has to be repeated that they heavily outnumbered their opponent, bringing three Union brigades against only about two-thirds of one Confederate brigade.

Hood was wise to take the tactical offensive at this stage of the campaign. Johnston should have done so much more often before the course of events brought the opposing armies to the Chattahoochee River. But any attempt to stall or turn back Sherman at any stage of the campaign had to be well planned and executed by spirited troops and commanders. The Rebels had many things working against them on July 20, not the least of which was an enemy for the most part well positioned and ready to respond if challenged.

It was impossible for Hood to know this, but striking McPherson offered a better chance of success than attacking Thomas. McPherson mishandled his part of Sherman's program. He took far too long to move to Decatur and then steer a course toward Atlanta, allowing Wheeler's badly outnumbered cavalry to delay him considerably. Even upon assuming a position on good ground within artillery range of the city by July 21, McPherson failed to properly protect his left flank. By the time Hood realized this important opportunity, the battle of Peach Tree Creek had been fought, followed by a grueling small battle for possession of Bald Hill east of Atlanta on July 21. Time was of the essence; Hood moved Hardee's fatigued troops in a long flanking march that took the entire evening and night of July 21 to find and strike McPherson's exposed flank by noon of July 22. Hardee's Corps attacked in piecemeal fashion, allowing the harried troops of the Seventeenth

Corps enough breathing room to repel one assault after the other and save Sherman's flank.

In the best of all possible worlds, from the Confederate viewpoint, if Hood could have canceled the strike against Thomas on July 20 and awaited McPherson's approach, he could have struck the Union flank with fresher troops, with more time to gather information and to plan, and with more chances of accomplishing something. He needed but one clear-cut victory to take a giant stride toward success in the campaign, and this scenario could have given it to him. Instead, his army wasted much of its strength, energy, and morale on a strike that resulted in nothing worth the expenditure of life on July 20.

If Hood hoped to duplicate Robert E. Lee's mode of operations in Georgia, there were many reasons why it would be a faint hope. The Federals dominated the strategic context of the war in the West far more than they controlled the strategic context in Virginia. They had not only more men but, importantly, a higher level of troop morale, a vibrant logistical system to sustain their deep penetration of Georgia, and a steady and confident leader in William T. Sherman. The Confederates could not hope to compete on a level of equality with their enemy in these areas. The team of Grant and Sherman posed a combination too tough for Lee to handle in Virginia and too tough for the Army of Tennessee (no matter who commanded it) in Georgia. The days of spectacular battle and campaign victories like those Lee achieved in the Seven Days campaign or at Chancellorsville were a thing of the past.

This is not to assert that there was no hope of Confederate success in 1864, but the chances of success were far more remote than they had been one or two years before. Those chances were lessened even more by the fact that the battle of Peach Tree Creek was conducted by a general who had no experience at commanding an army, leading men who were depressed at the loss of his predecessor, and having to rely on subordinates who either were not up to their newly acquired command responsibilities or irritated that he had been elevated above them. No matter how hard he tried, the elements of success slipped from Hood's desperate grasp at Peach Tree Creek.

The battle of July 20 pitted old enemies. Ever since the second day at Shiloh, when the Confederate Army of the Mississippi engaged the Union Army of the Ohio, these two competing field forces had met on many battlefields of the Civil War. They became known as the Army of Tennessee and the Army of the Cumberland by the midpoint of the conflict. From Stones River through Chickamauga, these two armies carried the main burden of their respective government's military efforts in the middle theater of war, along the rail lines linking Nashville with Chattanooga. Even after the shifting of massive reinforcements from Virginia and Mississippi to enable Grant to defeat Bragg at Chattanooga in late November 1863, the Army of the Cumberland constituted the bulk of the Union army group that Sherman led southward toward Atlanta in May 1864.

At Perryville on October 8, 1862, Stones River on December 31, 1862, and again at Peach Tree Creek on July 20, 1864, the Army of the Mississippi/Army of Tennessee had taken the Army of the Ohio/Army of the Cumberland by surprise. The damage inflicted was far worse on the first two occasions than on the third, but the Federals survived all three encounters. Peach Tree Creek would be the last meeting of these two opposing field forces, although elements of both would clash again at Jonesboro, Franklin, Nashville, and Bentonville.[8]

Arguments over who was responsible for success and failure on July 20, 1864, began immediately after the battle. But several decades elapsed before the veterans of Peach Tree Creek were willing to write about their experiences, visit the battlefield, or reconcile their wartime feelings toward the enemy. By the 1880s and 1890s, national reunion on an emotional level became a major feature of American life, allowing an interesting mix of interactions between North and South that helped in fundamental ways to shape American culture well into the twenty-first century.

Stephen Pierson was among the first Yankees to visit the battlefield of Peach Tree Creek and leave behind a description of his experience. He did so with some Southern men who had served in the Confederate army, among whom was Capt. Evan Howell of the *Atlanta Constitution*. Howell's battery had been located in a good position to pound the Twentieth Corps, and that position happened to be his grandfather's plantation, "where I was born and raised," as Pierson recalled the conversation, "and you may believe I made my guns talk for all they were worth that day." Pierson was so impressed by this he took off his hat and shook Howell's hand.[9]

A group of Union veterans from the 27th Indiana visited Peach Tree Creek in September 1895 and sought the exact spot their regiment held during the heat of the battle. The ground was still undisturbed; the fieldworks they constructed on the night of July 20 remained intact. But the burial places of their comrades had been dug up, leaving in place some of the sandstone slabs hastily erected to mark their location. The bodies had long before been removed to a national cemetery.[10]

A pamphlet issued in 1895 to promote the Atlanta area battlefields as a tourist attraction contained a map indicating that a number of streets and houses had already expanded into the western part of the July 22 battlefield and the eastern part of the Ezra Church battlefield by that time. But urban sprawl was still at least one mile away from the southern portion of the Peach Tree Creek battlefield. A couple of rail lines had been constructed across the southern extent of the ground, but the rest of these hallowed acres were still relatively undisturbed.[11]

As the nineteenth century slowly merged into the twentieth, the pace of remembrance and reconciliation quickened. Both Northerners and Southerners used the pages of the *Confederate Veteran* to air memories or attempt to contact former enemies. Federal Capt. George H. Blakeslee wanted to return a Confederate belt buckle he took from a captain in Featherston's Brigade on July 20 and to locate a young Rebel soldier he had helped off the field because the boy had lost both feet in the battle. A number of Confederate veterans wrote to the magazine to state the loss of brothers and sons at Peach Tree Creek as a way of coming to terms with their grief. J. L. Lemonds of the 5th Tennessee received the fourth wound of his war career on July 20, 1864, yet lived another thirty-eight years. Several men wanted to know where their relatives who were killed at Peach Tree Creek had been buried and sought help in the pages of the *Veteran*, while others used the magazine to urge the federal government to give up the Confederate flags captured at the battle and stored for decades in an attic of the War Department at Washington.[12]

Expressing and promoting national reconciliation, 5,000 Civil War veterans gathered in a blue and gray reunion at Atlanta in 1900. Held on July 20, the event was also attended by Oliver O. Howard, Thomas J. Wood, Alexander P. Stewart, and Samuel G. French. The Aragon Hotel served as headquarters, but the opening ceremony took place at the Grand Hotel on the night of July 19, where Howard gave a rousing address. The keynote of his talk, and of the reunion, was "American Brotherhood," or "No North, No South," as Wood put it. Carriages took the visitors to the Peach Tree Creek battlefield on the morning of July 20, and a "big Georgia barbecue" climaxed the reunion that afternoon in the coliseum building at Piedmont Park, halfway between Atlanta and the battlefield.[13]

The reunion coincided with major efforts by Atlanta officials to obtain federal government money for the surveying and marking of the ground at Peach Tree Creek. They estimated that $2,000 was needed for this purpose. The earthworks left behind by the Federals and Confederates were intact and, judging by photographs taken at the time, in very good shape. Jefferson E. Brant of the 85th Indiana actually stood once again in the trench his regiment constructed near Collier Road during the night of July 20, thirty-six years before. Pine trees a foot in diameter had grown over parts of the ground, and Brant had difficulty recalling the lay of the land. A group of Confederate veterans kindly pointed it out to him.[14]

The federal government did not comply with the city's request for funds, and the battlefield continued to be subject to metropolitan expansion. The city of Atlanta purchased Howell's Mill dam in 1910 because sewage emptied into Peach Tree Creek and backed up at the place. The city dismantled the dam, destroying one of the cultural features of the battlefield. The U.S. Senate reconsidered the $2,000 needed to mark the field in 1910, but the appropriation was not approved. Meanwhile, the city already was beginning to encroach on the ground. Piedmont Hospital was constructed on the southern portion of the field in 1905. The Howell family donated 200 acres of land in the heart of the battlefield to the city in 1929. This became the Atlanta Memorial Park, originally planned as a "memorial forest." However, only two years later, in 1931, the Bobby Jones Golf Course, one of the city's five major golf venues, took up most of the park, followed by the addition of a large tennis center and many walking trails, but no memorial to the battlefield.[15] The small number of Atlanta residents who were interested in Civil War preservation sounded a note of alarm as the city slowly engulfed the Peach Tree Creek battlefield. The War Department proposed the creation of a triad park to link the battles of Peach Tree Creek, July 22, and Ezra Church with a touring road and three monuments located at each site. The estimated cost amounted to $315,000 and included the acquisition of forty-eight acres of ground, but nothing came of the proposal.[16]

Then, after two years of negotiation, Ivan Allen Sr. and other concerned citizens finally convinced the family of Andrew J. Collier to donate twenty acres of land "along Collier road and both sides of Tanyard Creek" to Fulton County for a battlefield park by 1938. This would have preserved a small but important portion of the ground where Loring's Division met the right wing of Ward's division and the left wing of Geary's division. Tanyard Creek was the modern name of what was more often called Shoal Creek, Early Creek, or Tanyard Branch in 1864. The proposed park would have connected with the Atlanta Memorial Park, which was owned by the city. Winship Nunnally also was willing to give up to twenty acres of his land as an important connecting strip so the combination of city and county park land would total some 400 acres sweeping across the heart of the fighting ground.[17]

"This is one of the most important battlefields of the Civil War," Allen asserted with heartfelt enthusiasm. "The blood of brave men on both sides of every State in the Union was shed here." But the elaborate plans slowly fell apart. County officials did send convict labor to clear some brush from the

Collier land, but efforts to secure $225,000 from the Works Progress Administration of the federal government fell through. The WPA assistance had been slated to construct two and three-quarters of a mile of paved roads and walkways at Collier Mill. As months drained by without any movement toward securing WPA help, the Collier heirs became frustrated, as did Allen and his compatriots in the Atlanta preservation community. Allen tried to convince everyone that the federal government would likely take over responsibility for the battlefield if the county could shepherd it through the early years of maintenance, but his dream broke apart within a few months of those heady days in late 1938.[18]

The Colliers had actually deeded their property to the county, but a significant memorial to the battle of Peach Tree Creek never materialized. Only a few small memorials exist today. Tanyard Creek Park, which is actually in the center of the battlefield, is a tiny enclave within the busy northern suburbs of Atlanta, hardly noticeable to those who drive by. Inside the park, there are some millstones from the old Collier Mill (which was a landmark during the engagement) and a few markers commemorating the battle. The Atlanta Historical Society erected a "handsome marble monument" along Peachtree Road (the old Buck Head and Atlanta Road) on July 20, 1944, the eightieth anniversary of the battle. Modern-day Peachtree Battle Road, named to commemorate the engagement, actually lies entirely north of the creek and thus off the battlefield itself. Today's Collier Road approximates the actual road that lay on the second ridge south of the creek, where the Federal skirmish line was located. As late as 1995 dedicated Civil War students could find only a few traces of earthwork remnants on the Peach Tree Creek battlefield if they looked for them. Like the battlefields of July 22 and Ezra Church, the residents of Atlanta claimed, destroyed, and covered up the ground upon which the men of Peach Tree Creek fought and died.[19]

(Go)

Order of Battle Peach Tree Creek, July 20, 1864

Federal Forces: 20,000 engaged, lost 1,900 (9.5 percent)

MILITARY DIVISION OF THE MISSISSIPPI: Maj. Gen. William T. Sherman

ARMY OF THE CUMBERLAND: Maj. Gen. George H. Thomas

FOURTH CORPS: Maj. Gen. Oliver O. Howard

SECOND DIVISION: Brig. Gen. John Newton, 2,700 engaged, lost 102 (3.7 percent)
First Brigade: Brig. Gen. Nathan Kimball, 1,400 engaged, lost 34 (2.4 percent)
    36th Illinois: Col. Silas Miller
    44th Illinois: Col. Wallace W. Barrett
    73rd Illinois: Maj. Thomas W. Motherspaw
    74th Illinois: Capt. Thomas J. Bryan
    88th Illinois: Lieut. Col. George W. Smith
    15th Missouri: Col. Joseph Conrad
    24th Wisconsin: Maj. Arthur MacArthur Jr.
Second Brigade: Col. John W. Blake
    100th Illinois: Maj. Charles M. Hammond
    40th Indiana: Lieut. Col. Henry Leaming
    57th Indiana: Lieut. Col. Willis Blanch
    28th Kentucky: Maj. George W. Barth
    26th Ohio: Capt. Lewis D. Adair
    97th Ohio: Col. John Q. Lane
Third Brigade: Brig. Gen. Luther P. Bradley, lost 24
    27th Illinois: Lieut. Col. William A. Schmitt
    42nd Illinois: Capt. Jared W. Richards, lost 2
    51st Illinois: Capt. Theodore F. Brown
    79th Illinois: Maj. Terrence Clark
    3rd Kentucky: Capt. John W. Tuttle
    64th Ohio: Lieut. Col. Robert C. Brown
    65th Ohio: Capt. Charles O. Tannehill
    125th Ohio: Lieut. Col. David H. Moore
    Battery M, 1st Illinois Light Artillery: Capt. George W. Spencer
    Battery A, 1st Ohio Light Artillery: Lieut. Charles W. Scovill

FOURTEENTH CORPS: Maj. Gen. John M. Palmer

FIRST DIVISION: Brig. Gen. Richard W. Johnson, lost 125
First Brigade: Col. Anson G. McCook, lost 67
    104th Illinois: Lieut. Col. Douglas Hapeman, lost 46
    42nd Indiana: Capt. James H. Masters
    88th Indiana: Lieut. Col. Cyrus E. Briant, lost 4

15th Kentucky: Col. Marion C. Taylor
2nd Ohio: Capt. James F. Sarratt
33rd Ohio: Lieut. Col. James H. M. Montgomery, lost 6
94th Ohio: Lieut. Col. Rue P. Hutchins, lost 8
10th Wisconsin: Capt. Jacob W. Roby
21st Wisconsin: Lieut. Col. Harrison C. Hobart, lost 3

TWENTIETH CORPS: Maj. Gen. Joseph Hooker

FIRST DIVISION: Brig. Gen. Alpheus S. Williams, 3,500 engaged, lost 580
   (16.5 percent)
First Brigade: Brig. Gen. Joseph F. Knipe, 1,000 engaged, lost 288 (28.8 percent)
   5th Connecticut: Col. Warren A. Packer, lost 61
   3rd Maryland (detachment): Lieut. David Gove
   123rd New York: Lieut. Col. James C. Rogers, lost 44
   141st New York: Col. William K. Logie (mortally wounded); Lieut. Col.
      Andrew J. McNett (wounded); Capt. Elisha G. Baldwin, lost 74
   46th Pennsylvania: Col. James L. Selfridge, lost 109
Second Brigade: Brig. Gen. Thomas H. Ruger
   27th Indiana: Col. Silas Colgrove (wounded); Lieut. Col. John R. Fesler
   2nd Massachusetts: Col. William Cogswell
   13th New Jersey: Col. Ezra A. Carman
   107th New York: Col. Nirom M. Crane
   150th New York: Col. John H. Ketcham
   3rd Wisconsin: Col. William J. Hawley, lost 3
Third Brigade: Col. James S. Robinson
   82nd Illinois: Lieut. Col. Edward S. Salomon
   101st Illinois: Lieut. Col. John B. Le Sage
   143rd New York: Col. Horace Boughton
   61st Ohio: Col. Stephen J. McGroarty (wounded); Capt. John Garrett
   82nd Ohio: Lieut. Col. David Thomson
   31st Wisconsin (joined brigade July 21): Col. Francis H. West
   Battery I, 1st New York Light Artillery: Lieut. Charles E. Winegar
   Battery M, 1st New York Light Artillery: Capt. John D. Woodbury

SECOND DIVISION: Brig. Gen. John W. Geary, 3,000 engaged, lost 476
   (15.8 percent)
First Brigade: Col. Charles Candy
   5th Ohio: Lieut. Col. Robert L. Kilpatrick or Capt. Robert Kirkup
   29th Ohio: Capt. Myron T. Wright (wounded); Capt. Wilbur F. Stevens
   66th Ohio: Lieut. Col. Eugene Powell
   28th Pennsylvania: Lieut. Col. John Flynn
   147th Pennsylvania: Col. Ario Pardee Jr.
Second Brigade: Col. Patrick H. Jones
   33rd New Jersey: Col. George W. Mindil

119th New York: Col. John T. Lockman

134th New York: Lieut. Col. Allan H. Jackson (wounded);
Capt. Clinton C. Brown

154th New York: Maj. Lewis D. Warner, lost 7

73rd Pennsylvania: Maj. Charles C. Cresson

109th Pennsylvania: Capt. Walter G. Dunn, lost 16

Third Brigade: Col. David Ireland, lost 233

60th New York: Col. Abel Godard

102nd New York: Col. Herbert von Hammerstein, lost 55

137th New York: Lieut. Col. Koert S. Van Voorhis

149th New York: Col. Henry A. Barnum, lost 19 killed, 25 wounded, 11 missing,
total 55

29th Pennsylvania: Lieut. Col. Samuel Zulick

111th Pennsylvania: Col. George A. Cobham Jr. (killed); Lieut. Col. Thomas M.
Walker, 200 engaged, lost 74 (37.0 percent)

13th New York Battery: Lieut. Henry Bundy

Battery E, Pennsylvania Light Battery: Lieut. Thomas S. Sloan

THIRD DIVISION: Brig. Gen. William T. Ward, 4,000 engaged, lost 551
(13.7 percent)

First Brigade: Col. Benjamin Harrison, 1,342 engaged, lost 181 (13.4 percent)

102nd Illinois: Capt. William A. Wilson

105th Illinois: Maj. Everell F. Dutton

129th Illinois: Col. Henry Case

70th Indiana: Lieut. Col. Samuel Merrill

79th Ohio: Lieut. Col. Azariah W. Doan

Second Brigade: Col. John Coburn, 1,315 engaged, lost 216 (16.4 percent)

33rd Indiana: Capt. Edward T. McCrea

85th Indiana: Lieut. Col. Alexander B. Crane

19th Michigan: Maj. Eli A. Griffin (wounded); Capt. John J. Baker (wounded);
Capt. David Anderson

22nd Wisconsin: Lieut. Col. Edward Bloodgood

Third Brigade: Col. James Wood Jr., 1,324 engaged, lost 143 (10.6 percent)

20th Connecticut: Lieut. Col. Philo B. Buckingham, lost 55

33rd Massachusetts: Lieut. Col. Godfrey Rider Jr.

136th New York: Lieut. Col. Lester B. Faulkner

55th Ohio: Lieut. Col. Edwin H. Powers

73rd Ohio: Maj. Samuel H. Hurst

26th Wisconsin: Lieut. Col. Frederick C. Winkler, 260 engaged, lost 45
(17.3 percent)

Battery I, 1st Michigan Light Artillery: Capt. Luther R. Smith

Battery C, 1st Ohio Light Artillery: Lieut. Jerome B. Stephens

Confederate Forces: 26,000 engaged, lost 2,500 (9.6 percent)

ARMY OF TENNESSEE: Gen. John B. Hood

HARDEE'S CORPS: Lieut. Gen. William J. Hardee, 15,000 engaged, lost 1,500 (10 percent)

CHEATHAM'S DIVISION: Brig. Gen. George Maney
Maney's Brigade: Col. Francis M. Walker, lost 11
    1st and 27th Tennessee: Lieut. Col. John L. House
    4th Tennessee: Lieut. Col. Oliver A. Bradshaw
    6th and 9th Tennessee: Col. George C. Porter
    19th Tennessee: Maj. James G. Deaderick
    50th Tennessee: Col. Stephen H. Colms
Strahl's Brigade: Brig. Gen. Otho F. Strahl, lost 21
    4th and 5th Tennessee: Maj. Henry Hampton
    24th Tennessee: Col. John A. Wilson
    31st Tennessee: Lieut. Col. Fountain E. P. Stafford
    33rd Tennessee: Lieut. Col. Henry C. McNeill
    41st Tennessee: Lieut. Col. James D. Tillman
Vaughan's Brigade: Col. Michael Magevney Jr., lost 122
    11th Tennessee: Col. George W. Gordon
    12th and 47th Tennessee: Col. William M. Watkins (wounded);
        Lieut. Col. J. N. Wyatt (wounded); Capt. Joseph Carthell, lost 52
    29th Tennessee: Col. Horace Rice
    13th and 154th Tennessee: Maj. William J. Crook, 154th Tennessee lost 45
Wright's Brigade: Col. John C. Carter, lost 122
    8th Tennessee: Col. John H. Anderson
    16th Tennessee: Capt. Benjamin Randals
    28th Tennessee: Lieut. Col. David C. Crook
    38th Tennessee: Lieut. Col. Andrew D. Gwynne
    51st and 52nd Tennessee: Lieut. Col. John W. Estes

CLEBURNE'S DIVISION: Maj. Gen. Patrick R. Cleburne
Govan's Brigade: Brig. Gen. Daniel C. Govan
    2nd and 24th Arkansas: Col. E. Warfield
    5th and 13th Arkansas: Col. John E. Murray
    6th and 7th Arkansas: Col. Samuel G. Smith
    8th and 19th Arkansas: Col. George F. Baucum
    3rd Confederate: Capt. M. H. Dixon
Lowrey's Brigade: Brig. Gen. Mark P. Lowrey
    16th Alabama: Lieut. Col. Frederick A. Ashford
    33rd Alabama: Col. Samuel Adams
    45th Alabama: Col. Harris D. Lampley
    32nd Mississippi: Col. William H. H. Tison
    45th Mississippi: Maj. Elisha F. Nunn

Polk's Brigade: Brig. Gen. Lucius E. Polk
    1st and 15th Arkansas: Lieut. Col. William H. Martin
    5th Confederate: Col. James C. Cole
    2nd Tennessee: Col. William D. Robison
    48th Tennessee: Capt. Henry G. Evans
Smith's Brigade: Brig. Gen. James A. Smith
    6th and 15th Texas Cavalry (dismounted): Col. Robert R. Garland, lost 17
    7th Texas: Capt. T. B. Camp
    10th Texas: Col. Roger Q. Mills
    17th and 18th Texas Cavalry (dismounted): Capt. George D. Manion, lost 2
    24th and 25th Texas Cavalry (dismounted): Lieut. Col. William M. Neyland

WALKER'S DIVISION: Maj. Gen. William H. T. Walker
Gist's Brigade: Brig. Gen. States R. Gist
    2nd Georgia Battalion Sharpshooters: Maj. Richard H. Whiteley
    8th Georgia Battalion: Col. Zachariah L. Watters
    46th Georgia: Maj. Samuel J.C. Dunlop
    65th Georgia: Capt. William G. Foster
    5th Mississippi: Lieut. Col. John B. Herring
    8th Mississippi: Col. John C. Wilkinson
    16th South Carolina: Col. James McCullough
    24th South Carolina: Col. Ellison Capers
Mercer's Brigade: Brig. Gen. Hugh W. Mercer, 2000 engaged, lost 3 killed,
      15 wounded, 5 missing, total 23 (1.1 percent)
    1st Georgia (Volunteer): Col. Charles H. Olmstead
    54th Georgia: Lieut. Col. Morgan Rawls
    57th Georgia: Lieut. Col. Cincinnatus S. Guyton
    63rd Georgia: Maj. Joseph V. H. Allen
Stevens's Brigade: Brig. Gen. Clement H. Stevens (mortally wounded);
      Col. J. Cooper Nisbet
    1st Georgia Battalion Sharpshooters: Maj. Arthur Shaaff
    1st Georgia (Confederate): Col. George A. Smith
    25th Georgia: Col. William J. Winn
    29th Georgia: Capt. J. W. Turner
    30th Georgia: Lieut. Col. James S. Boynton
    66th Georgia: Col. J. Cooper Nisbet

BATE'S DIVISION: Maj. Gen. William B. Bate
Finley's Brigade: Brig. Gen. Jesse J. Finley
    1st Florida Cavalry (dismounted) and 3rd Florida: Capt. Matthew H. Strain
    1st and 4th Florida: Lieut. Col. Edward Badger
    6th Florida: Lieut. Col. Daniel L. Kenan
    7th Florida: Lieut. Col. Robert Bullock
Lewis's Brigade: Brig. Gen. Joseph H. Lewis
    2nd Kentucky: Col. James W. Moss

4th Kentucky: Lieut. Col. Thomas W. Thompson
5th Kentucky: Lieut. Col. Hiram Hawkins
6th Kentucky: Col. Martin H. Cofer
9th Kentucky: Col. John W. Caldwell
Smith's Brigade: Col. Thomas B. Smith
4th Georgia Battalion Sharpshooters: Maj. Theodore D. Caswell
37th Georgia: Col. Joseph T. Smith
25th and 37th Tennessee: Lieut. Col. R. Dudley Frayser
20th Tennessee: Lieut. Col. William M. Shy
30th Tennessee: Lieut. Col. James J. Turner

ARTILLERY, HARDEE'S CORPS: Col. Melancthon Smith
Cobb's Battalion: Maj. Robert Cobb
Gracey's Kentucky Battery: Lieut. R. B. Matthews
Mebane's Tennessee Battery: Lieut. J. W. Phillips
Slocomb's Louisiana Battery: Capt. Cuthbert H. Slocomb
Hotchkiss's Battalion: Maj. T. R. Hotchkiss
Goldthwaite's Alabama Battery: Capt. Richard W. Goldthwaite
Key's Arkansas Battery: Capt. Thomas J. Key
Swett's Mississippi Battery: Lieut. H. Shannon
Hoxton's Battalion: Lieut. Col. Llewellyn Hoxton
Perry's Florida Battery: Capt. Thomas J. Perry
Phelan's Alabama Battery: Lieut. Nathaniel Venable
Turner's Mississippi Battery: Capt. William B. Turner
Martin's Battalion: Maj. Robert Martin
Bledsoe's Missouri Battery: Capt. Hiram M. Bledsoe
Ferguson's South Carolina Battery: Lieut. John A. Alston
Howell's Georgia Battery: Capt. Evan P. Howell

ARMY OF MISSISSIPPI: Lieut. Gen. Alexander P. Stewart, 11,000 engaged, lost 1,000 (9.0 percent)

FRENCH'S DIVISION: Maj. Gen. Samuel G. French, lost 19
Cockrell's Brigade: Col. Elijah Gates, lost 15
1st Missouri Cavalry (dismounted) and 3rd Missouri Battalion Cavalry (dismounted): Lieut. Col. D. Todd Samuel
1st and 4th Missouri: Lieut. Col. Hugh A. Garland
2nd and 6th Missouri: Col. Peter C. Flournoy
3rd and 5th Missouri: Col. James McCown
Ector's Brigade: Brig. Gen. Matthew D. Ector, lost 4
29th North Carolina: Lieut. Col. Bacchus S. Proffitt
39th North Carolina: Col. David Coleman
9th Texas: Col. William H. Young
10th Texas Cavalry (dismounted): Col. C. R. Earp
14th Texas Cavalry (dismounted): Col. John L. Camp

32nd Texas Cavalry (dismounted): Col. Julius A. Andrews
Sears's Brigade: Brig. Gen. Claudius W. Sears
    7th Mississippi Battalion: Lieut. A. J. Farmer
    4th Mississippi: Col. Thomas N. Adaire
    35th Mississippi: Lieut. Col. Reuben H. Shotwell
    36th Mississippi: Col. William W. Witherspoon
    39th Mississippi: Maj. R. J. Durr
    46th Mississippi: Col. William H. Clark

LORING'S DIVISION: Maj. Gen. William W. Loring, 2,550 engaged, lost 1,016
    (39.8 percent)
Adams's Brigade: Brig. Gen. John Adams
    6th Mississippi: Col. Robert Lowry
    14th Mississippi: Lieut. Col. Washington L. Doss
    15th Mississippi: Col. Michael Farrell
    20th Mississippi: Col. William N. Brown
    23rd Mississippi: Col. Joseph M. Wells
    43rd Mississippi: Col. Richard Harrison
Featherston's Brigade: Brig. Gen. Winfield S. Featherston, 1,230 engaged, lost 626
    (50.8 percent)
    1st Mississippi Battalion Sharpshooters: Maj. James M. Stigler
    3rd Mississippi: Col. Thomas A. Mellon (wounded);
        Lieut. Col. Samuel M. Dyer
    22nd Mississippi: Maj. Martin A. Oatis (wounded); Capt. J. T. Formby
    31st Mississippi: Lieut. Col. James W. Drane (wounded); Maj. F. M. Gillespie
        (wounded); Lieut. William D. Shaw, 215 engaged, lost 164 (76.7 percent)
    33rd Mississippi: Col. Jabez L. Drake (killed); Capt. Moses Jackson
    40th Mississippi: Lieut. Col. George P. Wallace (wounded);
        Maj. W. McD. Gibbens (killed); Capt. Charles A. Huddleston
Scott's Brigade: Brig. Gen. Thomas M. Scott, 1,320 engaged, lost 390 (29.5 percent)
    27th, 35th, and 49th Alabama: Col. Samuel S. Ives, lost 33
    55th Alabama: Col. John Snodgrass
    57th Alabama: Lieut. Col. William C. Bethune, 330 engaged, lost 157
    12th Louisiana: Col. Noel L. Nelson, 318 engaged, lost 73

WALTHALL'S DIVISION: Maj. Gen. Edward C. Walthall
Cantey's Brigade: Col. Edward A. O'Neal, 1,050 engaged, lost 279 (26.5 percent)
    17th Alabama: Maj. Thomas J. Burnett
    26th Alabama: Maj. David F. Bryan
    29th Alabama: Col. John F. Conoley
    37th Mississippi: Col. Orlando S. Holland, 210 engaged, lost 48 (22.8 percent)
    Sharpshooters: Capt. Sid B. Smith
Quarles's Brigade: Brig. Gen. William A. Quarles, lost 24
    1st Alabama: Maj. Samuel L. Knox
    4th Louisiana: Col. S. E. Hunter

30th Louisiana: Lieut. Col. Thomas Shields

42nd Tennessee: Col. Isaac N. Hulme

45th and 55th Tennessee: Col. Robert A. Owens

48th Tennessee: Lieut. Col. Aaron S. Godwin

49th Tennessee: Col. William F. Young

53rd Tennessee: Col. John R. White

Reynolds's Brigade: Brig. Gen. Daniel H. Reynolds, 540 engaged, lost 67
        (12.4 percent)

1st Arkansas Mounted Rifles (dismounted): Lieut. Col. Morton G. Galloway, lost 2 killed, 12 wounded, 2 missing, total 16

2nd Arkansas Mounted Rifles (dismounted): Col. James A. Williamson

4th Arkansas: Col. Henry G. Bunn

9th Arkansas: Col. Isaac L. Dunlop

25th Arkansas: Col. Charles J. Turnbull

ARTILLERY, ARMY OF MISSISSIPPI: (commander unknown)

Myrick's Battalion: Maj. John D. Myrick

  Bouanchaud's Louisiana Battery: Capt. Alcide Bouanchaud

  Cowan's Mississippi Battery: Capt. James J. Cowan

  Lookout Tennessee Battery: Lieut. Richard L. Watkins, lost 15

Preston's Battalion: Maj. William C. Preston (killed)

  Selden's Alabama Battery: Lieut. Charles W. Lovelace

  Tarrant's Alabama Battery: Lieut. Seth Shepard

  Yates's Mississippi Battery: Capt. James H. Yates

Storrs's Battalion: Maj. George S. Storrs

  Guibor's Missouri Battery: Lieut. Aaron W. Harris

  Hoskins' Mississippi Battery: Capt. James A. Hoskins

  Ward's Alabama Battery: Capt. John J. Ward

Waties's Battalion: Capt. John Waties

  Croft's Georgia Battery: Capt. Edward Croft

  King's Missouri Battery: Capt. Houston King

  Waties's South Carolina Battery: Lieut. R. B. Waddell

Notes

Abbreviations

AAS   American Antiquarian Society, Worcester, Massachusetts
ADAH   Alabama Department of Archives and History, Montgomery
AHC   Atlanta History Center, Atlanta, Georgia
ALPL   Abraham Lincoln Presidential Library, Springfield, Illinois
AU   Auburn University, Special Collections and Archives,
           Auburn, Alabama
BHL-UM   University of Michigan, Bentley Historical Library, Ann Arbor
CHM   Chicago History Museum, Chicago
CHS   Connecticut Historical Society, New Haven
CU   Cornell University, Rare and Manuscript Collections, Ithaca,
           New York
CWM   College of William and Mary, Special Collections,
           Williamsburg, Virginia
DPL   Detroit Public Library, Burton Historical Collection, Detroit
DU   Duke University, Rubenstein Rare Book and Manuscript Library,
           Durham, North Carolina
EU   Emory University, Manuscript, Archives, and Rare Books Library,
           Atlanta, Georgia
FHS   Filson Historical Society, Louisville, Kentucky
GA   Georgia Archives, Morrow
GHS   Georgia Historical Society, Savannah
GLIAH   Gilder Lehrman Institute of American History, New-York
           Historical Society, New York
HSP   Historical Society of Pennsylvania, Philadelphia
IHS   Indiana Historical Society, Indianapolis
ISL   Indiana State Library, Indianapolis
LC   Library of Congress, Manuscript Division, Washington, D.C.
LMU   Lincoln Memorial University, Abraham Lincoln Library and
           Museum, Harrogate, Tennessee
LSU   Louisiana State University, Louisiana and Lower Mississippi Valley
           Collections, Baton Rouge
MDAH   Mississippi Department of Archives and History, Jackson
MHS   Massachusetts Historical Society, Boston
MSU   Mississippi State University, Special Collections, Starkville
NARA   National Archives and Records Administration, Washington, D.C.
NC   Navarro College, Pearce Civil War Collection, Corsicana, Texas
NL   Newberry Library, Chicago
N-YHS   New-York Historical Society, New York
NYPL   New York Public Library, Rare Books and Manuscripts, New York
NYSL   New York State Library, Albany

OHS	Ohio Historical Society, Archives/Library, Columbus
OR	*War of the Rebellion: A Compilation of the Official Records of the Union and Confederate Armies.* 70 vols. in 128. Washington, D.C.: Government Printing Office, 1880–1901. Unless otherwise cited, all references are to Series 1. *OR* citations take the following form: volume number (part number, where applicable):page number.
RBHPC	Rutherford B. Hayes Presidential Center, Fremont, Ohio
SAF	State Archives of Florida, Tallahassee
SCHS	South Carolina Historical Society, Charleston
SHSM-RCC	State Historical Society of Missouri, Research Center Columbia
SHSM-RCR	State Historical Society of Missouri, Research Center Rolla
SOR	*Supplement to the Official Records of the Union and Confederate Armies* 100 Vols. Wilmington, N.C.: Broadfoot, 1993–2000.
SU	Syracuse University, Special Collections Research Center, Syracuse, New York
TC	The Citadel, Archives and Museum, Charleston, South Carolina
TSLA	Tennessee State Library and Archives, Nashville
UA	University of Alabama, W. S. Hoole Special Collections Library, Tuscaloosa
UC	University of California, Bancroft Library, Berkeley
UG	University of Georgia, Hargrett Rare Book and Manuscript Library, Athens
UH	University of Houston, Special Collections, Texas
UI	University of Iowa, Special Collections, Iowa City
UM	University of Mississippi, Archives and Special Collections, Oxford
UNC	University of North Carolina, Southern Historical Collection, Chapel Hill
UND	University of Notre Dame, Rare Books and Special Collections, South Bend, Indiana
USAMHI	U.S. Army Military History Institute, Carlisle, Pennsylvania
USC	University of South Carolina, South Caroliniana Library
USM	University of Southern Mississippi, Archives, Hattiesburg
UTC	University of Tennessee, Special Collections, Chattanooga
UTK	University of Tennessee, Special Collections, Knoxville
UTM	University of Tennessee, Special Collections, Martin
VHS	Virginia Historical Society, Richmond
WHS	Wisconsin Historical Society, Madison
WLC-UM	University of Michigan, William L. Clements Library, Ann Arbor

Chapter 1

1. Sherman to Halleck, September 15, 1864, *OR*, 38(1):62–63; Castel, *Decision in the West*, 111, 115, 121.

2. For a good overview of the Overland campaign, consult Grimsley, *And Keep Moving On.*

3. Sherman to Ellen, May 20, 1864, in Simpson and Berlin, *Sherman's Civil War*, 638.

4. Hess, *Trench Warfare under Grant and Lee*, 205–14.

5. Bearss, "Siege of Jackson," 55–105.

6. Sherman to Halleck, September 15, 1864, *OR*, 38(1):69.

7. Castel, *Decision in the West*, 121–209.

8. Ibid., 217–326; Hess, *Kennesaw Mountain*, 71–137.

9. Castel, *Decision in the West*, 261–62.

10. Johnston to Bragg, July 10, 1864, *OR*, 38(5):873.

11. Howard to Whipple, September 18, 1864, *OR*, 38(1):200–201.

12. Thomas to Sawyer, August 17, 1864, *OR*, 38(1):155; Hascall to Campbell, September 10, 1864, *OR*, 38(2):571; Johnston to Cooper, July 14, 1864, *OR*, 38(5):879; Connelly, *Autumn of Glory*, 397–98.

13. Connelly, *Autumn of Glory*, 398; Williams to Burford, July 10, 1864, 2 P.M.; Kelly to Burford, July 10, 1864, 6 P.M.; and Anderson to Burford, July 10, 1864, *OR*, 38(5):873–74.

14. Johnston to Wheeler, July 13, 1864, *OR*, 38(5):879.

15. Landingham to mother, July 14, 1864, Irenus Watson Landingham Collection, AU; J. Walker Coleman to Quintard, July 9, 1864, Charles Todd Quintard Papers, DU; Walker to daughter, July 15, 1864, W. H. T. Walker Papers, DU.

16. Johnston, "Opposing Sherman's Advance to Atlanta," 274.

17. Sherman to Ellen, June 30, 1864, in Simpson and Berlin, *Sherman's Civil War*, 660; Sherman to Halleck, July 6, 1864, *OR*, 38(5):66.

18. Cox, *Atlanta*, 144.

19. Ibid., 145; Joslyn, *Charlotte's Boys*, 268; Franklin, *Civil War Diaries*, 188; William McLeod Civil War Pocket Diary, July 18, 1864, SAF; E. D. Willett Diary, July 18, 1864, ADAH.

20. Cox, *Atlanta*, 146.

21. Ibid., 144–45.

22. Ibid., 147.

23. Bradley to Mary, July 17, 1864, Luther P. Bradley Collection, USAMHI; Sherman to Halleck September 15, 1864, *OR*, 38(1):71; O'Connor to not stated, September 7, 1864, *OR*, 38(2):229–30.

24. Capers to wife, July 17, 1864, Ellison Capers Papers, DU; Walker to Mary, July 12, 1864, W. H. T. Walker Papers, DU; Champion to wife, June 27, July 14, 1864, Sidney S. Champion Papers, DU.

25. Davis to Johnston, July 11, 1864, *OR*, 38(5):875.

26. Bragg to Davis, July 13, 1864, *OR*, 38(5):878; McMurry, *John Bell Hood*, 117; Hess, *Braxton Bragg*, 230–31.

27. McMurry, *John Bell Hood*, 118; Hess, *Braxton Bragg*, 231.

28. Hood to Bragg, July 14, 1864, *OR*, 38(5):879–80.

29. Hess, *Braxton Bragg*, 232; McMurry, *John Bell Hood*, is the best biography of the general.

30. Castel, *Decision in the West*, 198–206, 242–43; Hess, *Kennesaw Mountain*, 28–46.

31. Numerous historians have written about the relationship between Bragg and Polk. See, for example, Hess, *Braxton Bragg*, 30–31, 65–72, 172–75, 178–79; Cozzens, *This Terrible Sound*, 264–65, 306–7, 513–14.

32. McMurry, *John Bell Hood*, 118; McMurry, *Atlanta 1864*, 137; Connelly, *Autumn of Glory*, 415; Hay, "Davis-Hood-Johnston Controversy," 81.

33. Bragg to Davis, July 15, 1864, *OR*, 38(5):881; Johnston to Cooper, October 20, 1864, *OR*, 38(3):620–21; Joseph E. Johnston to Wigfall, August 27, 1864, Louis Trezevant Wigfall Family Papers, LC; Hess, *Braxton Bragg*, 233.

34. Davis to Johnston, July 16, 1864, *OR*, 38(5):882.

35. Johnston to Davis, July 16, 1864, *OR*, 38(5):883.

Chapter 2

1. Douglas Hapeman Diaries, July 17, 1864, ALPL; Sherman to Halleck, September 15, 1864, *OR*, 38(1):71; Blair to Clark, September 12, 1864, *OR*, 38(3):553; Sherman to Thomas, July 17, 1864, *OR*, 38(5):159.

2. Sherman to Thomas, July 17, 1864, *OR*, 38(5):159. While modern day Atlantans refer to the stream as Peachtree Creek, R. Jenkins, *Battle of Peach Tree Creek*, xv, correctly prefers to use the Civil War era spelling of Peach Tree Creek.

3. Thomas to Sawyer, August 17, 1864; Howard to Whipple, September 18, 1864; "Itinerary of the Fourteenth Army Corps, May 6–September 8"; and Davis to McClurg, September, no date, 1864, *OR*, 38(1):155–56, 201, 507, 634; Hight, *History of the Fifty-Eighth*, 342; entry July 17, 1864, Jacob Andervount Diary, AHC; diary, July 17, 1864, James R. Carnahan Papers, IHS; diary, July 17, 1864, Charles Richard Pomeroy Jr., Papers, DU; entry July 17, 1864, Douglas Hapeman Diaries, ALPL; Barnes, Carnahan, and McCain, *Eighty-Sixth Regiment*, 414; Cox, *Atlanta*, 150.

4. Hight, *History of the Fifty-Eighth*, 343; Dan Griffin to Scribner, July 19, 1864, Benjamin Franklin Scribner Papers, IHS.

5. Thomas to Sawyer, August 17, 1864: Banning to Wilson, September 9, 1864, *OR*, 38(1):156; 704; Cox, *Atlanta*, 150; Johnson to McClurg, August, no date, 1864, *OR*, 38(1):524; Angle, *Three Years*, 239.

6. Williams to Perkins, September 12, 1864; Compton to Palmer, September 9, 1864; Geary to Perkins, September 15, 1864; Ward to Perkins, September 7, 1864; and Miller to Crawford, July 27, 1864, *OR*, 38(2):33, 53, 136, 327, 403; diary, July 17, 1864, Albert M. Cook Papers, SU; Alanson B. Cone Personal Narrative, NYSL; E. P. Failing diary, July 17, 1864, Failing-Knight Papers, MHS; Buckingham to Horace J. Munsey, August 6, 1864, Philo Beecher Buckingham Papers, AAS; Charles A. Booth Journal, July 17, 1864, WHS; diary, July 17, 1864, Curtis J. Judd Papers, CHM.

7. Hascall to Campbell, September 10, 1864, *OR*, 38(2):571; diary, July 17, 1864, John Watkins Papers, UTK; Cox to Schofield, July 17, 1864, 6 P.M., *OR*, 38(5):164.

8. McPherson to Sherman, July 17, 1864, 7:30 P.M., and Twining to Schofield, July 17, 1864, *OR*, 38(5):165.

9. Wheeler to Mason, October 9, 1864, *OR*, 38(3):951–52; Ferguson to Wheeler, July 17, 1864, 6:30 P.M. and 6:40 P.M., *OR*, 38(5):885–86; Dodson, *Campaigns of Wheeler*, 205.

10. Sherman to Halleck, July 17, 1864, 10 P.M., *OR*, 38(5):158.

11. Garrett, *Atlanta*, 1:8–10; Kaufman, *Peachtree Creek*, 168, 170–72.

12. Johnston to Cooper, October 20, 1864, *OR*, 38(3):618; Johnston, "Opposing Sherman's Advance," 274; Circular, Headquarters, Hardee's corps, July 17, 1864, 10:30, *OR*, 38(5):887.

13. Johnston, "Opposing Sherman's Advance," 274, and Johnston to Cooper, October 20, 1864, *OR*, 38(3):618; Thomas B. Mackall Journal (McMurry transcript), July 17–18, 1864, Joseph E. Johnston Papers, CWM; Cooper to Johnston, July 17, 1864, and General Orders No. 4, Headquarters, Army of Tennessee, July 17, 1864, *OR*, 38(5):885, 887; Johnston to Wigfall, August 27, 1864, Louis Trezevant Wigfall Family Papers, LC.

14. Thomas B. Mackall Journal (McMurry transcript), July 17, 1864, Joseph E. Johnston Papers, CWM; Seddon to Hood, July 17, 1864, *OR*, 38(5):885.

15. Hood to Johnston, July 28, 1864, 1 A.M., *OR*, 38(5):889; J. B. Hood, *Advance and Retreat*, 126; Connelly, *Autumn of Glory*, 417; F. Halsey Wigfall to Mama, August 7, 1864, Louis Trezevant Wigfall Family Papers, LC.

16. J. B. Hood, *Advance and Retreat*, 126; Thomas B. Mackall Journal (McMurry transcript), July 18, 1864, Joseph E. Johnston Papers, CWM; Hood to Cooper, July 18, 1864, *OR*, 38(5):888; F. Halsey Wigfall to Mama, July 31, 1864, Louis Trezevant Wigfall Family Papers, LC.

17. Thomas B. Mackall Journal (McMurry transcript), July 18, 1864, Joseph E. Johnston Papers, CWM; F. Halsey Wigfall to Mama, July 31, 1864, Louis Trezevant Wigfall Family Papers, LC; Johnston to Cooper, July 18, 1864, *OR*, 38(5):888; Johnston, "Opposing Sherman's Advance," 274–75.

18. Johnston to Cooper, October 20, 1864, *OR*, 38(3):618; Johnston to Wigfall, August 27, 1864, Louis Trezevant Wigfall Family Papers, LC; Johnston, "Opposing Sherman's Advance," 275–76; Hay, "Davis-Hood-Johnston Controversy," 67.

19. Hay, "Davis-Hood-Johnston Controversy," 67; Phillips, *Correspondence*, 645.

20. Connelly, *Autumn of Glory*, 400, 403; R. Jenkins, *Battle of Peach Tree Creek*, 8–17. Col. Newton N. Davis of the 24th Alabama reflected the opinion of many when he assumed Johnston would strike at the enemy now that the Army of Tennessee had crossed the Chattahoochee River. He admitted that there was no official word to that effect. Davis to Bettie, July 11, 1864, Newton N. Davis Papers, ADAH. For a questionable postwar account asserting that Johnston had definite plans to attack when he was relieved, see Bright, "States in the Confederate War," 395–96.

21. Johnston, "Opposing Sherman's Advance," 275; Johnston to Cooper, October 20, 1864, *OR*, 38(3):618.

22. Davis to Hood, July 18, 1864, *OR*, 38(5):888.

23. J. B. Hood, *Advance and Retreat*, 127–28.

24. Thomas B. Mackall Journal (McMurry transcript), July 18–19, 1864, Joseph E. Johnston Papers, CWM; F. Halsey Wigfall to Mama, July 31, 1864, Louis Trezevant Wigfall Family Papers, LC; Phillips, *Correspondence*, 647.

25. J. B. Hood, *Advance and Retreat*, 162–63; Hood to Cooper, July 18, 1864, and Hood to Soldiers, July 18, 1864, *OR*, 38(5):889, 891; Hay, "Davis-Hood-Johnston Controversy," 67; Connelly, *Autumn of Glory*, 424–25.

26. "Grape" letter, July 19, 1864, *Augusta Daily Constitutionalist*, July 22, 1864.

27. J. B. Hood, *Advance and Retreat*, 162–65; Hood to Cooper, February 15, 1865, *OR*, 38(3):636.

28. Johnston to Cooper, October 20, 1864, and Hood to Cooper, February 15, 1865, *OR*, 38(3):619, 630, 636; J. B. Hood, *Advance and Retreat*, 162.

29. J. B. Hood, *Advance and Retreat*, 162; French, *Two Wars*, 217.

30. McNeill, "Survey of Confederate Soldier Morale," 10–11, 15–16, 21; McMurry, "Confederate Morale," 228–29, 233, 235, 238; McMurry, "Atlanta Campaign of 1864," 8, 10–14; Castel, *Decision in the West*, 353–58, 360–65; McMurry, *Atlanta 1864*, 129.

31. W. B. Corbitt Diary, July 18, 1864, Confederate Miscellany Collection, Series I, EU; Taylor Beatty Diary, July 18, 1864, UNC; Sykes to [wife], fragment dated [July 19, 1864], Jim Huffman, comp., "Pre-& Civil War Letters of Lt. Col. Columbus Sykes 16th [*sic*] Regiment Mississippi Infantry," MDAH; Neal to Pa, July 20, 1864, Andrew Jackson Neal Papers, EU; Rountree, "Letters from a Confederate Soldier," 290.

32. Joslyn, *Charlotte's Boys*, 268; Ross to Mary, July 19, 1864, Emmett Ross Papers, MSU; Mumford H. Dixon Diary, July 18, 1864, EU. See also William McLeod Civil War Pocket Diary, July 19, 1864, SAF; Durham, *Blues in Gray*, 223; Jesse L. Henderson Civil War Diary, July 18, 1864, UM; Franklin, *Civil War Diaries*, 188; W. Cate, *Two Soldiers*, 89; Taylor Beatty Diary, July 19, 1864, UNC; [Murphree], "Autobiography and Civil War Letters," 184; Robert G. Mitchell to Nettie, July 11, 1864, Mitchell-Fondren Papers, GA.

33. Stevens to Johnston, July 18, 1864, *OR*, 38(5):890–91; Thomas B. Mackall Journal (McMurry transcript), July 18, 1864, Joseph E. Johnston Papers, CWM; "Grape" letter, July 19, 1864, *Augusta Daily Constitutionalist*, July 22, 1864; Kirwan, *Johnny Green*, 147; Nisbet, *4 Years on the Firing Line*, 206; Black to Mary A. Black, July 20, 1864, Hugh Black Letters, AHC.

34. Neal to Pa, July 20, 1864, Andrew Jackson Neal Papers, EU; Ross to Mary, July 19, 1864, Emmett Ross Papers, MSU; W. H. Reynolds to sister, July 20, 1864, William J. Dickey Family Papers, UGA; Cuttino, *Saddle Bag*, 268; Furman to wife, July 21, 1864, Charles Manning Furman Papers, USC; Brannock to wife, July 18, 1864, James Madison Brannock Papers, VHS; F. Halsey Wigfall to Mama, July 31, 1864, Louis Trezevant Wigfall Family Papers, LC; correspondent of *Savannah Republican*, reprinted in *Augusta Daily Constitutionalist*, July 22, 1864; "Grape" letter, July 19, 1864, *Augusta Daily Constitutionalist*, July 22, 1864.

35. McMurry, "Confederate Morale," 235; McMurry, "Atlanta Campaign of 1864," 10; John Henry Marsh to Quintard, July 26, 1864, Charles Todd Quintard Papers, DU; Dunlop to sister, August 13, 1864, Colin Dunlop Civil War Letters, AHC.

36. For memoirs and unit histories, see Samuel Wragg Ferguson Memoirs, 56, SCHS; Watkins, *Co. Aytch*, 171–72; Head, *Campaigns and Battles*, 136–37; Cannon, *Inside of Rebeldom*, 236–37; Kendall, "Recollections of a Confederate Officer," 1175–76, 1191; Goodloe, *Confederate Echoes*, 129–30; autobiography, 29, Edwin Hansford Rennolds Sr. Papers, UTK; Thompson, *Orphan Brigade*, 260–61; Little and Maxwell, *History of Lumsden's Battery*, 45–46; Joseph B. Cumming Recollections, 59, UNC; R. M. Collins, *Chapters*, 226; memoir, Joshua W. Mewborn Papers,

USAMHI. For diaries that are obviously rewritten after the war, see E. D. Willett Diary, July 17, 1864, ADAH; Mumford H. Dixon Diary, July 18, 1864, EU; Spurlin, *Civil War Diary*, 43.

37. Gale to Gale, July 30, 1864, Crist, *Papers of Jefferson Davis*, 10:570.

38. "Memoranda to Special Field Orders No. 36, July 17," and Sherman to Thomas, July 18, 1864, 6 A.M., *OR*, 38(5):167, 170.

39. "Order of the Day for July 18, 1864," Headquarters, Department of the Cumberland, July 17, *OR*, 38(5):167.

40. Howard to Whipple, September 18, 1864; Newton to assistant adjutant general, Army of the Cumberland, September, no date, 1864; Bradley to Lee, September 12, 1864; Moore to Waterman, September 12, 1864; and "Journal of the Atlanta Campaign, kept at headquarters of the Fourth Army Corps, by Lieut. Col. Joseph S. Fullerton, Assistant Adjutant General," *OR*, 38(1):201, 296–97, 355, 371–72, 901; Howard to Whipple, July 18, 1864, 7 P.M., *OR*, 38(5):171; Longacre and Haas, *To Battle for God and the Right*, 199–200; Benjamin T. Smith Reminiscences, 155–56, ALPL; Baumgartner and Strayer, *Yankee Tigers*, 123–24; *History of the Seventy-Third*, 322; diary, July 18, 1864, John Wesley Marshall Papers, OHS.

41. Sherman, *Memoirs*, 2, 72; Sherman, "Grand Strategy," 253; Sherman to Halleck, September 15, 1864, *OR*, 38(1):72; Cox, *Atlanta*, 148; Johnson, *A Soldier's Reminiscences*, 280.

42. "Estimated strength of Hood's army," *OR*, 38(5):178.

43. Stanley to Fullerton, no date; Wagner to Lee, September 10, 1864; "Journal of the Atlanta Campaign, kept at headquarters of the Fourth Army Corps, by Lieut. Col. Joseph S. Fullerton, Assistant Adjutant General," *OR*, 38(1):225, 337, 901–2; *History of the Seventy-Third*, 157, 322; Gates, *Rough Side of War*, 244; "Special," correspondence of *Memphis Daily Appeal*, July 19, 1864, reprinted in *Augusta Daily Constitutionalist*, July 22, 1864; diary, July 18, 1864, James R. Carnahan Papers, IHS; diary, July 18, 1864, John Wesley Marshall Papers, OHS; diary, July 21 [18], 1864, Silas Sweeney Mallory Papers, RBHPC.

44. Williams to Perkins, September 12, 1864; Geary to Perkins, September 15, 1864; Barnum to Forbes, September 11, 1864; Chatfield to Wheelock, September 16, 1864; Zulich to Wheelock, September 7, 1864; Ward to Perkins, September 7, 1864; Miller to Crawford, July 27, 1864; Bloodgood to Crawford, September 9, 1864; Wood to Beecher, September 23, 1864; and Buckingham to Young, September 8, 1864, *OR*, 38(2):33, 136, 272, 290, 314, 327, 403, 426, 441, 453; Buckingham to Horace J. Munsey, August 6, 1864, Philo Beecher Buckingham Papers, AAS; Charles A. Booth Journal, July 18, 1864, WHS; Trowbridge to wife and baby, July 17–18, 1864, George Martin Trowbridge Papers, WLC-UM.

45. Charles A. Booth Journal, July 18, 1864, WHS; Trowbridge to wife and baby, July 17–18, 1864, George Martin Trowbridge Papers, WLC-UM; diary, July 18, 1864, Dwight S. Allen Papers, WHS; E. P. Failing Diary, July 18, 1864, Failing-Knight Papers, MHS; William Clark McLean Diary, July 18, 1864, McLean Family Papers, NYSL; Alanson B. Cone Personal Narrative, July 18, 1864, NYSL; diary, July 18, 1864, Albert M. Cook Papers, SU; Ketcham to Fay, September 6, 1864, *OR*, 38(2):80.

46. Candy to Forbes, August 1, 1864; Pardee to Creigh, August 10, 1864; and Warner to Mindil, September 8, 1864, *OR*, 38(2):158, 199, 251–52; John W. Houtz Diaries, July 18, 1864, OHS.

47. Johnson to McClurg, August, no date, 1864, and Moore to Smith, September 8, 1864, *OR*, 38(1):524, 601; diary, July 18, 1864, Charles Richard Pomeroy Papers, DU; Douglas Hapeman Diaries, July 18, 1864, ALPL; Dan Griffin to Scribner, July 19, 1864, Benjamin Franklin Scribner Papers, IHS; Johnson to Palmer, July 18, 1864, *OR*, 38(5):172; Kaufman, *Peachtree Creek*, 139, 141–43, 145.

48. Johnson to Palmer, July 18, 1864, *OR*, 38(5):172.

49. Thomas to Sawyer, August 17, 1864; Davis to McClurg, September, no date, 1864; Morgan to McClurg, September 15, 1864; Lum to Wiseman, August 8, 1864; Banning to Wilson, September 9, 1864; and Baird to McClurg, September 7, 1864, *OR*, 38(1):156, 634, 652, 670, 704–5, 742; Slack to father and mother, July 23, 1864, Albert L. Slack Letters, EU; Thomas to Sherman, July 18, 1864, 2:15 P.M., *OR*, 38(5):170–71; Kaufman, *Peachtree Creek*, 148–49, 151, 153, 156.

50. Schofield to Sherman, September 10, 1864, and Hascall to Campbell, September 10, 1864, *OR*, 38(2):516, 571; diary, July 19, 1864, John Watkins Papers, UTK; "Journal of the Atlanta Campaign, kept at headquarters of the Fourth Army Corps, by Lieut. Col. Joseph S. Fullerton, Assistant Adjutant General," *OR*, 38(1):902.

51. Howard to Dayton, September 17, 1864, and Dodge to Clark, November 25, 1864, *OR*, 38(3):38, 383.

52. Stewart to Mason, January 12, 1865, and Walthall to Gale, January 14, 1865, *OR*, 38(3):870–71, 924; General Orders No. 4, Headquarters, Army of the Mississippi, July 18, 1864, *OR*, 38(5):891.

53. French to Gale, December 6, 1864; Young to Sanders, September 17, 1864; and Cockrell to Sanders, September 20, 1864, *OR*, 38(3):903, 909, 917.

54. Joslyn, *Charlotte's Boys*, 268; Franklin, *Civil War Diaries*, 188; Roy to Cleburne, July 18, 1864, and General Orders No. 57, Hood's Corps, July 18, 1864, *OR*, 38(5):890, 892; entry July 18, 1864, William McLeod Civil War Pocket Diary, SAF; E. D. Willett Diary, July 28, 1864, ADAH; narrative, 7, Henry De Lamar Clayton Sr. Papers, UA.

55. Garrett, *Atlanta*, 1:10, 610; Cox, *Atlanta*, 147; Hood to Cooper, February 15, 1865, *OR*, 38(3):636.

56. J. B. Hood, *Advance and Retreat*, 165.

57. Dodson, *Campaigns of Wheeler*, 206; Mackall to Wheeler, July 18, 1864, 11:45, *OR*, 38(5):889–90.

58. Hood to Seddon, July 18, 1864, and Circular, Headquarters, Hardee's Corps, July 18, 1864, *OR*, 38(5):889, 892.

59. Walker to Mary, July 18, 1864, W. H. T. Walker Papers, DU.

60. Hay, "Davis-Hood-Johnston Controversy," 81–82; McMurry, *John Bell Hood*, 122; McMurry, *Atlanta 1864*, 140.

61. Hay, "Davis-Hood-Johnston Controversy," 76; McMurry, *John Bell Hood*, 123; McMurry, *Atlanta 1864*, 140.

62. Sherman to Halleck, July 18, 1864, 7 P.M., and Sherman to Thomas, July 18, 1864, *OR*, 38(5):169–70.

Chapter 3

1. Balloch to wife, July 19, 1864, George Williamson Balloch Papers, DU; Special Field Orders No. 37, Headquarters, Military Division of the Mississippi, July 18, 1864, and Sherman to Thomas, July 19, 1864, OR, 38(5):179, 183; Castel, *Decision in the West*, 367–68.

2. Harry Stanley Diary, July 20, 1864, AHC; Memoranda to Special Field Orders No. 36, July 17, 1864, OR, 38(5):167; Geary to Perkins, September 15, 1864, OR, 38(2):137; *History of Battery A*, 116; Newbury, "At Peach Tree Creek"; Grunert, *One Hundred and Twenty-Ninth Regiment Illinois*, 84; Byrne, *Uncommon Soldiers*, 171; Rice, "With Sherman: Another Chapter of the Peach Tree Creek Battle."

3. Fullerton, "Orders of the day for the Fourth Army Corps for July 19, 1864, unless changed in orders to-night," July 18, 1864, 9 P.M.; Howard to Thomas, July 19, 1864, 7:40 A.M.; Howard to Whipple, July 19, 1864, 9:30 A.M.; and Howard to Sherman, July 19, 1864, OR, 38(5):180–81, 186–88; Howard to Whipple, September 18, 1864; Wood to Fullerton, September 10, 1864; Knefler to Bestow, September 10, 1864; Dick to Erb, September 12, 1864; and "Journal of the Atlanta Campaign, kept at headquarters of the Fourth Army Corps, by Lieut. Col. Joseph S. Fullerton, Assistant Adjutant General," OR, 38(1):201, 381, 450, 457, 902; *History of the Seventy-Ninth*, 157–58; diary, July 19, 1864, James R. Carnahan Papers, IHS; Jacob Andervount Diary, July 19, 1864, AHC.

4. Wood to Fullerton, September 10, 1864; Knefler to Bestow, September 10, 1864; Cram to Erb, September 14, 1864; and "Journal of the Atlanta Campaign, kept at headquarters of the Fourth Army Corps, by Lieut. Col. Joseph S. Fullerton, Assistant Adjutant General," OR, 38(1):381–82, 450, 462–63, 903; *History of the Seventy-Ninth*, 158; Chesley D. Bailey Diary, July 19, 1864, FHS.

5. Wood to Fullerton, September 10, 1864; General Orders No. 42, Headquarters, Third Division, Fourth Corps, July 19, 1864; Johnson to McGrath, September 15, 1864; Knefler to Bestow, September 10, 1864; Cram to Erb, September 14, 1864; Bridges to Fullerton, September 9, 1864; Bradley to Immell, September 6, 1864; and "Journal of the Atlanta Campaign, kept at headquarters of the Fourth Army Corps, by Lieut. Col. Joseph S. Fullerton, Assistant Adjutant General," OR, 38(1):382, 389, 420, 450, 462–63, 484, 504, 904; Cross, *Nobly They Served*, 104; *History of the Seventy-Ninth*, 158; Barnes, Carnahan, and McCain, *Eighty-Sixth Regiment*, 419; [McConnell], *Diary of William McConnell*, 86; Chesley D. Bailey Diary, July 19, 1864, FHS; Jacob Andervount Diary, July 19, 1864, AHC. Hale spent the rest of the war in prison, taking the oath of allegiance to the U.S. Government on July 5, 1865. Oath of allegiance, July 5, 1865, William J. Hale Service Record, NARA.

6. Hotchkiss to Bestow, September 10, 1864, OR, 38(1):395.

7. Hazen, *Narrative*, 272; Wood to Fullerton, September 10, 1864, OR, 38(1):382; [McConnell], *Diary of William McConnell*, 86; diary, July 19, 1864, James R. Carnahan Papers, IHS.

8. Howard to Whipple, September 18, 1864; Newton to assistant adjutant general, Army of the Cumberland, September, no date, 1864; Kimball to assistant adjutant general, Second Division, Fourth Corps, August 4, 1864; and Bryan to Opdycke, September, no date, 1864, OR, 38(1):201, 297, 305, 320–21.

9. Howard to Whipple, September 18, 1864; Stanley to Fullerton, no date, 1864; Bennett to Lawton, September 13, 1864; and "Journal of the Atlanta Campaign, kept at headquarters of the Fourth Army Corps, by Lieut. Col. Joseph S. Fullerton, Assistant Adjutant General," *OR*, 38(1):201–2, 225, 268, 903–4; Day, *One Hundred and First Ohio*, 244; Howard to Whipple, July 19, 1864, 9:30 A.M., *OR*, 38(5):187; Gates, *Rough Side of War*, 244.

10. Hooker to Whipple, July 19, 1864, 6 P.M., *OR*, 38(5):190; Geary to Perkins, September 15, 1864, *OR*, 38(2):136–37.

11. Geary to Perkins, September 15, 1864; Reynolds to Brannan, September 9, 1864; and Bundy to Reynolds, September 7, 1864, *OR*, 38(2):137, 470, 482.

12. Geary to Perkins, September 15, 1864; Barnum to Forbes, September 11, 1864; Chatfield to Wheelock, September 16, 1864; and Barnum to Wheelock, September 7, 1864, *OR*, 38(2):137, 272, 290, 302; Furman to wife, July 21, 1864, Charles Manning Furman Papers, USC.

13. Candy to Forbes, August 1, 1864; Flynn to Creigh, September 8, 1864; Pardee to Creigh, August 10, 1864; and Warner to Mindil, September 8, 1864, *OR*, 38(2):158, 192, 199, 252; John W. Houtz Diaries, July 19, 1864, OHS.

14. Williams to Perkins, September 12, 1864, and Ketcham to Fay, September 6, 1864, *OR*, 38(2):33, 80; Carrier to wife, July 21, 1864, William H. Carrier Letters, WHS.

15. H. Osborn, "Sherman's Atlanta Campaign," 131.

16. Ward to Perkins, September 7, 1864, and Bloodgood to Crawford, September 9, 1864, *OR*, 38(2):327, 426; Charles A. Booth Journal, July 20, 1864, WHS.

17. Hooker to not stated, no date, and Whipple to Hooker, July 19, 1864, *OR*, 38(5):190.

18. Whipple to Palmer, July 18, 1864, *OR*, 38(5):172; Cox, *Atlanta*, 151; Garrett, *Atlanta*, 1:343–44, 481, 2:13; Morgan to Morrison, August 23, 1864, *OR*, 38(1):649.

19. Davis to McClurg, September, no date, 1864, *OR*, 38(1):634; Aten, *History of the Eighty-Fifth*, 196–97.

20. Langley to Wiseman, September 9, 1864, and Holmes to Swift, September 7, 1864, *OR*, 38(1):712, 729; Stewart, *Dan McCook's Regiment*, 129–30; Aten, *History of the Eighty-Fifth*, 197.

21. Holmes to Swift, September 7, 1864, *OR*, 38(1):729.

22. Walthall to Gale, January 14, 1865, and Reynolds to Barksdale, July 23, 1864, *OR*, 38(3):924, 935.

23. Reynolds to Barksdale, July 23, 1864, *OR*, 38(3):935.

24. Ibid.; Holmes to Swift, September 7, 1864, *OR*, 38(1):729–30.

25. Reynolds to Barksdale, July 23, 1864, *OR*, 38(3):935–37.

26. Reynolds to Barksdale, July 23, 25, 1864, *OR*, 38(3):893, 936.

27. Reynolds to Barksdale, July 23, 1864, *OR*, 38(3):936.

28. Holmes to Swift, September 7, 1864, *OR*, 38(1):730; Stewart, *Dan McCook's Regiment*, 130.

29. Langley to Wiseman, September 9, 1864, and Griffith to Swift, September 7, 1864, *OR*, 38(1):712, 716, 718; Aten, *History of the Eighty-Fifth*, 197–98; "De Lafayette Musselman," 595–96.

30 "List of casualties in the Fifty-second Regiment Ohio Infantry Volunteers from May 3, 1864, to September 6, 1864," *OR*, 38(1):731; Holmes to Aten, January 20, 1896, quoted in Aten, *History of the Eighty-Fifth*, 199.

31. Langley to Wiseman, September 9, 1864, *OR*, 38(1):712, 716; Kinnear, *History of the Eighty-Sixth*, 61–62; Rogers, *125th Regiment Illinois*, 100–101; Harrison, "Peach Tree Creek."

32. Reynolds to Barksdale, July 23, 25, 1864, *OR*, 38(3):893, 936; M. Jones and Martin, *Gentle Rebel*, 61.

33. "Itinerary of the Fourteenth Army Corps, May 6–September 8"; Mitchell to Wiseman, September 4, 1864; Vernon to Wilson, September 5, 1864; Pearce to Wilson, September 9, 1864; Jones to Wilson, September 10, 1864; and Banning to Wilson, September 9, 1864, *OR*, 38(1):507, 681, 688–89, 694, 698, 704; John J. Mercer Diary, July 19, 1864, Antebellum and Civil War Collection, box 2, folder 13, AHC.

34. Davis to McClurg, September, no date, 1864, and Langley to Wiseman, September 9, 1864, *OR*, 38(1):635, 716; Aten, *History of the Eighty-Fifth*, 204; extract of report of Surg. Charles W. Jones, no date, *SOR*, pt. 1, 7.

35. Langley to Wiseman, September 9, 1864, *OR*, 38(1):712; Stewart, *Dan McCook's Regiment*, 131–32.

36. Morgan to Morrison, August 23, 1864, and Lum to Wiseman, August 8, 1864, *OR*, 38(1):649, 670–71; Algoe, "Capturing a Mill: A Gallant Exploit on Peach Tree Creek."

37. Aten, *History of the Eighty-Fifth*, 199–200; Reynolds to Barksdale, July 23, 1864, *OR*, 38(3):937.

38. Adams to Robinson, July 19, 1864, and Reynolds to Barksdale, July 23, 25, 1864, *OR*, 38(3):891–92, 894, 937.

39. Adams to Robinson, July 19, 1864, *OR*, 38(3):891; M. Jones and Martin, *Gentle Rebel*, 60.

40. Adams to Robinson, July 19, 1864; Loring's endorsement, July 20, 1864; and Reynolds to Barksdale, July 25, 1864, *OR*, 38(3):892, 894.

41. Reynolds to Barksdale, July 23, 1864, *OR*, 38(3):936–37; Hood to Seddon, July 20, 1864, *OR*, 38(5):894; Jim Huffman, comp., "Pre-& Civil War Letters of Lt. Col. Columbus Sykes 16th [*sic*] Regiment Mississippi Infantry," MDAH.

42. McClurg to Baird, July 18, 1864, 8 P.M., *OR*, 38(5):173; Baird to McClurg, September 7, 1864; Walker to [Lowrie], August 20, 1864; Hunter to Curtis, August 17, 1864; Carlton to Curtis, August 18, 1864; and Gleason to Lowrie, August 13, 1864, *OR*, 38(1):742, 761, 768–69, 783, 790.

43. Whipple to Palmer, July 19, 1864, *OR*, 38(5):189; Moore to Smith, September 8, 1864, *OR*, 38(1):601.

44. Sherman to Thomas, July 19, 1864, and Sherman to Howard, July 19, 1864, 12 P.M., *OR*, 38(5):183, 188.

45. Cox, *Atlanta*, 151; Thomas to Sherman, July 19, 1864, 4:45 P.M., *OR*, 38(5): 184.

46. Schofield to Sherman, September 10, 1864, and Hascall to Campbell, September 10, 1864, *OR*, 38(2):516, 571.

47. Schofield to Sherman, September 10, 1864, and Hascall to Campbell, Sep-

tember 10, 1864, *OR*, 38(2):516, 571; reminiscences, Thomas Doak Edington Papers, UTK.

48. Cox, *Atlanta*, 153.

49. Sherman to Thomas, July 19, 1864, and Sherman to Howard, July 19, 1864, 12 P.M., *OR*, 38(5):183, 188; Bennett to Lawton, September 13, 1864, *OR*, 38(1):268.

50. Howard to Dayton, September 17, 1864, *OR*, 38(3):38.

51. Dodge to Clark, November 25, 1864, *OR*, 38(3):383; Sherman to Thomas, July 19, 1864; Thomas to Sherman, July 19, 1864, 4:45 P.M.; Sherman to Howard, July 19, 1864, 12 P.M.; Howard to Sherman, July 19, 1864; and Hooker to Whipple, July 19, 1864, 6 P.M., *OR*, 38(5):183–84, 188, 190.

52. Sherman to Thomas, July 19, 1864, and Thomas to Sherman, July 19, 1864, 3:30 P.M., and 4:45 P.M., and 8:10 P.M., *OR*, 38(5):182–84, 186.

53. Sherman to Thomas, July 19, 1864, 7 P.M. and 8:10 P.M.; and Thomas to Sherman, July 19, 1864, *OR*, 38(5):185–86.

54. Stone, "Atlanta Campaign," 439.

55. Diary, July 19, 1864, James M. Randall Diary and Letters, www.ehistory.com; Sherman, *Memoirs*, 2, 72.

56. Whitehead to Irene Cowan, July 19, 1864, Dr. P. F. Whitehead Letters, USM; W. Cate, *Two Soldiers*, 89–90.

57. Thomas B. Mackall Journal (McMurry transcript), July 19, 1864, Joseph E. Johnston Papers, CWM; Castel, *Decision in the West*, 368; Hood to Seddon, July 19, 1864, *OR*, 38(5):892.

58. Mason to Wheeler, July 19, 1864, 11 A.M. and 7:15 P.M., and Mackall to Wheeler, July 19, 1864, 2:15 P.M., *OR*, 38(5):892–93; Wheeler to Mason, October 9, 1864, *OR*, 38(3):951.

59. J. B. Hood, *Advance and Retreat*, 166; Tower, *A Carolinian Goes to War*, 223.

60. Jesse L. Henderson Civil War Diary, July 19, 1864, UM; Mathis, *In the Land of the Living*, 104; E. D. Willett Diary, July 19, 1864, ADAH; diary, July 19, 1864, and Ross to Mary, July 19, 1864, Emmett Ross Papers, MSU; Franklin, *Civil War Diaries*, 188; diary, July 19, 1864, and autobiography, 29, Edwin Hansford Rennolds Sr. Papers, UTK; Joslyn, *Charlotte's Boys*, 268; Circular, Headquarters, Hardee's Corps, July 19, 1864, *OR*, 38(5):894.

61 J. B. Hood, *Advance and Retreat*, 166; McMurry, *John Bell Hood*, 127; McMurry, *Atlanta 1864*, 147.

62 J. B. Hood, *Advance and Retreat*, 166–68.

63. Ibid., 168.

64. McMurry, *Atlanta 1864*, 143.

65. Taylor Beatty Diary, July 19, 1864, UNC.

Chapter 4

1. Fleharty, *Our Regiment*, 89; H. Osborn, *Trials and Triumphs*, 160; William H. Lynch Diaries, July 20, 1864, SHSM-RCC.

2. Special Field Orders No. 39, Headquarters, Military Division of the Mississippi, July 19, 1864, and Sherman to Thomas, July 20, 1864, *OR*, 38(5):193, 195; Hight, *History of the Fifty-Eighth*, 344.

3. Howard to Whipple, September 18, 1864, and "Journal of the Atlanta Campaign, kept at headquarters of the Fourth Army Corps, by Lieut. Col. Joseph S. Fullerton, Assistant Adjutant General," OR, 38(1):202, 904; Fullerton to Newton, July 20, 1864, 6 A.M., OR, 38(5):201–2.

4. Newton to assistant adjutant general, Army of the Cumberland, September, no date, 1864; Kimball to assistant adjutant general, Second Division, Fourth Corps, August 4, 1864; Bradley to Lee, September 12, 1864; and Moore to Waterman, September 12, 1864, OR, 38(1):297, 305, 355, 372; diary, July 20, 1864, John Wesley Marshall Papers, OHS; Bradley to sister Buel, July 21, 1864, Luther P. Bradley Collection, USAMHI.

5. Thomas to Newton, July 20, 1864, 10:30 A.M.; and Newton to Whipple, July 20, 1864, OR, 38(5):198–99.

6. Stoneman to Sherman, July 20, 1864, 11 A.M.; and Sherman to McPherson, July 20, 1864, 8 P.M., OR, 38(5):207–8.

7. Newton to assistant adjutant general, Army of the Cumberland, September, no date, 1864; Kimball to assistant adjutant general, Second Division, Fourth Corps, August 4, 1864; and Wagner to Lee, September 10, 1864, OR, 38(1):297, 305, 337.

8. Kimball to assistant adjutant general, Second Division, Fourth Corps, August 4, 1864; Bryan to Opdycke, September, no date, 1864; and Blanch to Cox, September 15, 1864, OR, 38(1):305, 321, 348; Daniel E. Barnard to sister, July 24, 1864, Howe-Barnard Family Papers, NL.

9. Kimball to assistant adjutant general, Second Division, Fourth Corps, August 4, 1864, OR, 38(1):305–6.

10. Newton to assistant adjutant general, Army of the Cumberland, September, no date, 1864, OR, 38(1):298; Rice, "With Sherman: Another Chapter of the Peach Tree Creek Battle"; J.W.M. to editor, July 21, 1864, Indianapolis Daily Journal, July 26, 1864. Federal officers often referred to Clear Creek as Pea Vine Creek, confusing the location of the latter stream with the former. The modern location of Newton's position is the approximate junction of Brighton Road and Peachtree Road. See Garrett, Atlanta, 1:612.

11. Newton to assistant adjutant general, Army of the Cumberland, September, no date, 1864; Kimball to assistant adjutant general, Second Division, Fourth Corps, August 4, 1864; and Wagner to Lee, September 10, 1864, OR, 38(1):297, 306, 337.

12. Newton to Fullerton, July 21, 1864, and Kimball to assistant adjutant general, Second Division, Fourth Corps, August 4, 1864, OR, 38(1):290, 306; unidentified correspondence of Cincinnati Commercial, reprinted in Cleveland Daily Plain Dealer, July 28, 1864; George A. Cooley Civil War Diary, July 20, 1864, WHS.

13. Newton to Fullerton, July 21, 1864; Newton to assistant adjutant general, Army of the Cumberland, September, no date, 1864; and Bradley to Lee, September 12, 1864, OR, 38(1):290, 297, 355; Hynes to brother, July 29, 1864, William D. Hynes Papers, ISL; Baumgartner and Strayer, Yankee Tigers, 127; George O. Pratt Diary, July 20, 1864, ALPL.

14. Newton to assistant adjutant general, Army of the Cumberland, September, no date, 1864; Wagner to Lee, September 10, 1864; and Blanch to Cox, September 15, 1864, OR, 38(1):297, 337, 348.

15. Newton to Fullerton, July 21, 1864; Newton to assistant adjutant general, Army of the Cumberland, September, no date, 1864; and Conrad to Jackson, September 12, 1864, *OR*, 38(1):290, 297, 326; *History of the Seventy-Third*, 324; Marcoot, *Five Years*, 70.

16. "Journal of the Atlanta Campaign, kept at headquarters of the Fourth Army Corps, by Lieut. Col. Joseph S. Fullerton, Assistant Adjutant General," *OR*, 38(1):905; Howard, *Autobiography*, 1:609–10.

17. "Journal of the Atlanta Campaign, kept at headquarters of the Fourth Army Corps, by Lieut. Col. Joseph S. Fullerton, Assistant Adjutant General," *OR*, 38(1):905; Howard, *Autobiography*, 1:610.

18. Howard, *Autobiography*, 1:610; Wood to Fullerton, September 10, 1864, and "Journal of the Atlanta Campaign, kept at headquarters of the Fourth Army Corps, by Lieut. Col. Joseph S. Fullerton, Assistant Adjutant General," *OR*, 38(1):382, 905–6; Jacob Andervount Diary, July 20, 1864, AHC; Chesley D. Bailey Diary, July 20, 1864, FHS; Barnes, Carnahan, and McCain, *Eighty-Sixth Regiment*, 420; Hazen, *Narrative*, 272; diary, July 20, 1864, James R. Carnahan Papers, HIS; R. Jenkins, *Battle of Peach Tree Creek*, 42–43.

19. Schofield to Sherman, September 10, 1864, and Cox to Campbell, September 10, 1864, *OR*, 38(2):516, 686–87; R. Jenkins, *Battle of Peach Tree Creek*, 46–47.

20. Hobson to Kerstetter, August 15, 1864; Estes to Hubbell, July 31, 1864; and Cox to Campbell, September 10, 1864, *OR*, 38(2):616–17, 632, 686–87; reminiscences, July 20, 1864, Thomas Doak Edington Papers, UTK; diary, July 20, 1864, John Watkins Papers, UTK.

21. Neill to Campbell, [July 20, 1864], *OR*, 38(5):205.

22. Ramsey to Newton, July 20, 1864, 3:45 P.M.; Whipple to [Thomas], July 20, 1:30 P.M., 3 P.M.; Thomas to Hooker, July 20, 1864, 3 P.M.; and Hooker to Thomas, July 20, 1864, 3:30 P.M., *OR*, 38(5):199, 200, 204; Thomas to Sawyer, August 17, 1864, *OR*, 38(1):156.

23. Ward to Perkins, September 7, 1864; Wood to Beecher, September 23, 1864; and Buckingham to Young, September 8, 1864, *OR*, 38(2):327, 442, 453; H. Osborn, *Trials and Triumphs*, 160; Buckingham to Horace J. Munsey, August 6, 1864, Philo Beecher Buckingham Papers, AAS; Winkler to C. H. Young, July 28, 1864, Frederick C. Winkler Papers, WHS; Fleharty, *Our Regiment*, 89.

24. Coburn to Speed, July 28, 1864; Miller to Crawford, July 27, 1864; Bloodgood to Crawford, September 9, 1864; and Winkler to Young, September 25, 1864, *OR*, 38(2):389, 403–4, 426–27, 466; Newbury, "At Peach Tree Creek."

25. Trowbridge to wife and baby, July 20, 1864, George Martin Trowbridge Papers, WLC-UM; Coburn to Speed, July 28, 1864, *OR*, 38(2):389; Charles A. Booth Journal, July 20, 1864, WHS; J. Cate, *If I Live to Come Home*, 196; James A. Congleton Diary, July 20, 1864, LC; Newton, "Battle of Peach Tree Creek," 151; Lysander Wheeler Letter, to parents, brother and sister, July 21, 1864, GLIAH; Bohrnstedt, *Soldiering with Sherman*, 125.

26. Williams to Perkins, September 12, 1864; Compton to Palmer, September 9, 1864; Ruger to Pittman, September 11, 1864; Ketcham to Fay, September 6, 1864; and Boughton to Lee, July 24, 1864, *OR*, 38(2):33, 53, 62, 80, 106; diary, July 19

[20], 1864, Max Schlund Papers, NL; Alanson B. Cone Personal Narrative, July 20, 1864, NYSL; Carrier to wife, July 21, 1864, William H. Carrier Letters, WHS; Toombs, *Reminiscences*, 151; diary, July 20, 1864, Albert M. Cook Papers, SU.

27. Williams to Perkins, September 12, 1864, and Rogers to Palmer, September 7, 1864, *OR*, 38(2):33, 50; Quaife, *From the Cannon's Mouth*, 339; E. Brown, *Twenty-Seventh Indiana*, 517–18; R. Jenkins, *Battle of Peach Tree Creek*, 87.

28. Bauer, *Soldiering*, 145; Morhous, *Reminiscences*, 110; Irving Bronson, "Recollections of the Civil War," 49, TC.

29. Bauer, *Soldiering*, 145–46; Robinson to Pittman, July 24, 1864, *OR*, 38(2):91.

30. Diary, July 20, 1864, Max Schlund Papers, NL; Salomon to Boughton, September 15, 1864, *OR*, 38(2):99; Alanson B. Cone Personal Narrative, July 20, 1864, NYSL.

31. Bauer, *Soldiering*, 145; William Merrell, "Personal Memoirs of the Civil War," LMU.

32. Geary to Perkins, September 15, 1864; Candy to Forbes, August 1, 1864; and Wright to Creigh, September 8, 1864, *OR*, 38(2):137–38, 158, 184; diary, July 20, 1864, John D. Foering Diary/Papers, HSP.

33. Boyle, *Soldiers True*, 232; Zulich to Wheelock, September 7, 1864, *OR*, 38(2):314.

34. Geary to Perkins, September 15, 1864, and Fourat to Stockton, July 23, 1864, *OR*, 38(2):138, 224–25; R. Jenkins, *Battle of Peach Tree Creek*, 169.

35. Geary to Perkins, September 15, 1864; Jones to Forbes, August 1, 1864; Fourat to Stockton, July 23, 1864; and O'Connor to not stated, September 7, 1864, *OR*, 38(2):138, 213, 224–25, 230.

36. Geary to Perkins, September 15, 1864, and Jones to Forbes, August 1, 1864, *OR*, 38(2):138, 213; Pierson, "From Chattanooga to Atlanta," 350.

37. Palmer to Whipple, July 20, 1864, 7:30 A.M., *OR*, 38(5):202; Cox, *Atlanta*, 154; Baird to McClurg, September 7, 1864, *OR*, 38(1):742–43; James Biddle Diary, July 20, 1864, DPL.

38. Johnson to McClurg, August, no date, 1864; "Journal of the First Brigade," July 20, 1864; Briant to not stated, no date; and Minshall to Ford, September, no date, 1864, *OR*, 38(1):524, 532, 542, 551; Palmer to Johnson, July 20, 1864, and Johnson to McClurg, July 20, 1864, 11 A.M., *OR*, 38(5):203; diary, July 20, 1864, Charles Richard Pomeroy Papers, DU; entry July 20, 1864, Douglas Hapeman Diaries, ALPL.

39. Palmer to Johnson, July 20, 1864, *OR*, 38(5):203; "Journal of the First Brigade," July 20, 1863, *OR*, 38(1):532.

40. Morgan to Morrison, August 23, 1864, and Lum to Wiseman, August 8, 1864, *OR*, 38(1):649, 671.

41. Palmer to Whipple, July 20, 1864, 7:30 A.M., *OR*, 38(5):202; Pearce to Wilson, September 9, 1864; Banning to Wilson, September 9, 1864; Langley to Wiseman, September 9, 1864; and McKnight to Houghtaling, September 6, 1864, *OR*, 38(1):694, 704, 712, 837; Aten, *History of the Eighty-Fifth*, 200.

42. Thomas to Sherman, July 20, 1864, noon, *OR*, 38(5):196.

43. Hood to Cooper, February 15, 1865, *OR*, 38(3):630.

44. Ibid.; Stewart to Mason, January 12, 1865, *OR*, 38(3):630, 871. Hood reported that the interval between divisions should be 150 yards not 200 yards as Stewart stated. R. Jenkins, *Battle of Peach Tree Creek*, 63–64, incorrectly describes what an echelon formation was intended to accomplish. For a discussion of the echelon formation, see Hess, *Civil War Infantry Tactics*, 118–20, 245.

45. Sheppard, *By the Noble Daring*, 190; Furman to wife, July 21, 1864, Charles Manning Furman Papers, USC; Loring to West, September 15, 1864, and Nelson to Graham, July 24, 1864, *OR*, 38(3):876, 898; Goodloe, *Some Rebel Relics*, 308–9; William McLeod Civil War Pocket Diary, July 20, 1864, SAF.

46. Mason to Wheeler, July 20, 1864, 10:20 A.M.; Wade to Wheeler, July 20, 1864, 11 A.M.; and Mackall to Wheeler, July 20, 1864, 1:10 P.M., *OR*, 38(5):894–95.

47. Connelly, *Autumn of Glory*, 440.

48. Hood to Cooper, February 15, 1865, *OR*, 38(3):630; J. B. Hood, *Advance and Retreat*, 171; Cheatham to Roy, September 5, 1880, in notes to Roy's article about Atlanta campaign, Hardee Family Papers, ADAH.

49. Hood to Cooper, February 15, 1865, *OR*, 38(3):630; J. B. Hood, *Advance and Retreat*, 171; Cheatham to Wheeler, July 20, 1864, *OR*, 38(5):896.

50. Connelly, *Autumn of Glory*, 441; Losson, *Tennessee's Forgotten Warriors*, 174–75; Castel, *Decision in the West*, 371–72.

51. Hood to Cooper, February 15, 1865, *OR*, 38(3):630.

52. Jesse L. Henderson Civil War Diary, July 20, 1864, UM; E. D. Willett Diary, July 20, 1864, ADAH; Narrative, 7, Henry De Lamar Clayton Sr. Papers, UA; Cox, *Atlanta*, 152–53.

53. Hardee to Cooper, April 5, 1865, *OR*, 38(3):698; Samuel L. Black letter, May 31, 1880, in Roy, "General Hardee," 348.

54. Samuel L. Black letter, May 31, 1880, in Roy, "General Hardee," 348; diary, July 20, 1864, Edwin Hansford Rennolds Sr. Papers, UTK; Joslyn, *Charlotte's Boys*, 269; Franklin, *Civil War Diaries*, 188; record of events, Company B, 31st Mississippi, *SOR*, pt. 2, 34:17; Lowrey to Benham, September 20, 1864, *OR*, 38(3):733.

55. Stewart to Mason, January 12, 1865, *OR*, 38(3):871.

56. Loring to West, September 15, 1864, *OR*, 38(3):876.

57. Featherston to Loring, November 20, 1867, Winfield Scott Featherston Collection, UM; Featherston to Robinson, July 23, 1864; Scott to Robinson, July 23, 1864; French to Gale, December 6, 1864; and Walthall to Gale, January 14, 1865, *OR*, 38(3):880–81, 895, 903, 925; Featherston to Hood, December 18, 1866, John B. Hood Papers, NARA; French, *Two Wars*, 218; undated map, Ladies Memorial Association Collection, AHC.

58. Stewart to Mason, January 12, 1865; Loring to West, September 15, 1864; Featherston to Robinson, July 23, 1864; Scott to Robinson, July 23, 1864; and Walthall to Gale, January 14, 1865, *OR*, 38(3):871, 876, 881–82, 894, 925; Featherston to Loring, November 20, 1867, Winfield Scott Featherston Collection, UM; Unsigned Account of Battle of Peach Tree Creek, Thomas R. Markham Papers, LSU; Cannon, *Inside of Rebeldom*, 237; French, *Two Wars*, 218.

59. Dispatch, July 20, 1864, *Savannah Republican*, reprinted in *Charleston Mer-*

cury, July 26, 1864; S. Davis, *Atlanta Will Fall*, 133–34; Thomas B. Mackall Journal (McMurry transcript), July 20, 1864, Joseph E. Johnston Papers, CWM; McMurry, *John Bell Hood*, 128.

60. McMurry, *Atlanta 1864*, 150–52; Loring to West, September 15, 1864, *OR*, 38(3):876; Castel, *Decision in the West*, 375.

61. G. Smith, "Georgia Militia," 334; Connelly, *Autumn of Glory*, 444n; Castel, *Decision in the West*, 382.

62. Connelly, *Autumn of Glory*, 442; Howard, "Struggle for Atlanta," 313; Cox, *Atlanta*, 152–53.

63. Howard, *Autobiography*, 1:608, 610.

64. Johnston to Cooper, October 20, 1864, and "Abstract from returns of the Army of Tennessee, General Joseph E. Johnston, C.S. Army, July 10, 1864," *OR*, 38(3):619, 679; Castel, *Decision in the West*, 366; Stone, "Atlanta Campaign," 441, 443–44; McMurry, *Atlanta 1864*, 151.

65. McMurry, *Atlanta 1864*, 151.

Chapter 5

1. Cox, *Atlanta*, 161; Hardee to Cooper, April 5, 1865, *OR*, 38(3):698.

2. Hay, "Atlanta Campaign," 36; Castel, *Decision in the West*, 373, 375; "Abstract from returns of the Army of Tennessee, General Joseph E. Johnston, C.S. Army, July 10, 1864," *OR*, 38(3):679; Newton to Whipple, July 20, 1864, *OR*, 38(5):199; Newton to Fullerton, July 21, 1864, *OR*, 38(1):290. For a different estimate of Hardee's strength, see R. Jenkins, *Battle of Peach Tree Creek*, 55.

3. Castel, *Decision in the West*, 375. Of forty-five references in primary sources concerning the starting time of the attack, twenty (or 44.4%) agree it was 3 P.M. Twelve of the sources (or 26.6%), state it as 4 P.M. The other thirteen sources (28.8%) give various times ranging from 2 P.M. to 4:30 P.M.

4. Warner, *Generals in Blue*, 344–45; Howard, *Autobiography*, 1:613.

5. Unsigned letter to *Cincinnati Commercial*, reprinted in *Cleveland Daily Plain Dealer*, July 28, 1864; Howard, *Autobiography*, 1:613–14.

6. Newton to Fullerton, July 21, 1864, *OR*, 38(1):291; J.W.M. to editor, July 21, 1864, *Indianapolis Daily Journal*, July 26, 1864.

7. Warner, *Generals in Gray*, 19.

8. Castel, *Decision in the West*, 370, 376; R. Jenkins, *Battle of Peach Tree Creek*, 56, 105, 121–22; Thompson, *Orphan Brigade*, 261; entry of July 20, 1864, William McLeod Civil War Pocket Diary, SAF; Hardee to Cooper, April 5, 1865, *OR*, 38(3):698. Castel places Bate west of Clear Creek, but Jenkins correctly points out that his entire division lay east of the stream.

9. Pickett to [Hardee], July 20, 1864, 6 P.M., *OR*, 38(5):897; Blanch to Cox, September 15, 1864, *OR*, 38(1):348; R. Jenkins, *Battle of Peach Tree Creek*, 105–6.

10. R. Brown, *To the Manner Born*, 1–85; Newton to Fullerton, July 21, 1864, *OR*, 38(1):290; George Anderson Mercer Diary, July 20, 1864, UNC; "The Battle of Peach Creek," *Cincinnati Commercial*, reprinted in *Cleveland Daily Plain Dealer*, July 28, 1864; Scaife, *Campaign for Atlanta*, 90.

11. R. Jenkins, *Battle of Peach Tree Creek*, 57, 113, 122, 124; Castel, *Decision in the West*, 376; R. Brown, *To the Manner Born*, 260–61; Walker, *Hell's Broke Loose*, 153–54.

12. Howard to Whipple, September 18, 1864, and Blanch to Cox, September 15, 1864, *OR*, 38(1):202, 348–49; Kerwood, *Annals of the Fifty-Seventh*, 268–70.

13. Newton to Fullerton, July 21, 1864, and Newton to assistant adjutant general, Army of the Cumberland, September, no date, 1864, *OR*, 38(1):290, 297; J.W.M. to editor, July 21, 1864, *Indianapolis Daily Journal*, July 26, 1864; Hynes to brother, July 29, 1864, William D. Hynes Papers, ISL.

14. *History of Battery A*, 118; J.W.M. to editor, July 21, 1864, *Indianapolis Daily Journal*, July 26, 1864; Baumgartner and Strayer, *Yankee Tigers*, 127.

15. Bradley to sister Buel, July 21, 1864, and Bradley to mother, July 30, 1864, Luther P. Bradley Collection, USAMHI; Hynes to brother, July 29, 1864, William D. Hynes Papers, ISL; Atwater to Waterman, August 12, 1864, *OR*, 38(1):361.

16. Bradley to Lee, September 12, 1864, *OR*, 38(1):356; Baumgartner and Strayer, *Yankee Tigers*, 127; Longacre and Haas, *To Battle for God and the Right*, 201; R. Jenkins, *Battle of Peach Tree Creek*, 124–25, 136.

17. Longacre and Haas, *To Battle for God and the Right*, 201; Baumgartner and Strayer, *Yankee Tigers*, 127–28; Rice, "With Sherman: Another Chapter of the Peach Tree Creek Battle"; Hynes to brother, July 29, 1864, William D. Hynes Papers, ISL. According to Moritz Tschoepe, the 24th Wisconsin of Kimball's brigade was rushed to help Opdycke to cover the bridge crossing, but this is not confirmed in any other source. See Tschoepe, "A Hot Day: Reminiscences of the Battle of Peach Tree Creek before Atlanta," and Beaudot, *24th Wisconsin*, 321–22.

18. Newton to assistant adjutant general, Army of the Cumberland, September, no date, 1864, *OR*, 38(1):297–98; J.W.M. to editor, July 21, 1864, *Indianapolis Daily Journal*, July 26, 1864.

19. Howard, *Autobiography*, 1:619; Reynolds to Brannan, September 9, 1864, and Smith to Reynolds, September 7, 1864, *OR*, 38(2):471, 474; Spencer to Bridges, September 7, 1864, and Goodspeed to Immell, September 7, 1864, *OR*, 38(1):493, 500; Wills, *George Henry Thomas*, 269–70; Cleaves, *Rock of Chickamauga*, 230; H. Osborn, "Sherman's Atlanta Campaign," 131; McKinney, *Education in Violence*, 349; Howard, "Struggle for Atlanta," 314.

20. Hynes to brother, July 29, 1864, William D. Hynes Papers, ISL.

21. Bradley to Lee, September 12, 1864, *OR*, 38(1):356.

22. Warner, *Generals in Gray*, 291–92; E. Jones, *Enlisted for the War*, 4–5.

23. Gardner to parents, July 23, 1864, Lyman Gardner Papers, WLC-UM; Hynes to brother, July 29, 1864, William D. Hynes Papers, ISL; record of events, 28th Kentucky, *SOR*, pt. 2, 22:663; Wagner to Lee, September 10, 1864, *OR*, 38(1):338.

24. Nisbet, *4 Years on the Firing Line*, 209; Realf to Dear Friends, July 21, 1864, Richard Realf Letters and Poems, NL.

25. Conrad to Jackson, September 12, 1864, *OR*, 38(1):326–27; George A. Cooley Civil War Diary, July 20, 1864, WHS; *History of the Seventy-Third*, 324–25; Allendorf, *Long Road to Liberty*, 205–11.

26. Nisbet, *4 Years on the Firing Line*, 209; record of events, 28th Kentucky, *SOR*, pt. 2, 22:663; Daniel E. Barnard to sister, July 24, 1864, Howe-Barnard Family Papers, NL; Kimball to assistant adjutant general, Second Division, Fourth Corps, August 4, 1864, *OR*, 38(1):307; Benjamin T. Smith Reminiscences, 158, ALPL.

27. "X" letter to *Savannah Republican*, July 25, 1864, reprinted in *Augusta Daily Constitutionalist*, August 4, 1864; E. Jones, *Enlisted for the War*, 1; Joslyn, *Charlotte's Boys*, 269; Hamilton Branch to mother, July 21, 1864, Branch Family Papers, UGA; George Anderson Mercer Diary, July 20, 1864, UNC; Nisbet, *4 Years on the Firing Line*, 209–10.

28. News notice in *Macon Confederate*, reprinted in *Augusta Daily Constitutionalist*, July 27, 1864; Tower, *A Carolinian Goes to War*, 224; Adamson, *Brief History*, 41; Kerwood, *Annals of the Fifty-Seventh*, 271; E. Jones, *Enlisted for the War*, 1; R. Brown, *To the Manner Born*, 261, 364n.

29. Newton to assistant adjutant general, Army of the Cumberland, September, no date, 1864, and Atwater to Waterman, August 12, 1864, *OR*, 38(1):298, 361; Hynes to brother, July 29, 1864, William D. Hynes Papers, ISL.

30. Wiley, *Confederate Letters*, 52; Rountree, "Letters from a Confederate Soldier," 290; Clark, *Under the Stars and Bars*, 103.

31. Hamilton Branch to mother, July 21, 1864, Branch Family Papers, UGA; George Anderson Mercer Diary, July 20, 1864, UNC; "List of casualties in Mercer's brigade from July 20 to September 1, 1864," *OR*, 38(3):756; R. Jenkins, *Battle of Peach Tree Creek*, 136, 138–42.

32. Hawes, "Memoirs of Charles H. Olmstead," pt. 10, 44; Furman to wife, July 21, 1864, Charles Manning Furman Papers, USC; B. Benjamin Smith to Capers, April 3, 1880, Ellison Capers Papers, TC; George Anderson Mercer Diary, July 20, 1864, UNC.

33. Wagner to Lee, September 10, 1864, *OR*, 38(1):338.

34. Ibid., and Peatman to Cox, September 20, 1864, *OR*, 38(1):338, 351.

35. Warner, *Generals in Gray*, 210; Castel, *Decision in the West*, 376; Losson, *Tennessee's Forgotten Warriors*, 175; Rennolds, *History of the Henry County Commands*, 88. R. Jenkins, *Battle of Peach Tree Creek*, 144, 148, posits a different order of battle for Maney's Division than I do.

36. Franklin, *Civil War Diaries*, 188; Martin Van Buren Oldham Journal, July 20, 1864, UTM; autobiography, 29, Edwin Hansford Rennolds Sr. Papers, UTK; Rennolds, *History of the Henry County Commands*, 88; R. Jenkins, *Battle of Peach Tree Creek*, 154–56.

37. Autobiography, 29, and diary, July 20, 1864, Edwin Hansford Rennolds Sr. Papers, UTK; Rennolds, *History of the Henry County Commands*, 88–89; Martin Van Buren Oldham Journal, July 20, 1864, UTM; Losson, *Tennessee's Forgotten Warriors*, 176; Fowler, *Mountaineers in Gray*, 152; Franklin, *Civil War Diaries*, 188; Semmes to wife, July 22, 1864, Benedict Joseph Semmes Papers, UNC; Carroll Henderson Clark Memoirs, 44–45, TSLA. R. Jenkins, *Battle of Peach Tree Creek*, 148–49, 153, 155, argues that Carter and Strahl advanced beyond the rest of Maney's Division and managed to threaten the right flank of Kimball's brigade, but the evi-

dence for this is inconclusive. I believe the force that threatened Kimball's flank came from Loring's Division, as explained in the next chapter.

38. Elmore to parents, July 26, 1864, Day Elmore Letters, CHM; Warner, *Generals in Blue*, 267–68; Kimball to assistant adjutant general Second Division, Fourth Corps, August 4, 1864, and Bryan to Opdycke, September, no date, 1864, *OR*, 38(1):306, 321; Daniel F. Barnard to sister, July 24, 1864, Howe-Barnard Family Papers, NL.

39. Record of events, 28th Kentucky, *SOR*, pt. 2, 22:663; Tilton to Waterman, September 12, 1864, *OR*, 38(1):363; Bennett and Haigh, *History of the Thirty-Sixth Regiment*, 615; Elmore to parents, July 26, 1864, Day Elmore Letters, CHM; Fleming, *Confederate Ninth Tennessee*, 116–17.

40. Hughes, *Civil War Memoir*, 214–15; Walton et al., "Sketches of the History," 221.

41. Hughes, *Civil War Memoir*, 215.

42. Newton to Fullerton, July 21, 1864; Newton to assistant adjutant general, Army of the Cumberland, September, no date, 1864; and Kimball to assistant adjutant general, Second Division, Fourth Corps, August 4, 1864, *OR*, 38(1):290, 298, 306; Losson, *Tennessee's Forgotten Warriors*, 176; Bennett and Haigh, *History of the Thirty-Sixth Regiment*, 615.

43. R. M. Collins, *Chapters*, 227–28; [Cox] to Sneed, August 2, 1864, and Lowrey to Benham, September 10, 1864, *OR*, 38(3):730, 733; Bowser, "Notes on Granbury's Brigade," 747.

44. Buck, *Cleburne and His Command*, 231; Irving Buck to Roy, March 27, 1880, in Roy, "General Hardee," 384; R. M. Collins, *Chapters*, 228.

45. Spurlin, *Civil War Diary*, 43; Flynt to Sneed, July 29, 1864; Brown to not stated, July 28, 1864; and Perry to not stated, August 2, 1864, *OR*, 38(3):748, 749, 751; McCaffrey, *Band of Heroes*, 114–15.

46. R. M. Collins, *Chapters*, 228–30.

47. Lowrey to Benham, September 20, 1864, *OR*, 38(3):733; Nisbet, *4 Years on the Firing Line*, 210. ·

48. [Cox] to Sneed, August 2, 1864, *OR*, 38(3):730.

49. Pickett to [Hardee], July 20, 1864, 6 P.M., *OR*, 38(5):897; entry of July 20, 1864, William McLeod Civil War Pocket Diary, SAF; Frano, *Letters of Captain Hugh Black*, 67; McMurray, *History of the Twentieth Tennessee*, 320. For an estimate of losses in Bate's Division, see R. Jenkins, *Battle of Peach Tree Creek*, 106, 110.

50. E. A. Carman to Clayton, December 6, 1875, Henry De Lamar Clayton Sr. Papers, UA; diary, July 20, 1864, Emmett Ross Papers, MSU.

51. Hardee to Cooper, April 5, 1865, *OR*, 38(3):698; Roy, "General Hardee," 349; Castel, *Decision in the West*, 378.

52. Hardee to Cooper, April 5, 1865, *OR*, 38(3):698; Roy, "General Hardee," 380; Irving A. Buck to Roy, March 27, 1880, and D. G. White to Roy, April 6, 1880, in Roy, "General Hardee," 350, 382; Buck, *Cleburne and His Command*, 231–32.

53. Taylor to Sneed, July 29, 1864, *OR*, 38(3):752; W. Cate, *Two Soldiers*, 92; Buck, *Cleburne and His Command*, 231.

54. Hardee to Cooper, April 5, 1865, *OR*, 38(3):698–99; Cox, *Atlanta*, 160–62; Connelly, *Autumn of Glory*, 443; Castel, *Decision in the West*, 378.

55. [Cox] to Sneed, August 2, 1864, *OR*, 38(3):730; Mumford H. Dixon Diary, July 20, 1864, EU.

56. Neal to Pa, July 20, 1864, Andrew Jackson Neal Papers, EU; Mathis, *In the Land of the Living*, 103–4.

57. Hawes, "Memoirs of Charles H. Olmstead," pt. 10: 44; Hughes, *General William J. Hardee*, 223–25.

58. Thomas B. Mackall Journal (McMurry transcript), July 20, 1864, Joseph E. Johnston Papers, CWM; Hughes, *General William J. Hardee*, 224–25; Hardee to Cooper, April 5, 1865, *OR*, 38(3):699; J. B. Hood, *Advance and Retreat*, 185–86.

59. Howard to Whipple, July 21, 1864, 7 P.M., *OR*, 38(5):214; Circular, Headquarters, Department of the Cumberland, July 25, 1864; Howard to Whipple, September 18, 1864; Newton to Fullerton, July 21, 1864; Newton to assistant adjutant general, Army of the Cumberland, September, no date, 1864; and Kimball to assistant adjutant general, Second Division, Fourth Corps, August 4, 1864, *OR*, 38(1):174, 203, 290–91, 298, 306; "The Battle of Peach Creek," *Cincinnati Commercial*, reprinted in *Cleveland Daily Plain Dealer*, July 28, 1864.

60. Henry Perrin Mann Civil War Diaries, July 20, 1864, SHSM-RCR; MacArthur to [Jackson], September 12, 1864, and Atwater to Waterman, August 12, 1864, *OR*, 38(1):330, 361; Hynes to brother, July 29, 1864, William D. Hynes Papers, ISL; George O. Pratt Diary, July 20, 1864, ALPL.

61. Bradley to mother, July 30, 1864, Luther P. Bradley Collection, USAMHI; Howard to Whipple, September 18, 1864; Newton to assistant adjutant general, Army of the Cumberland, September, no date, 1864; Kimball to assistant adjutant general, Second Division, Fourth Corps, August 4, 1864; "Report of Killed and Wounded in Third Brigade in Engagement With the Enemy, July 20, 1864"; and Atwater to Waterman, August 12, 1864, *OR*, 38(1):203, 298, 307, 359, 361; George A. Cooley Civil War Diary, July 21, 1864, WHS.

62. Howard to Whipple, September 18, 1864, *OR*, 38(1):203.

63. Diary, July 21, 1864, John Wesley Marshall Papers, OHS.

Chapter 6
1. "Abstract from returns of the Army of Tennessee, General Joseph E. Johnston, C.S. Army, July 10, 1864," *OR*, 38(3):679; Hay, "Atlanta Campaign," 36.

2. Garrett, *Atlanta*, 1:612; Harrison to Speed, August 12, 1864, *OR*, 38(2):344–45; Wells, "A Western Man's Account of Peach Tree Creek"; Kaufman, *Peachtree Creek*, 117, 122.

3. Cox, *Atlanta*, 154–55.

4. Winkler to C. H. Young, July 28, 1864, Frederick C. Winkler Papers, WHS; H. Osborn, *Trials and Triumphs*, 160; Harrison to Speed, August 12, 1864; Coburn to Speed, July 28, 1864; Miller to Crawford, July 27, 1864; Crane to Coburn, no date; and Wood to Beecher, September 23, 1864, *OR*, 38(2):344–45, 389, 404, 412–13, 441; Newton, "Battle of Peach Tree Creek," 150–51; Charles A. Booth Journal, July 20, 1864, WHS.

5. Bloodgood to Crawford, September 9, 1864, *OR*, 38(2):427; Newton, "Battle of Peach Tree Creek," 151.

6. Elliott, *Soldier of Tennessee*, 201–5; Johnston to Cooper, October 20, 1864; Stewart to Mason, January 12, 1865; and Loring to Stewart, September 15, 1864, *OR*, 38(3):617, 871, 876–77; Castel, *Decision in the West*, 373, 375.

7. Featherston to Robinson, July 23, 1864, *OR*, 38(3):883; Featherston to Hood, December 18, 1866, John B. Hood Papers, NARA; Warner, *Generals in Gray*, 86. Featherston wrote three versions of his report, all of them essentially saying the same thing, because his original was captured by the enemy in the latter stages of the war. See Winfield S. Featherston to William W. Loring, September 1, 1866, box 10, folder 26, Ezra A. Carman Papers, NYPL.

8. Featherston to Hood, December 18, 1866, John B. Hood Papers, NARA; Oatis to [Robinson], September 12, 1864, *OR*, 38(3):886.

9. Featherston to Robinson, July 23, 1864; Oatis to [Robinson], September 12, 1864; and Huddleston to Neilson, September 15, 1864, *OR*, 38(3):881, 886, 890.

10. Featherston to Robinson, July 23, 1864; Oatis to [Robinson], September 12, 1864; and Jackson to Neilson, July 23, 1864, *OR*, 38(3):881–82, 886, 889; Featherston to Hood, December 18, 1866, John B. Hood Papers, NARA.

11. Featherston to Robinson, July 23, 1864; Stigler to Neilson, September 15, 1864; Dyer to Neilson, July 23, 1864; Oatis to [Robinson], September 12, 1864; Jackson to Neilson, July 23, 1864; and Huddleston to Neilson, September 15, 1864, *OR*, 38(3):882, 884–87, 889–90; Featherston to Loring, November 20, 1867, Winfield Scott Featherston Collection, UM; Featherston to Hood, December 18, 1866, John B. Hood Papers, NARA; record of events, Company H, 31st Mississippi, *SOR*, pt. 2, 34:47.

12. Featherston to Hood, December 18, 1866, John B. Hood Papers, NARA; Bloodgood to Crawford, September 9, 1864, *OR*, 38(2):427; Byrne, *Uncommon Soldiers*, 172–73; Bradley, *Star Corps*, 142–43.

13. Dyer to Neilson, July 23, 1864; Oatis to [Robinson], September 12, 1864; Jackson to Neilson, July 23, 1864; and Huddleston to Neilson, September 15, 1864, *OR*, 38(3):885, 887, 889–90.

14. Featherston to Robinson, July 23, 1864, *OR*, 38(3):883.

15. My estimate of Ward's strength is based on Coburn's report that his brigade had 1,315 men engaged on July 20. See Coburn to Speed, July 28, 1864, *OR*, 38(2):390.

16. Warner, *Generals in Blue*, 538–39; Roberts to sister, August 13, 1864, John H. Roberts Civil War Letters, WHS.

17. McBride, *History of the Thirty-Third*, 128; Brant, *History of the Eighty-Fifth Indiana*, 67–68; Welcher and Ligget, *Coburn's Brigade*, 235; Harrison to Speed, August 12, 1864; Coburn to Speed, July 28, 1864; and Miller to Crawford, July 27, 1864, *OR*, 38(2):345, 389–90, 404. Coburn gave Crist a certificate testifying "that he was the first man to notify him that the Rebels were coming." See Newton, "Battle of Peach Tree Creek," 153–54, 157.

18. McBride, *History of the Thirty-Third*, 128–29; James A. Congleton Diary, July 20, 1864, LC; Ward to Perkins, September 7, 1864; Coburn to Speed, July 28, 1864; and Miller to Crawford, July 27, 1864, *OR*, 38(2):327, 389–90, 404; Brant, *History of the Eighty-Fifth Indiana*, 68.

19. Ward to Perkins, September 7, 1864, and Coburn to Speed, July 28, 1864, *OR*, 38(2):327–28, 390; McBride, *History of the Thirty-Third*, 129.

20. Coburn to Speed, July 28, 1864, and Miller to Crawford, July 27, 1864, *OR*, 38(2):390, 404–5.

21. Crane to Coburn, no date, *OR*, 38(2):413–14.

22. Coburn to Speed, July 28, 1864, *OR*, 38(2):390.

23. Crane to Coburn, no date, *OR*, 38(2):413; Brant, *History of the Eighty-Fifth Indiana*, 68; McBride, *History of the Thirty-Third*, 129. Other men estimated the distance at which firing started between Coburn's brigade and the Confederates as fifty yards, not fifty feet. See Austin to wife, July 21, 1864, Judson L. Austin Papers, BHL-UM.

24. Miller to Crawford, July 27, 1864, *OR*, 38(2):405–6; McBride, *History of the Thirty-Third*, 129.

25. Ward to Perkins, September 7, 1864; Coburn to Speed, July 28, 1864; and Anderson to Crawford, July 27, 1864, *OR*, 38(2):328, 390, 422; Austin to wife, July 21, 1864, Judson L. Austin Papers, BHL-UM; Charles A. Booth Journal, July 20, 1864, WHS; Brant, *History of the Eighty-Fifth Indiana*, 68; Byrne, *Uncommon Soldiers*, 172–73.

26. Crane to Coburn, no date, *OR*, 38(2):414; McBride, *History of the Thirty-Third*, 130.

27. Coburn to Speed, July 28, 1864; Miller to Crawford, July 27, 1864; and Crane to Coburn, no date, *OR*, 38(2):390, 405, 413; McBride, *History of the Thirty-Third*, 129.

28. McBride, *History of the Thirty-Third*, 129; Harrison to Speed, August 12, 1864, *OR*, 38(2):345.

29. Harrison to wife, July 21, 1864, Benjamin Harrison Collection, IHS; West to not stated, September 21, 1864, *SOR*, pt. 1, 7:29; Smith to Harrison, September 15, 1864, and West to Grubbs, September 22, 1864, *OR*, 38(2):356, 377; Merrill, *Seventieth Indiana*, 139; John L. Ketcham letter, July 21, 1864, in Merrill, *Seventieth Indiana*, 151.

30. Newton, "Battle of Peach Tree Creek," 155; Fleharty, *Our Regiment*, 90.

31. John L. Ketcham letter, July 21, 1864, in Merrill, *Seventieth Indiana*, 150; Merrill to J. L. Mitchell, August 1, 1864, Samuel Merrill Papers, ISL; Harrison to Speed, August 12, 1864, *OR*, 38(2):345.

32. Harrison to Speed, August 12, 1864, *OR*, 38(2):345.

33. Ibid.; Harrison to wife, July 21, 1864, Benjamin Harrison Collection, IHS; John L. Ketcham letter, July 21, 1864, in Merrill, *Seventieth Indiana*, 152; Bohrnstedt, *Soldiering with Sherman*, 127; McWilliams, *Recollections*, 139.

34. Smith to Harrison, September 15, 1864, and Case to Dunlevy, July 30, 1864, *OR*, 38(2):356, 367–68.

35. Case to Dunlevy, July 30, 1864, *OR*, 38(2):368.

36. Harrison to Speed, August 12, 1864; Dutton to Mitchell, August 5, 1864; and Case to Dunlevy, July 30, 1864, *OR*, 38(2):346, 363–64, 368; Merrill, *Seventieth Indiana*, 139–40; Merrill to J. L. Mitchell, August 1, 1864, Samuel Merrill Papers, ISL.

37. Newton, "Battle of Peach Tree Creek," 156.

38. Dutton to Mitchell, August 5, 1864, and Case to Dunlevy, July 30, 1864, *OR*, 38(2):364, 368; DeRosier, *Through the South*, 132–33; diary, July 20, 1864, and Johnson to Folks at Home, July 25, 1864, Andrew Jackson Johnson Papers, IHS; Wheeler to parents, brother, and sister, July 21, 1864, Lysander Wheeler Letter, GLIAH; James A. Congleton Diary, July 20, 1864, LC; Bohrnstedt, *Soldiering with Sherman*, 125; Newbury, "At Peach Tree Creek"; Bode to editor, July 21, 1864, *Indianapolis Daily Journal*, August 2, 1864.

39. Harrison to Speed, August 12, 1864; Smith to Harrison, September 15, 1864; and West to Grubbs, September 22, 1864, *OR*, 38(2):346, 356, 377; Wells, "A Western Man's Account of Peach Tree Creek"; Fleharty, *Our Regiment*, 90–91; Reyburn and Wilson, *"Jottings from Dixie,"* 240, 242, 243n. R. Jenkins, *Battle of Peach Tree Creek*, 235, contends that the 79th Ohio and 102nd Illinois helped to repel the extreme right of Scott's Brigade as it attacked Geary's division to the west, before they turned their fire on Featherston's men who were striking at the rest of Harrison's brigade. But the sources cited in this note all clearly agree that the 79th Ohio and the 102nd Illinois fired only toward Featherston's command to the left.

40. Case to Dunlevy, July 30, 1864, *OR*, 38(2):368; Merrill, *Seventieth Indiana*, 140; Newton, "Battle of Peach Tree Creek," 156.

41. Harrison to Speed, August 12, 1864, *OR*, 38(2):345–46.

42. Ibid., 346–47; Fleharty, *Our Regiment*, 91; Reyburn and Wilson, *"Jottings from Dixie,"* 241.

43. Wood to Beecher, September 23, 1864, *OR*, 38(2):442; Winkler to C. H. Young, July 28, 1864, Frederick C. Winkler Papers, WHS.

44. Arnold to Young, September 25, 1864, and Winkler to Young, September 25, 1864, *OR*, 38(2):460, 466; H. Osborn, *Trials and Triumphs*, 160; Underwood, *Three Years' Service*, 227; Priest, *John T. McMahon's Diary*, 163.

45. Winkler to C. H. Young, July 28, 1864, Frederick C. Winkler Papers, WHS; George Hoenig Journal, July 21, 1864, www.russscott.com; Hurst, *Journal-History*, 139–40; H. Osborn, *Trials and Triumphs*, 161; Pula, *Sigel Regiment*, 257; Wood to Beecher, September 23, 1864, and Winkler to Young, September 25, 1864, *OR*, 38(2):442, 466.

46. Winkler to Young, September 25, 1864, *OR*, 38(2):466–67; Winkler to C. H. Young, July 28, 1864, Frederick C. Winkler Papers, WHS.

47. Winkler to C. H. Young, July 28, 1864, Frederick C. Winkler Papers, WHS; Winkler to Young, September 25, 1864, *OR*, 38(2):467.

48. Wood to Beecher, September 23, 1864, and Winkler to Young, September 25, 1864, *OR*, 38(2):443–44, 466.

49. Winkler to Young, September 25, 1864, *OR*, 38(2):467; Winkler to C. H. Young, July 28, 1864, Frederick C. Winkler Papers, WHS.

50. Winkler to C. H. Young, July 28, 1864, Frederick C. Winkler Papers, WHS; Winkler to Young, September 25, 1864, *OR*, 38(2):467.

51. Howard to Whipple, September 18, 1864; Newton to Fullerton, July 21, 1864; Newton to assistant adjutant general, Army of the Cumberland, September, no date, 1864; and Kimball to assistant adjutant general, Second Division, Fourth Corps,

August 4, 1864, *OR*, 38(1):202, 290, 298, 306; Benjamin T. Smith Reminiscences, 157, ALPL; Beaudot, *24th Wisconsin*, 321–22. Castel, *Decision in the West*, 377, contends that Magevney and Carter advanced far enough to outflank Kimball's right. There is no evidence to support this idea; Newton believed the threat came from Loring's Division.

52. Wood to Beecher, September 23, 1864, and Buckingham to Young, September 8, 1864, *OR*, 38(2):442–43, 453; Buckingham to Horace J. Munsey, August 6, 1864, Philo Beecher Buckingham Papers, AAS; Storrs, *"Twentieth Connecticut,"* 136; Fenton, "From the Rapidan," 501.

53. Wood to Beecher, September 23, 1864; Buckingham to Young, September 8, 1864; and: Hurst to Young, September 23, 1864, *OR*, 38(2):443, 454, 462; Buckingham to Horace J. Munsey, August 6, 1864, Philo Beecher Buckingham Papers, AAS; Hurst, *Journal-History*, 140.

54. Wood to Beecher, September 23, 1864, and Winkler to Young, September 25, 1864, *OR*, 38(2):443, 467.

55. Wood to Beecher, September 23, 1864, and Buckingham to Young, September 8, 1864, *OR*, 38(2):443, 454; Buckingham to Horace J. Munsey, August 6, 1864, Philo Beecher Buckingham Papers, AAS; J. Cate, *If I Live to Come Home*, 196.

56. Ward to Perkins, September 7, 1864, and Stephens to Gary, September 7, 1864, *OR*, 38(2):328, 484.

57. Featherston to Robinson, July 23, 1864, *OR*, 38(3):883–84.

58. Ibid., and Pulliam to Neilson, July 23, 1864, *OR*, 38(3):883, 888.

59. Featherston to Robinson, July 23, 1864, and Jackson to Neilson, July 23, 1864, *OR*, 38(3):883, 889; Dunn to Stumpy, August 1, 1864, Matthew Andrew Dunn Letters, MDAH; W. Jordan, "Matthew Andrew Dunn Letters," 123–24.

60. Featherston to Robinson, July 23, 1864; Dyer to Neilson, July 23, 1864; Oatis to [Robinson], September 12, 1864; and Huddleston to Neilson, September 15, 1864, *OR*, 38(3):882–83, 885, 887, 891.

61. Featherston to Robinson, July 23, 1864; Dyer to Neilson, July 23, 1864; Stigler to Neilson, September 15, 1864; and Oatis to [Robinson], September 12, 1864, *OR*, 38(3):882, 885, 887; Ward to Perkins, September 7, 1864, *OR*, 38(2):328.

62. Wheeler to parents, brother, and sister, July 21, 1864, Lysander Wheeler Letter, GLIAH; Johnson to Folks at Home, July 25, 1864, Andrew Jackson Johnson Papers, IHS; Merrill, *Seventieth Indiana*, 140.

63. Grunert, *One Hundred and Twenty-Ninth Regiment Illinois*, 86; Harrison to wife, July 21, 1864, Benjamin Harrison Collection, IHS; Harrison to Speed, August 12, 1864, *OR*, 38(2):347.

64. Case to Dunlevy, July 30, 1864, *OR*, 38(2):368; Merrill, *Seventieth Indiana*, 140.

65. Harrison to Speed, August 12, 1864; Ragan to not stated, September 22, 1864; and West to Grubbs, September 22, 1864, *OR*, 38(2):347, 374, 377; West to not stated, September 12, 1864, *SOR*, pt. 1, 7:27; Bohrnstedt, *Soldiering with Sherman*, 125; Merrill, *Seventieth Indiana*, 140–41; Harrison to wife, July 21, 1864, Benjamin Harrison Collection, IHS; Merrill to J. L. Mitchell, August 1, 1864, Samuel Merrill Papers, ISL.

66. Merrill, *Seventieth Indiana*, 152; Johnson to Folks at Home, July 25, 1864, Andrew Jackson Johnson Papers, IHS.

67. Stewart to Mason, January 12, 1865; Loring to West, September 15, 1864; Oatis to [Robinson], September 12, 1864; and Jackson to Neilson, July 23, 1864, *OR*, 38(3):871, 877, 887, 889.

68. Loring to West, September 15, 1864, *OR*, 38(3):877; Ward to Perkins, September 7, 1864; Miller to Crawford, July 27, 1864; Crane to Coburn, no date; and Wood to Beecher, September 23, 1864, *OR*, 38(2):328, 405, 413, 443; Wheeler to parents, brother, and sister, July 21, 1864, Lysander Wheeler Letter, GLIAH.

69. Featherston to Loring, November 20, 1867, Winfield Scott Featherston Collection, UM; Featherston to Robinson, July 23, 1864; "Return of casualties in Featherston's brigade in the engagement near Peach Tree Creek, Ga., July 20, 1864"; Stigler to Neilson, September 15, 1864; Pulliam to Neilson, July 23, 1864; and Jackson to Neilson, July 23, 1864, *OR*, 38(3):883–85, 888, 890; record of events, Company B, H, 31st Mississippi, and Company D, 40th Mississippi, *SOR*, pt. 2, 34:18, 47, 169; record of events, field and staff, 3rd Mississippi, *SOR*, pt. 2, 32:759; Howell, *To Live and Die*, 333.

70. Featherston to Robinson, July 23, 1864, *OR*, 38(3):881, 883.

71. Ward to Perkins, September 7, 1864; Harrison to Speed, August 12, 1864; Case to Dunlevy, July 30, 1864; Ragan to not stated, September 22, 1864; West to Grubbs, September 22, 1864; Coburn to Speed, July 28, 1864; Miller to Crawford, July 27, 1864; and Bloodgood to Crawford, September 9, 1864, *OR*, 38(2):329, 347, 368, 374, 377, 390–91, 406, 427; Welcher and Ligget, *Coburn's Brigade*, 240; Brant, *History of the Eighty-Fifth Indiana*, 68; Reyburn and Wilson, *"Jottings from Dixie,"* 242; Hurst, *Journal-History*, 141; West to not stated, September 21, 1864, *SOR*, pt. 1, 7:29; Merrill to J. L. Mitchell, August 1, 1864, Samuel Merrill Papers, ISL.

72. Ward to Perkins, September 7, 1864; Harrison to Speed, August 12, 1864; Miller to Crawford, July 27, 1864; Buckingham to Young, September 8, 1864; and Winkler to Young, September 25, 1864, *OR*, 38(2):329, 347, 406, 454, 467; McBride, *History of the Thirty-Third*, 130.

73. Featherston to Hood, December 18, 1866, John B. Hood Papers, NARA; Featherston to Robinson, July 23, 1864, *OR*, 38(3):882; Featherston to Loring, November 20, 1867, Winfield Scott Featherston Collection, UM.

74. Cox, *Atlanta*, 156; Oatis to [Robinson], September 12, 1864, *OR*, 38(3):887.

75. Ward to Perkins, September 7, 1864, and Coburn to Speed, July 28, 1864, *OR*, 38(2):328, 390; Merrill to Emma, July 24, 1864, Samuel Merrill Papers, ISL; Alfred H. Trego Diary, July 20, 1864, CHM; Bohrnstedt, *Soldiering with Sherman*, 126.

76. Brant, *History of the Eighty-Fifth Indiana*, 68; Bradley, *Star Corps*, 143–44.

77. Miller to Crawford, July 27, 1864, *OR*, 38(2):406; Beasecker, *"I Hope to Do My Country Service,"* 300.

78. Beasecker, *"I Hope to Do My Country Service,"* 301; Johnson to Folks at Home, July 25, 1864, Andrew Jackson Johnson Papers, IHS; Harrison to wife, July 21, 1864, Benjamin Harrison Collection, IHS.

79. Henry Lyon to editor, July 22, 1864, *Indianapolis Daily Journal*, August 1,

1864; Anderson, *They Died to Make Men Free*, 223–24; McBride, *History of the Thirty-Third*, 133.

Chapter 7

1. Blair, *A Politician Goes to War*, 188; Warner, *Generals in Blue*, 169–70.

2. Blair, *A Politician Goes to War*, 188; Geary to Perkins, September 15, 1864, and Pardee to Creigh, August 10, 1864, *OR*, 38(2):137–38, 199–200; Cox, *Atlanta*, 156; Boyle, *Soldiers True*, 231; Clarke, "The Fight for the Battery at Peach Tree Creek."

3. Candy to Forbes, August 1, 1864; Pardee to Creigh, August 10, 1864; and Reynolds to Brannan, September 9, 1864, *OR*, 38(2):158, 200, 470; Foering diary, July 20, 1864, John D. Foering Diary/Papers, HSP.

4. Jones to Forbes, August 1, 1864, and Warner to Mindil, September 8, 1864, *OR*, 38(2):212–13, 252; Elliott to Lamont [March 21, 1895], *SOR*, pt. 1, 7:22; Dunkelman, *Patrick Henry Jones*, 57; R. Jenkins, *Battle of Peach Tree Creek*, 169–71. For a differing view of the formation adopted by Geary's division, see Dunkelman, "'Worst Sight,'" 71, 75.

5. Geary to Perkins, September 15, 1864; Barnum to Forbes, September 11, 1864; Chatfield to Wheelock, September 16, 1864; Van Voorhis to [Wheelock], September 8, 1864; and Barnum to Wheelock, September 7, 1864, *OR*, 38(2):137–38, 272–73, 291, 299, 302; J.W.M. to editor, July 21, 1864, *Indianapolis Daily Journal*, July 26, 1864.

6. Warner, *Generals in Gray*, 269–70.

7. Scott to Robinson, July 23, 1864; Ives to Graham, July 24, 1864; Milligan to [Graham], July 24, 1864; and Nelson to Graham, July 24, 1864, *OR*, 38(3):895–98; Cannon, *Inside of Rebeldom*, 237.

8. Cannon, *Inside of Rebeldom*, 237.

9. Scott to Robinson, July 23, 1864, *OR*, 38(3):895; Long, "A Good Word for the Twentieth Corps."

10. Geary to Perkins, September 15, 1864; Jones to Forbes, August 1, 1864; Fourat to Stockton, July 23, 1864; and O'Connor to not stated, September 7, 1864, *OR*, 38(2):138, 213, 224–25, 230; Pierson, "From Chattanooga to Atlanta," 350.

11. Cannon, *Inside of Rebeldom*, 238; Geary to Perkins, September 15, 1864, *OR*, 38(2):138; Pierson, "From Chattanooga to Atlanta," 350.

12. Fourat to Stockton, July 23, 1864, *OR*, 38(2):225; Loring to West, September 15, 1864, and Ives to Graham, July 24, 1864, *OR*, 38(3):877, 896; "Special" letter to editor, July 20, 1864, *Augusta Daily Constitutionalist*, July 23, 1864; Noyes, "Excerpts from the Civil War Diary," 347.

13. Pierson, "From Chattanooga to Atlanta," 351; Fourat to Stockton, July 23, 1864, and O'Connor to not stated, September 7, 1864, *OR*, 38(2):225, 230.

14. Jones to Forbes, August 1, 1864, and Fourat to Stockton, July 23, 1864, *OR*, 38(2):213, 225; Zinn, *Mutinous Regiment*, 131. The state flag lost by the 33rd New Jersey is today housed at the New Jersey Historical Society in Newark. See *Atlanta: Voices of the Civil War*, 100.

15. Clarke, "The Fight for the Battery at Peach Tree Creek"; Lockman to not stated, no date, *OR*, 38(2):236.

16. Geary to Perkins, September 15, 1864, *OR*, 38(2):138; Blair, *A Politician Goes to War*, 189; Castel, *Decision in the West*, 377; R. Jenkins, *Battle of Peach Tree Creek*, 178, 180–81; Ives to Graham, July 24, 1864, and Nelson to Graham, July 24, 1864, *OR*, 38(3):896, 898; Banning, *35th Alabama*, 52.

17. Geary to Perkins, September 15, 1864, and Pardee to Creigh, August 10, 1864, *OR*, 38(2):140, 200; Snodgrass to Graham, July 24, 1864, *OR*, 38(3):897.

18. Wright to Creigh, September 8, 1864; McConnell to Creigh, September 12, 1864; and Flynn to Creigh, September 8, 1864, *OR*, 38(2):184, 187–88, 192; John W. Houtz Diaries, July 20–21, 1864, OHS; Ike to Ed. P., August 16, 1864, Unidentified Civil War Union Soldier Letter, GHS.

19. Lockman to not stated, no date, and Warner to Mindil, September 8, 1864, *OR*, 38(2):236, 252; Darling to friends, July 23, 1864, Marcellus Warner Darling Papers, UI; J.W.M. to editor, July 21, 1864, *Indianapolis Daily Journal*, July 26, 1864; William Harper quoted in Dunkelman, "'Worst Sight,'" 73.

20. Elliott to Lamont, [March 21, 1895], *SOR*, pt. 1, 7:22–23.

21. Candy to Forbes, August 1, 1864, and Pardee to Creigh, August 10, 1864, *OR*, 38(2):158, 200–201; Ives to Graham, July 24, 1864, *OR*, 38(3):896.

22. Lockman to not stated, no date, and Cresson to Lee, September 8, 1864, *OR*, 38(2):236, 261.

23. Barnum to Forbes, September 11, 1864, and Elliott to Wheelock, September 8, 1864, *OR*, 38(2):273, 285.

24. Zulich to Wheelock, September 7, 1864, *OR*, 38(2):314.

25. Barnum to Forbes, September 11, 1864, and Barnum to Wheelock, September 7, 1864, *OR*, 38(2):273, 302.

26. Barnum to Wheelock, September 7, 1864, *OR*, 38(2):302–4; G. Collins, *Memoirs*, 278; Beyer and Keydel, *Deeds of Valor*, 378–79.

27. Chatfield to Wheelock, September 16, 1864, and Van Voorhis to [Wheelock], September 8, 1864, *OR*, 38(2):291, 299.

28. Walker to Wheelock, no date, *OR*, 38(2):318; Boyle, *Soldiers True*, 232, 235–36.

29. Boyle, *Soldiers True*, 237–38; Walker to Wheelock, no date, *OR*, 38(2):318.

30. Barnum to Wheelock, September 7, 1864, *OR*, 38(2):302–3; G. Collins, *Memoirs*, 278–79, 281.

31. Kirkup to Creigh, September 9, 1864, and Pardee to Creigh, August 10, 1864, *OR*, 38(2):174, 200.

32. Bundy to Reynolds, September 7, 1864, *OR*, 38(2):482.

33. Ibid., and Reynolds to Brannan, September 9, 1864, *OR*, 38(2):482, 471; Loring to West, September 15, 1864, *OR*, 38(3):877.

34. Clarke, "The Fight for the Battery at Peach Tree Creek."

35. Kirkup to Creigh, September 9, 1864; Pardee to Creigh, August 10, 1864; Barnum to Forbes, September 11, 1864; Elliott to Wheelock, September 8, 1864; Bundy to Reynolds, September 7, 1864; and Reynolds to Brannan, September 9, 1864, *OR*, 38(2):175, 200, 273, 285, 482, 471.

36. Kirkup to Creigh, September 9, 1864; Pardee to Creigh, August 10, 1864; and

Bundy to Reynolds, September 7, 1864, *OR*, 38(2):174–75, 200–201, 482; Elliott to Lamont, [March 21, 1895], *SOR*, pt. 1, 7:23.

37. Candy to Forbes, August 1, 1864; Lockman to not stated, no date; Reynolds to Brannan, September 9, 1864; Bundy to Reynolds, September 7, 1864; and Sloan to Reynolds, September 6, 1864, *OR*, 38(2):158, 236, 471, 482, 487.

38. Geary to Perkins, September 15, 1864, *OR*, 38(2):140; Elliott to Lamont, [March 21, 1895], *SOR*, pt. 1, 7:23.

39. Pierson, "From Chattanooga to Atlanta," 352.

40. Scott to Robinson, July 23, 1864; Ives to Graham, July 24, 1864; and Nelson to Graham, July 24, 1864, *OR*, 38(3):895–96, 898; record of events, Comp. L, 12th Louisiana, *SOR*, pt. 2, 24:272–73.

41. Scott to Robinson, July 23, 1864; Milligan to [Graham], July 24, 1864; and Snodgrass to Graham, July 24, 1864, *OR*, 38(3):895, 897; Vanaernam to Liz, July 24, 1864, Henry Vanaernam Letters, GLIAH; diary, July 20, 1864, Marcellus Warner Darling Papers, UI; Cresson to Lee, September 8, 1864, and Barnum to Forbes, September 11, 1864, *OR*, 38(2):261, 273.

42. Cox, *Atlanta*, 156; Geary to Perkins, September 15, 1864; Jones to Forbes, August 1, 1864; Barnum to Forbes, September 11, 1864; and Barnum to Wheelock, September 7, 1864, *OR*, 38(2):138–40, 213–14, 273, 303; Blair, *A Politician Goes to War*, 189; Elliott to Lamont, [March 21, 1895], *SOR*, pt. 1, 7:24.

43. Geary to Perkins, September 15, 1864, and Pardee to Creigh, August 10, 1864, *OR*, 38(2):140, 201.

44. Geary to Perkins, September 15, 1864, *OR*, 38(2):140.

45. Geary to Perkins, September 15, 1864; Alexander to [Lee], September 7, 1864; and Barnum to Forbes, September 11, 1864, *OR*, 38(2):141, 267, 273; Dunkelman and Winey, *Hardtack Regiment*, 230; Dunkelman, "'Worst Sight,'" 74.

46. Scott to Robinson, July 23, 1864, and Nelson to Graham, July 24, 1864, *OR*, 38(3):895, 898; McGuire, *McGuire Papers*, 27; record of events (regimental field and staff), 12th Louisiana and Comp. G, 12th Louisiana, *SOR*, pt. 2, 24:249, 264; "Terrible Losses of the Rebel Army Near Atlanta," unidentified newspaper clipping, Lewis A. Labadie Papers, DPL. For differing estimates of losses in the 55th Alabama, see Miller, *Forgotten Regiment*, 61, and in Scott's Brigade, see R. Jenkins, *Battle of Peach Tree Creek*, 186–87.

47. Milligan to [Graham], July 24, 1864, *OR*, 38(3):897; [Murphree], "Autobiography and Civil War Letters," 185–87; Talbot letter quoted in R. Jenkins, *Battle of Peach Tree Creek*, 187–88.

48. Cannon, *Inside of Rebeldom*, 238; McGuire, *McGuire Papers*, 27; [Murphree], "Autobiography and Civil War Letters," 185; Milligan to [Graham], July 24, 1864, *OR*, 38(3):897.

49. Stewart to Mason, January 12, 1865, and Loring to West, September 15, 1864, *OR*, 38(3):871, 877. For a differing estimate of losses in Loring's Division, see R. Jenkins, *Battle of Peach Tree Creek*, 399.

Chapter 8

1. Warner, *Generals in Gray*, 325–26; Walthall to Gale, January 14, 1865, *OR*, 38(3):925–26.

2. Walthall to Gale, January 14, 1865, *OR*, 38(3):925; Garrett, *Atlanta*, 1:613.

3. Garrett, *Atlanta*, 1:613.

4. Warner, *Generals in Gray*, 226; O'Neal to Barksdale, July 31, 1864, *OR*, 38(3):941; Zorn, *Hold at All Hazards*, 86; G. Osborn, "Civil War Letters," 216.

5. O'Neal to Barksdale, July 31, 1864, *OR*, 38(3):941; G. Osborn, "Civil War Letters," 216; Orlando S. Holland to Hood, no date, John B. Hood Papers, NARA; Holland to not stated, July 22, 1864, in S. Hood, *Lost Papers*, 72, 74; cards and Orlando S. Holland to Samuel Cooper, July 6, 1864, plus endorsements by Edward A. O'Neal, Edward C. Walthall, Alexander P. Stewart, and Joseph E. Johnston, Samuel W. Jones service record, 37th Mississippi, NARA.

6. O'Neal to Barksdale, July 31, 1864, *OR*, 38(3):941; Garrett, *Atlanta*, 1:613; Crumpton, "In the Atlanta Campaign," 381; Bryan to Smith, July 22, 1864, in S. Hood, *Lost Papers*, 80.

7. Warner, *Generals in Blue*, 559–60.

8. Williams to Perkins, September 12, 1864, *OR*, 38(2):33; diary, July 20, 1864, Max Schlund Papers, NL; J.W.M. to editor, July 21, 1864, *Indianapolis Daily Journal*, July 26, 1864; Cox, *Atlanta*, 156.

9. Cox, *Atlanta*, 156–57; Williams to Perkins, September 12, 1864; Ruger to Pittman, September 11, 1864; Reynolds to Brannan, September 9, 1864; and Woodbury to Pittman, September 13, 1864, *OR*, 38(2):33–34, 62, 470–71, 479.

10. Williams to Perkins, September 12, 1864, and Ruger to Pittman, September 11, 1864, *OR*, 38(2):33, 62.

11. Irving Bronson, "Recollections of the Civil War," 49, TC.

12. Warner, *Generals in Blue*, 406–7; Robinson to Pittman, July 24, 1864, *OR*, 38(2):91.

13. Boughton to Lee, July 24, 1864, *OR*, 38(2):106–7.

14. Garrett to Lee, September 10, 1864, *OR*, 38(2):109; Wallace, "At Peach Tree Creek."

15. Williams to Perkins, September 12, 1864, and Robinson to Pittman, July 24, 1864, *OR*, 38(2):34, 91.

16. *Atlanta: Voices of the Civil War*, 102; Thomson to Lee, September 10, 1864, *OR*, 38(2):111; Foos testimony in Dewitt C. Foos Court-Martial Case File, NARA.

17. Warner, *Generals in Blue*, 272–73; Marvin, *Fifth Regiment Connecticut*, 327.

18. Bauer, *Soldiering*, 146–47; Knipe to Pittman, September 13, 1864, and Rogers to Palmer, September 7, 1864, *OR*, 38(2):43, 50; William Clark McLean Diary, July 20, 1864, McLean Family Papers, NYSL; Goundrey, "The Twentieth Corps: Some Further Criticisms concerning Its Disputed Actions and Achievements."

19. Bauer, *Soldiering*, 148–51.

20. Ibid., 147–48; Morhous, *Reminiscences*, 110–11; Rogers to Palmer, September 7, 1864, *OR*, 38(2):50; Alanson B. Cone Personal Narrative, July 20, 1864, NYSL; diary, July 20, Albert M. Cook Papers, SU.

21. O'Neal to Barksdale, July 31, 1864, *OR*, 38(3):941.

22. Walthall to Gale, January 14, 1865, and O'Neal to Barksdale, July 31, 1864, *OR*, 38(3):925, 941; B. Smith, *Palmetto Boy*, 98–99; E. Jones, *Enlisted for the War*, 177, 179; Furman to wife, July 21, 1864, Charles Manning Furman Papers, USC; J. A. Stevenson to Capers, August 28, 1885, Ellison Capers Papers, DU.

23. Boughton to Lee, July 24, 1864, *OR*, 38(2):107; Morhous, *Reminiscences*, 111.

24. Williams to Perkins, September 12, 1864; Ruger to Pittman, September 11, 1864:; and Ketcham to Fay, September 6, 1864, *OR*, 38(2):34, 62, 80; Bartlett, *"Dutchess County Regiment,"* 99–100.

25. Morhous, *Reminiscences*, 112.

26. Bauer, *Soldiering*, 149–50.

27. Selfridge to Palmer, September 8, 1864, *OR*, 38(2):57; Bauer, *Soldiering*, 150.

28. Bauer, *Soldiering*, 149.

29. Ibid., 149, 150–51.

30. Morhous, *Reminiscences*, 113–14.

31. Ibid., 116–17.

32. Padgett, "With Sherman," 301–2; Rogers to Palmer, September 7, 1864, *OR*, 38(2):50; Bauer, *Soldiering*, 151.

33. Knipe to Pittman, September 13, 1864, and Selfridge to Palmer, September 8, 1864, *OR*, 38(2):43, 56; Shimp to wife, July 26, 1864, William T. Shimp Papers, USAMHI.

34. Williams to Perkins, September 12, 1864, and Ruger to Pittman, September 11, 1864, *OR*, 38(2):34, 62; Cox, *Atlanta*, 157; E. Brown, *Twenty-Seventh Indiana*, 518, 521–22.

35. E. Brown, *Twenty-Seventh Indiana*, 519–21; Bryant, *History of the Third Regiment*, 256; Fesler to Fay, September 6, 1864, *OR*, 38(2):64.

36. E. Brown, *Twenty-Seventh Indiana*, 520; Fesler to Fay, September 6, 1864, *OR*, 38(2):64.

37. E. Brown, *Twenty-Seventh Indiana*, 522.

38. Williams to Perkins, September 12, 1864; Robinson to Pittman, July 24, 1864; and Le Sage to Lee, September 7, 1864, *OR*, 38(2):34, 91, 103.

39. Salomon to Boughton, September 15, 1864, *OR*, 38(2):100; diary, July 20, 1864, Max Schlund Papers, NL.

40. Salomon to Boughton, September 15, 1864, *OR*, 38(2):100; diary, July 20, 1864, Max Schlund Papers, NL; Hess, *Rifle Musket*, 100–104; Hess, *Ezra Church*, 198–99.

41. Warner, *Generals in Blue*, 415–16; Bryant, *History of the Third Regiment*, 254, 256; Carrier to wife, July 21, 1864, William H. Carrier Letters, WHS; Sawyer to Nancy, July 21, 1864, James F. Sawyer Letters, WHS; Holzhueter, "William Wallace's Civil War Letters," 102; Cogswell to Fay, September 8, 1864, and Carman to Fay, September 6, 1864, *OR*, 38(2):65, 72; Quint, *Record of the Second Massachusetts*, 240; Morse, *Letters Written during the War*, 181; Comey, *A Legacy of Valor*, 182; John Emerson Anderson Memoirs, 154, LC; Tappan, *Civil War Journal*, 140–41.

42. William Merrell, "Personal Memoirs of the Civil War," LMU.

43. Ibid.; Compton to Palmer, September 9, 1864, *OR*, 38(2):53; Shimp to wife, July 26, 1864, William T. Shimp Papers, USAMHI.

44. E. Bauer, *Soldiering*, 149; Compton to Palmer, September 9, 1864, *OR*, 38(2):53.

45. Crumpton, *Book of Memories*, 86–87.

46. Ibid., 88–89; O'Neal to Barksdale, July 31, 1864, *OR*, 38(3):941; Holland to not stated, July 22, 1864, and Bryan to Smith, July 22, 1864, in S. Hood, *Lost Papers*, 74, 80; Bauer, *Soldiering*, 149.

47. Carrier to wife, July 21, 1864, William H. Carrier Letters, WHS; Williams to Perkins, September 12, 1864; Gill to Foye, September 27, 1864; and Robinson to Pittman, July 24, 1864, *OR*, 38(2):34, 38–39, 91.

48. Winegar to Mickle, September 7, 1864, and Woodbury to Pittman, September 13, 1864, *OR*, 38(2):476–77, 479.

49. Williams to Perkins, September 12, 1864; Knipe to Pittman, September 13, 1864; Packer to assistant adjutant general, First Brigade, First Division, Twentieth Corps, September 12, 1864; Rogers to Palmer, September 7, 1864; and Selfridge to Palmer, September 8, 1864, *OR*, 38(2):34, 43, 46, 50, 57; Quaife, *From the Cannon's Mouth*, 335; Shimp to wife, July 26, 1864, William T. Shimp Papers, USAMHI; Marvin, *Fifth Regiment Connecticut*, 328–29.

50. O'Neal to Barksdale, July 31, 1864, *OR*, 38(3):941–42; G. Osborn, "Civil War Letters," 216. For an evocative photograph of the torn jeans belonging to John E. Johnson of the 29th Alabama, damaged when he was killed at Peach Tree Creek, see *Atlanta: Voices of the Civil War*, 103. See also R. Jenkins, *Battle of Peach Tree Creek*, 298, for more information about Johnson.

51. Warner, *Generals in Gray*, 255–56; Quarles to Barksdale, July 25, 1864, and Reynolds to Barksdale, July 25, 1864, *OR*, 38(3):930, 938.

52. Quarles to Barksdale, July 25, 1864, and Reynolds to Barksdale, July 25, 1864, *OR*, 38(3):930–31, 938; Galloway to Wilburn, July 25, 1864, in S. Hood, *Lost Papers*, 77; Dacus, *Reminiscences*, not paginated.

53. Reynolds to Barksdale, July 25, 1864, *OR*, 38(3):938; Bunn to Wilburn, July 25, 1864, in S. Hood, *Lost Papers*, 75; Dacus, *Reminiscences*, not paginated; Leeper, *Rebels Valiant*, 239.

54. Thomas to Hooker, July 20, 1864, 3 P.M., *OR*, 38(5):204; Ruger to Pittman, September 11, 1864, *OR*, 38(2):62; Hapeman to Ford, September 5, 1864, and Moore to Smith, September 8, 1864, *OR*, 38(1):537, 602.

55. *Record of the Ninety-Fourth*, 71; Adolphson, "Incident of Valor," 413; Hapeman to Ford, September 5, 1864, *OR*, 38(1):537; Calkins, *One Hundred and Fourth Regiment of Illinois*, 220–21, 333; McDowell, "Fifteenth Kentucky," 252–53.

56. Hapeman to Ford, September 5, 1864, and Briant to not stated, no date, *OR*, 38(1):537, 542–43; Bunn to Wilburn, July 25, 1864, and Galloway to Wilburn, July 25, 1864, in S. Hood, *Lost Papers*, 75, 77.

57. Douglas Hapeman Diaries, July 20, 1864, ALPL; Hapeman to Ford, September 5, 1864: Halpin to Ford, September 8, 1864, *OR*, 38(1):537–38, 546–47; Adolphson, "Incident of Valor," 414–15.

58. Douglas Hapeman Diaries, July 20, 1864, ALPL; Calkins, *One Hundred and Fourth Regiment of Illinois*, 221, 223–25; Gould and Kennedy, *Memoirs of a Dutch Mudsill*, 270.

59. Hapeman to Ford, September 5, 1864, *OR*, 38(1):537–38; Calkins, *One Hundred and Fourth Regiment of Illinois*, 221; Adolphson, "Incident of Valor," 415–16; Bunn to Wilburn, July 25, 1864, in S. Hood, *Lost Papers*, 75; Rory, "Peach Tree Creek."

60. Douglas Hapeman Diaries, July 20, 1864, ALPL; Calkins, *One Hundred and Fourth Regiment of Illinois*, 221–21; Briant to not stated, no date; Minshall to Ford, September, no date, 1864; Hutchins to Ford, September 11, 1864; and Fitch to Ford, September 5, 1864, *OR*, 38(1):543, 551, 554, 557; diary, July 20, 1864, Charles Richard Pomeroy Papers, DU; diary, July 20, 1864, James M. Randall Diary and Letters, www.ehistory.com; McDowell, "Fifteenth Kentucky," 253; Horrall, *History of the Forty-Second*, 234; *Record of the Ninety-Fourth*, 72; Ruger to Pittman, September 11, 1864, *OR*, 38(2):62; Bryant, *History of the Third Regiment*, 256. For a highly exaggerated account of the participation of the 21st Wisconsin in the battle of July 20, see Gould and Kennedy, *Memoirs of a Dutch Mudsill*, 270.

61. Hapeman to Ford, September 5, 1864, *OR*, 38(1):538; Douglas Hapeman Diaries, July 20, 1864, ALPL; Calkins, *One Hundred and Fourth Regiment of Illinois*, 222–25 (includes Strawn quote); Hess to wife, July 24, 1864, Frederick Christian Hess Letters, UC.

62. Adolphson, "Incident of Valor," 418.

63. Calkins, *One Hundred and Fourth Regiment of Illinois*, 222, 224.

64. Douglas Hapeman Diaries, July 20, 1864, ALPL; *Record of the Ninety-Fourth*, 72; Briant to not stated, no date; Minshall to Ford, September, no date, 1864; Hutchins to Ford, September 11, 1864; and Fitch to Ford, September 5, 1864, *OR*, 38(1):543, 551, 554, 557.

65. Dacus, *Reminiscences*, not paginated; Galloway to Wilburn, July 25, 1864, in S. Hood, *Lost Papers*, 77–79; Reynolds to Barksdale, July 25, 1864, *OR*, 38(3):938.

66. Kendall, "Recollections of a Confederate Officer," 1175, 1192.

67. Stewart to Mason, January 12, 1865; Walthall to Gale, January 14, 1865; and O'Neal to Barksdale, July 31, 1864, *OR*, 38(3):871, 925, 941.

68. Walthall to Gale, January 14, 1865; Reynolds to Barksdale, July 25, 1864; and Lovelace to West, September 15, 1864, *OR*, 38(3):925–26, 938, 969; J. A. Stevenson to Capers, August 28, 1885, Ellison Capers Papers, DU; F. Halsey Wigfall to Lou, July 20, 1864, and to Mama, July 31, 1864, Louis Trezevant Wigfall Family Papers, LC; Castel, *Decision in the West*, 378; Daniel, *Cannoneers in Gray*, 157.

69. Reynolds to Barksdale, July 25, 1864; Watkins to Myrick, September 14, 1864; and Lovelace to West, September 15, 1864, *OR*, 38(3):938, 967–69.

70. Moore to Smith, September 8, 1864, *OR*, 38(1):602; Griffin to wife, July 30, 1864, Daniel F. Griffin Papers, ISL.

71. Johnson, *A Soldier's Reminiscences*, 281.

72. Warner, *Generals in Gray*, 93–94.

73. Jack to French, [July 20, 1864], *OR*, 38(5):896; Stewart to Mason, January 12, 1865; French to Jack, July 25, 1864; French to Gale, December 6, 1864; and Cockrell to Sanders, September 20, 1864, *OR*, 38(3):871, 902–3, 917; French, *Two Wars*, 218–19. R. Jenkins, *Battle of Peach Tree Creek*, 340–41, argues that Gates's Brigade supported Reynolds's attack. He bases this on some accounts that give a relatively

high casualty rate for the brigade. But other accounts offer low estimates of brigade casualties, and it is difficult to see how Gates could have supported Reynolds when Ector's Brigade was positioned next to Reynolds, not Gates. R. Jenkins, *Battle Rages Higher*, 231–32, argues that Ector supported Reynolds, but I see no evidence to suggest this scenario. See also Bevier, *History of the First and Second Missouri*, 240.

74. French to Jack, July 25, 1864, *OR*, 38(3):902; Gottschalk, *In Deadly Earnest*, 382.

75. French to Jack, July 25, 1864, *OR*, 38(3):902.

76. Moore to Smith, September 8, 1864, *OR*, 38(1):602; Griffin to wife, July 27, 1864, Daniel F. Griffin Papers, ISL; Blackburn, *Letters from the Front*, 215; Winter, *Joseph Boyce*, 169; French to Jack, July 25, 1864, and Cockrell to Sanders, September 20, 1864, *OR*, 38(3):902, 917; Gottschalk, *In Deadly Earnest*, 382.

77. Johnson to McClurg, August, no date, 1864, and "Journal of the First Brigade," *OR*, 38(1):524, 532; extracts of report by Surg. Charles W. Jones, *SOR*, pt. 1, 7:72.

78. Baird to McClurg, September 7, 1864, and Gleason to Lowrie, August 16, 1864, *OR*, 38(1):743, 790; Patrick and Willey, *Fighting for Liberty and Right*, 231; Angle, *Three Years*, 239.

79. T. Brown, Murphy, and Putney, *Behind the Guns*, 102; John J. Mercer Diary, July 20, 1864, AHC.

80. Ramsey to Palmer, July 20, 1864, 5 P.M., *OR*, 38(5):202.

Chapter 9

1. Castel, *Decision in the West*, 379.

2. Cox, *Atlanta*, 160; Howard, *Autobiography*, 1:609.

3. Hascall to Campbell, September 10, 1864; Sherwood to Hobson, August 25, 1864; Strickland to Kerstetter, August 14, 1864; and Waller to not stated, no date, *OR*, 38(2):571–72, 639–40, 648, 657; journal, July 20, 1864, Tilghman Blazer Collection, UTK.

4. Sherman, *Memoirs*, 2, 72–73; Sherman to Thomas, July 20, 1864, 6:10 [P.M.], *OR*, 38(5):196–97; Gallup to wife, July 20, 1864, George W. Gallup Papers, FHS.

5. Stanley to Fullerton, no date, 1864; Taylor to Mason, September 15, 1864; and Stookey to Lawton, September 12, 1864, *OR*, 38(1):225, 248–49, 272; Gates, *Rough Side of War*, 245; R. Jenkins, *Battle of Peach Tree Creek*, 42–43.

6. Stanley to Fullerton, no date, 1864, and Taylor to Mason, September 15, 1864, *OR*, 38(1):225, 249; Howard, *Autobiography*, 1:611; William Lewis English Diary, August 13, 1864, ALPL; Day, *One Hundred and First Ohio*, 244; R. Jenkins, *Battle of Peach Tree Creek*, 44–45. The 30th Alabama lost at least nine men in the afternoon skirmish with the Federals. Stephens, *Bound for Glory*, 259.

7. Stanley to Fullerton, no date, 1864; Suman to [Lawton], September 10, 1864; and Hurd to Lawton, September 13, 1864, *OR*, 38(1):225, 276, 282; Day, *One Hundred and First Ohio*, 244; Simmons, *84th Reg't Ill.*, 187; Howard to Mendenhall, July 20, 1864, *OR*, 38(5):198.

8. Gates, *Rough Side of War*, 245; Howard to Mendenhall, July 20, 1864, *OR*,

38(5):198; "Journal of the Atlanta Campaign, kept at headquarters of the Fourth Army Corps, by Lieut. Col. Joseph S. Fullerton, Assistant Adjutant General," and Hotchkiss to Bestow, September 10, 1864, *OR*, 38(1):396, 906.

9. Howard, *Autobiography*, 1:611; R. Jenkins, *Battle of Peach Tree Creek*, 46–47.

10. Cox, *Atlanta*, 153; Castel, *Decision in the West*, 371, 378–79.

11. Castel, *Decision in the West*, 367, 371.

12. Howard to Dayton, September 17, 1864; Logan to Clark, [September 13, 1864]; and De Gress to Lofland, September 1, 1864, *OR*, 38(3):38–39, 102, 265; Howard, "Struggle for Atlanta," 314.

13. McPherson to Sherman, July 20, 1864, 8:45 P.M., and Sherman to McPherson, July 21, 1864, 1 A.M., *OR*, 38(5):208, 218–19; Castel, *Decision in the West*, 380.

14. James B. David Diary, July 20, 1864, UTK; Wagner to Lee, September 10, 1864, *OR*, 38(1):338; diary, July 20, 1864, John Wesley Marshall Papers, OHS; *History of the Seventy-Third*, 325–26; Hynes to brother, July 29, 1864, William D. Hynes Papers, ISL.

15. Kimball to assistant adjutant general, Second Division, Fourth Corps, August 4, 1864, *OR*, 38(1):306–7; Baumgartner and Strayer, *Yankee Tigers*, 128–29.

16. Baumgartner and Strayer, *Yankee Tigers*, 129–30; Hinman, *Story of the Sherman Brigade*, 580.

17. Buckingham to Young, September 8, 1864, *OR*, 38(2):454; Coe, *Mine Eyes Have Seen the Glory*, 179; Newton, "Battle of Peach Tree Creek," 158–59.

18. Harrison to wife, July 21, 1864, Benjamin Harrison Collection, IHS; Harry Stanley Diary, July 21, 1864, AHC; Brant, *History of the Eighty-Fifth Indiana*, 69; Buckingham to Horace J. Munsey, August 6, 1864, Philo Beecher Buckingham Papers, AAS; Dutton to Mitchell, August 5, 1864, and Miller to Crawford, July 27, 1864, *OR*, 38(2):364, 406.

19. Coburn to Speed, July 28, 1864, *OR*, 38(2):390; Bohrnstedt, *Soldiering with Sherman*, 126; James A. Congleton Diary, July 20, 1864, LC; Fleharty, *Our Regiment*, 95; Hitchcock to parents, July 21, 1864, Watson C. Hitchcock Papers, CHS; Merrill, *Seventieth Indiana*, 144–47.

20. Williams to Perkins, September 12, 1864; Selfridge to Palmer, September 8, 1864 Fesler to Fay, September 6, 1864; Salomon to Boughton, September 15, 1864; Candy to Forbes, August 1, 1864; and Chatfield to Wheelock, September 16, 1864, *OR*, 38(2):34, 56, 64, 100, 159, 291; diary, July 20, 1864, Max Schlund Papers, NL; E. Brown, *Twenty-Seventh Indiana*, 527.

21. William Merrell, "Personal Memoirs of the Civil War," LMU.

22. Morhous, *Reminiscences*, 112–13.

23. Edie to Smith, September 19, 1864; McManus to Fetterman, September 19, 1864; Hall to Fetterman, September 17, 1864; and Vernon to Wilson, September 5, 1864, *OR*, 38(1):562, 572, 582, 689; James Biddle Diary, July 20, 1864, DPL; Kinnear, *History of the Eighty-Sixth*, 63.

24. Thomas to Sherman, July 20, 1864, 6:15 P.M., and Ramsey to Stoneman, July 20, 1864, *OR*, 38(5):197, 207.

25. "Journal of the Atlanta Campaign, kept at headquarters of the Fourth

Army Corps, by Lieut. Col. Joseph S. Fullerton, Assistant Adjutant General," *OR*, 38(1):906; Sherman to Thomas, [July 20], 1864, 3:25 [P.M.], *OR*, 38(5):196; Castel, *Decision in the West*, 380.

26. Sherman to Thomas, July 20, 1864, 6:10 [P.M.], *OR*, 38(5):196–97.

27. Sherman to Thomas, July 20, 1864, 8 P.M., *OR*, 38(5):198.

28. Sherman to Halleck, July 20, 1864, 9 P.M., and Van Duzer to Eckert, July 20, 1864, 10 P.M., *OR*, 38(5):195, 210.

29. Hood to Cooper, February 15, 1865, *OR*, 38(3):631; William McLeod Civil War Pocket Diary, July 20, 1864, SAF; George Anderson Mercer Diary, July 20, 1864, UNC; Joslyn, *Charlotte's Boys*, 269; Durham, *Blues in Gray*, 223; Franklin, *Civil War Diaries*, 188–89; autobiography, 29, Edwin Hansford Rennolds Sr. Papers, UTK.

30. Durham, *Blues in Gray*, 223; Thomas B. Mackall Journal (McMurry transcript), July 20–21, 1864, Joseph E. Johnston Papers, CWM; Hawes, "Memoirs of Charles H. Olmstead," pt. 10, 44.

31. Stewart to Mason, January 12, 1865; Loring to West, September 15, 1864; Featherston to Robinson, July 23, 1863, and Jackson to Neilson, July 23, 1864, *OR*, 38(3):871, 877, 882–83, 889; Featherston to Loring, November 20, 1867, Winfield Scott Featherston Collection, UM; Howell, *To Live and Die*, 334; Sykes to wife, July 26, 1864, William E. Sykes Papers, MSU.

32. Featherston to Robinson, July 23, 1864; Stigler to Neilson, September 15, 1864; Jackson to Neilson, July 23, 1864; Scott to Robinson, July 23, 1864; and Nelson to Graham, July 24, 1864, *OR*, 38(3):882, 885, 889, 895, 898; record of events, Company L, 12th Louisiana, *SOR*, pt. 2, 24:273.

33. Walthall to Gale, January 14, 1865; Quarles to Barksdale, July 25, 1864; and Reynolds to Barksdale, July 25, 1864, *OR*, 38(3):926, 930–31, 938; Kendall, "Recollections of a Confederate Officer," 1192.

34. West to French, July 20, 1864, 7 P.M., *OR*, 38(5):896; French to Jack, July 25, 1864, and Cockrell to Sanders, September 20, 1864, *OR*, 38(3):902, 917.

35. Tower, *A Carolinian Goes to War*, 223.

36. Ibid.; Cuttino, *Saddle Bag*, 268; Ross to Mary, July 22, 1864, Emmett Ross Papers, MSU; diary, July 20, 1864, James Conquest Cross Black Papers, UNC.

37. Wheeler to Mason, October 9, 1864, *OR*, 38(3):951.

38. Cheatham to Wheeler, July 20, 1864, 5:30 P.M. and 6:45 P.M., and Mackall to Wheeler, July 20, 1864, 6:30 P.M., *OR*, 38(5):896–97.

39. Lowrey to Benham, September 20, 1864; Flynt to Sneed, July 29, 1864; and Taylor to Sneed, July 29, 1864, *OR*, 38(3):733, 748, 752.

40. Hood to Seddon, July 20, 1864, 11 P.M., *OR*, 38(5):894.

Chapter 10

1. John W. Houtz Diaries, July 21, 1864, OHS; George A. Cooley Civil War Diary, July 21, 1864, WHS; DeRosier, *Through the South*, 132–33; J. Cate, *If I Live to Come Home*, 196; E. Brown, *Twenty-Seventh Indiana*, 522–23; Alanson B. Cone Personal Narrative, July 21, 1864, NYSL; Johnson to Folks at Home, July 25, 1864, Andrew Jackson Johnson Papers, IHS; Alfred H. Trego Diary, July 21, 1864, CHM.

2. Wagner to Lee, September 10, 1864, *OR*, 38(1):338; Longacre and Haas, *To Battle for God and the Right*, 201–2; Jones to wife, July 24, 1864, Joseph Jones Letter, GLIAH; George A. Cooley Civil War Diary, July 21, 1864, WHS; diary, July 21, 1864, Albert M. Cook Papers, SU; Coe, *Mine Eyes Have Seen the Glory*, 179.

3. Bode to editor, July 21, 1864, *Indianapolis Daily Journal*, August 2, 1864; George Hoenig Journal, July 21, 1864, www.russscott.com; Charles P. Wickham quote in H. Osborn, *Trials and Triumphs*, 162; J. Cate, *If I Live to Come Home*, 196.

4. Harry Stanley Diary, July 22, 1864, AHC.

5. Circular, Headquarters, Department of the Cumberland, July 25, 1864, *OR*, 38(1):174; copy of Circular, Headquarters, Department of the Cumberland, July 25, 1864, George L. Reis Letters, UTK; Coburn to Speed, July 28, 1864, *OR*, 38(2): 390.

6. Balloch to wife, July 24, 1864, George Williamson Balloch Papers, DU; Douglas Hapeman Diaries, July 21, 1864, ALPL; Angle, *Three Years*, 239; Blair, *A Politician Goes to War*, 189; Johnson to Folks at Home, July 25, 1864, Andrew Jackson Johnson Papers, IHS; George A. Cooley Civil War Diary, July 21, 1864, WHS; Daniel E. Barnard to sister, July 24, 1864, Howe-Barnard Family Papers, NL; Cox, *Atlanta*, 158–59.

7. Sherman, "Grand Strategy," 253; Stone, "Atlanta Campaign," 442, 485; dispatch to *St. Louis Union*, in *St. Louis Daily Missouri Democrat*, July 26, 1864; Van Horne, *History of the Army of the Cumberland*, 2, 116; Howard, *Autobiography*, 1:619.

8. Thomas to Sawyer, August 17, 1864, and Circular, Headquarters, Department of the Cumberland, July 25, 1864, *OR*, 38(1):156, 174; Stone, "Atlanta Campaign," 442, 485; dispatch to *St. Louis Union*, in *St. Louis Daily Missouri Democrat*, July 26, 1864; Balloch to wife, July 24, 1864, George Williamson Balloch Papers, DU; Bradley to sister, July 21, 1864, Luther P. Bradley Collection, USAMHI; Van Horne, *History of the Army of the Cumberland*, 2:116; Cox, *Atlanta*, 158; Sherman, "Grand Strategy," 253; Douglas Hapeman Diaries, July 21, 1864, ALPL; Howard, *Autobiography*, 1:619; R. Jenkins, *Battle of Peach Tree Creek*, 395; Castel, *Decision in the West*, 381.

9. Taylor Beatty Diary, July 21, 1864, UNC; Whitehead to Irene Cowan, July 21, 1864, Dr. P. F. Whitehead Letters, USM; dispatch to *Savannah Republican*, in *Charleston Mercury*, July 26, 1864; "Abstract from Returns of the Army of Tennessee, General Joseph E. Johnston, C.S. Army, July 10, 1864," and "Abstract from Returns of the Army of Tennessee, General John B. Hood, C.S. Army, Commanding, July 31, 1864," *OR*, 38(3):679–80; Castel, *Decision in the West*, 381; Daniel, *Days of Glory*, 414; McMurry, *Atlanta 1864*, 152. For another estimate of losses in Stewart's command, see R. Jenkins, *Battle of Peach Tree Creek*, 397.

10. Thomas to Sawyer, August 17, 1864, *OR*, 38(1):156; Gardner to parents, July 23, 1864, Lyman Gardner Papers, WLC-UM; diary, July 21, 1864, John Wesley Marshall Papers, OHS.

11. Wood to Beecher, September 23, 1864, *OR*, 38(2):443; Hitchcock to Frank and Betsey, July 21, 1864, Watson C. Hitchcock Papers, CHS; Winkler to C. H. Young, July 28, 1864, Frederick C. Winkler Papers, WHS; Thackery, *Light and Uncertain Hold*, 205.

12. Harrison to Speed, August 12, 1864; Dutton to Mitchell, August 5, 1864; and Coburn to Speed, July 28, 1864, *OR*, 38(2):347, 364, 390; Bradley, *Star Corps*, 143; Charles A. Booth Journal, July 20, 1864, WHS; Austin to wife, July 21, 1864, Judson L. Austin Papers, BHL-UM; Brant, *History of the Eighty-Fifth Indiana*, 68; Byrne, *Uncommon Soldiers*, 173; Harrison to wife, July 21, 1864, Benjamin Harrison Collection, IHS; Merrill to J. L. Mitchell, August 1, 1864, Samuel Merrill Papers, ISL; diary, July 21, 1864, Andrew Jackson Johnson Papers, IHS; Merrill, *Seventieth Indiana*, 149; Bohrnstedt, *Soldiering with Sherman*, 126.

13. Williams to Perkins, September 12, 1864, and Geary to Perkins, September 15, 1864, *OR*, 38(2):34, 141; Alexander Dobbin Diary, July 21, 1864, EU; Wallace, "At Peach Tree Creek"; Hapeman to Ford, September 5, 1864, *OR*, 38(1):538.

14. Harrison to [Speed], September 14, 1864, *OR*, 38(2):348; Daniel W. Sheahan Diary, July 21, 1864, ALPL.

15. Circular, Headquarters, Department of the Cumberland, July 25, 1864, *OR*, 38(1):174.

16. Holzhueter, "William Wallace's Civil War Letters," 102; Alanson B. Cone Personal Narrative, July 21, 1864, NYSL; Newbury, "At Peach Tree Creek"; diary, July 21, 1864, John Wesley Marshall Papers, OHS; Bauer, *Soldiering*, 152; Padgett, "With Sherman," 302; Conger, "The Private," 59.

17. Boyle, *Soldiers True*, 239; Mannis and Wilson, *Bound to Be a Soldier*, 151; E. P. Failing Diary, July 21, 1864, Failing-Knight Papers, MHS; Benjamin Harrison letter to Malcolm A. Lowes, in Merrill, *Seventieth Indiana*, 147; Daniel W. Sheahan Diary, July 20, 1864, ALPL.

18. Rice, "With Sherman: Another Chapter of the Peach Tree Creek Battle"; Grunert, *One Hundred and Twenty-Ninth Regiment Illinois*, 87; McWilliams, *Recollections*, 140.

19. William A. Brand letter, July 23, 1864, in Thackery, *Light and Uncertain Hold*, 205; E. P. Failing Diary, July 24, 1864, Failing-Knight Family Papers, MHS; William Cline Diary, July 22, 26, 1864, UND; Elmore to parents, July 26, 1864, Day Elmore Letters, CHM.

20. "Confederate colors captured by the Army of the Cumberland in the campaign against Atlanta from May 4 to September 8, 1864," and Circular, Headquarters, Department of the Cumberland, July 25, 1864, *OR*, 38(1):171, 174; "Report of trophies captured during the campaign from Chattanooga, Tenn., to Atlanta, Ga., by the troops of the Twentieth Army Corps," *OR*, 38(2):22; R. Jenkins, *Battle of Peach Tree Creek*, 414.

21. "Report of trophies captured during the campaign from Chattanooga, Tenn., to Atlanta, Ga., by the troops of the Twentieth Army Corps," *OR*, 38(2):22; Bradley, *Star Corps*, 143.

22. "Report of trophies captured during the campaign from Chattanooga, Tenn., to Atlanta, Ga., by the troops of the Twentieth Army Corps," *OR*, 38(2):22; Sylvester, "'Gone for a Soldier,'" 211; Charles A. Booth Journal, July 21, 1864, WHS.

23. John W. Leeper quoted in Leeper, *Rebels Valiant*, 239; Clemmer, *Valor in Gray*, xv, xix–xxi.

24. Douglas Hapeman Diaries, July 21, 1864, ALPL; Selfridge to Palmer, Septem-

ber 8, 1864, and Dustin to Grubbs, September 15, 1864, *OR*, 38(2):57, 362; diary, July 22, 1864, John Wesley Marshall Papers, OHS; Merrill to J. L. Mitchell, August 1, 1864, Samuel Merrill Papers, ISL; Wallace, "At Peach Tree Creek"; "Report of arms captured, lost, and becoming surplus in the Army of the Cumberland for the month of July, 1864," *OR*, 38(1):159.

25. Thomas to Sawyer, August 17, 1864; "Report of prisoners of war and rebel deserters received and disposed of during the month of July, 1864"; and Circular, Headquarters, Department of the Cumberland, July 25, 1864, *OR*, 38(1):156, 159, 174.

26. "First Battle before Atlanta," *Washington Daily National Intelligencer*, July 28, 1864; Byrne, *Uncommon Soldiers*, 173; Newbury, "At Peach Tree Creek"; diary, July 21, 1864, Albert M. Cook Papers, SU; Charles A. Booth Journal, July 21, 1864, WHS.

27. Foye to Cooper, September 29, 1864, and Goodman to Foye, September 22, 1864, *OR*, 38(2):25, 152; E. Brown, *Twenty-Seventh Indiana*, 523; diary, July 20, 1864, Andrew Jackson Johnson Papers, IHS.

28. Gill to Foye, September 27, 1864, *OR*, 38(2):39; Githins to wife, July 22, 1864, William Harrison Githins Letters, Gail and Stephen Rudin Collection of Civil War Letters, CU.

29. Foye to Cooper, September 29, 1864; Gill to Foye, September 27,1864; Goodman to Foye, September 22, 1864; and Grinstead to not stated, September 29, 1864, *OR*, 38(2):25, 39, 152, 337.

30. Henry Perrin Mann Civil War Diaries, July 21, 1864, SHSM-RCR; Bauer, *Soldiering*, 152; William Clark McLean Diary, July 21, 1864, McLean Family Papers, NYSL; Padgett, "With Sherman," 302.

31. Foye to Cooper, September 29, 1864, and Grinstead to not stated, September 29, 1864, *OR*, 38(2):25, 337.

32. Garrett to Lee, September 10, 1864; Goodman to Foye, September 22, 1864; and Grinstead to not stated, September 29, 1864, *OR*, 38(2):109, 152, 339; Hutchinson to father, July 24, 1864, Edwin Hutchinson Papers, LSU.

33. Austin to wife, July 21, 1864, Judson L. Austin Papers, BHL-UM; Merrill, *Seventieth Indiana*, 152; Bohrnstedt, *Soldiering with Sherman*, 128; Carrier to wife, July 28, 1864, William H. Carrier Letters, WHS; Foye to Cooper, September 29, 1864; Goodman to Foye, September 22, 1864; and: Grinstead to not stated, September 29, 1864, *OR*, 38(2):25, 152, 337; Winkler to C. H. Young, July 28, 1864, Frederick C. Winkler Papers, WHS; William Cline Diary, July 22, 1864, UND.

34. Austin to wife, July 21, 1864, Judson L. Austin Papers, BHL-UM; Harmon, "Battle of Peach Tree Creek." Actually, Union women disguised as men also took part in the Civil War but not in this battle.

35. Hitchcock to parents, July 26, 1864, Watson C. Hitchcock Papers, CHS; Ewing, "Wounding a Young lady"; Fleharty, *Our Regiment*, 94–95; George A. Cooley Civil War Diary, July 21, 1864, WHS; Frederick N. Kollock Diary, July 21, 1864, Charles S. Harris Collection, UTC.

36. Marvin, *Fifth Regiment Connecticut*, 330; Thackery, *Light and Uncertain Hold*, 209.

37. E. P. Failing Diary, July 20–22, 1864, Failing-Knight Papers, MHS.

38. Trowbridge to wife and baby, July 21, 1864, George Martin Trowbridge Papers, WLC-UM.

39. Ibid.

40. Trowbridge to wife and baby, July 21, 22, 1864, George Martin Trowbridge Papers, WLC-UM.

41. Trowbridge to wife and baby, July 21, 22, 23, 1864, George Martin Trowbridge Papers, WLC-UM.

42. Trowbridge to wife and baby, July 22, 23, 1864, George Martin Trowbridge Papers, WLC-UM.

43. Beasecker, *"I Hope to Do My Country Service,"* 301.

44. Willis Perry Burt Diary, July 20, 1864, Laura Burt Brantley Collection, GHS; R. Davis, *Requiem for a Lost City*, 125.

45. Whitehead to Irene Cowan, July 21, 1864, Dr. P. F. Whitehead Letters, USM; Brannock to wife, July 26, 1864, James Madison Brannock Papers, VHS.

46. "List of Killed and Wounded of 12th and 47th Tenn. Regts Vaughans Brigd Cheatham's Div. H.C.A.T.," James Madison Brannock Papers, VHS.

47. Jones quoted in Dunkelman, *Brothers One and All*, 139; Bauer, *Soldiering*, 152; P. Jordan, "Forty Days," 138.

48. [Murphree], "Autobiography and Civil War Letters," 186; Brannock to wife, July 26, 1864, James Madison Brannock Papers, VHS.

49. Cook to Fred, July 25, 1864, Albert M. Cook Papers, SU; *Medical and Surgical History*, 7:108.

50. Clipping of the *Salem Press*, August 2, 1864; Welch to father, July 29, [1864]; and cards, Henry Welch service record, 123rd New York, copies in Henry Welch Papers, USAMHI.

51. Marshall to Mary, July 29, 1864, John Law Marshall Correspondence, N-YHS.

52. Morhous, *Reminiscences*, 114–16.

53. *Medical and Surgical History*, 10:478; Thackery, *Light and Uncertain Hold*, 204–5.

54. *Medical and Surgical History*, 10:530, 563, and 12:578.

55. Ibid., 7:236; Thackery, *Light and Uncertain Hold*, 205.

56. *Medical and Surgical History*, 7:198.

57. Ibid.

58. Osborne, "George Young," 28–29; "List of Articles lost & destroyed in the Public Service near Atlanta Ga. While in the possession of Lt. Geo Young in the month of July 1864," George Young Papers, AHC.

59. Transcript of article in *Ellenville Journal*, January 11, 1884, and May 23, 1884, George Young Papers, AHC; Osborne, "George Young," 29–30. Young's coat, hat, and trousers, worn on July 20, are on display at the museum of the Atlanta History Center.

60. *Medical and Surgical History*, 12:545.

61. James Palmer Civil War Diary, undated and unpaginated, MDAH.

62. Howell, *To Live and Die*, 330–31.

63. Oscar Bowen quoted in Howell, *To Live and Die*, 331.

64. R. M. Collins, *Chapters*, 229–31.

65. Ibid., 231–35.

66. Harry Stanley Diary, July 21, 1864, AHC.

67. Potter, *Reminiscences*, 93, 95–96.

68. G. Collins, *Memoirs*, 282.

69. Morhous, *Reminiscences*, 113.

Chapter 11

1. Sylvester, "'Gone for a Soldier,'" 211; Realf to Dear Friends, July 21, 1864, Richard Realf Letters and Poems, NL; J. Cate, *If I Live to Come Home*, 196; Padgett, "With Sherman," 302; Edgerton to mother, [July 1864], William W. Edgerton Civil War Letters, UH; Hitchcock to parents, July 21, 1864, Watson C. Hitchcock Papers, CHS; Hynes to brother, July 29, 1864, William D. Hynes Papers, ISL; Foster to Mose, August 23, 1864, William F. Morgan Papers, NC.

2. Wheeler to parents, brother, and sister, July 21, 1864, Lysander Wheeler Letter, GLIAH; Holzhueter, "William Wallace's Civil War Letters," 102; Elias J. Prichard to brother and sister, July 19 (continued July 22), 1864, EU; Trowbridge to wife and baby, July 22, 1864, George Martin Trowbridge Papers, WLC-UM; unsigned copy of untitled poem, Lewis A. Labadie Papers, DPL.

3. Austin to wife, July 23, 1864, Judson L. Austin Papers, BHL-UM.

4. Buckingham to wife, August 9, 1864, Philo Beecher Buckingham Papers, AAS.

5. Merrill to Emma, July 24, 1864, Samuel Merrill Papers, ISL; Marshall to Mary, July 29, 1864, John Law Marshall Correspondence, N-YHS; Harrison to wife, July 21, 1864, Benjamin Harrison Collection, IHS.

6. Harrison to wife, July 21, 1864, Benjamin Harrison Collection, IHS.

7. Bode to editor, July 21, 1864, *Indianapolis Daily Journal*, August 2, 1864; Henry Lyon to editor, July 22, 1864, *Indianapolis Daily Journal*, August 1, 1864; unsigned letter, July 21, 1864, *Washington Daily National Intelligencer*, July 28, 1864; Montrose to editor of *Cincinnati Commercial*, July 24, 1864, in *New York Daily Tribune*, July 27, 1864, and in *St. Louis Daily Missouri Democrat*, July 26, 1864; Sylvester, "'Gone for a Soldier,'" 211.

8. F. Halsey Wigfall to Lou, July 20, 1864, and to Mama, July 31, 1864, Louis Trezevant Wigfall Family Papers, LC; G. Osborn, "Civil War Letters," 215–16; McGuire, *McGuire Papers*, 27.

9. *Augusta Daily Constitutionalist*, July 22, 1864; Scarborough, *Diary of Edmund Ruffin*, 3, 508.

10. Marvin, *Fifth Regiment Connecticut*, 327–28; Compton to Palmer, September 9, 1864, and West to Grubbs, September 22, 1864, *OR*, 38(2):53, 377; diary, July 20, 1864, Andrew Jackson Johnson Papers, IHS; Stone, "Atlanta Campaign," 441; Hunter to Curtis, August 17, 1864, *OR*, 38(1):769; E. E. Russell, "Where Hood Gathered No Acorns"; Coe, *Mine Eyes Have Seen the Glory*, 178; Palmer, "A Gallant Record: What the 20th Conn. Did in the Atlanta Campaign"; Alanson B. Cone Personal Narrative, July 20, 1864, NYSL.

11. Sherman to Halleck, September 15, 1864, *OR*, 38(1):71; Poe to wife, July 24, 1864, Orlando Metcalfe Poe Papers, LC.

12. Sherman, *Memoirs*, 2, 72–73.

13. Geary to Perkins, September 15, 1864, *OR*, 38(2):140; Tuttle to Monroe [after July 28, 1864], Miletus Tuttle Letters, UGA; Longacre and Haas, *To Battle for God and the Right*, 201; Gould and Kennedy, *Memoirs of a Dutch Mudsill*, 270–71; Byrne, *Uncommon Soldiers*, 173; Johnson to Folks at Home, July 25, 1864, Andrew Jackson Johnson Papers, IHS; Benjamin T. Smith Reminiscences, 158, ALPL; Balloch to wife, July 24, 1864, George Williamson Balloch Papers, DU; Van Horne, *History of the Army of the Cumberland*, 2:115–16.

14. Geary to Perkins, September 15, 1864, *OR*, 38(2):140; J. Cate, *If I Live to Come Home*, 196; West to not stated, September 21, 1864, *SOR*, pt. 1, 7:29; Knapp to parents, July 24, 1864, Charles Webster Knapp Letters, WHS; Potter, *Reminiscences*, 95–95.

15. Diary, July 21, 1864, and Cook to Fred, July 25, 1864, Albert M. Cook Papers, SU.

16. Harry Stanley Diary, July 20, 1864, AHC; George A. Cooley Civil War Diary, July 21, 1864, WHS.

17. Longacre and Haas, *To Battle for God and the Right*, 206.

18. Roberts to sister, August 13, 1864, John H. Roberts Civil War Letters, WHS; Comfort to father, August 13, 1864, John R. Comfort Papers, WLC-UM; Foster to Moses C. Morgan, August 23, 1864, William F. Morgan Papers, NC; John Emerson Anderson Memoir, 154, LC. Historians have generally treated Hooker well for his performances in the Atlanta campaign. See Hebert, *Fighting Joe Hooker*, 282–83. and Rafuse, "Always 'Fighting Joe,'" 246–50.

19. Diary, July 21, 1864, John Wesley Marshall Papers, OHS; George A. Cooley Civil War Diary, July 21, 1864, WHS; *History of the Seventy-Third*, 326; Douglas Hapeman Diaries, July 20, 1864, ALPL; Alanson B. Cone Personal Narrative, July 20, 1864, NYSL; Cox, *Atlanta*, 149.

20. Maley to William M. Maley, July 21, 1864, Henry H. Maley Letters, UND; Angle, *Three Years*, 239–40.

21. Young, *Reminiscences*, 90; Nisbet, *4 Years on the Firing Line*, 210; Dunlop to sister, August 13, 1864, Colin Dunlop Civil War Letters, AHC; "Special" letter, July 20, 1864, *Augusta Daily Constitutionalist*, July 23, 1864; T. J. Walker, "Reminiscences of the Civil War," UTK.

22. Hawes, "Memoirs of Charles H. Olmstead," pt. 10, 43.

23. Godwin to Bettie, August 15, 1864, D. G. Godwin Correspondence, AHC; Mathis, *In the Land of the Living*, 104; Winfield S. Featherston to Hood, December 18, 1866, John B. Hood Papers, NARA.

24. Hood to Cooper, February 15, 1865, *OR*, 38(3):630–31.

25. Hardee to Cooper, April 5, 1865, *OR*, 38(3):697–98.

26. J. B. Hood, *Advance and Retreat*, 168, 171.

27. Ibid., 171, 185, 251.

28. Ibid., 168–69, 186; French, *Two Wars*, 219; Tower, *A Carolinian Goes to War*, 223.

29. Roy, "General Hardee," 381.

30. Ibid., 379, 383–85; Thomas B. Roy to Govan, March 8, 1880, Daniel Chevi-

lette Govan Papers, UNC; B. Benjamin Smith to Capers, April 3, 1880, Ellison Capers Papers, TC.

31. Franklin, *Civil War Diaries*, 188–89; Buck, *Cleburne and His Command*, 231; Hewitt, Schott, and Kunis, *To Succeed or Perish*, 56; Tower, *A Carolinian Goes to War*, 224.

32. Sherman to McPherson, July 21, 1864, 1 A.M., *OR*, 38(5):218.

33. Thomas to Sherman, July 21, 1864, *OR*, 38(5):212; Howard, "Struggle for Atlanta," 314; diary, July 21, 1864, John Wesley Marshall Papers, OHS; Newton to Fullerton, July 21, 1864; Newton to assistant adjutant general, Army of the Cumberland, September, no date, 1864; and Kimball to assistant adjutant general, Second Division, Fourth Corps, August 4, 1864, *OR*, 38(1):291, 299, 307.

34. Newton to assistant adjutant general, Army of the Cumberland, September, no date, 1864, *OR*, 38(1):299; diary, July 21, 1864, John Wesley Marshall Papers, OHS; George A. Cooley Civil War Diary, July 21, 1864, WHS; Newton to Whipple, July 21, 1864; Whipple to Newton, July 21, 1864; and Ramsey to Newton, July 21, 1864, *OR*, 38(5):214–15.

35. "Journal of the Atlanta Campaign, kept at headquarters of the Fourth Army Corps, by Lieut. Col. Joseph S. Fullerton, Assistant Adjutant General," *OR*, 38(1):906–7; Day, *One Hundred and First Ohio*, 245.

36. "Journal of the Atlanta Campaign, kept at headquarters of the Fourth Army Corps, by Lieut. Col. Joseph S. Fullerton, Assistant Adjutant General," *OR*, 38(1):907; Fullerton to Stanley, July 21, 1864, 2 P.M.; Fullerton to Wood, July 21, 1864, 2 P.M.; and Howard to Schofield, July 21, 1864, 2:45 P.M., *OR*, 38(5):214, 218.

37. Howard to Whipple, September 18, 1864; Taylor to Mason, September 15, 1864; and Stookey to Lawton, September 12, 1864, *OR*, 38(1):203, 249, 272; diary, July 21, 1864, James R. Carnahan Papers, IHS; Chesley D. Bailey Diary, July 21, 1864, FHS; *History of the Seventy-Ninth*, 159; Barnes, Carnahan, and McCain, *Eighty-Sixth Regiment*, 421–22; John H. Tilford Diaries, July 21, 1864, FHS; Hazen, *Narrative*, 272; Gates, *Rough Side of War*, 245–46.

38. Hotchkiss to Bestow, September 10, 1864, and Johnson to McGrath, September 15, 1864, *OR*, 38(1):396, 420–21; Jacob Andervount Diary, July 21, 1864, AHC; James Biddle Diary, July 20, 1864, DPL; Hazen, *Narrative*, 273; Howard to Whipple, July 21, 1864, 7 P.M., *OR*, 38(5):213–14.

39. Sherman to Thomas, July 21, 1864, *OR*, 38(5):212; Schofield to Sherman, September 10, 1864, and Hobson to Kerstetter, August 15, 1864, *OR*, 38(2):516, 617.

40. Hascall to Campbell, September 10, 1864, *OR*, 38(2):572; reminiscences, July 21, 1864, Thomas Doak Edington Papers, UTK; diary, July 21, 1864, John Watkins Papers, UTK; journal, July 21, 1864, Tilghman Blazer Collection, UTK.

41. Howard to Dayton, September 17, 1864, *OR*, 38(3):39.

42. Whipple to Hooker, July 20, 1864, *OR*, 38(5):205; Geary to Perkins, September 15, 1864, *OR*, 38(2):141; Carrier to wife, July 21, 1864, William H. Carrier Letters, WHS; diary, July 21, 1864, Albert M. Cook Papers, SU.

43. Irving Bronson, "Recollections of the Civil War," 51–52, TC.

44. Diary, July 21, 1864, Andrew Jackson Johnson Papers, IHS; Merrill, *Seventieth Indiana*, 149; Bohrnstedt, *Soldiering with Sherman*, 127.

45. Shimp to wife, July 26, 1864, William T. Shimp Papers, USAMHI; Bradley, *Star Corps*, 144.

46. Sherman to Thomas, July 21, 1864, and Whipple to Palmer, July 21, 1864, *OR*, 38(5):212, 217.

47. Johnson to McClurg, August, no date, 1864; "Journal of the First Brigade": Hapeman to Ford, September 5, 1864; Minshall to Ford, September, no date, 1864; Brigham to not stated, September 10, 1864; Moore to Smith, September 8, 1864;: Baird to McClurg, September 7, 1864; and Gleason to Lowrie, August 16, 1864, *OR*, 38(1):524, 532, 538, 551, 565, 602, 743, 791; diary, July 21, 1864, Charles Richard Pomeroy Papers, DU; Douglas Hapeman Diaries, July 21, 1864, ALPL; Calkins, *One Hundred and Fourth Regiment of Illinois*, 226; Young to Sanders, September 17, 1864, *OR*, 38(3):909–10.

48. Davis to McClurg, July 21, 1864, and Van Duzer to Eckert, July 21, 1864, 7:30 P.M., *OR*, 38(5):216–17, 222; Lum to Wiseman, August 8, 1864, *OR*, 38(1):671; Slack to father and mother, July 23, 1864, Albert L. Slack Letters, EU.

49. Thomas to Sherman, July 21, 1864, *OR*, 38(5):213.

50. Narrative, 7, Henry De Lamar Clayton Sr. Papers, UA; E. D. Willett Diary, July 21, 1864, ADAH.

51. Circular, Headquarters, Featherston's Brigade, July 21, 1864, Featherston Order Book, Winfield Scott Featherston Collection, UM.

52. Grant to Sherman, July 21, 1864, 10 A.M., and Sherman to Halleck, July 21, 1864, 8:30 P.M., *OR*, 38(5):210–11.

53. Sherman to Halleck, July 21, 1864, 8:30 P.M.; Sherman to Thomas, July 21, 1864; and Special Field Orders No. 40, Headquarters, Military Division of the Mississippi, July 21, 1864, *OR*, 38(5):211–12, 222; Sherman to Halleck, September 15, 1864, *OR*, 38(1):71–72.

54. Hood to Seddon, July 22, 1864, 10:30 P.M., *OR*, 38(5):900; Walthall to Gale, January 14, 1865, *OR*, 38(3):926; Jim Huffman, comp., "Pre-& Civil War Letters of Lt. Col. Columbus Sykes 16th [*sic*] Regiment Mississippi Infantry," MDAH; Stewart to Mason, January 12, 1865, and French to Gale, December 6, 1864, *OR*, 38(3):872, 903; E. D. Willett Diary, July 21, 1864, ADAH.

55. Sherman to Halleck, September 15, 1864, *OR*, 38(1):72; Van Duzer to Eckert, July 22, 1864, 9 P.M., *OR*, 38(5):232; Stone, "Atlanta Campaign," 444; Sherman, *Memoirs*, 2, 75.

56. Howard to Whipple, July 22, 1864, 8 P.M., *OR*, 38(5):226–27; Howard to Whipple, September 18, 1864; Suman to [Lawton], September 10, 1864; Hurd to Lawton, September 13, 1864; Rose to [Lawton], September 14, 1864; Askew to McGrath, September 12, 1864; Johnson to McGrath, September 15, 1864; and "Journal of the Atlanta Campaign, kept at headquarters of the Fourth Army Corps, by Lieut. Col. Joseph S. Fullerton, Assistant Adjutant General," *OR*, 38(1):203, 276–77, 282, 289, 410, 421, 907; diary, July 22, 1864, James R. Carnahan Papers, IHS; Jacob Andervount Diary, July 22, 1864, AHC; Hazen, *Narrative*, 273; *History of the Seventy-Ninth*, 160.

57. Parsons to brother, July 22, 1864, George W. Parsons Papers, IHS; Kimball to assistant adjutant general, Second Division, Fourth Corps, August 4, 1864; Bryan

to Opdycke, September, no date, 1864; and Moore to Waterman, September 12, 1864, *OR*, 38(1):307, 321, 372; James Biddle Diary, July 22, 1864, DPL; *History of the Seventy-Third*, 326; Newton to Whipple, July 22, 1864, and Fullerton to Stanley, July 22, 1864, 12:30 P.M., *OR*, 38(5):225.

58. "Journal of the Atlanta Campaign, kept at headquarters of the Fourth Army Corps, by Lieut. Col. Joseph S. Fullerton, Assistant Adjutant General," *OR*, 38(1):908–9; Howard to Whipple, July 22, 1864, 8 P.M., *OR*, 38(5):227.

59. Reminiscences, July 22, 1864, Thomas Doak Edington Papers, UTK; diary, July 22, 1864, John Watkins Papers, UTK; Nash to Erastus Winters, January 3, 1911, George W. Nash Letter, FHS.

60. McPherson to Logan, July 22, 1864, 6 A.M., *OR*, 38(5):231.

61. Hooker to Whipple, July 22, 1864, 5 A.M., and Circular, Headquarters, Twentieth Corps, July 22, 1864, *OR*, 38(5):227, 233; Harrison to [Speed], September 14, 1864; Dustin to Grubbs, September 15, 1864; Dutton to Mitchell, August 5, 1864; and Miller to Crawford, July 27, 1864, *OR*, 38(2):348, 362, 364, 406.

62. Diary, July 22, 1864, Andrew Jackson Johnson Papers, IHS; Charles A. Booth Journal, July 22, 1864, WHS; Harris to Carman, September 7, 1864; Salomon to Boughton, September 15, 1864; and Geary to Perkins, September 15, 1864, *OR*, 38(2):73, 100, 141–42; diary, July 22, 1864, Marcellus Warner Darling Papers, UI; E. P. Failing Diary, July 23, 1864, Failing-Knight Papers, MHS; Bauer, *Soldiering*, 153; Irving Bronson, "Recollections of the Civil War," 52, TC; Alanson B. Cone Personal Narrative, July 22, 1864, NYSL; Hinkley, *Narrative of Service*, 130–31; diary, July 22, 1864, Albert M. Cook Papers, SU.

63. William Clark McLean Diary, July 22, 1864, McLean Family Papers, NYSL; E. Brown, *Twenty-Seventh Indiana*, 515–16.

64. Williams to Perkins, September 12, 1864, *OR*, 38(2):35; diary, July 23, 1864, Albert M. Cook Papers, SU.

65. Trowbridge to wife and baby, July 22, 24, 25, 1864, George Martin Trowbridge Papers, WLC-UM.

66. Palmer to Whipple, July 22, 1864, 4:30 A.M., *OR*, 38(5):227; Johnson to McClurg, August, no date, 1864; Minshall to Ford, September, no date, 1864; Moore to Smith, September 8, 1864; and Hunter to Curtis, August 17, 1864, *OR*, 38(1):524, 551, 603, 769; Calkins, *One Hundred and Fourth Regiment of Illinois*, 227, 359; Douglas Hapeman Diaries, July 22, 1864, ALPL; diary, July 22, 1864, James M. Randall Diary and Letters, www.ehistory.com.

67. McIntire to Ford, September 5, 1864; Briant to not stated, no date; Davis to McClurg, September, no date, 1864; Baird to McClurg, September 7, 1864; Wilson to Spofford, August 20, 1864; and Barnett to [Houghtaling], *OR*, 38(1):540, 543, 635, 743, 820, 830; diary, July 22, 1864, Charles Richard Pomeroy Papers, DU; Patrick and Willey, *Fighting for Liberty and Right*, 232.

68. William Cline Diary, July 22, 26, 1864, UND; Henry Perrin Mann Civil War Diaries, July 22, 1864, SHSM-RCR.

69. Sherman to Thomas, July 22, 1864, 11 A.M., *OR*, 38(5):223; Sherman to Halleck, September 15, 1864, and Poe to not stated, October 8, 1865, *OR*, 38(1):72, 131–32.

70. Sherman to Thomas, July 22, 1864, 11 A.M., and Thomas to Sherman, July 22, 1864, 5 P.M., *OR*, 38(5):223–24; Thomas to Sawyer, August 17, 1864, *OR*, 38(1):157; Stone, "Atlanta Campaign," 445; Van Duzer to Meigs, July 20, 1865, *OR*, 52(1):694.

71. Angle, *Three Years*, 238–39.

Conclusion

1. Kerwood, *Annals of the Fifty-Seventh*, 267; Hughes, *Civil War Memoir*, 213; Tower, *A Carolinian Goes to War*, 224.

2. Ike to Ed. P., August 16, 1864, Unidentified Civil War Union Soldier Letter, GHS; Bauer, *Soldiering*, 152; Joseph B. Cumming Recollections, 60, UNC; entry of July 20, 1864, Harry Stanley Diary, AHC; "Memoranda of an interview with Gen Hooker at Garden City Long island Oct 1 1875," box 4, folder 9, Ezra J. Carman Papers, NYPL.

3. E. Brown, *Twenty-Seventh Indiana*, 525–26; Elmore to parents, July 26, 1864, Day Elmore Letters, CHM.

4. Stewart to Mason, January 12, 1865, *OR*, 38(3):871; Johnston, "Opposing Sherman's Advance to Atlanta," 277; Stone, "Atlanta Campaign," 442–43, 485–86; Cox, *Atlanta*, 162.

5. Connelly, *Autumn of Glory*, 443–44; Castel, *Decision in the West*, 382–83; McMurry, *Atlanta 1864*, 151; McMurry, *John Bell Hood*, 124, 130; Daniel, *Cannoneers in Gray*, 160.

6. Castel, *Decision in the West*, 382. R. Jenkins, *Battle of Peach Tree Creek*, 35, believes that Hood "might well have pulled off another Chancellorsville-like surprise and routed Thomas's Army of the Cumberland" if he had attacked on July 19 instead of July 20. He cites Reynolds's attack on Dilworth's crossing of Peach Tree Creek on the former day as an indication of aggressive defense. I see no reason to believe that contention. Thomas's men conducted themselves with due caution and were alert for trouble on both days. Moreover, Dilworth defeated Reynolds and established a bridgehead on the south side of the creek, rendering this vicious little battle anything but an argument in favor of major Confederate attacks on July 19. At best, the Reynolds-Dilworth battle shows that a more aggressive defense by the Confederates could have resulted in a slower, more cautious approach by Thomas.

7. Symonds, *Joseph E. Johnston*, 163–66. Stewart recalled that Johnston's instructions to him were to prepare a good defensive position south of Peach Tree Creek and expect the Federals to approach Atlanta from the north. He did not tell Stewart whether he intended to attack as they crossed the stream but "his dispositions were evidently made with a view to so attack, and were inconsistent with any other purpose." Robinson, "General Joseph E. Johnston," 361.

8. Daniel, *Days of Glory*, 430; E. Brown, *Twenty-Seventh Indiana*, 524.

9. Pierson, "From Chattanooga to Atlanta," 352; Kaufman, *Peachtree Creek*, 144–45.

10. E. Brown, *Twenty-Seventh Indiana*, 521.

11. *Battles of Atlanta*, not paginated.

12. George H. Blakeslee letter; A. B. Foster letter; D. W. Russell letter; "J. L. Lemonds," *Confederate Veteran*, 11, 468; Samuel Turner letter, *Confederate Veteran*, 22,

479; "Restore Our Battle-Stained Banners," *Confederate Veteran*, 6, 148; Howell, *To Live and Die*, 329.

13. *Confederate Veteran*, 8, 257; *Atlanta Constitution*, July 19, 20, 21, 1900; Garrett, *Atlanta*, 2:392–93.

14. *Confederate Veteran*, 8, 257; *Confederate Veteran*, 18, 273; Brant, *History of the Eighty-Fifth Indiana*, 69.

15. Garrett, *Atlanta*, 2:483, 565, 848; "One Thousand Dollars," 138; "Plans to Mark Battlefield," 273; Kaufman, *Peachtree Creek*, 6, 103, 111, 117.

16. R. Jenkins, *Battle of Peach Tree Creek*, 422; Kaufman, *Peachtree Creek*, 123, 137.

17. Allen to Walter Hill, June 24, 1938; copy of Meredith Collier to Board of Commissioners of Roads and Revenues, Fulton County, no date but attached to letter of December 21, 1938; and Allen to Troy Chastain, February 16, 1939, Ivan Allen Sr. Papers, AHC.

18. Allen to Walter Hill, June 24, 1938; Thomas Collier to Frank Fling, May 30, 1939; and Allen to Troy Chastain, February 16, June 1, 1939, Ivan Allen Sr. Papers, AHC.

19. Garrett, *Atlanta*, 1:614. Capt. Adolph Metzner of the 32nd Indiana was a gifted amateur artist who painted many scenes of army life and battle at Stones River and other engagements. He began a painting of the fight at Peach Tree Creek as well, even though not a participant in the engagement—the regiment belonged to Wood's division of the Fourth Corps. The painting remained unfinished. See Peake, *Blood Shed*, 111. For a good tour guide to the modern site of the battle of Peach Tree Creek, see McCarley, "'Atlanta is Ours.'"

Bibliography

Archives
Abraham Lincoln Presidential Library, Springfield, Illinois
    William Lewis English Diary
    Douglas Hapeman Diaries
    George O. Pratt Diary
    Daniel W. Sheahan Diary
    Benjamin T. Smith Reminiscences
Alabama Department of Archives and History, Montgomery
    Newton N. Davis Papers
    Hardee Family Papers
    E. D. Willett Diary
American Antiquarian Society, Worcester, Massachusetts
    Philo Beecher Buckingham Papers
Atlanta History Center, Atlanta, Georgia
    Ivan Allen Sr. Papers
    Jacob Andervount Diary, Antebellum and Civil War Collection
    Hugh Black Letters
    Colin Dunlop Civil War Letters
    D. G. Godwin Correspondence
    Ladies Memorial Association Collection
    John J. Mercer Diary, Antebellum and Civil War Collection
    Harry Stanley Diary
    George Young Papers
Auburn University, Special Collections and Archives, Auburn, Alabama
    Irenus Watson Landingham Collection
Chicago History Museum, Chicago
    Day Elmore Letters
    Curtis J. Judd Papers
    Alfred H. Trego Diary
The Citadel, Archives and Museum, Charleston, South Carolina
    Irving Bronson. "Recollections of the Civil War." Bruce Catton Collection
    Ellison Capers Papers
College of William and Mary, Special Collections, Williamsburg, Virginia
    Joseph E. Johnston Papers
Connecticut Historical Society, New Haven
    Watson C. Hitchcock Papers
Cornell University, Rare and Manuscript Collections, Ithaca, New York
    William Harrison Githins Letters, Gail and Stephen Rudin Collection
        of Civil War Letters
Detroit Public Library, Burton Historical Collection, Detroit, Michigan
    James Biddle Diary
    Lewis A. Labadie Papers

Duke University, Rubenstein Rare Book and Manuscript Library, Durham,
    North Carolina
    George Williamson Balloch Papers
    Ellison Capers Papers
    Sidney S. Champion Papers
    Charles Richard Pomeroy Papers
    Charles Todd Quintard Papers
    W. H. T. Walker Papers
Emory University, Manuscript, Archives, and Rare Books Library,
    Atlanta, Georgia
    W. B. Corbitt Diary, Confederate Miscellany Collection, Series 1
    Mumford H. Dixon Diary
    Alexander Dobbin Diary
    Andrew Jackson Neal Papers
    Elias J. Prichard Letters, Confederate Miscellany Collection, Series 1
    Albert L. Slack Letters
Filson Historical Society, Louisville, Kentucky
    Chesley D. Bailey Diary
    George W. Gallup Papers
    George W. Nash Letter
    John H. Tilford Diaries
Georgia Archives, Morrow
    Mitchell-Fondren Papers
Georgia Historical Society, Savannah
    Willis Perry Burt Diary, Laura Burt Brantley Collection
    Unidentified Civil War Union Soldier Letter
Gilder Lehrman Institute of American History, New-York Historical Society,
    New York
    Joseph Jones Letter
    Henry Vanaernam Letters
    Lysander Wheeler Letter
Historical Society of Pennsylvania, Philadelphia
    John D. Foering Diary/Papers
Indiana Historical Society, Indianapolis
    James R. Carnahan Papers
    Daniel F. Griffin Letter, Benjamin Franklin Scribner Papers
    Benjamin Harrison Collection
    Andrew Jackson Johnson Papers
    George W. Parsons Papers
Indiana State Library, Indianapolis
    Daniel F. Griffin Papers
    William D. Hynes Papers
    Samuel Merrill Papers
Library of Congress, Manuscript Division, Washington, D.C.
    John Emerson Anderson Memoir

James A. Congleton Diary
Orlando Metcalfe Poe Papers
Louis Trezevant Wigfall Family Papers
Lincoln Memorial University, Abraham Lincoln Library and Museum,
     Harrogate, Tennessee
William Merrell. "Personal Memoirs of the Civil War"
Louisiana State University, Louisiana and Lower Mississippi Valley Collections,
     Baton Rouge
Edwin Hutchinson Papers
Unsigned Account of Battle of Peachtree Creek, Thomas R.
     Markham Papers
Massachusetts Historical Society, Boston
E. P. Failing Diary, Failing-Knight Papers
Mississippi Department of Archives and History, Jackson
Matthew Andrew Dunn Letters
Jim Huffman, comp., "Pre-&Civil War Letters of Lt. Col. Columbus
     Sykes 16th [*sic*] Regiment, Mississippi Infantry"
James Palmer Civil War Diary
Mississippi State University, Special Collections, Starkville
Emmett Ross Papers
William E. Sykes Papers
National Archives and Records Administration, Washington, D.C.
Court-Martial Case Files, Dewitt C. Foos, 82nd Ohio, File No. ll2737, RG 153,
     Records of the Office of the Judge Advocate General, Army, 1809–94
William J. Hale Service Record, 2nd Tennessee, M268, Compiled Service
     Records of Confederate Soldiers Who Served in Organizations from the
     State of Tennessee
John B. Hood Papers, RG109, War Department Collection of
     Confederate Records
Samuel W. Jones Service Record, 37th Mississippi, M269, Compiled Service
     Records of Confederate Soldiers Who Served in Organizations from the
     State of Mississippi
Navarro College, Pearce Civil War Collection, Corsicana, Texas
William F. Morgan Papers
Newberry Library, Chicago
Daniel E. Barnard Letters, Howe-Barnard Family Papers
Richard Realf Letters and Poems
Max Schlund Papers
New-York Historical Society, New York
John Law Marshall Correspondence
New York Public Library, Rare Books and Manuscripts, New York
Ezra A. Carman Papers
New York State Library, Albany
Alanson B. Cone Personal Narrative
William Clark McLean Diary and Letters, McLean Family Papers

Ohio Historical Society, Archives/Library, Columbus
    John W. Houtz Diaries
    John Wesley Marshall Papers
Rutherford B. Hayes Presidential Center, Fremont, Ohio
    Silas Sweeney Mallory Papers
South Carolina Historical Society, Charleston
    Samuel Wragg Ferguson Memoirs
State Archives of Florida, Tallahassee
    William McLeod Civil War Pocket Diary
State Historical Society of Missouri, Research Center Columbia
    William H. Lynch Diaries
State Historical Society of Missouri, Research Center Rolla
    Henry Perrin Mann Civil War Diaries
Syracuse University, Special Collections Research Center, Syracuse, New York
    Albert M. Cook Papers
Tennessee State Library and Archives, Nashville
    Carroll Henderson Clark Memoirs, Civil War Collection
U.S. Army Military History Institute, Carlisle, Pennsylvania
    Luther P. Bradley Collection
    Joshua W. Mewborn Papers
    William T. Shimp Papers, Civil War Miscellaneous Collection
    Henry Welch Papers
University of Alabama, W. S. Hoole Special Collections Library, Tuscaloosa
    Henry De Lamar Clayton Sr. Papers
University of California, Bancroft Library, Berkeley
    Frederick Christian Hess Letters
University of Georgia, Hargrett Rare Book and Manuscript Library, Athens
    Branch Family Papers
    William J. Dickey Papers
    Miletus Tuttle Letters
University of Houston, Special Collections, Texas
    William W. Edgerton Civil War Letters
University of Iowa, Special Collections, Iowa City
    Marcellus Warner Darling Papers
University of Michigan, Bentley Historical Library, Ann Arbor
    Judson L. Austin Papers
University of Michigan, William L. Clements Library, Ann Arbor
    John R. Comfort Papers, James S. Schoff Civil War Collections
    Lyman Gardner Papers, James S. Schoff Civil War Collections
    George Martin Trowbridge Papers, James S. Schoff Civil War Collections
University of Mississippi, Archives and Special Collections, Oxford
    Winfield Scott Featherston Collection
    Jesse L. Henderson Civil War Diary
University of North Carolina, Southern Historical Collection, Chapel Hill
    Taylor Beatty Diary

James Conquest Cross Black Papers
Joseph B. Cumming Recollections
Daniel Chevilette Govan Papers
George Anderson Mercer Diary
Benedict Joseph Semmes Papers
University of Notre Dame, Rare Books and Special Collections,
    South Bend, Indiana
    William Cline Diary
    Henry H. Maley Letters
University of South Carolina, South Caroliniana Library
    Charles Manning Furman Papers
University of Southern Mississippi, Archives, Hattiesburg
    Dr. P. F. Whitehead Letters
University of Tennessee, Special Collections, Chattanooga
    Frederick N. Kollock Diary, Charles S. Harris Collection
University of Tennessee, Special Collections, Knoxville
    Tilghman Blazer Collection
    James B. David Diary
    Thomas Doak Edington Papers
    George L. Reis Letters
    Edwin Hansford Rennolds Sr. Papers
    T. J. Walker, "Reminiscences of the Civil War"
    John Watkins Papers
University of Tennessee, Special Collections, Martin
    Martin Van Buren Oldham Journal
Virginia Historical Society, Richmond
    James Madison Brannock Papers
Wisconsin Historical Society, Madison
    Dwight S. Allen Papers
    Charles A. Booth Journal
    William H. Carrier Letters
    George A. Cooley Civil War Diary
    Charles Webster Knapp Letters
    John H. Roberts Civil War Letters
    James F. Sawyer Letters
    Frederick C. Winkler Papers

Newspapers

Atlanta Constitution
Augusta Daily Constitutionalist
Charleston Mercury
Cincinnati Commercial
Cleveland Daily Plain Dealer
Indianapolis Daily Journal
Macon Confederate

Memphis Daily Appeal
New York Daily Tribune
St. Louis Daily Missouri Democrat
St. Louis Union
Savannah Republican
Washington Daily National
    Intelligencer

Websites

George Hoenig Journal, www.russscott.com

James M. Randall Diary and Letters, www.ehistory.com

Articles and Books

Adamson, A. P. *Brief History of the Thirtieth Georgia Regiment.* Griffin, Ga.: Mills Printing, 1912.

Adolphson, Steven J. "An Incident of Valor in the Battle of Peach Tree Creek, 1864." *Georgia Historical Quarterly* 57 (1973): 406–20.

Algoe, John. "Capturing a Mill: A Gallant Exploit on Peach Tree Creek." *National Tribune*, October 28, 1886.

Allendorf, Donald. *Long Road to Liberty: The Odyssey of a German Regiment in the Yankee Army — The 15th Missouri Volunteer Infantry.* Kent, Ohio: Kent State University Press, 2006.

Anderson, William M. *They Died to Make Men Free: A History of the 19th Michigan Infantry in the Civil War.* Berrien Springs, Mich.: Hardscrabble Books, 1980.

Angle, Paul M., ed. *Three Years in the Army of the Cumberland: The Letters and Diary of Major James A. Connolly.* Bloomington: Indiana University Press, 1959.

Aten, Henry J. *History of the Eighty-Fifth Regiment, Illinois Volunteer Infantry.* Hiawatha, Kans.: n.p., 1901.

Atlanta: Voices of the Civil War. Alexandria, Va.: Time-Life, n.d.

Banning, Leroy F. *Regimental History of the 35th Alabama Infantry, 1862–1865.* Bowie, Md.: Heritage Books, 1999.

Barnes, James A., James R. Carnahan, and Thomas H. B. McCain. *The Eighty-Sixth Regiment, Indiana Volunteer Infantry.* Crawfordsville, Ind.: Journal, 1895.

Bartlett, Edward O. *The "Dutchess County Regiment" (150th Regiment of the New York State Volunteer Infantry) in the Civil War.* Danbury, Conn.: Danbury Medical Printing, 1907.

Battles of Atlanta. Atlanta: n.p., 1895.

Bauer, K. Jack, ed. *Soldiering: The Civil War Diary of Rice C. Bull, 123rd New York Volunteer Infantry.* San Rafael, Calif.: Presidio Press, 1977.

Baumgartner, Richard A., and Larry M. Strayer, eds. *Yankee Tigers: Through the Civil War with the 125th Ohio.* Huntington, W.Va.: Blue Acorn Press, 1992.

Bearss, Edwin C. "The Siege of Jackson, July 10–17, 1863." In *The Battle of Jackson, May 14, 1863 — The Siege of Jackson, July 10–17, 1863 — Three Other Post-Vicksburg Actions*, by Edwin C. Bearss and Warren Grabau, 55–143. Baltimore: Gateway Press, 1981.

Beasecker, Robert, ed. *"I Hope to Do My Country Service": The Civil War Letters of John Bennitt, M.D., Surgeon, 19th Michigan Infantry.* Detroit: Wayne State University Press, 2005.

Beaudot, William J. K. *The 24th Wisconsin Infantry in the Civil War: The Biography of a Regiment.* Mechanicsburg, Pa.: Stackpole Books, 2003.

Bennett, L. G., and William M. Haigh. *History of the Thirty-Sixth Regiment Illinois Volunteers, during the War of the Rebellion*. Aurora, Ill.: Knickerbocker and Hodder, 1876.

Bevier, R. S. *History of the First and Second Missouri Confederate Brigades, 1861–1865, and from Wakarusa to Appomattox, a Military Anagraph*. St. Louis: Bryan, Brand, 1879.

Beyer, W. F., and O. F. Keydel, eds. *Deeds of Valor: How America's Heroes Won the Medal of Honor*. Detroit: Perrien-Keydel, 1905.

Blackburn, Theodore W. *Letters from the Front: A Union "Preacher" Regiment (74th Ohio) in the Civil War*. Dayton, Ohio: Morningside Bookshop, 1981.

Blair, William Alan, ed. *A Politician Goes to War: The Civil War Letters of John White Geary*. University Park: Pennsylvania State University Press, 1995.

Blakeslee, George H. Letter. *Confederate Veteran* 7 (1899): 165.

Bohrnstedt, Jennifer Cain, ed. *Soldiering with Sherman: Civil War Letters of George F. Cram*. DeKalb: Northern Illinois University Press, 2000.

Bowser, O. P. "Notes on Granbury's Brigade." In *A Comprehensive History of Texas, 1685 to 1897*, vol. 1, edited by Dudley G. Wooten, 741–54. Dallas: William G. Scarff, 1898.

Boyle, John Richards. *Soldiers True: The Story of the One Hundred and Eleventh Regiment Pennsylvania Veteran Volunteers, and of Its Campaigns in the War for the Union, 1861–1865*. New York: Eaton and Mains, 1903.

Bradley, G. S. *The Star Corps: or, Notes of an Army Chaplain, during Sherman's Famous "March to the Sea."* Milwaukee: Jermain and Brightman, 1865.

Brant, Jefferson E. *History of the Eighty-Fifth Indiana Volunteer Infantry*. Bloomington, Ind.: Cravens, 1902.

Bright, John M. "The States in the Confederate War." *Confederate Veteran* 17 (1909): 393–99.

Brown, Edmund Randolph. *The Twenty-Seventh Indiana Volunteer Infantry in the War of the Rebellion, 1861 to 1865*. [Monticello, Ind.: n.p., 1899.]

Brown, Russell K. *To the Manner Born: The Life of General William H. T. Walker*. Athens: University of Georgia Press, 1994.

Brown, Thaddeus C. S., Samuel J. Murphy, and William G. Putney. *Behind the Guns: The History of Battery I, 2nd Regiment, Illinois Light Artillery*. Carbondale: Southern Illinois University Press, 1965.

Bryant, Edwin E. *History of the Third Regiment of Wisconsin Veteran Volunteer Infantry, 1861–1865*. Madison, Wis.: Democrat Printing, 1891.

Byrne, Frank L., ed. *Uncommon Soldiers: Harvey Reid and the 22nd Wisconsin March with Sherman*. Knoxville: University of Tennessee Press, 2001.

Buck, Irving A. *Cleburne and His Command*. Jackson, Tenn.: McCowat-Mercer Press, 1959.

Calkins, William Wirt. *The History of the One Hundred and Fourth Regiment of Illinois Volunteer Infantry, War of the Great Rebellion, 1862–1865*. Chicago: Donohue and Henneberry, 1895.

Cannon, J. P. *Inside of Rebeldom: The Daily Life of a Private in the Confederate Army*. Washington, D.C.: National Tribune, 1900.

Castel, Albert. *Decision in the West: The Atlanta Campaign of 1864*. Lawrence: University Press of Kansas, 1992.

Cate, Jean M. Ed. *If I Live to Come Home: The Civil War Letters of Sergeant John March Cate*. Pittsburgh: Dorrance Publishing, 1995.

Cate, Wirt Armistead, ed. *Two Soldiers: The Campaign Diaries of Thomas J. Key, C.S.A., and Robert J. Campbell, U.S.A.* Chapel Hill: University of North Carolina Press, 1938.

Clark, Walter A. *Under the Stars and Bars: or, Memories of Four Years Service with the Oglethorpes, of Augusta, Georgia*. Augusta, Ga.: Chronicle, 1900.

Clarke, Henry E. "The Fight for the Battery at Peach Tree Creek." *National Tribune*. May 31, 1883.

Cleaves, Freeman. *Rock of Chickamauga: The Life of General George H. Thomas*. Norman: University of Oklahoma Press, 1948.

Clemmer, Gregg S. *Valor in Gray: The Recipients of the Confederate Medal of Honor*. Staunton, Va.: Hearthside, 1996.

Coe, David, ed. *Mine Eyes Have Seen the Glory: Combat Diaries of Union Sergeant Hamlin Alexander Coe*. Rutherford, N.J.: Fairleigh Dickinson University Press, [1975].

Collins, George K. *Memoirs of the 149th Regt. N.Y. Vol. Inft., 3rd Brig., 2d Div., 12th and 20th A.C.* Syracuse, N.Y.: Author, 1891.

Collins, R. M. *Chapters from the Unwritten History of the War Between the States*. St. Louis: Nixon-Jones, 1893.

Comey, Lyman Richard E. *A Legacy of Valor: The Memoirs and Letters of Captain Henry Newton Comey, 2nd Massachusetts Infantry*. Knoxville: University of Tennessee Press, 2004.

Conger, E. H. "The Private." In *War Sketches and Incidents as Related by the Companions of the Iowa Commandery, Military Order of the Loyal Legion of the United States*, 2: 57–64. Wilmington, N.C.: Broadfoot Publishing, 1994.

Connelly, Thomas Lawrence. *Autumn of Glory: The Army of Tennessee, 1862–1865*. Baton Rouge: Louisiana State University Press, 1971.

Cox, Jacob D. *Atlanta*. New York: Charles Scribner's Sons, 1882.

Cozzens, Peter. *This Terrible Sound: The Battle of Chickamauga*. Urbana: University of Illinois Press, 1992.

Crist, Lynda Lasswell, ed. *The Papers of Jefferson Davis*. 17 vols. Baton Rouge: Louisiana State University Press, 1971–2008.

Cross, Frederick C., ed. *Nobly They Served the Union*. [Walnut Creek, Calif.]: Frederick C. Cross, 1976.

Crumpton, Washington Bryan. *A Book of Memories, 1842–1920*. Montgomery, Ala.: Baptist Mission Board, 1921.

———. "In the Atlanta Campaign." *Confederate Veteran* 29 (1921): 381–83.

Cuttino, George Peddy, ed. *Saddle Bag and Spinning Wheel: Being the Civil War Letters of George W. Peddy, M.D. Surgeon, 56th Georgia Volunteer Regiment, C.S.A.* Macon, Ga.: Macon University Press, [1981].

Dacus, Robert H. *Reminiscences of Company "H," First Arkansas Mounted Rifles*. Dardanelle, Ark.: Post-Dispatch Printing, [1897].

Daniel, Larry J. *Cannoneers in Gray: The Field Artillery of the Army of Tennessee, 1861–1865*. Tuscaloosa: University of Alabama Press, 1984.

———. *Days of Glory: The Army of the Cumberland, 1861–1865*. Baton Rouge: Louisiana State University Press, 2004.

Davis, Robert Scott, ed. *Requiem for a Lost City: A Memoir of Civil War Atlanta and the Old South*. Macon, Ga.: Mercer University Press, 1999.

Davis, Stephen. *Atlanta Will Fall: Sherman, Joe Johnston, and the Yankee Heavy Battalions*. Wilmington, Del.: Scholarly Resources, 2001.

Day, L. W. *Story of the One Hundred and First Ohio Infantry*. Cleveland: W. M. Bayne, 1894.

"De Lafayette Musselman." In *Memorials of Deceased Companions of the Commandery of the State of Illinois, Military Order of the Loyal Legion of the United States, from July 1, 1901, to December 31, 1911*, 594–97. Wilmington, N.C.: Broadfoot Publishing, 1993.

DeRosier, Arthur H. Jr., ed. *Through the South with a Union Soldier*. Johnson City: East Tennessee State University Research Advisory Council, 1969.

Dodson, W. C., ed. *Campaigns of Wheeler and His Cavalry, 1862–1865*. Atlanta, Ga.: Hudgins, 1899.

Dunkelman, Mark H. *Patrick Henry Jones: Irish American, Civil War General, and Gilded Age Politician*. Baton Rouge: Louisiana State University Press, 2015.

———. "'The Worst Sight I Ever Saw': The 154th New York Infantry at the Battle of Peachtree Creek." *North & South* 9, no. 2 (May 2006): 64–79.

Dunkelman, Mark H., and Michael J. Winey. *The Hardtack Regiment: An Illustrated History of the 154th Regiment, New York State Infantry Volunteers*. Rutherford, N.J.: Fairleigh Dickinson University Press, 1981.

Durham, Roger S., ed. *The Blues in Gray: The Civil War Journal of William Daniel Dixon and the Republican Blues Daybook*. Knoxville: University of Tennessee Press, 2000.

Elliott, Sam Davis. *Soldier of Tennessee: General Alexander P. Stewart and the Civil War in the West*. Baton Rouge: Louisiana State University Press, 1999.

Ewing, W. W. "Wounding a Young Lady." *National Tribune*, July 28, 1910.

Fenton, E. B. "From the Rapidan to Atlanta." In *War Papers: Being Papers Read before the Commandery of the State of Michigan, Military Order of the Loyal Legion of the United States*, 1:483–504. Wilmington, N.C.: Broadfoot Publishing, 1993.

Fleharty, S. F. *Our Regiment: A History of the 102d Illinois Infantry Volunteers*. Chicago: Brewster and Hanscom, 1865.

Fleming, James R. *The Confederate Ninth Tennessee Infantry*. Gretna, La.: Pelican Publishing, 2006.

Foster, A. B. Letter. *Confederate Veteran* 6 (1898): 585.

Fowler, John D. *Mountaineers in Gray: The Nineteenth Tennessee Volunteer Infantry Regiment, C.S.A.* Knoxville: University of Tennessee Press, 2004.

Franklin, Ann York, comp. *The Civil War Diaries of Capt. Alfred Tyler Fielder, 12th Tennessee Regiment Infantry, Company B, 1861–1865*. Louisville, Ky.: Ann York Franklin, 1996.

Frano, Elizabeth Coldwell, ed. *Letters of Captain Hugh Black to His Family in Florida during the War Between the States, 1861–1864.* Evansville, Ind.: Evansville Bindery, 1998.

French, Samuel G. *Two Wars: An Autobiography.* Nashville, Tenn.: Confederate Veteran, 1901.

Garrett, Franklin M. *Atlanta and Environs: A Chronicle of Its People and Events.* 2 vols. New York: Lewis Historical Publishing, 1954.

Gates, Arnold, ed. *The Rough Side of War: The Civil War Journal of Chesley A. Mosman.* Garden City, N.Y.: Basin Publishing, 1987.

Goodloe, Albert Theodore. *Confederate Echoes: A Voice from the South in the Days of Secession and of the Southern Confederacy.* Nashville, Tenn.: Smith and Lamar, 1907.

———. *Some Rebel Relics from the Seat of War.* Nashville: Methodist Episcopal Church, South, 1893.

Gottschalk, Phil. *In Deadly Earnest: The History of the First Missouri Brigade, CSA.* Columbia, Mo.: Missouri River Press, 1991.

Gould, David, and James B. Kennedy, eds. *Memoirs of a Dutch Mudsill: The "War Memories" of John Henry Otto, Captain, Company D, 21st Regiment Wisconsin Volunteer Infantry.* Kent, Ohio: Kent State University Press, 2004.

Goundrey, Thomas D. "The Twentieth Corps: Some Further Criticisms concerning Its Disputed Actions and Achievements." *National Tribune,* June 21, 1883.

Grimsley, Mark. *And Keep Moving On: The Virginia Campaign, May–June, 1864.* Lincoln: University of Nebraska Press, 2002.

Grunert, William *History of the One Hundred and Twenty-Ninth Regiment Illinois Volunteer Infantry.* Winchester, Ill.: R. B. Dedman, 1866.

Harmon, T. R. "Battle of Peach Tree Creek." *National Tribune,* September 20, 1906.

Harrison, James. "Peach Tree Creek." *National Tribune,* May 10, 1888.

Hawes, Lilla Mills, ed. "The Memoirs of Charles H. Olmstead." Pt. 10. *Georgia Historical Quarterly* 45, no. 1 (March 1961): 42–56.

Hay, Thomas Robson. "The Atlanta Campaign." *Georgia Historical Quarterly* 7, no. 1 (March 1923): 18–43.

———. "The Davis-Hood-Johnston Controversy of 1864." *Mississippi Valley Historical Review* 11, no. 1 (June, 1924): 54–84.

Hazen, W. B. *A Narrative of Military Service.* Boston: Ticknor, 1885.

Head, Thomas A. *Campaigns and Battles of the Sixteenth Regiment, Tennessee Volunteers, in the War Between the States.* Nashville: Cumberland Presbyterian Publishing, 1885.

Hebert, Walter H. *"Fighting Joe Hooker."* Lincoln: University of Nebraska Press, 1999.

Hess, Earl J. *Braxton Bragg: The Most Hated Man of the Confederacy.* Chapel Hill: University of North Carolina Press, 2016.

———. *Civil War Infantry Tactics: Training, Combat, and Small-Unit Effectiveness.* Baton Rouge: Louisiana State University Press, 2015.

————. *Ezra Church and the Struggle for Atlanta*. Chapel Hill: University of North Carolina Press, 2015.

————. *Kennesaw Mountain: Sherman, Johnston, and the Atlanta Campaign*. Chapel Hill: University of North Carolina Press, 2013.

————. *The Rifle Musket in Civil War Combat: Reality and Myth*. Lawrence: University Press of Kansas, 2008.

————. *Trench Warfare under Grant and Lee: Field Fortifications in the Overland Campaign*. Chapel Hill: University of North Carolina Press, 2007.

Hewitt, Lawrence Lee, Thomas E. Schott, and Marc Kunis, eds. *To Succeed or Perish: The Diaries of Sergeant Edmund Trent Eggleston, 1st Mississippi Light Artillery Regiment, CSA*. Knoxville: University of Tennessee Press, 2015.

Hight, John J. *History of the Fifty-Eighth Regiment of Indiana Volunteer Infantry*. Princeton: Press of the Clarion, 1895.

Hinkley, Julian Wisner. *A Narrative of Service with the Third Wisconsin Infantry*. [Madison, Wis.]: Democrat Printing Company, 1912.

Hinman, Wilbur F. *The Story of the Sherman Brigade*. Alliance, Ohio: Daily Review, 1897.

History of Battery A, First Regiment of Ohio Vol. Light Artillery. Milwaukee: Daily Wisconsin Steam Printing, 1865.

A History of the Seventy-Third Regiment of Illinois Infantry Volunteers. N.p.: Regimental Reunion Association, [1890].

History of the Seventy-Ninth Regiment Indiana Volunteer Infantry in the Civil War of Eighteen Sixty-One in the United States. Indianapolis, Ind.: Hollenbeck Press, 1899.

Holzhueter, John O., ed. "William Wallace's Civil War Letters: The Atlanta Campaign." *Wisconsin Magazine of History* 57, no. 2 (Winter 1973–74): 90–116.

Hood, J. B. *Advance and Retreat: Personal Experiences in the United States and Confederate States Armies*. Philadelphia: Burk and M'Fetridge, 1880.

Hood, John B. "The Defense of Atlanta." In *Battles and Leaders of the Civil War*. Vol. 4, edited by Richard Underwood Johnson and Clarence Clough Buel, 336–44. New York: Thomas Yoseloff, 1956

Hood, Stephen M., ed. *The Lost Papers of Confederate General John Bell Hood*. El Dorado Hills, Calif.: Savas Beatie, 2015.

Horrall, Spillard F. *History of the Forty-Second Indiana Volunteer Infantry*. [Chicago: Donohue and Henneberry, 1892.]

Howard, Oliver O. *Autobiography*. 2 vols. New York: Baker and Taylor, 1907.

————. "The Struggle for Atlanta." In *Battles and Leaders of the Civil War*, vol. 4, edited by Richard Underwood Johnson and Clarence Clough Buel, 293–325. New York: Thomas Yoseloff, 1956.

Howell, H. Grady, Jr., *To Live and Die in Dixie: A History of the Third Regiment Mississippi Volunteer Infantry, C.S.A.* Jackson, Miss.: Chickasaw Bayou Press, 1991.

Hughes, Nathaniel Cheairs, Jr., ed. *The Civil War Memoir of Philip Daingerfield Stephenson, D.D.* Conway: University of Central Arkansas Press, 1995.

————. *General William J. Hardee: Old Reliable*. Baton Rouge: Louisiana State University Press, 1965.

Hurst, Samuel H. *Journal-History of the Seventy-Third Ohio Volunteer Infantry*. Chillicothe, Ohio: n.p., 1866.

"J. L. Lemonds." *Confederate Veteran* 11 (1903): 468.

Jenkins, Kirk C. *The Battle Rages Higher: The Union's Fifteenth Kentucky Infantry*. Lexington: University of Kentucky Press, 2003.

Jenkins, Robert D., Sr. *The Battle of Peach Tree Creek: Hood's First Sortie, 20 July 1864*. Macon, Ga.: Mercer University Press, 2013.

Johnson, R. W. *A Soldier's Reminiscences in Peace and War*. Philadelphia: J. B. Lippincott, 1886.

Johnston, Joseph E. "Opposing Sherman's Advance to Atlanta." In *Battles and Leaders of the Civil War*, vol. 4, edited by Richard Underwood Johnson and Clarence Clough Buel, 260–77. New York: Thomas Yoseloff, 1956.

Jones, Eugene W., Jr. *Enlisted for the War: The Struggles of the Gallant 24th Regiment, South Carolina Volunteers, Infantry, 1861–1865*. Hightstown, N.J.: Longstreet House, 1997.

Jones, Mary Miles, and Leslie Jones Martin, eds. *The Gentle Rebel: The Civil War Letters of 1st Lt. William Harvey Berryhill Co. D, 43rd Regiment, Mississippi Volunteers*. Yazoo City, Miss.: Sassafras Press, 1982.

Jordan, Philip D., ed. "Forty Days with the Christian Commission: A Diary by William Salter." *Iowa Journal of History and Politics* 33, no. 2 (April 1935): 123–54.

Jordan, Weymouth T., ed. "Mathew Andrew Dunn Letters." *Journal of Mississippi History* 1, no. 2 (April 1939): 110–27.

Joslyn, Mauriel Phillips, ed. *Charlotte's Boys: Civil War Letters of the Branch Family of Savannah*. Berryville, Va.: Rockbridge Publishing, 1996.

Kaufman, David R. *Peachtree Creek: A Natural and Unnatural History of Atlanta's Watershed*. Athens: University of Georgia Press, 2007.

Kendall, John Smith, [ed.]. "Recollections of a Confederate Officer." *Louisiana Historical Quarterly* 29, no. 4 (October 1946): 1041–228.

Kerwood, Asbury L. *Annals of the Fifty-Seventh Regiment Indiana Volunteers*. Dayton, Ohio: W. J. Shuey, 1868.

Kinnear, J. R. *History of the Eighty-Sixth Regiment Illinois Volunteer Infantry*. Chicago: Tribune, 1866.

Kirwan, A. D., ed. *Johnny Green of the Orphan Brigade: The Journal of a Confederate Soldier*. Lexington: University Press of Kentucky, 2002.

Leeper, Wesley Thurman. *Rebels Valiant: Second Arkansas Mounted Rifles (Dismounted)*. Little Rock: Pioneer Press, 1964.

Little, George, and James R. Maxwell. *A History of Lumsden's Battery, C.S.A.* Tuscaloosa, Ala.: R. E. Rhodes Chapter, United Daughters of the Confederacy, n.d.

Long, Charles A. "A Good Word for the Twentieth Corps." *National Tribune*, April 26, 1883.

Longacre, Glenn V., and John E. Haas, eds. *To Battle for God and the Right: The*

Civil War Letterbooks of Emerson Opdycke. Urbana: University of Illinois
Press, 2003.

Losson, Christopher *Tennessee's Forgotten Warriors: Frank Cheatham and His
Confederate Division*. Knoxville: University of Tennessee Press, 1989.

Mannis, Jedediah, and Galen R. Wilson, eds. *Bound to Be a Soldier: The Letters
of Private James T. Miller, 111th Pennsylvania Infantry, 1861–1864*. Knoxville:
University of Tennessee Press, 2001.

Marcoot, Maurice. *Five Years in the Sunny South: Reminiscences of Maurice
Marcoot, Late of Co. "B," 15th Reg. Missouri Veteran Volunteer Infantry from
1861 to 1866*. N.p.: n.p., n.d.

Marvin, Edwin E. *The Fifth Regiment Connecticut Volunteers*. Hartford, Conn.:
Wiley, Waterman & Eaton, 1889.

Mathis, Ray, d. *In the Land of the Living: Wartime Letters by Confederates from
the Chattahoochee Valley of Alabama and Georgia*. Troy, Ala.: Troy State
University Press, 1981.

McBride, John Randolph. *History of the Thirty-Third Indiana Veteran Volunteer
Infantry during the Four Years of Civil War, from September 16, 1861 to July 21,
1865*. Indianapolis, Ind.: William R. Burford, 1900.

McCaffrey, James M. *This Band of Heroes: Granbury's Texas Brigade, C.S.A.*
College Station: Texas A&M University Press, 1996.

McCarley, J. Britt. "'Atlanta Is Ours and Fairly Won': A Driving Tour of the Atlanta
Area's Principal Civil War Battlefields." *Atlanta Historical Journal* 28, no. 3
(Fall 1984): 7–98.

[McConnell, William.] *Diary of William McConnell, Private, Company I, 15th
O.V.V.I.* Tiro, Ohio: Charles McConnell, n.d.

McDowell, William P. "The Fifteenth Kentucky." *Southern Bivouac* 5 (1886):
251–53.

McGuire, Kate Flanagan, comp. *McGuire Papers: Containing Major Thomas
McGuire's Civil War Letters*. [Tusquahoma, La.]: K. F. McGuire, 1966.

McKinney, Francis F. *Education in Violence: The Life of George H. Thomas and the
History of the Army of the Cumberland*. Detroit: Wayne State University Press,
1961.

McMurray, W. J. *History of the Twentieth Tennessee Regiment Volunteer Infantry,
C.S.A.* Nashville, Tenn.: Publication Committee, 1904.

McMurry, Richard M. *Atlanta 1864*. Lincoln: University of Nebraska Press, 2000.

———. "The Atlanta Campaign of 1864: A New Look." *Civil War History* 22
(1976): 5–15.

———. "Confederate Morale in the Atlanta Campaign of 1864." *Georgia Historical
Quarterly* 54 (1970): 226–43.

———. *John Bell Hood and the War for Southern Independence*. Lexington:
University Press of Kentucky, 1982.

McNeil, William J. "A Survey of Confederate Soldier Morale during Sherman's
Campaign through Georgia and the Carolinas." *Georgia Historical Quarterly*
55 (1971): 1–25.

McWilliams, John. *Recollections of John McWilliams, His Youth, Experiences in*

California and the Civil War. [Princeton, N.J.: Princeton University Press, ca. 1921.]

Medical and Surgical History of the Civil War. 12 vols. Wilmington, N.C.: Broadfoot Publishing, 1991.

Merrill, Samuel. *The Seventieth Indiana Volunteer Infantry in the War of the Rebellion.* Indianapolis, Ind.: Bowen-Merrill, [1900].

Miller, Rex. *The Forgotten Regiment: A Day-by Day Account of the 55th Alabama Infantry Regiment, CSA (1861–1865).* Rev. ed. Depew, N.Y.: Patrex Press, 1989.

Morhous, Henry C. *Reminiscences of the 123d Regiment, N.Y.S.V.* Greenwich, N.Y.: People's Journal, 1879.

Morse, Charles F. *Letters Written during the Civil War, 1861–1865.* Boston: T. R. Marvin and Sons, 1898.

[Murphree, Joel.] "Autobiography and Civil War Letters of Joel Murphree of Troy, Alabama, 1864–1865." *Alabama Historical Quarterly* 19, no. 1 (Spring 1957): 170–208.

Newbury, Joseph B. "At Peach Tree Creek." *National Tribune,* July 28, 1910.

Newton, George A. "Battle of Peach Tree Creek." In *G.A.R. War Papers: Papers Read before Fred. D. Jones Post, No. 401, Department of Ohio, G.A.R.,* 1:148–63. Cincinnati, Ohio: Elm Street Printing, 1891.

Nisbet, James Cooper. *4 Years on the Firing Line.* Jackson, Tenn.: McCowat-Mercer, 1963.

Noyes, Edward, ed. "Excerpts from the Civil War Diary of E. T. Eggleston." *Tennessee Historical Quarterly* 17, no. 4 (December 1958): 336–58.

"One Thousand Dollars to Appropriately Mark Battle of Peachtree Creek." *Confederate Veteran* 18 (1910): 138.

Osborn, George C., ed. "Civil War Letters of Robert W. Banks: Atlanta Campaign." *Georgia Historical Quarterly* 27, no. 2 (June 1943): 208–16.

Osborn, Hartwell. "Sherman's Atlanta Campaign." *Western Reserve University Bulletin* 14, no. 6 (November 1911): 116–38.

———. *Trials and Triumphs: The Record of the Fifty-Fifth Ohio Volunteer Infantry.* Chicago: A. C. McClurg, 1904.

Osborne, Seward R., Jr. "George Young: Forgotten Hero of Peach Tree Creek." *North South Trader* (March-April, 1980): 28–32.

Padgett, James A., ed. "With Sherman through Georgia and the Carolinas: Letters of a Federal Soldier." Pt. 1. *Georgia Historical Society* 32 (1948): 284–322.

Palmer, George H. "A Gallant Record: What the 20th Conn. Did in the Atlanta Campaign." *National Tribune,* December 22, 1887.

Patrick, Jeffrey L., and Robert J. Willey, eds. *Fighting for Liberty and Right: The Civil War Diary of William Bluffton Miller, First Sergeant, Company K, Seventy-Fifth Indiana Volunteer Infantry.* Knoxville: University of Tennessee Press, 2005.

Peake, Michael A. *Blood Shed in This War: Civil War Illustrations by Captain Adolph Metzner, 32nd Indiana.* Indianapolis: Indiana Historical Society, 2010.

Phillips, Ulrich B., ed. *Correspondence of Robert Toombs, Alexander H. Stephens, and Howell Cobb: Annual Report of the American Historical Association for the Year 1911.* 2 vols. Washington, D.C.: Government Printing Office, 1913.

Pierson, Stephen. "From Chattanooga to Atlanta in 1864, a Personal Reminiscence." *Proceedings of the New Jersey Historical Society* 16 (1931): 324–56.

"Plans to Mark Battlefield of Atlanta." *Confederate Veteran* 18 (1910): 273.

Potter, John. *Reminiscences of the Civil War in the United States.* [Oskaloosa, Iowa: Globe Presses, 1897.]

Priest, John Michael, ed. *John T. McMahon's Diary of the 136th New York, 1861–1864.* Shippensburg, Pa.: White Mane, 1993.

Pula, James S. *The Sigel Regiment: A History of the Twenty-Sixth Wisconsin Volunteer Infantry, 1862–1865.* Campbell, Calif.: Savas Publishing, 1998.

Quaife, Milo M., ed. *From the Cannon's Mouth: The Civil War Letters of General Alpheus S. Williams.* Detroit: Wayne State University Press, 1959.

Quint, Alonzo H. *The Record of the Second Massachusetts Infantry, 1861–65.* Boston: James P. Walker, 1867.

Rafuse, Ethan S. "Always 'Fighting Joe'": Joseph Hooker and the Campaign in North Georgia, May–July 1864." In *Corps Commanders in Blue: Union Major Generals in the Civil War*, edited by Ethan S. Rafuse, 221–60. Baton Rouge: Louisiana State University Press, 2014.

Record of the Ninety-Fourth Regiment Ohio Volunteer Infantry, in the War of the Rebellion. Cincinnati: Ohio Valley Press, n.d.

Rennolds, Edwin H. *A History of the Henry County Commands Which Served in the Confederate States Army.* Kennesaw, Ga.: Continental Book Company, 1961.

"Restore Our Battle-Stained Banners." *Confederate Veteran* 6 (1898): 147–48.

Reyburn, Philip J., and Terry L. Wilson, eds. *"Jottings from Dixie": The Civil War Dispatches of Sergeant Major Stephen F. Fleharty, U.S.A.* Baton Rouge: Louisiana State University Press, 1999.

Rice, R. C. "With Sherman: Another Chapter of the Peach Tree Creek Battle." *National Tribune*, November 24, 1892.

Robinson, Leigh. "General Joseph E. Johnston." *Southern Historical Society Papers* 19 (1891): 337–70.

Rogers, Robert M. *The 125th Regiment Illinois Volunteer Infantry.* Champaign, Ill.: Gazette Steam Printing, 1882.

Rory, W. B. "Peach Tree Creek." *National Tribune*, May 3, 1883.

Rountree, Benjamin. "Letters from a Confederate Soldier." *Georgia Review* 18, no. 3 (Fall 1964): 267–97.

Roy, T. B. "General Hardee and the Military Operations around Atlanta." *Southern Historical Society Papers* 8 (1880): 337–87.

Russell, D. W. Letter. *Confederate Veteran* 17 (1909): 53.

Russell, E. E. "Where Hood Gathered No Acorns." *National Tribune*, May 17, 1883.

Scaife, William R. *The Campaign for Atlanta.* Atlanta, Ga.: William R. Scaife, 1993.

Scarborough, William Kauffman, ed. *The Diary of Edmund Ruffin.* 3 vols. Baton Rouge: Louisiana State University Press, 1972–89.

Sheppard, Jonathan C. *By the Noble Daring of Her Sons: The Florida Brigade of the Army of Tennessee.* Tuscaloosa: University of Alabama Press, 2012.

Sherman, William T. "The Grand Strategy of the Last Year of the War." In *Battles and Leaders of the Civil War*, vol. 4, edited by Richard Underwood Johnson and Clarence Clough Buel, 247–259. New York: Thomas Yoseloff, 1956.

————. *Memoirs.* 2 vols. New York: D. Appleton, 1875.

Sieburg, Evelyn Ratchford, ed. *Memoirs of a Confederate Staff Officer from Bethel to Bentonville.* Shippensburg, Pa.: White Mane Books, 1998.

Simmons, L. A. *The History of the 84th Reg't Ill. Vols.* Macomb, Ill.: Hampton Brothers, 1866.

Simpson, Brooks D., and Jean V. Berlin, eds. *Sherman's Civil War: Selected Correspondence of William T. Sherman, 1860–1865.* Chapel Hill: University of North Carolina Press, 1999.

Smith, Bobbie Swearingen, ed. *A Palmetto Boy: Civil War-Era Diaries and Letters of James Adams Tillman.* Columbia: University of South Carolina Press, 2010.

Smith, Gustavus W. "The Georgia Militia about Atlanta." In *Battles and Leaders of the Civil War*, vol. 4, edited by Richard Underwood Johnson and Clarence Clough Buel, 331–35. New York: Thomas Yoseloff, 1956.

Spurlin, Charles D., ed. *The Civil War Diary of Charles A. Leuschner.* Austin, Tex.: Eakin Press, 1992.

Stephens, Larry D. *Bound for Glory: A History of the 30th Alabama Infantry Regiment, C.S.A.* Ann Arbor, Mich.: Sheridan Books, 2005.

Stewart, Nixon B. *Dan McCook's Regiment, 52nd O.V.I.* Alliance, Ohio: Review Printing, 1900.

Stone, Henry. "The Atlanta Campaign." In *The Mississippi Valley, Tennessee, Georgia, Alabama, 1861–1864: Papers of the Military Historical Society of Massachusetts*, 8:341–492. Boston: Military Historical Society of Massachusetts, 1910.

Storrs, John W. *The "Twentieth Connecticut": A Regimental History.* Ansonia, Conn.: Naugatuck Valley Sentinel, 1886.

Supplement to the Official Records of the Union and Confederate Armies. 100 vols. Wilmington, N.C.: Broadfoot, 1993–2000.

Sylvester, Lorna Lutes, ed. "'Gone for a Soldier': The Civil War Letters of Charles Harding Cox." *Indiana Magazine of History* 68, no. 3 (September 1972): 181–239.

Symonds, Craig L. *Joseph E. Johnston: A Civil War Biography.* New York: W. W. Norton, 1992.

Tappan, George, ed. *The Civil War Journal of Lt. Russell M. Tuttle, New York Volunteer Infantry.* Jefferson, N.C.: McFarland, 2006.

Thackery, David E. *A Light and Uncertain Hold: A History of the Sixty-Sixth Ohio Volunteer Infantry.* Kent, Ohio: Kent State University Press, 1999.

Thompson, Ed Porter. *History of the Orphan Brigade.* Dayton, Ohio: Morningside Bookshop, 1973.

Toombs, Samuel. *Reminiscences of the War.* Orange, N.J.: Journal, 1878.

Tower, R. Lockwood, ed. *A Carolinian Goes to War: The Civil War Narrative of*

Arthur Middleton Manigault. Columbia: University of South Carolina Press, 1983.

Tschoepe, Mortiz. "A Hot Day: Reminiscences of the Battle of Peach Tree Creek before Atlanta." *National Tribune*, November 6, 1884.

Turner, Samuel. Letter. *Confederate Veteran* 22 (1914): 479.

Underwood, Adin B. *The Three Years' Service of the Thirty-Third Mass. Infantry Regiment, 1862–1865*. Boston: A. Williams, 1881.

Van Horne, Thomas B. *History of the Army of the Cumberland: Its Organization, Campaigns, and Battles*. 2 vols. Wilmington, N.C.: Broadfoot Publishing, 1988.

Walker, Scott. *Hell's Broke Loose in Georgia: Survival in a Civil War Regiment*. Athens: University of Georgia Press, 2005.

Wallace, F. S. "At Peach Tree Creek." *National Tribune*, June 10, 1909.

Walton, J. B., J. A. Chalaron, B. F. Eschelman, and W. M. Owen. "Sketches of the History of the Washington Artillery." *Southern Historical Society Papers* 11 (1883): 210–22.

War of the Rebellion: A Compilation of the Official Records of the Union and Confederate Armies. 70 vols. in 128. Washington, D.C.: Government Printing Office, 1880–1901.

Warner, Ezra J. *Generals in Blue: Lives of the Union Commanders*. Baton Rouge: Louisiana State University Press, 1964.

———. *Generals in Gray: Lives of the Confederate Commanders*. Baton Rouge: Louisiana State University Press, 1959.

Watkins, Sam R. *Co. Aytch: A Confederate Soldier's Memoirs*. New York: Collier Books, 1962.

Welcher, Frank J., and Larry G. Ligget. *Coburn's Brigade: 85th Indiana, 33rd Indiana, 19th Michigan, and 22nd Wisconsin in the Western Civil War*. Carmel, Ind.: Guild Press of Indiana, 1999.

Wells, W. H. "A Western Man's Account of Peach Tree Creek." *National Tribune*, June 7, 1883.

Wiley, Bell Irvin, ed. *Confederate Letters of John W. Hagan*. Athens: University of Georgia Press, 1954.

Wills, Brian Steel. *George Henry Thomas: As True as Steel*. Lawrence: University Press of Kansas, 2012.

Winter, William C., ed. *Captain Joseph Boyce and the 1st Missouri Infantry, C.S.A.* St. Louis: Missouri History Museum, 2011.

Young, L. D. *Reminiscences of a Soldier of the Orphan Brigade*. Louisville, Ky.: Courier-Journal, n.d.

Zinn, John G. *The Mutinous Regiment: The Thirty-Third New Jersey in the Civil War*. Jefferson, N.C.: McFarland, 2005.

Zorn, William A. *Hold at all Hazards: The Story of the 29th Alabama Infantry Regiment, 1861–1865*. Greenville, S.C.: A Press, 1987.

Index

Cannon, J. P., 133, 147
Cantey, James, 150
Capers, Ellison, 12, 159
Carrier, William H., 165, 202
Carter, John C., 29, 94, 273n37, 279n51
Case, Henry, 115, 117–18
Castel, Albert, 78–79, 181–82, 192–93, 234, 238, 279n51
Cate, John Marsh, 191, 213, 217
Champion, Sidney S., 12
Chapman, Henry, 161
Chattahoochee River, 6, 8, 10–13, 18–20, 38, 59
Cheatham, Benjamin F., x, 55, 57, 63, 73–75, 78, 98, 187, 235, 239
Clancy, Charles W., 44, 49
Clanharty, C. W., 165
Clarke, Henry E., 137, 143
Clayton, Henry D., 74, 98, 188, 239
Clayton, Sarah Conley, 205
Clear Creek, 36, 74, 84, 267n10
Cleburne, Patrick R., 80, 96, 98–99, 189, 220–21
Cline, William, 231
Cobb, Howell, 26–27
Cobham, George A., Jr., 141, 196
Coburn, John, 66, 104, 109–11, 119, 122, 127–28, 192, 276n17
Coe, Hamlin, 183, 191
Coleman, J. Walker, 9
Colgrove, Silas, 162–63
Collier, Andrew J., 144–45
Collins, E., 210
Collins, Robert M., 96–97, 211
Cone, Alanson B., 216
Conger, Edwin H., 196
Conn, James P., 208
Connecticut units
    5th Infantry, 158, 166, 184
    20th Infantry, 119–22
Connelly, Thomas L., 8, 26, 78
Connolly, James A., 18, 176, 218, 232
Conrad, Joseph, 60, 62, 90, 94
Cook, Albert M., 33, 206, 217, 230

Cooper, Joseph A., 51, 53
Cooper, Samuel, 23
Cox, Aaron A., 97
Cox, Charles Harding, 198, 213, 215
Cox, Jacob D., 10–11, 19, 36, 51, 53, 63, 78, 99, 127, 178, 192, 218, 234
Cram, George F., 115, 225
Crane, Alexander B., 111
Crawford, Francis C., 111
Cresson, Charles C., 139
Crist, Henry, 109, 276n17
Crosier, William, 140
Crumpton, Washington Bryan, 165
Cumming, Joseph B., 233

Dacus, Robert H., 167, 171
Daniels, Marcus, 203
Davis, C. V. H., 124
Davis, Jefferson, 12–16, 25–26, 30, 38, 70–71, 236–37
Davis, Jefferson C., 18, 31, 33, 44, 47–48, 176, 226, 231
Davis, Newton N., 259n20
De Fontaine, Felix G., 76
De Gress, Francis, 182
Dewey, Ben Park, 174
Dibrell, George G., 8
Dickerman, Ezra, 208–9
Dickinson, Lewis, 225
Dilger, Hubert, 174
Dilworth, Caleb J., 44–45, 47, 71, 300n6
Dimmit, Elias, 48
Dodge, Grenville M., 8, 19–20, 34
Dodson, W. C., 19
Donohue, Thomas, 208
Doty, John S. H., 170
Drake, Jabez L., 119, 124, 191, 193, 230
Drane, J. W., 124
Drullinger, Robert F., 180
Dunham, Charles Laforest, 191
Dunlevy, Howard, 114
Dunn, Matthew Andrew, 124
Dyer, Samuel M., 124

Ector, Matthew D., 174–76, 287n73
Elliott, Fergus, 139
Elmore, Day, 95, 234
English, William Lewis, 180
Ewing, Charles, 227

Failing, Edward P., 196, 203
Farrell, Michael, 46–47, 49
Featherston, Winfield S., 76, 106–8,
    127, 219, 226, 276n7
Ferguson, Samuel W., 19, 37, 188
Fesler, John R., 163
Fielder, Alfred Tyler, 221
Fleharty, Stephen, 66, 202
Flynn, Thomas H., 117
Foos, Dewitt C., 156
Fourat, Enos, 69–70, 135
Foye, John W., 201
French, Samuel G., 28, 76, 174–76, 187,
    220, 243
Fuchs, William John, 120
Fullerton, Joseph, 59

Gallaway, Morton D., 168, 171
Gallup, George W., 179
Gardner, Lyman, 193
Garrard, Kenner, 6, 17
Gates, Elijah, 174–76, 287n73
Geary, John W., 32–33, 42, 69–70, 129–
    31, 133, 135, 138–39, 144–45, 216–
    17
Georgia units
    1st Confederate Infantry, 91
    29th Infantry, 91
    46th Infantry, 43
    54th Infantry, 91
    66th Infantry, 90–91
Gettysburg, battle of, 145
Gibson, Randall L., 98, 188
Gibson, William H., 40–41, 180, 223
Gillespie, F. M., 124
Gilson, Andrew J., 202
Gist, States R., 86
Githins, Harrison, 200

Godard, Abel, 139–40, 143
Goldsmith, John H., 140, 143
Goodloe, Albert T., 72
Goodman, H. Earnest, 200–201
Gourd, Samuel, 139
Govan, Daniel C., 96
Grant, Lemuel, 9, 231
Grant, Ulysses S., 1, 2
Griffin, Daniel F., 176
Grinstead, William, 201–2
Grose, William, 42, 180

Hale, William J., 40
Hall, James I., 95
Hall, O. S., 161
Hammerstein, Herbert von, 140–41
Hammond, Charles M., 86
Hampton, Wade, 55
Hapeman, Douglas, 168, 170–71, 176,
    192–93
Hardee, William J., x, 13, 28, 37–38, 55,
    57, 73–76, 78, 85; at battle of Peach
    Tree Creek, 80, 84, 96–100, 188,
    219–20, 234, 236
Harper, William, 138
Harrison, Benjamin, 66, 109–15, 117–
    18, 122, 125, 128, 183, 196, 214
Harryman, Samuel K., 115
Hart, John, 212
Hascall, Milo S., 34, 51, 63, 178–79
Hay, Thomas Robson, 25
Hazen, William B., 41, 59, 63, 180, 223
Helmreich, Peter, 206
Hinman, Wilbur F., 183
Hitchcock, Watson C., 202
Hobson, William E., 63–64, 179, 224
Hoenig, George, 119, 191
Holland, Orlando S., 150, 152
Holmes, James T., 44, 46–47
Hood, John Bell, ix, x, 13–15, 23–28,
    30–32, 36–38, 50, 55–57, 71–74,
    76, 78, 97, 99–100, 150, 173, 182,
    186, 188–89, 199, 216, 218–21, 223,
    234–38, 240–41, 270n44

Pardee, Ario, 139, 143–44
Parker, George W., 40
Parsons, George W., 228
Peach Tree Creek, 20, 23, 30, 33, 39, 66, 68, 72, 74; Federal crossing of, 39–54
Peach Tree Creek, battle of, x, xii; alcohol at, 217; burial of dead at, 190–91, 193, 196–97, 229–30; casualties at, 93–94, 96–97, 101, 120, 122, 126–27, 141, 147–48, 166, 171, 173, 176, 192–93, 247–54; causes of Confederate defeat at, 126, 145, 173, 235, 237–39; commemoration of, 242–45; flags at, 112, 123–25, 140, 152, 197–98; fortifications at, 57, 61, 81, 90, 100–101, 145, 161–62, 183–84; historians evaluate, 234–42, 296n18; Medals of Honor won at, 171; morale at, xi, xii, 11–12, 28–30, 37, 53, 60, 94, 133, 139, 235, 237; newspaper coverage of, 215; participants evaluate, 213–22, 233–34; poetry about, 214; preparation for, 56–57, 71–72, 78–79; prisoners at, 101–2, 121, 127, 199; terrain at, 60–61, 72, 74, 103–4, 110; trees on field of, 191–92, 231; troop strength at, 79–81, 103, 106, 133, 150, 247–54; visual images of, 123, 142, 194, 301n19; women soldiers at, 202; wounded, care of, 199–212, 230
Peach Tree Creek Line, 36, 56, 62, 71, 73, 106, 126, 133, 149, 181–82, 184–85, 187, 226–27
Pea Vine Creek, 36, 53, 63, 74
Pennsylvania units
    Battery E, Light Artillery, 130, 144
    28th Infantry, 130, 138, 142
    29th Infantry, 140, 143
    46th Infantry, 158, 160, 162–63, 166
    73rd Infantry, 130, 139–40
    109th Infantry, 130, 139, 144, 147

111th Infantry, 141
147th Infantry, 130, 138–39, 143–44
Pickett, W. D., 97
Pierson, Stephen, 70, 135, 137, 144, 242
Poe, Orlando, 216, 231
Polk, Leonidas, 14–15
Polk, Lucius E., 96
Post, Oliver R., 211–12
Potter, John, 212, 217
Power's Ferry, 18, 20
Preston, John S., 173
Preston, Sally Buchanan, 173
Preston, William C., 173

Quarles, William A., 149–50, 167, 171, 187

Randall, Charles B., 140, 196
Randall, James M., 55, 230
Rawls, Morgan, 91
Realf, Richard, 90
Reid, Harvey, 112
Rennolds, Edwin Hansford, 186
Reynolds, Daniel H., 45–47, 49–50, 56, 149–50, 166, 171, 300n6
Reynolds, John A., 143
Rice, Ralsa C., 88, 182–83
Rider, Robert G., 46
Roberts, John H., 217
Robinson, James S., 67, 152, 154, 163, 165
Robson, Annie, 204
Rogers, James C., 156, 158–59, 162
Ross, Emmett, 29
Roy, Thomas B., 220–21
Ruger, Thomas H., 67, 154, 160, 164, 167

Salomon, Edward S., 163
Salter, William, 205
Schlund, Max, 163–64
Schofield, John M., 17, 31, 34, 51, 53, 63, 178, 224, 228

Warner, Louis D., 138
Watkins, Richard L., 173
Webster, Asbell A., 208
Welch, Henry, 206–7
West, Francis H., 160
Wheeler, Joseph, 8, 16, 19–20, 28, 37, 55–56, 72–73, 98–99, 181–82, 188–89, 235
Wheeler, Lysander, 125, 214
Whipple, William D., 64
Whitehead, P. F., 55, 205
Wickham, Charles P., 191
Wigfall, F. Halsey, 23, 27, 215
Wiley, Henry O., 161
Willett, Elbert D., 226
Williams, Alpheus S., 32–33, 43, 67, 104, 133, 152–54, 156, 160, 163, 166, 193, 230
Williams, John S., 8, 19, 32, 37
Williamson, Thomas J., 112, 198
Wilson, William A., 118

Winkler, Frederick C., 118, 120–21
Wisconsin units
    5th Battery, 71
    3rd Infantry, 164, 170
    10th Infantry, 168, 170–71
    21st Infantry, 168, 170
    22nd Infantry, 66, 104, 108, 112, 119–20, 198
    24th Infantry, 41, 60, 62, 90, 101, 272n17
    26th Infantry, 118–22, 197–98
    31st Infantry, 155, 160
Wood, James, 43, 66, 111–12, 118–20, 122, 128
Wood, Thomas J., 8, 18, 32, 40–42, 59, 63, 179–80, 222–23, 243

Young, George, 156, 209–10, 294n59
Young, L. D., 218
Young, William C., 212
Young, William H., 226